International Employment law

International Employment law

Editor:

Veronica Cinti

Delve Publishing

www.delvepublishing.com

International Employment law

Editor: Veronica Cinti

708 3rd Avenue, 6th Floor
New York, NY 10017
United States of America
www.delvepublishing.com

ISBN: 978-1-68095-705-1

Library of Congress Control Number: 2016953781

About the Editor

Veronica Cinti

Experienced researcher and content creator, Veronica Cinti has covered different roles in academia and the private sector. Among other things, she served as researcher and teaching associate at University, and as managing editor and journalist in the media industry.

Contents

List of Contributors

Sally McManus

Justine Nolan
Faculty of Law, University of New South Wales, Australia

Louise Vytopil
Utrecht University School of Law, NL

Aalt G. Colenbrander
Legal Research Master student at Utrecht University (the Netherlands), NL

Elizabeth Shi
Lecturer, Graduate School of Business and Law, RMIT University

Albertine Veldman
Utrecht University School of Law

Dr Graham Smith1
Partner at the Melbourne office of Clayton Utz

Leigh Howard
Lawyer at the Melbourne Officers of Clayton Utz

Patrycja Zwiech
Faculty of Economics Science and Management University of Szczecin, Poland

Linda Senden
Utrecht University School of Law

Sarah Speekenbrink
LL.M., PhD Candidate, Netherlands Institute of Human Rights, Utrecht University

Amy Dunne
External PhD Candidate in International Antitrust Law, Leiden University (the Netherlands)

Manuel Abrantes
Master in Sociology of the University of Amsterdam, Netherlands

Ton van den Brink
Utrecht Centre for Shared Regulation and Enforcement (RENFORCE) of Utrecht University

Hans van Meerten
Utrecht Centre for Shared Regulation and Enforcement (RENFORCE) of Utrecht University

Jose Roberto Herrera Diaz
Lawyer of Javeriana University

Verine Etsebeth
University of Johannesburg South Africa

Giovanni Di Lieto
Bendigo Kangan Institute
Navitas College of Public Safety

Robert CARLEY
Instructional Assistant Professor, International Studies, Texas A&M University 2013-Present

Hilario MOLINA II
PhD, Sociology, Texas A&M University

Frans Pennings
Utrecht University School of Law

Preface

The dynamics of the relationships between workers, employers, trade unions and the government, as well as the implementation of labor standards and the concept of decent work, have been at the center of international institutions attention. ILO and WTO are the leading figures in a movement regarding employment conditions and dynamics around the world, aimed at creating fair and sustainable working environments for the private and public sector, respecting the dignity of human beings and their rights.

Even though most aspects of employment law remain of pertinence of local governments, global guidelines have been drawn and applied worldwide. The harmonization of legal practices pertaining to labor, though, is still a work in progress. In spite of the progressions made, many issues remain not properly addressed, such as those related to discrimination. This book aims at providing the reader with an overview of topical issues regarding employment law. It starts with the presentation of the motives and movement behind the development of an ethical work consciousness and moves towards the analysis of some specific legal responses given to issues characterizing the relationships addressed by this branch of law, and the applicability of few concepts of the regulations in different contexts. In its final part, the book discusses the shaping of a few critical aspects of those relationships, such as discrimination and the normative concept of labor citizenship. Through this combination, the book aims to create the opportunity for the readers of understanding the applicability of legal solutions in diversified settings. The contextualization offered at the end of the book should serve to internalize the dynamics affecting some of the prominent issues of the current society, which have not been address in a comprehensive manner by law, yet. This should enable the readers to critically analyze arising matters in those settings, and formulate proper responses when faced with the chance of giving their contribution to the development of this branch of law.

Editor
Veronica Cinti

Littler's international employment and labor law practice can help multinational clients maneuver through the best of economic times, as well as during unstable periods. We help global clients adapt to the maze of employment laws, taking into account the varied economic circumstances and customs throughout the world.

We advise Fortune Global 500 companies on the full array of labor and employment issues, including managing independent contractors, litigating and arbitrating cross-border employment claims, drafting executive contracts, assisting with workforce reductions, and assessing and drafting global ethics and data privacy policies. We also advise medium- and smaller-sized companies making their first international ventures, as well as those that are expanding their overseas operations. We assist clients in developing the framework to operate internationally with employees in various countries, whether they are on temporary assignment or have longer-term expatriate arrangements.

Littler's attorneys provide clients with extensive support in:

- Assessing risks and benefits of global operational decisions
- Managing global labor relations
- Protecting corporate reputation and brand
- Managing global human resources
- Addressing international data protection issues
- Reviewing expatriate employee programs
- Developing multilingual management training

Employment and labor law legal advice

Ever sheds has the widest range of experience in the world. This means we offer clients whatever they need in terms of human resources advice: legal expertise, creative thinking and the resources to handle any job of any size. We have genuine specialists in even the most unusual aspects of employment law and have clients in nearly all sectors. We have extensive experience of working for international businesses throughout the world and are used to coordinating services across jurisdictions and time zones. Our labor and employment lawyers are trained to focus on solutions and to use straightforward effective language. We understand the importance of ready access to legal advice and the speed of delivery so we are committed to providing this.

International and cross border employment law issues

We are the largest and most respected human resources team, with the Chambers & Partners legal directory recognizing us as an employment team "synonymous with quality and value for money".

We offer an integrated and coordinated service delivery across all jurisdictions and a guarantee of quality and consistency wherever you work with us. You have the benefit of centralized control over your legal budget and direct access to our local specialists.

We offer advice in the following areas:

- Model employment contracts and service agreements for each jurisdiction
- All types of employment litigation including discrimination

- International secondments
- European Works Councils and other international labor relations issues
- Cross-border corporate re-organization
- Employment aspects of operational re-organizations such as redundancy
- Employment aspects of business critical incidents such as competition authority investigations and treatment of implicated employees

For U.S. and Global Corporations Operating Internationally

Our International Employment Issues Practice Group (working with Jackson Lewis attorneys in other practice groups and our international affiliate firms) devises solutions for our clients in the full range of global matters, including:

- Global restructurings, plant closings and collective redundancies;
- Drafting and global implementation of employee codes of conduct, policies and work rules;
- Global labor relations and works council (including European Works Council) matters;
- Implementation of data protection policies and practices;
- Expatriate and other global mobility issues, including corporate compliance immigration requirements;
- Obtaining employment-based temporary work visas and permanent resident status;
- Advising on cross-border or international executive separations;
- Cross-border litigation and arbitration;
- Global compensation and benefit matters;
- Advising on labor/employment issues associated with global M&A or other transactions, such as transfer of undertaking; and
- Conducting or managing internal compliance investigations.

For Multinational Companies with U.S. Interests

Multinational entities operating in the United States face a challenging array of laws and regulations governing the rights and responsibilities of employers and workers. Our attorneys are well-positioned to work with clients on these issues, among others:

- Ensuring U.S. operations comply with federal, state and local employment laws;
- Securing the visas and employment authorizations needed to transfer foreign nationals to the U.S.;
- Employing U.S. citizens abroad; and
- Due diligence on the employment implications of mergers, acquisitions, closings and other business transactions.

CHAPTER 1 YOUR RIGHTS AT WORK

Sally McManus

I was a union branch secretary for the whole of the 'Your Rights at Work' campaign, from the dark days of 2004 and I still am now. I was involved in many of the debates that happened at the leadership level within the NSW union movement, and also as a union secretary implementing decisions with members and their communities. With any campaign it is important not to make generalisations and to say because this worked in the campaign, therefore it should be used as a template for other campaigns. That is a mistake the union movement sometimes makes and a mistake we all can make in our own struggles. The other danger is to look at campaigns in retrospect and to say it was a particular aspect that really won the day. Of course, afterwards, and especially when a campaign is successful, you have all sorts of people that might have an interest in arguing a certain aspect was the key reason it was successful. For instance media companies saying it was the television advertising that did it. Isolating one part in this way, and using it to explain the whole, is a mistake.

I want to try and give you a broad perspective about what actually went on in the campaign, the decisions that the union movement took, what that involved, and draw from that some lessons. In the end I want to say two key things: firstly that it was a tried and true campaigning model. It was not anything new, not anything shiny, not anything made up by some brilliant leaders, by this generation of trade union leaders or by union members in general. It wasn't some model that we got from another movement, it was a strategy that all successful movements have used and really it would be known to all of you. Secondly, and in this context it's important for us not to look for silver bullets.

Citation: Sally McManus, Your Rights at Work, http://dx.doi.org/10.5130/ccs.v1i2.1246.

NEW TACTICS

What was new though, and what was special, were some of the tactics used throughout the campaign. They were new for us, for the trade union movement, and they were special because they were unique in the circumstances. But in the end, they are really just tactics. In terms of the overall strategy, what we ended up implementing was the same model you have seen for a lot of successful campaigns.

So what was special in the YRAW campaign? The first thing was the level of unity amongst the trade union movement. We have the advantage of being one of only a few trade union movements in the world to have just one peak body. Many trade union movements are split between several peak bodies, split along religious or along political grounds, and that really hampers their ability to act as a united movement. And whilst there was unity, this did not happen through any Stalinist enforcement or the force of personality of any particular leader. There were vigorous internal debates at every key point during the campaign. In the early days, for instance, we debated whether to campaign at all. There were debates about the levy imposed on all unions, which was used for television advertising and various other things. There was a significant debate about whether we should have television advertising at all, and you can imagine many of us were saying why should we give our money to Kerry Packer? There were debates about whether mass mobilisation was the right way to go or not. And of course, all the way up until Election Day there was an internal dialectic within our movement about what was the right strategy or the right tactic at that particular time.

The strength of our movement was that once we made a decision, we all stuck to it. Whether we were on one side of the debate or the other, once the decision was made, we were much disciplined about it. I think this particular strength was built on our history and we had some test runs during the Howard years. The MUA dispute, for example, was a test-run of building unity within our movement. I remember before that dispute right wing and left wing unions and activists didn't speak to each other. The dispute, because it was so dramatic, then threw all of us together and a lot of those old tribal hatreds or misconceptions were broken down. That set the scene, enabling the unity that we had during the campaign.

The second thing that is special about the YRAW campaign is that it was highly coordinated. It is a massive logistical exercise to run a campaign of its size over a threeyear period. Just getting information out, for it to be simple, and for it to go right down to workplaces, was a big exercise in itself and of course we had central messaging throughout the campaign. That level of co-ordination was essential in the campaign's success. Thirdly, what was special was the resources that were mobilised throughout the campaign. Even though union membership has been falling, we are still easily the largest social movement in the country and there are a lot of resources that we can bring to bear when we are co-ordinated and unified. Within my union, for instance, we levied our members a dollar a week for the length of the campaign. The levy went to the Australian Council of Trade Unions (ACTU) and raised millions of dollars that was then spent on TV ads, campaigning material, setting up the infrastructure, setting up the information centres, hiring venues, all the things you need to run a campaign on the scale we needed to. Also, in terms of resources, we had something important that our opponents didn't have. And of course that was the people who we could mobilise.

The final thing that I thought was special about this campaign, although it may not be very special in terms of campaigns in general, was a mixture of both top-down and bottom-up campaigning. I think that we really needed both.

CAMPAIGN TECHNIQUES

So what was new or unique in the YRAW campaign? We had union meetings at key points throughout the campaign, and these were not just in the capital cities and were not only within unions. Many of you were probably at campaign meetings that used a Sky Channel satellite broadcast. This idea of a simultaneous public broadcast to meetings across the country really came out of the NSW Teachers' Federation, and the way they organised. These meetings were key in terms of getting a consistent message out, and building a sense of solidarity beyond the big cities, and beyond the union movement.

For us to spend a lot of money on mass media was a big decision, as I mentioned before. Those of us who were critical in the beginning had renounced our criticism probably by mid-2006. The media experts said that the very first advertisement, the one that we call the 'Tracy' ad, of the woman who's been sacked with the two kids, was very powerful. In a way it became the defining image for us, right through the two years, and it became very hard for the Federal Government, for business with all their money and all their resources, to be able to compete with us on that level. Also we had consistent branding throughout the campaign. To have a single slogan and recognisable campaign materials across the country, and consistently throughout the campaign timeline, was a new thing

Another new aspect to the campaign was that we relied on focus groups and on a media company in terms of us shaping our message. We had a lot of arguments about this because of course union secretaries think they know exactly what people think and what their members think. The idea that we should get someone else to go and tell us was an affront to many people. But many of us realised that we needed to be a bit more sophisticated. That's not to say that you just take whatever the media people say, but it's useful information that can then inform your decisions. At those early focus groups, before Work Choices came out, they'd asked people a questions that states 'if the government was going to bring in laws to abolish unfair dismissal, to destroy awards, what would you say about it'? And we, as paid trade union officials, were surprised that people were saying this is outrageous and that they were really angry. They said, 'well, yes, it's about rights, my rights have been taken off me and they're worth fighting for'. I don't think we would have got the bit about 'worth fighting for' back in 2005 as part of our slogan and part of our attitude towards the campaign if it hadn't been for the focus groups.

Online campaigning, the YRAW website, the online forums and email groups also worked very well for those who are at their computers every day and that was a new thing for us. We raised a lot of money through online fundraising, to get billboards up, to keep TV ads running, and just through direct online appeals. This is an approach we adopted from the Dean campaign in the United States and from Get Up!,

Issues at Stake

The issue, obviously being the Work Choices laws, was everything. We really saw it as do or die. Work Choices was aimed at destroying the trade union movement and at destroying for the rights of working families. For us, that was a huge motivating force and the issue in itself. Not every campaign has that, not every campaign has an issue that's felt so strongly and so widely, that it is able to unite people across the whole of the country and across a whole class. I don't know if we would've been able to build consensus, and mobilise all of those resources and effort, if it wasn't for the seriousness of the issue. It was the big motivating factor, and what I'm really saying about that is that you can't just make these campaigns happen. People have got to feel strongly enough around the issue in order to cross the political boundaries, to take the risks, and do a lot of the things we ended up doing in the YRAW campaign.

Defining the issue is obviously important in any campaign and for us, something that was also a bit new was the use of a rights-based campaign frame. We had to translate lots of technical changes that the government was making, 726 pages of legislation, into five clear messages. Meaning, that Work Choices was going to take away unfair dismissal, it was going abolish awards, it was going to take away the independent umpire. We had to distil it into that, and ensure they were really clearly understood issues. We had to say them over and over again for three years. As I said before, understanding our audience was important and advice from outside was important in informing our decisions. The whole slogan about working families didn't come from Obama, and it didn't come from the Labor Party, it came from the trade union movement in Australia. We started talking in terms of working families back in 2005 because we knew from our research that that's who we had to pitch our message to. We were quite cut-throat in saying well, we basically have to win back all those people who voted for Howard in 1996. So we found out who they were, we knew what their demographics were, and we asked them about how they identified themselves. What we found is they identified themselves as working families, so that's where that aspect of the campaign came from.

The other important thing about defining the issue and campaigning around the issue, was making it real. Work Choices, in terms of the actual legislation, didn't actually affect the majority of people for some time. Of course it did in the sense of the general environment it created for bosses, but there were relatively few people on AWAs and most Awards were only scheduled to be abolished half way through 2008. In lots of ways the worst aspects of Work Choices would only start kicking-in after the 2007 federal election. So, making it real in terms of showing the real-life examples of what we were talking about was critical, and that was to do with the rights framework. It was about government taking away your rights, rights you already had, and they were taking it off you. Now, it doesn't matter if you are a union member or not, no one likes to have their rights taken off them.

A Three-Year Campaign

By about June 2005 we had a really clear strategy. It was quite simple in some ways. First, during 2005 we had to concentrate on educating members. Then, in 2006, when Work Choices was being implemented, we had to defend people against it while continuing that education. In 2007 we had to win the election. In that period, at every union meeting I would go to I would explain to members about what the strategy was and discuss its elements. Then people could see where they fitted and why attending a day of action was important, or why building-up union density in their workplaces was important to defend against what your employer might try to do. And why we were spending money on TV ads, or why we were doing certain things was seen within the framework of a clear strategy that people could believe in.

In 2005 I went up to the Northern Rivers region of NSW to start talking to community workers about what was not even announced yet in terms of what the government was planning. We knew what was coming because Howard had given a speech to the Business Council of Australia where he announced they were going to take away unfair dismissal laws, and abolish awards. Talking to community workers about the effect that was going to have on them, and why we needed to campaign against it, was really hard. No one believed us and people thought it just couldn't be possible. It was like ploughing the ground in a drought, like a drought of 10 years, but over time it was getting traction. I look back now and think about those hundreds of meetings that union activists did, union organisers did, that delegates had done over those early stages, of educating people, and it was worth every single minute. Throughout the campaign, the more people knew about the changes the more they hated them (surprise, surprise) so that was crucially important.

Mass mobilisations were also very important in my view. They provided a real interim goal to organise around for union activists, a tangible thing that people could do in terms of showing opposition, and it gave activists a clear role in their workplaces or in their communities in terms of mobilising people. It built the sense of solidarity that we are in this together as a movement. That is something that you can't put a price on. Also it builds hope, because through that solidarity and seeing that there are all these other people who are mobilised on the issue, it creates a feeling that we can really change things. And it also really developed the activists that became the local 'Your Rights at Work' groups.

2006 was a really hard year. It was very much a defensive year because Work Choices was in and we had to stop as many bosses as possible implementing it. We had that sense that if we could keep the bosses at bay they wouldn't be able to do enough damage to make it undoable. We all knew about the New Zealand experience and that almost overnight the tide had swept over the trade union movement, and that ground lost in terms of wages and conditions was hard to win back. So we had to create such a smell around Work Choices so that bosses would be afraid to implement the laws, and this meant we had to rally around any workers who had it imposed on them. We were looking for an iconic dispute, and we were expecting there would be something like Patricks with the MUA dispute, where a big employer would announce 'we're introducing AWAs and we're going to sack our workforce'. What did we get instead? We got relatively small employers like the Cowra Meatworks and Spotlight. By targeting these employers we educated of our members, and scared other employers. They thought, 'Well, I've got to add up the risks now, of starting to implement this. It may attract a national campaign and it may attract action in our communities. Maybe we don't want to be the first to do this, lets let some other people do it first.' So that helped as well. Then of course what we did when the laws affected real workers, we publicised it in a big way on the TV and in every meeting and in every possible way that we could. Soon we had muddied the Work Choices brand, and employers were afraid to be seen to be embracing it.

2007 was our big year. We knew we were going to have a chance to get rid of the government, and start getting rid of Work Choices. We had to continue the same things we were doing the other two years. We still had to defend workers, but the closer it got to the election the less employers wanted to touch Work Choices. Of course you had some employers introducing AWAs, but you didn't have it in a wholesale way. So in a way the heavy lifting was already done, in my view, in the campaign in 2005, and the first half of 2006. Both those two years made 2007 possible.

Grassroots Mobilisation

I wanted to talk a little bit about the bottom-up aspects of the campaign, as sometimes they get lost. Most of the work in this campaign was done by grassroots activists in workplaces and in their communities talking to people and organising around the issue. Most of the hard work was done at the workplace level, building union membership in workplaces, demanding that employers not implement Work Choices. There would have been thousands of union members that were doing that in their own workplaces. And the decisions about how they were going to organise were made by the workers themselves.

The 'Your Rights at Work' groups are a good example of this bottom-up organising. The first 'Your Rights at Work' group, as far as I know, was set up in Lismore in 2005 at the first day-of-action. Really what happened was that a whole lot of people came together in the community, union delegates and union members from a whole range of workplaces. They sat there, I think it was in the Lismore Worker's Club, and watched the Sky Channel campaign broadcast. At the end of the meeting a few of the more experienced activists said 'well let's get everyone's names'. All these people had lived and worked together in a small town, and were also union members, but didn't know they had that in common. They may have worked in the nursery down the road, or they might have been a teacher, or they might have been a community worker. Normally if they walked down the street, they wouldn't have much in common, but this brought them together. A group of activists taking some leadership said 'well, look, why don't we meet, every few weeks, and start looking at what we can do in our town around this'. So that's where it started and they called themselves the Northern Rivers Unionists Network, and that was long before they were being called 'Your Rights at Work' groups.

All-of-a-sudden there was a lot of activity in Lismore. For the next day-of-action they organised towards it, they leafleted the place, they went and spoke at various workplaces, they put in a lot of work, and on the 1st July 2005 thousands of people came. They had a very large turnout for a small place, and people started saying, 'what's going on in Lismore?' Well really what had gone on was organising at a grass roots level amongst union activists. Other unions started to think about this, and there were other towns where groups were set up. I think quite often it was Teachers' Federation activists taking it on, because they were the more experienced union activists in some of the smaller towns. These all had started organically, doing a similar thing in their regions.

So a decision was made to support these groups, and Unions NSW started building membership lists, but it was only later that central resources or any central organising was put in place for what came to be called 'Your Rights at Work' groups. From the beginning these groups were obviously cross-union, they were pretty much rank and file. It was only in 2007 that there was any full-time presence at all in terms of union officials in most of these places. They had limited formal structures and didn't have position holders, anything like that. So the decisions they made then about how they were going to campaign were completely controlled by those activists in those towns and suburbs. The fantastic thing was that this produced very effective campaigns, because the decisions they made were based on their local circumstances.

For example in the Blue Mountains there's this thing called the Winter Magic Festival, which is unique to the Mountains. The local 'Your Rights at Work' group decided that they were going to organise a contingent in it and they all dressed up, I don't know as magicians and similar, and that went down very well in that particular community. If you tried to do that in Penrith, or if you tried to do that in Newtown, everyone would think you were an idiot. If you had some centralised 'you must do it this way' model, it just would not have worked. The same in Lismore, they approached things much more around local markets and things that would already be happening around the place. Groups launched letter-writing campaigns to the local media, they signed-up people to campaign against the local member, and launched actions to defend local workers affected by Work Choices. In other places, like in Queanbeyan, the Empower group there approached things in a different way because they knew their area and they could campaign well within it. In Lindsay they approached things in a different way again. This was a particularly beautiful thing about the campaign, the way that local union members controlled and innovated within the centralised messaging, using the top-down frames in a very, very effective way.

In 2007, as the year went on, we got more and more focussed on marginal seats. We were convinced that we knew which sixteen seats had to change in order to bring down the government. We knew that we had to put everything we possibly could into winning those particular seats. So we did something new: pretty much all unions phoned all of our members in marginal seats. We called them three times during 2007. We spent a lot of time building relationships with people we identified as undecided voters, visiting them in their houses, talking to them about the importance of their vote and the importance of changing the government. That was something very new for us and it was something that took a lot of resources. Empirically it probably didn't matter in the end, and although that part of the campaign did add to the swing, in my view I think we'd won it by mid-2006 and those people had already changed their minds. The heavy lifting we did in those two years had really already shifted it. But if I had the time over again I'd still do exactly the same things, because you can't leave anything to chance.

There were 'Your Rights at Work' full-time co-ordinators paid collectively by the union movement in those sixteen marginal seats across the county. They worked for a year, living and working in the electorate, resourcing the local 'Your Rights at Work' group. The groups became very successful in these areas because they had the fulltime resources. Then on Election Day, it was a big debate within the union movement, we decided to independently staff and resource all of the booths in seven marginal seats located in NSW. Every single one of those booths was staffed. The ALP couldn't staff all their booths, but they didn't want anything to do with us for the first four weeks of the six-week election campaign. I was saying to my organisers, 'don't worry, they'll come begging', and they did, about a week or two before the elections, when they realised they didn't have the resources to staff the booths.

So, for example, in places like Grafton where every single booth last election was won by the National Party, was packed with 'Your Rights at Work' people and completely covered with 'Your Rights at Work' material. National Party people turned up at six o'clock and said 'What's going on, that's our area, and that's the Labor Party's area. We've had an arrangement here for the last 50 years you know.' Well, that arrangement was gone, and we were able to dominate things. In the end it probably didn't matter because people had made up their mind by Election Day. It was more a demonstration of the depth of commitment and extent of the mobilisation. You had people that had never done a basic thing like hand-out on election day. If you look at the numbers of people that were involved, just ordinary working people who would never have done that it was enormous.

So, to go back to what I said in the beginning, old campaigning is new campaigning. The activists of a generation before us learnt the same lessons that we learnt. There were new things for us though. We did take-on a new form of political campaigning in the marginal seats. What used to happen at election time in the trade union movement is that a month before the election some of us would give money, some of us would drag a few people out, maybe some of your most active members and your paid staff, and you'd hand-out at a polling booth and that would be it. So the 2007 election was quite different. The other, final thing to emphasise is that the bottom-up elements of the campaign were essential. It shouldn't now be seen as just a media campaign, because it wasn't. Most of the hard work of the campaign was carried out by workers themselves in their communities, and the most innovative strategies and tactics and energy that went into the campaign also came from there.

Finally I want to finish with this, which I love, a picture of the 'Your Rights at Work' march at the Grafton Jacaranda Festival. All those people that you see are rank and file people from various unions. They each made up a placard about what type of work they did - 'I'm a timber worker, I'm a community worker, I'm a hospital worker', all the way through the march. For them this was a really big step to go and march in a community festival, because it's a very conservative place, Grafton, with very little activist or union history. There was a big internal debate amongst those activists, and they decided they weren't going to carry their individual union flags or anything like that; they were going to identify the jobs that they did in the community. And they got a fantastic reception, and they'll probably do it again.

CHAPTER 2

THE CORPORATE RESPONSIBILITY TO RESPECT HUMAN RIGHTS

Justine Nolan

Keywords: Corporate responsibility, human rights, regulation, Guiding Principles

INTRODUCTION

There is one and only one social responsibility of business -- to use its resources and engage in activities designed to increase its profits so long as it stays within the rules of the game, which is to say, engages in open and free competition without deception or fraud.1

Milton Friedman's well known and oft quoted statement regarding corporate social responsibility is commonly interpreted as implying that companies do not possess any social responsibilities but rather should simply focus on increasing profits. However, an important element of Friedman's mantra is the pivotal phrase 'as long as it stays within the rules of the game'. Friedman, writing in 1970, narrowly defined that phrase in legal terms but significant developments since then, mean that the 'rules of the game' in terms of defining the social expectations of a company, have changed. The rules (such as they exist) are not simply confined to codified law but flow from sources as diverse as privately drafted codes of conduct to internationally formulated guiding principles, all so-called soft law standards that help guide corporate respect for human rights. The 'rules of the game' have become more amorphous and the responsibility for implementing them more diffuse since Friedman's initial foray into this field.

Responsibility for protecting and advancing respect for human rights has long been assumed to be the duty of the state and the rules for doing so, stemming predominantly from international treaties that might then be translated into national laws, such as labour and anti-discrimination laws. It is only quite recently that discussion has shifted to focus on the human rights responsibilities of corporations and what that might entail both in terms of formulating precisely what standards should be met by companies, who should set such standards and how to manage compliance with those standards. The adoption by the United Nations (UN) Human Rights Council in 2011 of the Guiding Principles on Business and Human Rights, 2 assisted in entrenching the notion of the existence of a corporate responsibility to respect human rights,3 but interpreting and implementing that responsibility on the ground is a longer term task that requires re-interpreting and refining the 'rules of the game'. The Guiding Principles, developed by the UN Special Representative on the issue of human rights and transnational corporations and other business enterprises, John Ruggie ('the Special Representative'), set out a three-pronged framework for delineating between the roles of the state and business with respect to human rights. First, states have a duty to protect people from human rights violations by corporations. Second, corporations have a responsibility to respect, uphold and not interfere with human rights. And, third, both states and corporations have a responsibility to ensure that people who are victims of corporate violations have access to an effective remedy. This demarcation between a state's duty and a corporation's responsibility explicitly acknowledges the traditional (and theoretically at least), primary role of states in protecting human rights but also recognises the urgent need for the private sector to take a prominent role in advancing respect for rights.

While the Guiding Principles provide a useful foundation for future action and reaffirm the responsibility (if not legal obligation) of companies to improve working conditions, well before their adoption in 2011 many global companies were already involved in establishing or working within private compliance programs, that were sometimes complementary to existing national laws and at other times, superseded state efforts to protect workplace rights. In some sectors and in some countries, the willingness of companies to either proactively (or more often) reactively improve working conditions in their supplier factories has outstripped the willingness of some

Citation: Justine Nolan, The Corporate Responsibility to Respect Human Rights, DOI: http://doi.org/10.5334/ujiel.ca.

national governments to confront and more clearly articulate their own understanding of what such corporate responsibility might entail. The reliance on private regulation to fill this lacuna is in part an acknowledgement of the sluggish pace at which international (and often national) law develops and the political reality that there is little appetite at present among states for the development of a new treaty focused specifically on business and human rights concerns.4

As the global business and human rights agenda has evolved in the last three to four decades, we have witnessed the rise of, and reliance on, private regulation,5 as a means of driving consensus on how corporations should or could advance respect for (and sometimes, protect) human rights. International human rights law and its state centric framework for protecting rights is proving inadequate to stem (or redress) corporate rights violations and is proving to be more the backdrop for the development of mechanisms to prevent and protect individuals from corporate rights violations, rather than the prism through which corporate accountability might be filtered. The unwillingness and/or inability of many governments to fulfil their human rights obligations has led to protection gaps. All around the global marketplace, non-state actors such as non-government organizations ('NGOs'), unions, companies, multi-stakeholder6 groups and industry bodies, have stepped in to fill this gap. This transfer, or sharing of regulatory authority from states to non-state actors is not so much 'deregulation' but rather what some commentators refer to as re-regulation7 or even a regulatory renaissance.8 Private regulatory mechanisms utilize a combination of hard and soft laws to establish relevant standards that companies strive to achieve. The source of such hard law tends to be readily accessible international and national legislation focused on defining consistent standards for health and safety, wage, hours and conditions of work; the soft law standards are more nebulous. While there is no entrenched definition of what constitutes soft law, in this context it might commonly include instruments as diverse as those internationally formulated (other than a treaty) that contain 'principles, norms, standards or other statements of expected behaviour'9but also widely accepted codes of conduct that have been developed by a group of stakeholders as a mechanism to prevent corporate rights abuses. The Guiding Principles thus appear to be the latest in a long line of soft regulatory techniques that rely in a large part on private regulation that encourages, but does not necessarily require, a corporation to comply with human rights. 10

This paper examines this process of 're-regulation' in the business and human rights context (principally focused on working conditions and labour standards). Section II examines the reliance on non-state actors to regulate corporate activity with respect to human rights and Section III considers the pivotal role played by soft law in regulating corporate compliance with human rights and the promise and pitfalls of doing so. Section IV considers the role of the state and the possibilities for it to both complement and supplement private regulation so as to better protect human rights. Ultimately, this paper proposes that the regulation of corporate activity with respect to human rights requires a multiplicity of stakeholders and a very nuanced mix of public and private regulation that may be difficult to replicate easily across different sectors, states and cultural boundaries. While, in this field, the state may no longer play the primary protection role ascribed to it in either international human rights law or the Guiding Principles, it remains an essential piece of the human rights enforcement puzzle and greater attention needs to be paid to analysing what mix of international/domestic, state/non-state and hard/soft regulatory mechanisms will be most effective in protecting human rights in the workplace.

THE RISE OF, AND RELIANCE ON PRIVATE REGULATION

For the last several decades, globalization has posed both challenges and opportunities for advancing the protection of human rights in the global marketplace. Significant developments have been taking place in factories, fields and offices all over the world where a variety of stakeholders have been pushing and prodding corporations to adopt operational changes that will lead to sustained compliance with international human rights standards. Sometimes business has been proactive in seeking such changes, at other times reluctant or simply absent. In today's global economy, large companies in most industries have come to rely on a series of contractors and suppliers in a range of countries to produce their products. Today's global supply chains link individual workers with large and small companies across national, political and cultural boundaries and 'in a world of 80,000 transnational corporations, ten times as many subsidiaries and countless national firms, many of which are small and medium-sized enterprises', any attempt to regulate corporate behaviour will always be a challenge.11 What is becoming increasingly apparent is that for sustained improvements to occur, a multiplicity of stakeholders must be involved, including but not necessarily relying only on the state. Some of the most powerful global actors today are companies, not governments.12Logically recourse to local laws and a system of enforcement and judicial relief in the host countries where global corporations operate should be the first option for ensuring greater respect for human rights. However the reality is that in many countries this simply is not happening. In developing countries (but not exclusively so), laws are sometimes weak, but enforcement weaker still and corruption can be endemic - reflecting chronic failures in developing a governmental order based on the rule of law. Thus, reliance on the state to ensure human rights are protected remains a long term proposition.

The development and implementation of private regulatory methods that do not rely on the role of the state as *the* 'human rights protector' include the incremental but now widespread adoption of codes, guidelines and principles – both at the micro and macro level – which are being used as mechanisms to drive corporate compliance with international human rights standards.13 Such developments have, and continue to, urge a change in corporate culture that recognises workers, wherever they are located, must be treated with dignity and respect. Slowly but surely a paradigm shift is taking place that affects the way companies and society are increasingly viewing this issue with the state being viewed as (possibly) part of the solution, but not *the* solution. Companies, in particular global transnational companies, are 'required' to play a significant role in developing a solution. 'In the recent past, it was sufficient for vanguard companies to do their best to avoid causing environmental and social damage. Now they are being asked to become a force for good, and discovering they cannot do it alone.'14 Thirty to forty years ago, very few companies acknowledged any affirmative obligation to address workplace conditions in the factories of their foreign suppliers – factories they generally neither owned nor operated – but this concept is no longer anathema to companies. For many (but not all) companies, the question is no longer 'Do we have an obligation to address workers' rights in suppliers' factories? It is how do we do it, at what cost, and with whom do we collaborate in addressing the problems that exist?'15

Take for example, the different corporate responses to two workplace disasters nearly thirty years apart. In December 1984, fourteen years after Friedman's acknowledgment of the limited scope of a corporation's social responsibility, a corporate catastrophe occurred in the Indian city of Bhopal. On the night of 2 December 1984, a massive leakage of toxic gases from a storage tank at a chemical plant resulted in the deaths of more than 3,000 people in its immediate aftermath and injured and subsequently killed thousands of others.16 Some blame was attributed to the central and state Indian governments and their lax enforcement of safety laws and haphazard planning permissions,17 but public attention also focused on the plant operator, Union Carbide India Limited, and its US based parent company, Union Carbide (UCC). Although UCC exercised extensive control over its Indian subsidiary (evidenced not simply by share ownership or representation on the board of directors but also by involvement in 'key decisions regarding issues such as, technology, plant design, safety…training of employees'18), UCC started shifting the blame for the accident to its subsidiary. The reaction of the principal companies involved was generally denial, obfuscation and a lack of responsibility for the calamity that ensued and liability was strictly defined in terms of legal accountability for the disaster. Litigation was pursued in both the American and Indian courts with mixed results.19 The action against the parent company, UCC was ultimately dismissed and the Indian case settled. Bhopal remains one of the modern world's worst industrial accidents and as a legal precedent it is most noteworthy for highlighting the limitations of the law and the lack of justice ultimately delivered to those worst affected. So, in the nearly thirty years since, as corporate violations of human rights have continued to occur, what, if anything has changed in terms of corporate and public perceptions of a company's responsibility to act and provide redress in the face of such a tragedy?

In April 2013, the Rana Plaza building in Dhaka, Bangladesh collapsed. The building housed five garment factories and over 1,100 workers were killed. Interest from the world's media immediately centred on the global companies outsourcing production to the garment workers in that building. Questions focused on the corporate responsibilities of these global buyers – legal or otherwise – in both preventing and redressing this workplace disaster.20 The ease with which modern technology distributed disturbing images of those killed and maimed in these factories no doubt played a key role in capturing corporate attention. In the aftermath of the tragedy, global press reports continued to focus primarily on the role and involvement of the private sector in remedying this problem rather than on the Bangladeshi government and its clearly inadequate regulatory enforcement of human rights and labour standards. The fact that direct legal liability may be very difficult to prove in linking the global firms with the collapse of the factory was not perceived as a barrier to responsibility.

In the six months following the Rana Plaza building collapse, three different initiatives formed, all with the stated aim of improving working conditions inside Bangladeshi factories. In May 2013, a group of predominantly European apparel companies developed the Accord on Fire and Building Safety21, quickly followed in June by the establishment of the Alliance for Bangladesh Worker Safety, made up of North American retailers including Walmart and Gap.22 These two initiatives, demonstrate 'regulatory renaissance' at work, by both recognizing the limited governmental capacity to provide a short-term remedy to prevent further disasters and accepting that corporate social responsibilities extend beyond those that can be defined in stark legal terms. These multi-stakeholder initiatives adopt a collective workplace safety standard and auditing plan that essentially privatizes aspects of workplace safety in respect of the remediation of safety threats. Together, the plans 'encompass financial commitments of almost $250 million, plus up to an additional $100 million in low-cost loans to help pay for building upgrades.'23 This utilization of non-state actors to protect human rights builds on state efforts in promulgating human rights standards, but also explicitly acknowledges the state's limited enforcement capacity and outsources the implementation of the proposed protection regime to the non-state sector.

Several months later, in October 2013, the International Labour Organization (ILO) announced a three year initiative to improve Bangladesh's garment factories.24 The ILO initiative, co-sponsored by the Bangladesh government, will conduct a fire and building safety assessment on 1,000 to 1,500 factories and run safety and health awareness training. The $24.1 million project – funded mainly by the British and Dutch governments – also aims to provide skills training to survivors of the Rana Plaza building collapse. This initiative uses government funds to enforce national and international regulations and aims to build the capacity of the Bangladesh government to enforce safety standards across a broad spectrum of local factories. In the interim, the private funds of European and American brands are at work, improving a narrower range of factories that are linked to the companies via their supply chain. While the competing nature of these three initiatives potentially makes implementation all the more challenging it also recognizes that potential solutions must be multi-pronged and may need to co-exist offering workplaces a mix of public and private regulation that has the potential to fill gaps that another program may overlook. A sub-contracting factory that does not have direct relationships with Western brands may not garner the attention of either the Accord or the Alliance, but may fall within the parameters of the ILO project. This is the essence of re-regulation, utilizing public and private regulation that sources standards from international and national legislation to create real reform of workplace safety encompassing, in this case, a large proportion of Bangladesh's garment industry. While limited to one country and one sector, one can see the promise of this regulatory renaissance. However it is not without its pitfalls.

FROM PRINCIPLES TO PRACTICE: REFINING THE RULES OF THE GAME

In the forty years following Friedman's assertion of the limited scope of a corporation's social responsibilities, a substantial body of soft law has developed that is effectively refining the rules of the game. As was exemplified by the non-state sector's response to the Bangladeshi tragedy, the practical protection of human rights is being pursued at ground level, both by civil society and international institutions acting in concert with business. The reasons that the various codes, guidelines and principles have proliferated in the last three to four decades are multifaceted (including an increase in pressure on companies from NGOs and a willingness on the part of some companies to adapt corporate strategies to incorporate such codes) but it is also clear that the development of these initiatives is in part a response to an inadequate legal framework. There remain very few legal obligations dealing with human rights that bind corporations operating trans-nationally.25 This lack of clear legal liability has been central to the creation of the permissive international 'human rights free' environment26 in which some corporations now operate and the parallel increase in the development of soft law mechanisms to regulate corporate behaviour. In spite of this, or more accurately because of this, a plethora of codes and guidelines have been established that, with varying levels of success, take on the role of the state in encouraging adherence to human rights standards.27

For example in 2011, after persistent criticism about the working conditions at Foxconn, (one of Apple's principal suppliers),28 Apple agreed to allow the non-profit Fair Labor Association (FLA) access to some Foxconn factories to assess compliance with Chinese legal requirements and the FLA's Workplace Code.29 Multi-stakeholder initiatives such as the FLA, which is a collaborative effort of companies, universities, colleges and civil society organisations, epitomize the private regulatory mechanisms that have developed with the lofty goal of establishing a practical framework for human rights protection. FLA's subsequent audits of Foxconn revealed multiple labour and human rights violations incompatible with both Chinese laws and FLA code standards. These included infractions relating to hours of work, health and safety, compensation and industrial relations.30 The FLA, along with the principal companies involved, then started to develop a plan to remedy these violations. The FLA is only one of a series of multi-stakeholder initiatives that emerged in the 1990s focused on the apparel sector,31 in which companies work in partnership with civil society to attempt to regulate unregulated jurisdictions. In this form of re-regulation, private actors are delivering public goods such as labour inspections; traditionally a state function but the assessable standards are a mix of public and private regulations. This acceptance (albeit often reluctantly) by (some) businesses of their human rights responsibilities is indicative of the transformation of the rules of the game and an acknowledgement that the rules can no longer be framed in narrow and legalistic terms.

The Guiding Principles on Business and Human Rights, the latest and most authoritative to date, of a long line of soft law standards designed to curb corporate rights violations unabashedly asserts a corporation's responsibility to respect human rights.32 This corporate responsibility, the UN Special Representative reasoned, emerged not from law but from the basic expectation society has of business: an expectation that companies will do no harm.33 The Guiding Principles stipulate that the corporate responsibility to respect human rights 'means that they [companies] should avoid infringing on the human rights of others and should address adverse human rights impacts with which they are involved'.34 The explanatory Commentary accompanying the Principles states that 'the responsibility to respect human rights is a global standard of expected conduct for all business enterprises wherever they operate [and that] [i]t exists independently of States' abilities and/or willingness to fulfil their own human rights obligations, and does not diminish those obligations.'35

What does this mean in practice and how do such top-down announcements from the UN filter down to impact workers' rights on the floor of a sub-contracting factory in Bangladesh? To some, the loose language of corporate responsibility rather than obligation implies an acceptance of a 'world where companies are encouraged, but not obliged, to respect human rights'36 and requires few real changes in the way business operates. 'The soothing promise of responsibility can deflect public attention from the need for stricter laws and regulations'.37 Responsibility is distinguished from accountability, and corporations interpreting these principles in practice, may choose to take their cue (or not) from a mix of international standards selectively embodied in a soft law format.

Following this line of reasoning, some argue that it is illegitimate for private companies to be conducting labour inspections and that resources should rather be devoted to strengthening public labour administration systems.38 The combination of utilizing soft law standards and enforcement by private actors while filling a governance gap left open by the state, attracts reasonable criticism around the selective nature of the standards monitored and the perennial problems of leaving the 'fox guarding the hen house'.39 In some cases, the standards monitored by some multi-stakeholder initiatives set a lower bar than that required by local law40 and some initiatives lack independent auditing and transparency.41 Many of the soft law codes and guidelines that have multiplied in this sector in the last three to four decades exhibit these types of problems.

While some credence can be given to the argument that these codes, guidelines and principles have emerged simply because there is a lack of anything better and/or as a tactic for avoiding government regulation, the use of soft law can also be a deliberate strategic choice – made by NGOs and business - because it is attractive to the participation of a broad group of stakeholders (particularly business and sometimes government). The attraction of such soft law (to some participants) can be easily understood if the standards are viewed as containing aspirational goals that aim for the best possible scenario with limited constraints if such goals are not met but soft law is not necessarily commensurate with soft results. Any clear demarcation between hard and soft law is challenging42 and while some may argue that 'the essence of any soft law rule is that it is not binding'43 in this particular field, differentiation between soft and so-called hard (or legally binding) law is not binary but one that should be viewed as developing on a continuum. What is legally sanctioned is distinguishable from activities that are not, but reputational sanctions can be crucial to business.44 The reality is that not unlike the global framework for enforcing international human rights law, such initiatives are only as strong as their members choose to make them, and they do not apply to those that do not want to join them. The soft language of the Guiding

Principles and the casing in which the corporate responsibility to respect principle is couched (that is, principle not 'law') was deliberately adopted in contrast to the legal protection duties it ascribes to states that are grounded in international human rights law. What distinguishes the Guiding Principles from earlier UN efforts to regulate corporations with respect to human rights45 is the deliberate decision to move away from pursuing an explicit legal connection between international human rights law and corporations and rely on a more amorphous, but broader societal expectation that attaches to companies. Such looseness in language can affect both how consistently the Principles are interpreted, who they attach to and how compliance is coerced.

One of the many challenges associated with the Guiding Principles is their practical implementation. While theoretically, emphasis is placed on the primary protective duty of the state to safeguard human rights, it is increasingly obvious from a practical perspective that in many markets this needs to be supplemented by private actors46. The Guiding Principles' recognition of the corporate responsibility to respect is acknowledgement of this. The limited capacity of many national governments and institutions like the ILO to stem rights violations, the decline of state backed labour inspections, and the ferocious appetite of the global marketplace has quite simply overwhelmed most national systems of labour market regulation.47 Even developed market economies have trouble maintaining adequate levels of inspection.48 The need for private actors to take responsibility for labour inspection remains, and will probably grow. Foxconn is China's largest private employer49 and in spite of this, or perhaps because of this, state regulated labour inspections were inadequate to address the ongoing rights violations within factories. No socially responsible company wants to be associated with child labour, forced labour or unsafe working conditions in the production of their goods, so the need to perform due diligence to ensure that labour and human rights standards are respected, even in jurisdictions where labour inspectors are active, is often a necessity.

The ideal situation would be one in which non-state actors complement the work of the state by mobilising resources to protect human rights that are comprehensively defined by reference to international standards. The work of the non-state actors is not to relieve states' of their duties, or selectively determine what workplace standards are relevant to their operations, but to assist in building the capacity of governments to assume or resume their obligations to improve working conditions. That synergy has been hard to capture and in many states where violations are rampant their public agencies are either in denial or in bad faith about the lamentable state of labour law enforcement in their jurisdiction.50 Reducing corporate violations of workers' rights is a process of progressive realisation. While a diverse range of initiatives aimed at curbing violations of workers' rights have proliferated in recent decades, it is also clear that such initiatives 'have been unable to stem the flow of human rights violations by TNCs [transnational corporations]'.51 This should not be taken as an indication that such measures are altogether devoid of merit. Initiatives that have relied on the development of soft law via such tools as codes of conduct can play a vital role in internalising human rights norms within corporations and solidifying the notion that corporations have duties with respect to shareholders *and* stakeholders (including workers in their supply chain) alike – a process that in time 'can shape the standards of care that are legally expected of business'.52 However, not all codes or initiatives are alike and there remains a vast gulf of difference between the motherhood type statement of the Guiding Principles to the specific standards or aspirations of some codes and how they actually engage business in the process of reform highlighting the need for state involvement in this field to supplement and at times, coerce business into operating responsibly and provide guidance and consistency with respect to adhering to internationally recognized standards.53

Relying purely on either the blind faith of market forces or the state to curb corporate violations has its challenges and ultimately, is likely to have limited longevity in bringing about sustained workplace improvements.54 To move from the development of these soft law principles to their practical implementation, requires articulated regulation by a multiplicity of stakeholders. In essence, re-regulation relies on a form of 'networked governance'55 that places corporate behaviour under the scrutiny of not only states, but also NGOs, unions, industry bodies and international organizations. Private regulatory mechanisms that borrow standards from both hard and soft law instruments may transcend, but also complement, the traditional and formal regulatory role played by states in protecting human rights. This form of regulatory renaissance is not so much 'governance without government'56 but rather governance that recognizes the limitations of government and seeks to supplement those regulatory gaps by directly involving other crucial stakeholders.

BLENDING PUBLIC AND PRIVATE REGULATION: THE CHANGING ROLE OF THE STATE

In its 2013 World Report, Human Rights Watch stridently makes the case for a more prominent - practical not just theoretical - role to be played by states in regulating corporate compliance with human rights: '[w]e have nearly reached the paltry limits of what can be achieved with the current enforcement-free approach to the human rights problems of global companies. It is time for governments to pull their heads out of the sand, look the problem they face in the eye, and accept their responsibility to oversee and regulate company human rights practices.'57 Human Rights Watch's argument is fortified by the many examples of corporate irresponsibility it has tabulated over the years58 including several where companies have professed to be operating according to a human rights code of conduct. Reasserting the role of the state in improving workplace conditions does not necessarily mean, as one commentator puts it 'a return to traditional command control regulation [as] the limits of that approach are well known.'59 What is needed, is some level of involvement by the state to harden the 'societal expectations' foisted on some companies and more readily assumed by others60: a blending of public and private regulation or re-regulation.

It is reasonable to argue that compliance by companies with soft law human rights standards is more likely if some aspects of those initiatives encouraging certain behaviours are mandated in the form of a 'hard' law requirement.61 Such requirements can take various forms and one obvious area where this might be effective in the current climate is government imposed human rights due diligence or specific reporting requirements on companies.62 These obligations could be mandated via domestic legislation (operating extraterritorially) to 'harden' principles that are currently cast in a soft format.

The Guiding Principles for example, encourage companies to conduct due diligence as a means by which companies might discharge their responsibility to respect rights.63 Such due diligence involves companies conducting a human rights risk assessment as part of their business operations but the parameters of such due diligence are not clearly defined.64 There is no legal obligation in the Guiding Principles to either conduct such an assessment or to publish its results. However, the hope or expectation that some companies might willingly adopt such responsibilities stems from experience over the last few decades of some companies who have been involved in multi-stakeholder initiatives that require companies to integrate human rights responsibilities into their*modus operandus*. The Guiding Principles leave a significant amount of 'wiggle room' for companies in setting the parameters of due diligence and note that:

Human rights due diligence:

(a) Should cover adverse human rights impacts that the business enterprise may cause or contribute to through its own activities, or which may be directly linked to its operations, products or services by its business relationships…65

The text of this provision is nebulous and open to interpretation. Whether the operations of a sub-contracting factory in Bangladesh can be 'directly linked' to its US based buyer is debatable and with no legal requirement to conduct due diligence, compliance is likely to be patchy and inconsistent. Selective implementation of this principle is also likely to be furthered by the Commentary attached to the Guiding Principles which states that '[w]here business enterprises have large numbers of entities in their value chains it may be unreasonably difficult to conduct due diligence for adverse human rights impacts across them all.'66 States however could supplement and strengthen this process by legislating to require companies they regulate to carry out such due diligence and set the parameters for what it should incorporate.

Articulating the reach of a state to impose such obligations (and therefore defining which companies a state might regulate) opens the proverbial bag of worms. Should (or could) such regulations extend beyond a parent company to its subsidiary operating in India or down its supply chain to its contracted supplier factories? Although in most jurisdictions national law regulates corporate activities that affect human rights including labour rights, anti-discrimination law, environmental protection and criminal law, domestic legislation typically does not apply extraterritorially. However, several UN bodies have, in the last few decades, taken an expansive approach on who and what a state might regulate in the pursuit of protecting human rights. For example, the UN Committee on Economic, Social and Cultural Rights when considering how states might protect the right to health noted that state actions might need to cross national boundaries.

To comply with their international obligations … States parties have to respect the enjoyment of the right of health in other countries, and to prevent third parties from violating the right in other countries, if they are able to influence these third parties by way of legal or political means…67 Postulating two years later in respect to protecting an individual's right to water, the same UN Committee called upon states 'to prevent their own citizens and companies from violating the right to water of individuals and communities in other countries [w] here States parties can take steps to influence other third parties to respect the right, through legal or political means …'.68

Despite this expansive and pragmatic approach taken by the UN Committee on Economic, Social and Cultural Rights that encourages states to protect individuals from corporate harms wherever they occur, the Guiding Principles adopted a more conservative view as to whether a state might regulate corporate activities that extend beyond its borders and jurisdiction. The Guiding Principles note that 'States must protect against human rights abuse within their territory and/or jurisdiction by third parties, including business enterprises.'69 The Commentary attached to Guiding Principle 2 further elaborates on these territorial and jurisdictional limits by noting the possibilities open to states to broaden and deepen the scope of the duty to protect but does not go so far as to suggest states are obliged to act in this regard.70

The Guiding Principles rather limp stance in recognising but not requiring states to regulate companies extraterritorially turns its back on a window of opportunity offered by the UN Committee on Economic, Social and Cultural Rights in recommending an assertive extraterritorial approach to protection. The Maastricht Principles on Extraterritorial Obligations of States in the area of Economic, Social and Cultural Rights71developed by a group of experts in September 2011 takes up the challenge of more solidly integrating international human rights law with the realities of the global economy and the transnational operations of business by declaring that '[a]ll States must take necessary measures to ensure that non-State actors which they are in a position to regulate … such as transnational corporations and other business enterprises, do not nullify or impair the enjoyment of economic, social and cultural rights.'72 Maastricht Principle 25 then goes on to clarify that states will be in a position to regulate such corporations if the corporation, or its parent or controlling company, has its centre of activity, is registered or domiciled, or has its main place of business or substantial business activities, in the State concerned'.73

When looking for examples of how a state might reasonably regulate corporate activities beyond their borders, one model of extraterritorial legislation that has had a widespread impact on the private sector is the US *Foreign Corrupt Practices Act*.74 Adopted in 1977, it has influenced the way in which US businesses operate abroad, and has changed the global business environment more generally with respect to corruption. Setting a precedent for how a legislative model can reverberate globally, the US act was followed into operation by the OECD *Convention on Combating Bribery of Foreign Public Officials in International Business Transactions* and the UN *Convention against Corruption*75 which established international standards for combating corruption. Companies have responded to these global anti-corruption laws by developing due diligence programs to proactively identify potential risks. The global implementation of laws to combat corruption is a useful model in assessing how more rigor could be brought to bear in applying international human rights standards to business and the mandated due diligence requirements showcase how the Guiding Principles could be hardened into a national legislative model with extraterritorial reach.

States might also supplement private regulatory mechanisms by mandating increased transparency in global business operations with a view to increasing respect for human rights. For example, the UN Global Compact (a very soft version of soft law in this field) asks companies to commit to issuing an annual 'Communication on Progress'76 as a means of advancing corporate responsiblity for human rights. While the Compact can cajole companies (and as a last resort threaten companies with expulsion) into complying, states can *require* companies they regulate to report on their global activities and the steps they are taking to ensure the protection of human rights. For example, Section 1502 of the US Dodd-Frank law requires all listed companies to report on the sources of minerals used in their products in the areas around the Democratic Republic of Congo.77 The purpose of this provision is to provide greater transparency about how the trade in minerals is potentially fuelling and funding the armed struggle in the Democratic Republic of Congo and relies on the adverse reputational impact of such disclosure rather than mandating penalties for actually sourcing minerals from conflict-afflicted regions. In addition, as part of the decision to lift certain economic sanctions applicable to Burma/Myanmar, the Obama administration has established new reporting requirements for US companies that are investing more than $500,000 in business in Burma. The reporting requirements include a provision that compels companies to outline the steps they are taking to ensure that their commercial engagements do not contribute to human rights abuses.78 The European Union (EU) has also recently adopted new laws aimed at increasing the transparency of government income from the oil and gas and logging industries. The 2013 EU *Accounting and Transparency Directives* will require European companies to report payments of more than €100,000 made to the government in the country they are operating in, including taxes levied on their income, production or profits, royalties, and license fees.79 These laws feed off the earlier efforts of multi-stakeholder initiatives such as the Extractive Industries Transparency Initiative and Publish What You Pay, which have long championed the need to increase transparency of payments by companies to governments.80 Such reporting requirements – both state and non-state sanctioned - indelibly link transparency with accountability, and in a field where accountability is arguably pursued by civil society with often greater vigour than states, the more information that is made available on global business operations, the more doable the work of these non-state actors becomes to privately regulate corporate activities.81

As these examples illustrate, interactions between public and private regulation can take many different forms and mandating certain aspects of human rights due diligence and reporting is one way in which state regulation can supplement private regulatory efforts to improve corporate compliance with human rights standards.82 Private regulatory mechanisms might sometimes impose more in-depth transparency requirements that exceed state reporting requirements but public regulation could cast a broader net to include companies that have resisted private regulation and also include sanctions for non-compliance that go beyond the reputational sanctions most commonly associated with private regulation.83

The challenges of relying purely on soft law and private regulation to enforce human rights compliance can be somewhat mollified by the supplementary involvement of the state. However, like reliance on soft law and private regulatory mechanisms, the involvement of the state in regulating corporate compliance with human rights, also has its challenges. While legally, it is arguable that states have the ability to impose extraterritorial human rights due diligence and reporting requirements on companies, the political willpower to do so is often lacking. The larger question of how the state might most effectively be involved in this blending of public and private regulation is also significant. For example, the FLA (discussed earlier with regard to the regulation of Apple's Foxconn factories) was convened by government84 which provided an important moral imperative that drew together a variety of stakeholders to address the issue of working conditions both in the US and abroad. But it was probably equally important that the US government then withdrew and let the newly formed not-for-profit organisation (the FLA) get on with the job. This allowed the FLA to be more agile and creative than it could have been had government remained at the table. It also allowed the FLA to operate in exporting countries without being challenged as an agent of US foreign or trade policy. By contrast, another multi-stakeholder initiative, the Voluntary Principles on Security and Human Rights (operating in the extractive sector) has developed with governments assuming a firm seat at the table alongside companies and NGOs and taking a lead role in developing this essentially private form of regulation. What is most effective in terms of blending public and private regulation is thus likely to differ sector by sector, and this can significantly impact the replication capacity of such initiatives. What might work to firm up commitments on security and human rights for the extractive industry where companies often operate in a joint venture with government may not be applicable to the garment sector where a company's supply chain is not generally directly or formally linked with the state.

Regionally too, approaches may differ. Civil society movements (with a strong element of consumer support) based in northern Europe and North America have actively prodded and pushed both companies and governments to take action on solidifying the concept and requirements of corporate responsibility for human rights for several decades. Such issues have only figured more recently on the regional agenda of South East Asian nations despite the ASEAN85 population of approximately 600 million having long provided an abundant and often attractively priced labour force. This potential workforce, combined with lands rich in natural resources, have together acted as a compelling incentive for transnational corporations to source their goods from this region. While consumer advocacy movements are gradually becoming more vocal in this region, other state based compliance triggers, such as trade incentives, are proving to be effective in supplementing private regulation.

One prominent example that showcases regulatory renaissance at work with its mix of public and private regulation is Cambodia's Better Factory program.86 The program developed out of the 1999 US-Cambodia bilateral trade agreement in which increased access to the US market (quota) was linked to tangible improvements in working conditions in Cambodia's garment factories.87 The project, launched in 2001, monitors factory performance against international and national labour standards and was established by the ILO in cooperation with the US and Cambodian governments. Monitoring reports were used not just by the US government to assess quota increases but also by global corporate buyers to determine where they should place their orders. Although quotas were eliminated in 2005, the ILO program continues with the ongoing support of the Garment Manufacturers' Association in Cambodia, international buyers and unions. The program is jointly funded by the US Department of Labor, USAID, Agence Francaise de Development, the Garment Manufacturers' Association in Cambodia, the Royal Government of Cambodia and international buyers.88 Key to the continuation of the program, are the global reputation-conscious buyers who 'in the continuing absence of a [local] well-funded labor inspectorate…appear to be driving improved compliance with ILO labor standards.'89 While international standards such as those found in ILO and human rights treaties are the appropriate baselines against which to monitor corporate compliance they only have meaning if effective remedies and enforcement mechanisms are put in place, or if local governments take them up. To date this has not generally happened and the ILO with its tri-partite structure (business, labour, and government) is often constrained in its efforts to implement the standards it has created. The Better Factories Cambodia project provides a concrete example of how international standards, together with strong monitoring, trade incentives and encouragement by global buyers (in the form of orders), can usefully be combined to form a strong and sustainable basis for improving working conditions.90

More recently ASEAN as a whole has started to open its doors to embracing the concept of corporate social responsibility, even though particular states in this region have a history of reluctance in discussing human rights.91 In its 2009 ASEAN Socio-Cultural Community Blueprint, ASEAN noted that one of its strategic community objectives was to 'ensure that Corporate Social Responsibility is incorporated in the corporate agenda.'92Accordingly, in 2010, the newly formed ASEAN Intergovernmental Commission on Human Rights commenced an (ongoing) thematic study focused on 'Corporate Social Responsibility and Human Rights in ASEAN'.93 A recent study of regional state practices with respect to business and human rights found that while most ASEAN States have substantial legal frameworks governing the rights intersection with business, the key challenge is the weak regulatory effectiveness vis-à-vis corporations which results in greater reliance being placed on private regulation to encourage corporate rights compliance.94 In this region, with a less vocal consumer movement to drive corporate respect for human rights, a variety of regulatory techniques that blend public and private measures can complement each other and lead to improved working conditions.

CONCLUSION

The rise of, and reliance on, soft law and private regulation to drive corporate compliance with human rights is symptomatic of the fact that governments in many of the countries where the goods are produced are unable or unwilling to implement improved working conditions. The logical involvement of the non-state sector (including companies, NGOs, unions, industry bodies and/or international organisations) has been a useful, if not a sufficient tool to temper this governance gap. Private intervention alone is unlikely to be sufficient to develop longevity and consistency around corporate compliance for human rights. For real change to occur governments must get involved. Violations occurring in a far flung factory in Bangladesh are not a problem that can simply be isolated or fixed by focusing on improvements at the factory level. Attention also needs to be directed to the corporate and state policies and practices that are being foisted on the factory from within their borders and beyond, both by states and the global buyers who place the orders in those factories. A blend of private and public regulation is required to tackle these inherent labour problems, and how this unfolds in a world of volatile consumer markets that require increased flexibility in production, rigid labour markets prohibiting flexibility, and rising costs that incentivise cost cutting, is challenging.

There is a convoluted and complex relationship between human rights and corporations, and it is clear that the interplay between national and international law and state and non-state actors is crucial in establishing both a legal and quasi-legal basis and mechanism for holding corporations accountable for human rights violations. While it is uncontested that corporations should obey the law in the jurisdictions in which they operate, where the content of rights in such jurisdictions does not meet the standards of international law or the law is not enforced, there is a failure in the legal governance regime for protecting human rights. The steady evolution of a global social expectation that companies should respect international human rights standards, combined with the occasional foray by states in adopting an expansive extraterritorial approach to protecting rights, is changing the nature and possibility of developing a firmer basis for corporate legal accountability for human rights and in so doing, refining the rules of the game. The growth and depth of soft law mechanisms that have developed around the theme of corporate responsibility have come about partly in recognition of the failure of legal regulation (both internationally and domestically) to hold corporations to account, but these soft law initiatives have become an important tool in attempting to prevent and remedy corporate rights violations.

While this re-regulatory process is slowly but surely refining the rules of the game so that achieving greater respect for human rights is a responsibility not only assumed, but also implemented by state and non-state actors, greater attention needs to be focused on the practical impacts rendered by such a process. Initiatives that might combine elements of public and private regulation, whether in the form of the FLA, the Voluntary Principles on Security and Human Rights or the Cambodia Better Factory project, are still in their relative infancy but new forms of private/public regulation are continuing to emerge. The Global Network Initiative95, the International Code of Conduct for Private Security Service Providers96, the Guiding Principles themselves, and most recently the Bangladeshi garment factory initiatives, are all projects that both emulate and at times, seem to be 'reinventing the wheel' of earlier efforts that combine aspects of soft/hard law and private/public regulation to improve adherence to human rights. More research is needed on what particular aspects of this re-regulation process are most effective in providing greater protection for human rights. Is state involvement a necessity in all sectors to maximise human right protection? What lessons can be learned from those initiatives that have been in operation for the last decade? Does reliance on soft law impede efforts to develop global laws to regulate corporate rights adherence? Would the development of such global laws be effective in tempering rights violations at the ground level? Under what conditions and in what sectors, are government imposed transparency or due diligence regulations likely to be most useful in protecting rights? In what situations should private regulation act as a substitute for state regulations, and are such tactics sustainable in the long term as a rights protection mechanism?

Accepting that rights must be respected by corporations, wherever in the world they operate is one thing, making it happen is quite another. In practical terms, non-state actors have either deliberately or by default, assumed the protective duties of states while some states have sat idly by.97 Utilizing the involvement of other stakeholders in a re-regulatory manner does not absolve a state from acting but rather recognizes that at times, a joint regulatory effort may be more effective than simply relying on the command and control tactics of yesteryear. The questions raised above indicate that there is a vast field of unknowns in this field of research. One mechanism that is being trialled by some states is to legislate extraterritorially and mandate human rights transparency requirements. The information disclosed under such laws can benefit both state and non-state actors in monitoring the impact of corporate activities on human rights but whether such laws will require penalties to be attached to ensure compliance remains to be seen, as does the flow on effect from the disclosures themselves.

What is clear is that the protective role traditionally assigned to states in international human rights law and as recognised in the Guiding Principles will remain relevant only as long as states act on the duties delegated to them. Non-state actors are not so much usurping the role of states but rather simultaneously filling a lacuna and building capacity for governments to get involved and institutionalise the norms being established via soft law. States must not only be able, but be willing to step up to their duty to protect human rights and this will likely be done most effectively by working with the non-state actors who are currently carrying the lion's share of the regulatory burden in this sector.

Notes

[1]M Friedman, 'The Social Responsibility of Business is to Increase its Profits' *New York Times Magazine* (New York, 13 September 1970) <http://www.colorado.edu/studentgroups/libertarians/issues/friedman-soc-resp-business.html>.

[2]UN Human Rights Council, 'Guiding Principles on Business and Human Rights: Implementing the United Nations "Protect, Respect and Remedy" Framework: Report of the Special Representative of the Secretary-General on the Issue of Human Rights and Transnational Corporations and Other Business Enterprises' (21 March 2011) A/HRC/17/31. The Guiding Principles operationalise the 2008 'Protect, Respect and Remedy Framework for Business and Human Rights' also developed by the Special Representative: UN Human Rights Council, 'Protect, Respect and Remedy: A Framework for Business and Human Rights: Report of the Special Representative of the Secretary General on the Issue of Human Rights and Transnational Corporations and Other Business Enterprises' (7 April 2008) A/HRC/8/5.

[3]The Special Representative commented in 2010 that the corporate responsibility to respect rights is a notion that has been gradually emerging and is 'acknowledged in virtually every voluntary and soft-law instrument related to corporate responsibility, and now affirmed by the Human Rights Council itself'. J Ruggie, *The UN 'Protect, Respect and Remedy' Framework for Business and Human Rights* (September 2010) <http://198.170.85.29/Ruggie-protect-respect-remedy-framework.pdf> accessed 24 June 2013. This stands in contrast to earlier views by economist Milton Friedman who argued that it was a 'fundamental misconception of the character and nature of the free economy' for a corporation to have any concern other than maximisation of profit (see M Friedman, *Capitalism and Freedom* (**University of Chicago Press 1962**) 133 and more recently D Henderson, *Misguided Virtue: False Notions of Corporate Social Responsibility*(**Institute of Public Affairs Great Britain 2001**) 147).

[4]J Ruggie, 'Treaty road not travelled' (May 2008) <www.hks.harvard.edu/m-rcbg/news/ruggie/Pages%20from%20ECM%20May_FINAL_JohnRuggie_may%2010.pdf>.

[5]Regulation as referred to in this paper incorporates both formal and informal, legal and non-legal mechanisms or techniques designed to influence or at times coerce corporations to better respect and/or protect human rights.

[6]As defined by Utting, 'the term "multistakeholder initiatives" is often used to refer to voluntary CSR initiatives where two or more stakeholders, actors of interest groups cooperate in the design and application of standards. Such stakeholders often include companies, industry associations, NGOs, trade unions, government agencies and international organizations. Multistakeholder institutions are sometimes legally constituted as not-for-profit organizations, with different interests and actors in their governance structures', in P Utting, 'Rething Business Regulation: From Self-Control to Social Control' (Business and Society Programme Paper Number 15, September 2005) <http://www.unrisd.org/unrisd/website/document.nsf/462fc27bd1fce00880256b4a0060d2af/f02ac3db0ed406e0c12570a10029bec8/$FILE/utting.pdf>.

[7]ibid 14.

[8]ibid 1; R M Locke, *The Promise and Limits of Private Power* (**Cambridge 2013**) 169.

[9]D Shelton, 'Normative hierarchy in international law' (**2006**) 100 AJIL 291, 319. Also see, J Ellis, 'Shades of Grey: Soft Law and the Validity of Public International Law' (**2012**) 25 LJIL 313, 334. Also see D Vogel, 'Private Global Business Regulation' (**2008**) 11 ARPS 261, 262, who refers to civil regulation as soft law and defines it as 'socially focused voluntary global business regulations'.

[10]For an overview of the challenges of utilizing private regulation and soft law in this field see R M Locke, *The Promise and Limits of Private Power* (**Cambridge 2013**); A Sobczak, 'Are Codes of Conduct in Global Supply Chains Really Voluntary: From Soft Law Regulation of Labour Relations to Consumer Law' (**2006**) 16 BEQ 167, 184; E Pariotti, 'International Soft Law, Human Rights and Non-state Actors: Towards the Accountability of Transnational

Corporations?' (**2009**) 10 HRR 139; L Baccaro and V Mele, 'For Lack of Anything Better? International Organizations and Global Corporate Codes' (**2011**) 89 PA 451; S Deva, *Regulating Corporate Human Rights Violations* (**Routledge 2012**) 64-118; W Cragg 'Business and Human rights: a principle and value-based analysis' in W Cragg (ed), *Business and Human Rights* (**Edward Elgar 2012**) 3-46.

[11]UN Human Rights Council, 'Business and Human Rights: Further Steps Toward the Operationalization of the "Protect, Respect and Remedy" Framework; Report of the Special Representative of the Secretary-General on the Issue of Human Rights and Transnational Corporations and Other Business Enterprises' (9 April 2010) UN Doc A/HRC/14/27.

[12]For example, in its 2013 World Report Human Rights Watch noted that 'In 2011 alone, oil and gas behemoth ExxonMobil generated revenues of US$467 billion—the size of Norway's entire economy. Walmart, the world's third-largest employer with more than 2 million workers, has a workforce that trails only the militaries of the United States and China in size.' Human Rights Watch, *World Report 2013* (USA 2013) 29.

[13]The rise of private voluntary initiatives aimed at regulating corporate adherence to human rights has a rich but relatively brief history, is well documented and includes prominent examples such as the the Sullivan Principles regulating business conduct in South Africa during the apartheid era to more recent initiatives such as the Fair Labor Assocation or the Forestry Stewardship Council. See for example: D O'Rourke, 'Outsourcing Regulation: Analysing Nongovernmental Systems of Labor Standards and Monitoring' (**2003**) 31 PSJ 1; E Schrage, *Promoting International Worker Rights through Private Voluntary Initiatives: Public Relations or Public Policy* (**University of Iowa 2004**); D Vogel, 'Private Global Business Regulation' (**2008**) 11 ARPS 261.

[14]R Tieman, 'Supply chain: Groups face rising concern on safety' *Financial Times* (New York, June 11 2013) <http://www.ft.com/intl/cms/s/0/5bd48c1a-b7e2-11e2-9f1a-00144feabdc0.html#axzz2W3By2VWv>.

[15]M Posner, 'Testimony before the United States Congressional Human Rights Caucus "Human Rights And Brand Accountability: How Multinationals Can Promote Labor Rights" ' (8 February 2006) <http://digitalcommons.ilr.cornell.edu/cgi/viewcontent.cgi?article=1012&context=codes> accessed 24 June 2013.

[16]According to official government figures 3,000 people died in the immediate aftermath, but this figure was later revised upward. See Bhopal Gas Tragedy Relief and Rehabilitation Department, Bhopal, State of Mahdya Pradesh, 'Profile' <http://www.mp.nic.in/bptrrdmp/profile.htm>. However according to Amnesty International's estimate between 7,000-10,000 people died within the first three days of the gas leak: Amnesty International, '*Clouds of Injustice: Bhopal Disaster 20 Years On*' (UK 2004).

[17]Deva (n 10) 30.

[18]ibid 28.

[19]Union Carbide Corporation Gas Plant Disaster at Bhopal, India in December 1984. MDL Docket No. 626, US District Court, Southern District of New York, ordered November 8, 1985. Interlocutory Application No. 19, Filed in Court of District Judge, Bhopal, in Regular Suit No. 1113 of 1986, 4 February 1986; Order 05-04-1989 in Civil Appeal Nos. 3187-89, *Union Carbide Corporation v Union of India*, Supreme Court of India.

[20]See JA Manik and S Greenhouse and J Yardley, 'Western Firms Feel Pressure as Toll Rises in Bangladesh' *New York Times* (New York, April 25 2013) <http://www.nytimes.com/2013/04/26/world/asia/bangladeshi-collapse-kills-many-garment-workers.html?pagewanted=all&_r=0>; and D Viederman, 'Supply chains and forced labor after Rana Plaza: lessons learned' *The Guardian* (London, May 30 2013) <http://www.guardian.co.uk/global-development-professionals-network/2013/may/30/rana-plaza-bangladesh-forced-labour-supply-chains>.

[21]See Accord on Fire and Building Safety <http://www.bangladeshaccord.org/>.

[22]See Alliance for Bangladesh Worker Safety <http://www.bangladeshworkersafety.org/>.

[23]S Labowitz, 'The $250 million commitment to Bangladesh's factories misses the point' *Quartz* (New York, July 19 2013) <http://qz.com/105852/the-250-million-commitment-to-bangladeshs-factories-misses-the-point/>.

[24]See ILO, 'Improving Working Conditions in the Ready-Made Garment Sector' <http://www.ilo.org/dhaka/Informationresources/Publicinformation/Pressreleases/WCMS_226720/lang--en/index.htm>.

[25]D Kinley and J Tadaki, 'From Talk to Walk: The Emergence of Human Rights Responsibilities for Corporations at International Law' (**2003–04**) 44 VJIL 931, 944–47.

[26]O De Schutter, 'Extraterritorial Jurisdiction as a Tool for Improving the Human Rights Accountability of Transnational Corporations' (November 2006) <http://www.reports-and-materials.org/Olivier-de-Schutter-report-for-SRSG-re-extraterritorial-jurisdiction-Dec-2006.pdf>.

[27]See Utting (n 6) 14-15.

[28]For a summation of some of these criticisms see A Chakrabortty, 'The woman who nearly died making your iPad' *The Guardian* (London, Monday 5 August 2013) <http://www.theguardian.com/commentisfree/2013/aug/05/woman-nearly-died-making-ipad>; China Labour Watch, 'Beyond Foxconn : Deplorable Working Conditions Characterize Apple's Entire Supply Chain' (June 27 2012) <http://www.chinalaborwatch.org/pdf/2012627-5.pdf>.

[29]FLA Workplace Code of Conduct <http://www.fairlabor.org/labor-standards>.

[30]Fair Labor Association, 'Independent Investigation of Apple Supplier, Foxconn, Report Highlights' (March 2012) <http://www.fairlabor.org/sites/default/files/documents/reports/foxconn_investigation_report.pdf> accessed 24 June 2013.

[31]Other multi-stakeholder initiatives include Social Accountability International, the Ethical Trading Initiative and the Fair Wear Foundation. The Worldwide Responsible Apparel Production (WRAP) is an industry grouping. Such voluntary initiatives set up to regulate supply chains or hold companies accountable vary widely and some have failed to agree on the need for external audits with transparent results. This shortcoming has arguably made them less effective and credible.

[32]UN Human Rights Council, '2011 Report' (n 2) Principle 11.

[33]UN Human Rights Council, '2008 Report' (n 2) [9] and [24].

[34]UN Human Rights Council, '2011 Report' (n 2) Principle 11.

[35]ibid.

[36]A Ganesan, 'UN Human Rights Council: Weak Stance on Business Standards' (16 June 2011) <www.hrw.org/news/2011/06/16/un-human-rights-council-weak-stance-business-standards>; see also AFLCIO, *Responsibility Outsourced: Social Audits, Workplace Certification and Twenty Years of Failure to Protect Worker Rights* (April 23, 2013) <http://www.aflcio.org/Learn-About-Unions/International-Labor-Movement/Responsibility-Outsourced-Report>.

[37]R B Reich, Supercapitalism: The Transformation of Business, Democracy and Everyday Life (**Knopf 2007**) 170, quoted in Locke, n 10, 157.

[38]AFLCIO (n 36) 17.

[39]UNCHR 'Interim Report of the Special Representative of the Secretary General on the Issue of Human Rights and Transnational Corporations and Other Business Enterprises' (22 February 2006) E/CN.4/2006/97 [53].

[40]For example, in the Apple-Foxconn case, the FLA Workplace Code required a maximum of 60 hours worked per week (regular and overtime), while Chinese law limits work to 40 hours per week and a maximum of 36 hours overtime per month, potentially meaning a maximum of 49 hours per week. FLA's audit found both standards had been exceeded. The reality is that the Chinese legal limits are not enforced: Fair Labor Association, n 30, 8.

[41]See for example the Worldwide Responsible Apparel Production (WRAP) <http://www.wrapapparel.org/>.

[42]AE Boyle, 'Some Reflections on the Relationship of Treaties and Soft Law' (**1999**) 48 ICLQ 901-902.

[43]A D'Amato 'Softness in International Law: A Self-Serving Quest for New Legal Materials: A Reply to Jean d'Aspremont' (**2009**) 20 EJIL 897, 899.

[44]C Oka, 'Accounting for the Gaps in Labour Standard Compliance: The Role of Reputation-conscious Buyers in the Cambodian Garment Industry' (**2010**) 22 EJDR 59, 78.

[45]See ie UN Sub-Commission on the Promotion and Protection of Human Rights, 'Norms on the Responsibilities of Transnational Corporations and Other Business Enterprises with Regard to Human Rights' (2003) E/CN.4/Sub.2/2003/12/Rev.2. More generally on earlier UN efforts see P Utting, 'UN-Business Partnerships: Whose Agenda Counts?' (Paper presented at a seminar on Partnerships for Development or Privatization of the Multilateral System?, Oslo, 8 December 2000) <www.unrisd.org/unrisd/website/document.nsf/d2a23ad2d50cb 2a280256 eb300385855/a687857bd5e36114c1256c3600434b5f/$FILE/utting.pdf>.

[46]Locke (n 10) 157.

[47]One positive example of how the synergy between the public and private sector can work to improve labour conditions is the ILO's Better Work program, which is collaboration between the ILO and the International Finance Corporation (IFC) focused on the application of labour standards in private sector development. The Better Factories Cambodia project launched in 2001, has often been held up as providing a concrete example of how international standards together with strong monitoring and trade incentives can usefully be combined to form a strong and sustainable basis for improving working conditions (see discussion at n 88). For a contrary view see International Human Rights and Conflict Resolution Clinic Stanford Law School & Worker Rights Consortium, *Monitoring in the Dark: An evaluation of the International Labour Organization's Better Factories Cambodia monitoring and reporting program* (2013) <http://www.workersrights.org/linkeddocs/Monitoring-In-The-Dark-Stanford-WRC.pdf>.

[48]AE Compa, *Unfair Advantage: Workers' Freedom of Association in the United States under International Human Rights Standards* (Cornell University Press 2004); also Human Rights Watch, *Blood, Sweat, and Fear: Workers' Rights in US Meat and Poultry Plants* (25 January 2005) <http://www.hrw.org/en/reports/2005/01/24/ blood-sweat-and-fear> accessed 1 May 2012.

[49]Fair Labor Association (n 30) 1.

[50]Bangladesh is a prime example of this and the decision by the US government in June 2013 to suspend Bangladesh's trade privileges with the US was an attempt by the US administration to increase the pressure on the Bangladeshi government to act more quickly to improve workers' rights. The involvement of the Bangladesh government in the 2013ILO factory initiative might be interpreted as a sign that such pressure was effective. See S Greenhouse, 'Obama to Suspend Trade Privileges with Bangladesh' *The New York Times* (New York, June 27 2013) <http://www.nytimes.com/2013/06/28/business/us-to-suspend-trade-privileges-with-bangladesh-officials-say.html?emc=edit_na_20130627&_r=0>.

[51]D Kinley and R Chambers, 'The UN Human Rights Norms for Corporations: The Private Implications of Public International Law' (**2006**) 3 HRLR 491.

[52]H Ward, 'Legal Issues in Corporate Citizenship' (February 2003) <http://pubs.iied.org/pdfs/16000IIED.pdf> accessed 1 May 2012.

[53]This is a much broader issue that cannot be fully explored in this paper. It is almost impossible to even compare some of the different multi-stakeholder initiatives as they operate according to invidualistic structures peculiar to their particular sector. For example, the Voluntary Principles on Security and Human Rights (<http://www.voluntaryprinciples.org/>) has a high level of state and corporate involvement but has been persistently criticised for its lack of implementation and enforcement mechanisms. Meanwhile an initiative like the FLA which operates primarily in the apparel and footwear sector, has no governmental involvement (but was formed partly at the behest of government), is stronger on compliance but has been criticised for its lack of union and broad civil society participation.

[54]Locke (n 10) 157.

[55]Baccaro and Mele (n 10) 453.

[56]Vogel (n 9) 263.

[57]Human Rights Watch (n 12) 30.

[58]See Human Rights Watch Reports at <https://www.hrw.org/topic/business>.

[59]Locke (n 10) 2. Command and control regulation might be loosely defined as direct regulation of a company/ industry or activity by legislation that states what is permitted and what

is not.

[60]The fact that states have a duty to protect from third party violations is non-controversial. How far that obligation extends and whether it should be applied extraterritorially is far less settled, see UN Human Rights Council, '2008 Report' (n 2) [18].

[61]For example, a recent briefing paper by an European NGO (SOMO) examined the due diligence efforts of 186 companies that are listed in Europe and make use of the minerals covered by Sec. 1502 of the Dodd–Frank Wall Street Reform and Consumer Protection Act (see discussion at n 77). The results indicated that only a small percentage of EU-listed companies are directly affected by Dodd Frank 1502 and are therefore required to publicly disclose their use of conflict minerals and the large majority of companies that are not required to comply with Dodd Frank 1502 simply do not conduct human rights due diligence on conflict minerals. See T Steinweg and G ten Kate, 'Conflict Due Diligence by European Companies' (November 2013) <http://www.somo.nl/publications-en/Publication_4003?utm_source=SOMO+Alert&utm_campaign=e3922a78cd-SOMO_Alert_Conflict_Minerals10_23_2013&utm_medium=email&utm_term=0_20c962ad76-e3922a78cd-318982993>.

[62]For a discussion of (now) failed legislative attempts in the US, Canada and Australia to impose national human rights standards on companies regardless of where they operate, see A McBeth, 'A Look at Corporate Code of Conduct Legislation' (**2004**) 33 CLWR 222, 251.

[63]UN Human Rights Council, '2011 Report' (n 2) [17] and [18].

[64]For more on this see J Nolan 'The Corporate Responsibility to Respect Human Rights: Soft Law or Not Law?' in S Deva and D Bilchitz (eds), *Human Rights Obligations of Business: Beyond the Corporate Responsibility to Respect?* (**Cambridge University Press 2013**), 138-61.

[65]UN Human Rights Council, '2011 Report' (n 2) [17].

[66]UN Human Rights Council, '2011 Report' (n 2) [17] (Commentary).

[67]UN Committee on Economic, Social and Cultural Rights (CESCR), 'General Comment 14: The Right to the Highest Attainable Standard of Health' (11 August 2000) UN Doc E/C.12/2000/4.

[68]UN CESCR, 'General Comment 15: The right to water' (20 February 2003) UN Doc. E/C.12/2002/11 [31].

[69]UN Human Rights Council, '2011 Report' (n 2) Guiding Principle 1.

[70]The Commentary attached to the Guiding Principles states: 'At present States are not generally required under international human rights law to regulate the extraterritorial activities of businesses domiciled in their territory and/or jurisdiction. Nor are they generally prohibited from doing so, provided there is a recognized jurisdictional basis. Within these parameters some human rights treaty bodies recommend that home States take steps to prevent abuse abroad by business enterprises within their jurisdiction. There are strong policy reasons for home States to set out clearly the expectation that businesses respect human rights abroad, especially where the State itself is involved in or supports those businesses. The reasons include ensuring predictability for business enterprises by providing coherent and consistent messages, and preserving the State's own reputation.

[71]Maastricht Principles on Extraterritorial Obligations of States in the area of Economic, Social and Cultural Rights (29 February 2012) <http://www.lse.ac.uk/humanRights/articlesAndTranscripts/2011/MaastrichtEcoSoc.pdf>; O De Schutter and others, 'Commentary to the Maastricht Principles on Extraterritorial Obligations of States in the area of Economic, Social and Cultural Rights' (**2012**) 34 HRQ 1084, 1135.

[72]Masstricht Principles (n 71), Principle 24 at 5.

[73]ibid Principle 25 at 5 and on a related issue with respect to determining the nationality of a TNC for the purpose of determining the judicial fora in which claims against a TNC may be heard, see the *Barcelona Traction Case* (*Belgium v Spain*) (New Application 1962) [1970] ICJ Rep 3, where the International Court of Justice held that the nationality of a corporation is to be determined by reference to the state in which the TNC is incorporated. This does not, of course, surmount the problems posed by the separation of legal personality recognised throughout the common law world; nor does it dispense of the procedural issues that arise in transnational claims. It does, however, mean that a corporation incorporated, for example, in Australia can in theory be sued in the courts of Australia based on actions committed in another jurisdiction. However the expansive approach taken in the Maastricht Principles stands in contrast to the approach of the US Supreme Court in a 2013 decision examining the extraterritorial liability of corporations for human rights violations. The decision in *Kiobel v Royal Dutch Petroleum Co.* (621 F. 3d 111), while focused exclusively on the jurisdictional limits of peculiar piece of legislation the - Alien Torts Claims Act (ATCA) - complicates the territorial question a little further. In *Kiobel*, a majority of the court further restricted – though did not close the door – to future litigation involving the actions taken by global companies outside the United States, especially for non-US based companies. The justices split five to four in their reasoning with the majority relying on the presumption against extraterritoriality arguing that nothing in the wording, logic or history of the ATCA showed that Congress necessarily meant to sweep into US courts wholly non-US claims involving non-US partics. Justicc Brcycr, however, in a concurrence joined by three others, rejected that the presumption against extraterritoriality applied to the statue and instead advocated an analysis 'guided in part by principles and practices of foreign relations law' (at 1) to determine whether an ATCA plaintiff's allegations involved 'sufficient ties' to the US to trigger jurisdiction. In *Kiobel*, with non-US plaintiffs, defendants and conduct surrounding the claims, it was deemed insufficient to trigger such potential jurisdiction. Recently the United Kingdom (UK) Supreme Court took a more expansive view toward extraterritoriality (albeit not in relation to corporate responsibility) when it considered the extraterritorial application of the ECHR in *Smith (and others) v MOD* [2013] UKSC 41. The Court considered whether the UK government had jurisdiction over British soldiers killed while serving in Iraq. The Supreme Court held unanimously that the UK exercised extraterritorial jurisdiction based on the authority and control over which the UK, through the chain of military command had over the individuals despite the UK no longer exercising 'public powers' in the region.

[74](1977) 15 US Code § 78dd-1.

[75]OECD Convention on Combating Bribery of Foreign Public Officials in International Business Transactions (adopted by the Negotiating Conference on 21 November 1997) and the UN Convention Against Corruption (adopted 31 October 2003, entry into force 14 December 2005) A/58/422.

[76]The UN Global Compact offers businesses a strategic framework aligning their operations with ten universally accepted principles in the areas of human rights, labor, environment and anti-corruption. See United Nations Global Compact, 'What is COP?' (20 March 2013) <http://www.unglobalcompact.org/COP/index.html>.

[77]In addition, Sec. 1504 of the Dodd–Frank Wall Street Reform and Consumer Protection Act (see n 61) addresses financial transparency. This section requires all listed oil and mining companies to disclose the revenues they pay to governments worldwide.

[78]See HumanRights.gov, 'Burma Responsible Investment Reporting Requirements' <http://www.humanrights.gov/wp-content/uploads/2013/05/Responsible-Investment-Reporting-Requirements-Final.pdf>.

[79]See Council Directive 2013/34/EU of 26 June 2013 on the annual financial statements, consolidated financial statements and related reports of certain types of undertakings, amending Directive 2006/43/EC of the European Parliament and of the Council and repealing Council Directives 78/660/EEC and 83/349/EEC [2013] OJ L182/19; Commission, 'Proposal for a Directive of the European Parliament and of the Council amending Directive 2004/109/EC on the harmonisation of transparency requirements in relation to information about issuers whose securities are admitted to trading on a regulated market and Commission Directive 2007/14/EC' COM (2011) 683 final.

[80]Extractive Industries Transparency Initiative <http://eiti.org/;http://www.publishwhatyoupay.org/>.

[81]There are those that argue that the costs of such transparency initiatives (including funding the reporting and due diligence requiements and potentially directing trade away from developing countries in need of foreign investment) outweigh any potential benefits. For a summary of the pros and cons of such arguments, see a transcript of a discussion held on December 13 2011, hosted by Brookings and Global Witness, 'The Transparency, Conflict Minerals and Natural Resources: What You Don't Know About Dodd-Frank' (20 December 2011) <http://www.brookings.edu/research/opinions/2011/12/20-debating-dodd-frank-kaufmann>.

[82]See Locke (n 10) 156-73 for discussion of other ways in which public regulation can be layered on private mechanisms to strenghten compliance with human rights standards.

[83]As one commentator argues 'A soft-law standard will allow an infraction to be cost-effective: that is, a violator of a norm of soft law may suffer reputational loss, but reputational damage may well be worth the benefits that are derived from non-compliance with the norm. By contract, a hard-law system must, without exception, endeavour to make every violation cost-ineffective.' A D'Amato, 'Softness in International Law: A Self-Serving Quest for New Legal Materials: A Reply to Jean d'Aspremont' (**2009**) 20 EJIL 897, 902.

[84]President Clinton's original impetus brought a variety of stakeholders together to form the Apparel Industry Partnership. The US government generally supported the process, but was not directly involved in the governance of the organization. The Apparel Industry Partnership eventually transformed into a non-profit organization in the form of the FLA.

[85]The Association of Southeast Asian Nation (ASEAN) is a geo-political and economic organisation of ten countries located in Southeast Asia, which was formed on 8 August 1967 by Indonesia, Malaysia, the Philippines, Singapore and Thailand. Since then, membership has expanded to include Brunei, Burma (Myanmar), Cambodia, Laos, and Vietnam.

[86]Better Factories Cambodia <http://betterfactories.org/>.

[87]The US - Cambodia Textile Trade Agreement was the first agreement of its kind to link increased access to US markets to improved working conditions in an exporting country. Textile and garment quotas were eliminated in January 2005 with the end of the Multi - Firber Agreement (MFA).

[88]ILO, 'Better Factories Cambodia' (14 October 2008) <http://www.ilo.org/asia/whatwedo/projects/WCMS_099340/lang--en/index.htm>.

[89]See Locke (n 10) 171.

[90]In October 2013, the ILO and the International Finance Corporation (IFC) announced a partnership to launch Better Work Bangladesh which will provide factory-level services, including assessments of compliance with national labor laws and international standards, <http://betterwork.org/global/?p=3735>. However, while the ILO program has brought benefits to Cambodia's flourishing garment industry it is a program in process rather than a template for resolving prolematic working conditions. Recent labour unrest by Cambodian garment workers demanding an increase in their minimum wage illustrates the temporary nature of any 'solution' to improving working conditions, see: G Mullany, 'Workers face police gunfire amid unrest in Cambodia' *The New York Times*(New York, January 3 2014) <http://www.nytimes.com/2014/01/04/world/asia/cambodia-protests.html?_r=0>.

[91]C Renshaw, 'The ASEAN Human Rights Declaration 2012', (2013) 3 HRLR 557, 579; **B Saul and J Mowbray and I Baghoomians**, 'Resistance to Regional Human Rights Cooperation in the Asia-Pacific: Demythologizing Regional Exceptionalism by Learning from the Americas, Europe and Africa' in H Nasu and B Saul (eds), *Human Rights in the Asia-Pacific Region: Towards Institution Building*, (107-126). A Byrnes and A Durbach and C Renshaw 'A Tongue but No Teeth? The Emergence of a New Human Rights Mechanism in the Asia Pacific Region' (**2009**) 31 (2) SLR 211, 238.

[92]ASEAN, 'ASEAN Socio-Cultural Community Blueprint' (2009) <http://www.asean.org/archive/5187-19.pdf>. But there has been persistent criticism from civil society in the region about the lack of consultations on these issues, and the slow pace with which discussions are proceeding. See Solidarity for Asian Peoples Advocacy, 'Civil Society Statement on Corporate Accountability in ASEAN' (13 November 2012) <http://seaca.net/viewArticle.php?aID=1058>.

[93]Part of the newly established regional Intergovernmental Commission on Human Rights' mandate, since its establishment in October 2009, is to promote and protect human rights that will complement the building of the ASEAN Community.

This involves, it argues, developing a common framework to accelerate the promotion of CSR and human rights in the region, and policy development. The 'Five Year Work Plan of the ASEAN Intergovernmental Commission on Human Rights (2010 – 2015)' notes CSR as one of its thematic studies. The study is still ongoing, <http://aichr.org/documents/>.

[94]Human Rights Resource Centre Business and Human Rights in ASEAN, *A Baseline Study 2013* <http://hrrca.org/data/business-and-human-rights-asean-baseline-study>.

[95]Global Network Initiative <http://www.globalnetworkinitiative.org/>.

[96]International Code of Conduct for Private Security Service Providers <http://www.icoc-psp.org/>.

[97]Human Rights Watch (n 12) 30.

REFERENCES

1. Baccaro L and Mele V, 'For Lack of Anything Better? International Organizations and Global Corporate Codes' (2011) 89 PA 451
2. Boyle AE, 'Some Reflections on the Relationship of Treaties and Soft Law' (1999) 48 ICLQ 901
3. Byrnes A and Durbach A and Renshaw C, 'A Tongue but No Teeth? The Emergence of a New Human Rights Mechanism in the Asia Pacific Region' (2009) 31 (2) SLR 211
4. Cragg W, 'Business and Human rights: a principle and value-based analysis' in Wesley Cragg (ed), *Business and Human Rights* (Edward Elgar 2012)
5. D'Amato A, 'Softness in International Law: A Self-Serving Quest for New Legal Materials: A Reply to Jean d'Aspremont' (2009) 20 EJIL 897
6. De Schutter O and others, 'Commentary to the Maastricht Principles on Extraterritorial Obligations of States in the area of Economic, Social and Cultural Rights' (2012) 34 HRQ 1084.
7. Deva S, *Regulating Corporate Human Rights Violations* (Routledge 2012)
8. Ellis J, 'Shades of Grey: Soft Law and the Validity of Public International Law' (2012) 25 LJIL 313
9. Friedman M, *Capitalism and Freedom* (University of Chicago Press 1962)
10. Henderson D, *Misguided Virtue: False Notions of Corporate Social Responsibility* (Institute of Public Affairs Great Britain 2001)
11. Kinley D and Tadaki J, 'From Talk to Walk: The Emergence of Human Rights Responsibilities for Corporations at International Law' (2003–04) 44 VJIL 931
12. Kinley D and Chambers R, 'The UN Human Rights Norms for Corporations: The Private Implications of Public International Law' (2006) 3 HRLR 491
13. Locke RM, *The Promise and Limits of Private Power* (Cambridge 2013)
14. McBeth A, 'A Look at Corporate Code of Conduct Legislation' (2004) 33 CLWR 222
15. Nolan J, 'The Corporate Responsibility to Respect Human Rights: Soft Law or Not Law?' in Surya Deva and David Bilchitz (eds), *Human Rights Obligations of Business: Beyond the Corporate Responsibility to Respect?* (Cambridge University Press 2013)
16. Oka C, 'Accounting for the Gaps in Labour Standard Compliance: The Role of Reputation-conscious Buyers in the Cambodian Garment Industry' (2010) 22 EJDR 59
17. O'Rourke D, 'Outsourcing Regulation: Analysing Nongovernmental Systems of Labour Standards and Monitoring' (2003) 31 PSJ 1
18. Pariotti E, 'International Soft Law, Human Rights and Non-state Actors: Towards the Accountability of Transnational Corporations?' (2009) 10 HRR 139
19. Reich RB, *Supercapitalism: The Transformation of Business, Democracy and Everyday Life*(Knopf 2007)
20. Saul B and Mowbray J and Baghoomians I, 'Resistance to Regional Human Rights Cooperation in the Asia-Pacific: Demythologizing Regional Exceptionalism by Learning from the Americas, Europe and Africa' in Hitoshi Nasu and Ben Saul (eds), *Human Rights in the Asia-Pacific Region: Towards Institution Building* (Routledge 2011)
21. Schrage E, *Promoting International Worker Rights through Private Voluntary Initiatives: Public Relations or Public Policy* (University of Iowa 2004)
22. Shelton D, 'Normative hierarchy in international law' (2006) 100 AJIL 291
23. Sobczak A, 'Are Codes of Conduct in Global Supply Chains Really Voluntary: From Soft Law Regulation of Labour Relations to Consumer Law' (2006) 16 BEQ 167
24. Vogel D, 'Private Global Business Regulation' (2008) 11 ARPS 261

CHAPTER 3

CONTRACTUAL CONTROL AND LABOUR-RELATED CSR NORMS IN THE SUPPLY CHAIN

Louise Vytopil

Keywords: Corporate social responsibility, supply chain, contracts, codes of conduct, general terms and conditions

INTRODUCTION

This article explores the choices that multinational companies make in order to regulate corporate social responsibility aspects of their supply chains. The first part will look at the context in which these companies operate and explain the relevance of the questions which are central to this article. Furthermore, the methodology will be set out. The second part provides a theoretical private law background with respect to contracts, general terms and conditions and codes of conduct in the Netherlands. The final part will answer the following research questions: what do the codes of conduct and CSR contracts currently used by best-practice players look like? What are the contractual consequences (both in terms of possibilities and limitations) of these instruments? The article will answer these questions by describing the initiatives that fourteen Dutch multinational companies currently use in order to regulate their supply chains. Furthermore, it will qualify these initiatives in terms of contract law and highlight some patterns found in these initiatives.

SETTING THE STAGE

Over the past couple of decades, the world in which companies operate has changed dramatically. Since the early 1990s, there has been a strong increase in the amount of companies that operate multinationally. At the end of the 1960s, only 7,000 multinational companies (MNCs) had been registered, expanding to over 30,000 in the early 1990s and 60,000 at the start of the new millennium.1 An important role in this respect has been played by globalisation. The process of globalisation encompasses many different aspects, such as de-territorialisation, increased use of technology and heightened transparency. These factors combined create – what the Netherlands Socio-Economic Council (Sociaal-Economische Raad, SER) refers to as – increased interconnectedness.2 Companies may export their products to countries around the world or relocate part of their production process to lower-wage countries.3 Companies located in low-wage countries, such as India, China and Bangladesh, increasingly do business for firms based in Europe and the United States. Furthermore, many developing countries have set up export processing zones.4

By operating in multiple countries, MNCs can take advantage of the weak points that each specific legal system offers, while planning the legal structure of their daughter companies so that the corporate veil is best utilised to avoid liability for any violations of the law.5 This can lead to undesirable consequences: through their daily operations, MNCs may damage the local environment or they may commit human rights abuses. So how is the behaviour of MNCs governed when they operate across borders? While companies are traditionally governed by the law of their corporate seat, their home states, generally speaking, do not have any legislative power or control when their corporate citizens operate across the borders of nation states as the result of the territoriality principle. At the same time, host states may lack the expertise or resources to regulate adequately.6 Globalisation has also eroded the power of the nation state. As a result, regulating the behaviour of companies operating across the borders of nation states is complex. Thus the behaviour of MNCs is often not (effectively) regulated. What remains is a regulatory gap in which multinationals operate. Western multinationals thus make use of global supply chains in order to provide their goods and services to the public, but these global supply chains are often not regulated by public law. At the same time, information processes have changed as a result of globalisation. If things go wrong, the world becomes aware of this within a matter of minutes.

Citation: Louise Vytopil, Contractual Control and Labour-Related CSR Norms in the Supply Chain, DOI: http://doi.org/10.18352/ulr.186.

And as has been shown by various examples, things do go wrong. Consider, for example, the suicides at a Foxconn factory in Shenzen, Southern China, producing electronics for – inter alia – Dell and Apple.7 Or Shell's massive oil-spills in the Ogoni delta in Nigeria, resulting in the devastation of many square kilometres of water and farmland, for which it recently accepted liability.8 MNCs are held accountable (both by the media and – to a slightly lesser extent – in the legal arena) for these wrongdoings. MNCs themselves now take action in order to prevent human rights violations from occurring. These private initiatives are often brought together under the umbrella term of corporate social responsibility (CSR); in the words of Freer Spreckley described as the 'triple P bottom line' of People, Planet and Profit.9 In the words of the European Commission: initiatives that 'contribute to a better society and a cleaner environment'.10 This concept of CSR as encompassing the 'triple P' is currently widely accepted among academics and companies alike. This article will not elaborate on the question whether or not companies should undertake CSR measures.11 After all, I believe that it is clear that companies do undertake CSR measures and, therefore, the focus should not be on whether they should do so, but rather, on gaining greater insight into their CSR initiatives. What do they look like and how can they be qualified?

While in the early days of CSR many companies did not concern themselves with written policies, over the past few decades the code of conduct (COC) has taken off.12 Rule-setting in CSR is now mostly undertaken by private actors rather than public actors: MNCs increasingly rely on self-regulation, soft law and codes of conduct. And while CSR and these private law initiatives are largely voluntary13 by nature, they are not entirely non-committal. The same holds true for CSR in the supply chain. It is generally held that MNCs are no longer simply responsible for preventing wrongdoings by their own company, but rather that they also have a (limited) responsibility with regard to their business partners, including supply partners. This conclusion is supported by the business and human rights framework drafted by the United Nations Special Representative for Business & Human Rights, John Ruggie. The framework, entitled 'Protect, Respect and Remedy' (the 'UN Framework'), describes the obligations that businesses have with regard to human rights. This framework was endorsed by the UN Human Rights Council on 16 June 2011 and sets out the responsibilities that – inter alia – businesses have with regard to their operations and human rights. They are to respect human rights, acting with due diligence and dealing with any problems that may arise. This responsibility extends to the supply chain that companies use when producing their goods or services. According to Ruggie, companies are to take on responsibilities with regard to CSR in the supply chain.

These responsibilities are echoed in the 2011 update to the OECD Guidelines,14 which incorporates and builds upon the UN Framework. For the first time, the 2011 update contains both the general notion that enterprises are to exercise due diligence and the view that companies are to avoid any negative impact as a result of their business, regardless of whether such a negative impact is caused by their own operations or by others in their supply chain. Such a 'responsibility' in respect of CSR and responsible supply chain management is therefore widely accepted at this moment in time; however, it should be noted that it is only that: a 'responsibility', not a (legal) obligation. Many companies feel the demand for responsible supply chain management from society and NGOs. This is reflected in their CSR policies: nowadays, these often include supply chain issues. In the Netherlands, 60% of the largest companies investigated in the 2010 Transparency Benchmark addressed supply chain issues in some way or another in their CSR policy.15 There is currently no strict liability for MNCs who engage with suppliers in low-wage countries, although, from time to time, politicians have called for further responsibilities. In the Netherlands, such a call came from Parliament in 2007, when it requested the SER to advise on the necessity of legislation on supply chain responsibility. The Labour Party (PvdA) had proposed an Act on the Transparency of Product Chains (Wet Openbaarheid Ketens).16 The European Parliament, as well, has called for legislation that would create a strict liability for any MNC that included child labour in its supply chain, regardless of where this child labour would take place.17 Furthermore, calls have come for European legislation in respect of the use of conflict minerals throughout the supply chain; up until now, however, no such legislation exists.18

So while no legislation on CSR in the supply chain exists in the Netherlands, it is widely accepted that companies have a certain degree of responsibility with regard to their supply chain. The extent of this responsibility is not yet clear, however. The question whether and, if so, how these CSR issues in the supply chain are incorporated in contractual documents has not yet been answered. Moreover, it is not always clear what the contractual consequences of these choices are in terms of both tort and contract law. This article attempts to answer these questions in terms of contract law and their binding nature. It investigates the content of the codes of conduct and the CSR contracts of best-practice players in the Netherlands. It examines how these documents are incorporated in contractual relationships between multinationals and their suppliers and what is required in order for these documents to be contractually binding. Finally, it proposes a categorisation of these measures and investigates their binding nature.

METHODOLOGY

The first part of this research attempts to answer the following question: what do the contractual measures taken by MNCs in respect of CSR in the supply chain consist of? The sample of approached companies consisted of 45 Dutch multinationals: the top 25 stock exchange (AEX) listed companies19 and an additional 20 companies from industries that have traditionally developed CSR policies (the food and garment industries). It was expected that approximately 25% of these companies would be willing to participate. For this qualitative research, a sample of 10-15 companies would provide sufficient information upon which to build a model of possible choices. These multinationals were first approached by telephone, then sent a letter with more information on the research. This letter was – if necessary – again followed up with a phone call to further discuss the research. A total of 16 companies participated, of which 14 were interviewed before this research was concluded (30%). Seven of these companies were AEX listed at the time of participation and six were also represented in the Dow Jones Sustainability World Index 2010 (out of a total of 13 Dutch companies in that Index). A variety of sectors were represented: finance (2), energy (2), clothing (3), food

(2), electronics (2), services (1) and chemicals and construction (2). All companies requested that they remain anonymous.

Scripted interviews were held with each participating company, nearly all of which took place in person. Relevant documentation was gathered from the internet where possible; documents not publicly available were obtained from the company. Non-public documentation mostly consisted of model agreements (such as purchasing agreements) and general terms and conditions. All companies were requested to provide all relevant documentation regarding CSR in the supply chain (i.e. both in respect of 'people' and 'planet' aspects). However, in order to make the analysis manageable, not all possible aspects of CSR could be included in this research. After all, this would lead to comparing documents on corruption (common in, inter alia, the building industry) and CO2 reduction with documents on health and safety (common in the food industry). It was therefore necessary to find some 'common ground' in the CSR measures adopted by these companies. In respect of assessing the content of CSR measures (which aspects were included and how they were described), only labour rights embodied in the eight ILO Core Conventions were included.20 The reason for focusing on these core labour rights is threefold. First of all, all companies included in the sample included most or all of those rights in their CSR documentation. Furthermore, the ILO Core Conventions are historically widely accepted and lie at the heart of core CSR documents such as the OECD Guidelines and Ruggie's framework.21 Finally, the rights embedded in these core conventions are fairly unambiguous: one can include quantitative standards with regard to – for example – child labour and list the grounds of discrimination. This makes a comparison of the content of the CSR measures that companies take in respect of these aspects fairly easy.

The empirical research was conducted between February 2011 and August 2011. Any new policies or codes of conduct dated thereafter were not included in this research. The second part of this research analyses the contractual instruments in terms of content. The content of the codes was analysed based on an adaptation of the model by Kolk and Van Tulder.22 That model analyses codes on the basis of their stringency, focusing on which human rights standards have been incorporated, to what degree codes will be implemented, what type of control is established and how stringent that code is. Codes were then classified as strong, moderate or weak.

In the third part of this research, the contractual aspects of these model choices studied were analysed on the basis of Dutch private law. The possibilities and limitations of these options in terms of private law are explored: are codes binding? Are there any issues in terms of contract law? In a later stage of the research, aspects of contractual and extracontractual liability will also be investigated for these options. It should be noted that this research does not attempt to answer the question of why companies choose certain CSR measures and how effective the implementation of these measures is.23 The subject is approached from a private law angle and is not looked at from a business ethics or law and economics perspective.

INSTRUMENTS FOR CONTRACTUAL CONTROL AND DUTCH LAW

Once a company decides to take control of corporate social responsibility in its supply chain by means of contractual control,24 it has a wide range of private law instruments at its disposal. It may choose to connect with existing codes of conduct, for instance with those that exist in the sector in which the company operates, or it may find that a better fit can be obtained if the company drafts its own code of conduct or incorporates specific clauses in its contracts or general terms and conditions. In order to assess these instruments correctly, some aspects of international private law must be discussed. After all, the nature of these contracts is inherently international, and while MNCs would prefer to see their own law applied to the contract, this may not always happen. This section will therefore first explore some aspects of private international law. Next, the theory behind various instruments will be discussed. First, the option of a contract. What is required for a binding contract to come into existence under Dutch law? The second option is to shape a CSR instrument in the form of general terms or conditions. What consequences does this have for the validity of the instrument? How does a 'battle of the forms' play out under Dutch law? Finally, I will discuss codes of conduct. I will propose a model in order to analyse and compare them, based on the model proposed by Van Tulder and Kolk,25 and will answer the question whether codes of conduct are binding upon the MNC under Dutch law.

Private International Law

The nature of the contracts is international; supply contracts that concern CSR-sensitive products or services are generally concluded between a Western MNC and a low-cost country supplier. As a result, it is necessary to study which legal system is to apply to these contracts and codes of conduct. In respect of the Netherlands, the Rome I Regulation on the Law Applicable to Contractual Obligations (Rome I) will govern which law is applicable to contracts in civil and commercial cases (Article 1 Rome I). Rome I has been in effect since 17 December 2009 and it is universally applicable. As a result, the law specified by Rome I will be applied, regardless of whether it is the law of an EU Member State.

Article 3 Rome I states that if a choice of law has been made, the law chosen will be applicable to the contract. Parties are free to choose which legal system applies to the agreement, except in those cases where Rome I only provides for certain legal systems. This is not the case for the contracts at hand. If no choice of law has been made, Article 4 Rome I prescribes that the law governing the contract is the law of the state with which it is most closely connected. Article 4 Rome I provides a number of examples: in the case of a sales contract (Article 4(1)) this will be the law of the state in which the seller is located. If more than one specific element listed under Article 4 is present, the law of the state of the 'characteristic performance' will govern the contract, unless it is clear that the contract is more closely connected to another country; in that case, the law of the latter country will apply. If the contract does not include a choice of law, the law of the home state of the MNC will often therefore not be the law which governs the contract, but rather the law of the country in which the supplier is located. Generally speaking, however, most MNCs will include a choice of law in their contract. In approximately 90% of all contracts investigated, the MNC will choose the law of its home state as the law applicable to the contract.26 In most cases, the law that governs the contract will therefore be the law of the home state.27

If parties engage in a discussion as to whether a contract has been concluded at all or whether general terms and conditions apply, there may also be a discussion with regard to which law governs these pre-contractual questions. These issues are relevant in the case of CSR codes of conduct and contracts, since MNCs may argue that no legally binding contract has come into being since the parties did not intend to be legally bound. Article 10 Rome I indicates that the 'existence and validity of a contract shall be determined by the law which would govern it (…) if the contract were valid', in other words: the lex causae. This is only different (Article 10(2)) if one party states that it has not consented to the contract; in such a case, the law of its home state applies if, considering the circumstances, it would not be reasonable to base the consequences of that party's behaviour on the law specified in Article 10(1). These questions will therefore be governed by the law that would have governed the contract if it were assumed that a contract had validly been concluded; this is usually the home state of the MNC, unless one party disputes that it has consented at all, in which case the law of its home state may apply.

Contracts

The most straightforward choice a company could make if it wanted to regulate CSR issues with its supply partners would be to include one or more CSR clauses in its supply contracts. This section will briefly explore how and where contract law is regulated in the Netherlands. Furthermore, it will set out which requirements need to be met in order for a contract to come into place, and – to some extent – how third parties may be impacted by the content of the contract. Contracts are regulated in the Burgerlijk Wetboek (Dutch Civil Code, DCC). A contract comes into being by an offer and a subsequent acceptance (Article 6:217 Paragraph 1 DCC). An offer is only qualified as such if a proposal to enter into an agreement is made, containing all essential elements of that agreement, so that a simple 'yes' by the contracting party can suffice. Acceptance of the offer flows from the 'yes' by the contracting party. If the acceptance differs from the offer, the 'acceptance' should in fact be qualified as a new offer (Article 6:225 DCC) and as a rejection of the original offer.28

In practice, there may be some discussion as to whether a statement qualifies as an offer or not. A company may state that it did not wish to express an offer, but rather that its statement was the expression of an aspiration, and that those statements were not intended to have any legal consequences. How does Dutch law deal with such a scenario? In order for a contract to come into existence, parties must declare their intention (wilsverklaring), this declaration of intent being a kind of legal act as described in Article 3:33 DCC. If the intention of a (legal) person diverges from its declaration, such as when an MNC does not wish to be legally bound by its statement, the question is what should prevail. Should that be the appearance of the party's declaration or its intention? Article 3:35 DCC states that the outward appearance of the declaration prevails over the internal will of the person acting, as long as the other party has justifiably relied upon the intent of the person acting. This system is known as the will/reliance doctrine (wilsvertrouwensleer) and it not only applies to the question whether an offer has been made but also to the question whether an offer has been accepted (see also Section 4.3). Generally speaking, most companies will clarify whether a policy or document is intended to be legally binding by inserting wording to that effect. If this is not clear, however, it will depend on the circumstances of the case at hand whether or not a statement could have been interpreted as an offer.

The enforceability of a contract furthermore depends on whether the contract contains determinable terms (Article 6:227 DCC) and is sufficiently certain. This criterion is met if the content of the obligations is sufficiently clear or determinable.29 Assuming this is the case, the obligations arising from the contract are legally enforceable. Besides being held to the obligations that flow from the contract, contracting parties also have other legal obligations. Article 6:2 DCC states that contracting parties are required to act in conformity with the requirements of reasonableness and fairness. This requirement of reasonableness and fairness is elaborated upon in Article 6:248 Paragraph 1 DCC: the agreement has the consequences that the parties have agreed upon, although the nature of the agreement, law, custom and demands of reasonableness and fairness may colour the agreement. Furthermore, if the content of a contract is unclear or incomplete, the 'Haviltex criterion' will form the basis of its interpretation. In that case, the interpretation of such a written contract should not be based on a purely textual explanation of that contract, but rather on what the parties, in the given circumstances, could reasonably expect from one another, taking into account their social background and any legal knowledge they may have.30

A contract between two parties may, under certain circumstances, also have consequences for others that are not party to the contract. The following may be relevant within the context of CSR contracting.31 The first option is that of a perpetual clause (kettingbeding) in a contract. This option provides for the possibility that contractual obligations between two parties are continued by their successors. Dutch law poses no specific requirements on the validity of a perpetual clause. An example of a perpetual clause in a CSR context (and one that is used in practice, as we will see) is that the MNC provides that the COC not only applies to their contractual relationship, but that the supplier must also include this COC in the contracts with its sub-tier suppliers. In this way, the COC of one MNC can possibly apply to the entire supply chain. However, there are issues in the case of non-compliance with such perpetual clauses under Dutch law. The MNC only contracts with its supply partner, not with sub-tier suppliers. If, contrary to its contractual obligations, the supplier fails to include a certain clause in the contracts with its sub-suppliers, on the basis of contract law the MNC can only make claims vis-à-vis its own supplier. But the MNC cannot force the sub-tier supplier (which, after all, is not its contracting partner) to observe certain clauses from a contract to which it is not a party. At the same time, Dutch case law has deemed it impossible for the stipulator of a perpetual clause to claim damages from the third party on the basis of extra-contractual liability.32 A qualitative obligation is not the solution in these cases since qualitative obligations can only cover acts of tolerating facts or refraining from acts (Article 6:251 DCC). Despite their limited effectiveness – there is no possibility to restore the contractual clause, it is difficult to claim damages from sub-tier suppliers – perpetual clauses are the only contractual solution for such a situation.

It may also be possible for third parties to derive rights from a contract to which are not a party. If the MNC and the supplier include a clause in their contract that indicates that employees must be granted a certain minimum protection of employment rights or a minimum salary, one can question whether these employees can directly make claims under this contract, despite not being parties to it. The clause on behalf of a third party is regulated under Dutch law in Articles 6:253 and 6:254 DCC. If A and B agree upon a clause on behalf of C, B is contractually obliged to fulfil this obligation if C accepts the clause. Until C has accepted this clause, C cannot claim rights under the agreement. Such acceptance may be implicit, as with 'regular' two-party contracts. If a clause on behalf of a third party is not complied with, both the third party and the stipulator may request performance, unless the stipulator has no interest in performance or the third party resists the stipulators' claim for performance.33

If a contract has been validly concluded between parties through an offer and a subsequent acceptance of that offer, it has the consequences that the parties have agreed upon, as well as any other consequences stipulated by law. If the supplier does not comply with the contract, the MNC will have various legal options at its disposal to pressure the MNC into observing the contract.34 Contracts will therefore be a legally effective option that is at the MNC's disposal in order to regulate its supply chain. It may nevertheless be more convenient for a MNC not to have to draft a new contract for each separate supplier. If the MNC wants to use a standard set of clauses, it may either use a standard contract form which can be adapted for each individual supplier, or it may use a set of general terms and conditions that is applied to all contracts of a certain type. Most legal systems provide some sort of separate regulation for these terms and conditions. They will be discussed in the next section.

General Terms and Conditions

Most companies use general terms and conditions in some shape or form within the course of their daily business. Some incorporate CSR terms in their general terms and conditions, or make a reference to a CSR policy or COC. But what are general terms and conditions and how are they regulated under Dutch law?

General terms and conditions are a set of standardised conditions, which are used repeatedly and do not encompass the core terms from the contract. Title 6.5.3 of the DCC regulates general terms and conditions.35 Article 6:247 DCC of that title contains scope rules in respect of three situations. First of all, if both parties are professionals and located in the Netherlands, Title 6.5.3 applies, regardless of the law that governs the agreement (Paragraph 1). If both are professional parties but one or both are located outside of the Netherlands, Title 6.5.3 does not apply, regardless of the law that applies to the agreement (Paragraph 2). Lastly, if the contracting party is a consumer and is located in the Netherlands, Title 6.5.3 applies, regardless of the law that applies to the agreement (Paragraph 4). The reason for not applying Title 6.5.3 to professional contracting parties in international situations is to create greater legal certainty for parties which operate in such an international setting; foreign users of general terms and conditions do not have to take Title 6.5.3 into account when drafting their terms that may be used for Dutch contracting parties. Given the nature of the agreements studied in this research, it is very unlikely that either the situation mentioned in Paragraph 1 or in Paragraph 4 of Article 6:247 DCC would apply. In virtually all cases, the supplier will be a professional party located outside of the Netherlands (Paragraph 2). As a result, Title 6.5.3 will generally not apply to the agreements studied, even if Dutch law applies to the agreement.36 If this title does not apply to the general terms and conditions at hand, those terms and conditions will only be governed by the applicable contract law.37 As a result, in order to evaluate whether the terms and conditions used are valid and binding, one should refer to the general framework for contracting as set out above. Furthermore, the following should be noted.

General terms and conditions become part of the contract as a result of an offer and an acceptance; upon accepting the user's general terms and conditions, its contracting party is bound by them. In practice, it may occur that two parties each refer to their own general terms and conditions and want them to be applied to the agreement. This is referred to as a battle of the forms. Different legal systems adhere to different systems in respect of the battle of the forms. The Netherlands adheres to the 'first shot' system of the battle of the forms. Article 6:225 Paragraph 3 DCC covers the battle of the forms. This clause is not part of Title 6.5.3 and therefore also applies if the parties are international professionals. This article stipulates that the first reference is valid; the second reference only has effect if the first set of general terms and conditions is explicitly rejected. A standardised announcement that one's own terms and conditions will apply is not sufficient to meet the criterion of an 'explicit rejection'. Mentioning that one's own set will apply, to the exclusion of all other terms and conditions, will however suffice, subject to the condition that it is presented in a manner that is to be taken seriously.38

Another issue which is specific to general terms and conditions is the following. At times, general terms and conditions refer to yet other terms and conditions, which may or may not be provided to the contracting party at the time of contracting. Under Dutch law, such a reference to a second set of general terms and conditions will not mean, generally speaking, that this second set also becomes part of the contract. Only if the contracting party has read the second set of terms and conditions, or creates the impression of knowing their content, is this not an issue, since – as Jongeneel points out – the contracting party has either intended to be bound by these terms (Article 3:33 DCC) or has created the impression that it has such an intention (Article 3:35 DCC).39 All in all, the nature of general terms and conditions (i.e. their repeated use) makes them a practical instrument for CSR contracting. Under Dutch law, general terms and conditions that are used in an international setting are not specifically regulated and are only subject to general contracting laws, making them a fairly flexible and convenient option. But there is another option at the disposal of the MNC wishing to regulate its supply chain: the code of conduct.

Codes of Conduct

What constitutes a code of conduct? There are a number of aspects that scholars generally agree upon. The first is the principle of voluntariness. This is not necessarily voluntariness in the sense that once a company uses a code, it does not need to abide by it, but rather that the target group creating or adopting the code was under no (legal) obligation to do so. Another aspect often highlighted is that codes of conduct contain a set of norms and standards. Van Tulder and Van der Zwart40 define codes of conduct as 'a set of agreements with which an organization indicates which behavior it expects from its members (and possibly business partners) in certain, defined situations.' If a company decides to include a code of conduct as part of its broader CSR policy, it has a wide range of policies that it can choose from, varying from codes created by international organisations such as the OECD, sectoral initiatives such as the Electronic Industry Citizenship Coalition, or it may draft a code itself. Codes of conduct may contain a wide range of topics: societal responsibility, human rights, the environment, responsible investment, the integrity of employees, and so on.41

In order to make reasonable comparisons on the basis of a fairly small sample, this research only focuses on the labour norms and standards laid down in the eight core conventions of the International Labour Organization (ILO). The following four categories are covered by a total of eight ILO core conventions: (i) freedom of association and collective bargaining, (ii) prohibition of child labour, (iii) prohibition of forced labour, and (iv) non-discrimination. These principles are widely recognised and have been included in the ILO's Tripartite Declaration of Principles Concerning Multinational Enterprises and Social Policy as well as in the UN Global Compact principles. In order to identify the legal status of (voluntary) codes of conduct, one must distinguish the question whether a MNC can be held accountable by a third party on the basis of such a code, from the question of the binding nature between the MNC and its supply partner. I will first answer the question whether a MNC is bound by its own COC in relation to third parties. This is also the question that most of the discussions concerning the binding nature of codes of conduct in the literature have revolved around. Although the first question is more relevant in respect of liability for CSR violations by MNCs, and this research relates to the use of private law instruments in the supply chain (rather than the use of COCs in general), I will briefly discuss these theories since they provide background information on how codes of conduct are classified in private law in general. I will then discuss the question of the binding nature of a COC on supply partners. This section will restrict itself to situations where the code of conduct is not embedded in another kind of private law initiative, such as a contract or general terms.

The answer to the question whether codes of conduct are legally binding upon the MNC that publicly adheres to them is not clear-cut. Generally speaking, there are two streams of thought in the international literature. The maximalist perspective argues that codes of conduct are legally binding and that the clauses of these codes should be enforceable in the courts. The minimalist view believes that the character of codes of conduct is not legally binding and that compliance with these codes should be voluntary. A third perspective is that of the 'zebra code', which contains both legally binding and nonbinding clauses.42 From an international perspective, the minimalist view is dominant.43 An example of this is the reference in the OECD Guidelines, which indicates that 'observance (...) is voluntary and not legally enforceable'.44 Similarly, in the Netherlands the general notion is that voluntarily drafted or accepted codes are not legally binding for those that adhere to them.45 It is often also claimed that the provisions contained in a code are not legally binding, at least that such a binding nature does not naturally flow from the instrument of a code of conduct. Koelemeijer asserts that if any binding nature of clauses in a code is to be induced, this does not flow from the code itself but rather from general or more specific (inter)national legislation, if a code contains legally binding clauses.46

The general view, therefore, is that a COC is not in and of itself binding for the MNC that adheres to it. What, if anything, does that mean for the status of the COC in supply relationships? I believe that a mere reference to a code of conduct ('Please take note of the Code of Conduct of Company X, enclosed as Annex A') in a contractual document is insufficient for a contract to be concluded. After all, it is not clear to the supplier that the MNC expects him to uphold the COC and does not constitute an offer in the private law sense. In order for the COC to be binding upon the supplier, this code of conduct should therefore be contractually embedded. As has been set out supra, an offer and an acceptance is needed under Dutch law in order to conclude a contract. Therefore, it must be clear to the supplier that the reference to or provision of the COC is, in fact, an offer, which he may or may not accept. This may be done by requesting that the supplier signs for the receipt of and compliance with the COC. Another option is to refer to the COC in a contract and to declare that that COC is applicable to the contract, as a form of special terms and conditions. Having set out the theory above, it is time to look at what CSR contracting in the supply chain looks like in practice. What are the contractual consequences of choices made by Dutch MNCs? Are the instruments used binding?

CONTRACTUAL CONTROL IN THE SUPPLY CHAIN IN PRACTICE

Introduction

In the Netherlands, 16 companies were willing to participate in this research. A total of 14 were interviewed before August 2011; those companies were included in this article. All of them provided their codes of conduct, and, if applicable, the general (purchase) terms and conditions that contained CSR clauses and/or CSR clauses from their contracts. A twofold analysis was carried out on the basis of these documents.

The first type of analysis related to content. As indicated, the analysis of the content was carried out on the basis of an adaptation of the model proposed by Van Tulder and Kolk.47 The adapted model is included as Figure 1 infra. Secondly, the structure of the contractual control mechanisms was analysed. Which instruments were most frequently used by companies? Could a pattern be discovered that would distinguish various types of initiatives? To what extent were instruments legally binding? Did they also include clauses in relation to third parties?

Content of CSR Instruments

In order to compare and assess codes of conduct, one needs a set of indicators and variables. Kolk and Van Tulder have proposed such a model, binding together the content of the issues included, the nature of the wording, references to legal systems which they make and compliance aspects.48 For the purpose of assessing the COCs of the participating companies, I have adapted this model, thereby only including issues in respect of the 8 ILO core conventions. This adjusted model is proposed in the final section of this article. The content of all 14 contractual control initiatives was inserted into the model inserted as Figure 1.

			Classification
Binding	*Code signed separately?*		yes / no
Issues		– non-discrimination, equal remuneration	Ranging from: 0 out of 4 to 4 out of 4.
		– industrial relations (freedom of association, collective bargaining)	
		– child labour	
		– forced labour	
Nature	*Quantitative standards?*	100% (predominant), 75% (majority)	predominant, majority, medium or frail
		50% (medium)	
		0-25% (frail)	
Measures	*Reference?*	Reference to local legal system or international standards or other COC?	none defined; home country; host country; international or combinations
Compliance	*Monitoring systems and processes*	Good insight into systems (clear), reference to some parts but criteria or time frames lacking (clear to vague), only general reference to monitoring without details (vague).	clear / clear to vague / vague
	Position of monitoring actor	Firms themselves (1st), business associations (2nd), external professionals (3rd), combination (4th).	1st, 2nd, 3rd, 4th
	Sanctions	Warnings and exclusion of membership (mild), threat to business activities (severe).	none / mild / severe

Figure 1:

The analysis led to three types of content: weak, moderate and strong content.

Weak Codes

Content described as weak often did not include all four issues of the ILO core conventions; sometimes, issues such as freedom of association, collective bargaining or force were not included. The wording was general and left much room for interpretation; e.g., phrases such as 'promoting respect for people and their work environment', 'supplier will not indulge in acts of discrimination' and 'supplier will recognise its employees' rights to freedom of association'. Such phrasing does not make it clear what the MNC exactly expects from the supplier. There was no reference to legal standards (home state, host state or international). Codes did not generally include any compliance mechanisms, such as auditing or selfassessment questionnaires. The codes are not signed for by suppliers. Out of the 14 codes, 4 were classified as weak (29%).

Moderate Codes

The contents of three codes (21%) were considered moderate. These codes used either general phrasing or predominantly general phrasing; they did, for instance, describe exactly what was expected from the suppliers in terms of non-discrimination and they mentioned all possible grounds for discrimination, but only referred to freedom of association in general terms. Limited quantitative standards were included (for instance, only relating to child labour). Codes mentioned legal standards but did not make it clear which legal standards those are; e.g., codes stated that 'all legal standards must be observed'.

Strong Codes

The contents of seven codes (50%) were classified as strong. These codes included clear norms for all four issues. They usually included relevant references to ILO conventions and all included references to a mix of legal standards (home state, host state, international and international trade standards). The norms also usually set out what was expected in the case of conflict between the various norms. Quantitative standards were usually included with respect to child labour.49 These codes frequently referred to or included external, third-party COCs as well. All codes of conduct were signed for by supply partners. Furthermore, all strong codes included compliance mechanisms, either by means of auditing (usually by a third party; sometimes by the company itself) and/or self-assessment questionnaires. With the exception of one COC, all strong codes included obligations in respect of sub-tier suppliers: any further sub-suppliers that the supplier engaged with would also need to agree to the content of the code of conduct.

Form of Initiatives: COCs, General Terms and Conditions or Contracts?

All three types of instruments – contracts, general terms and conditions, and codes of conduct – were seen in practice. Most companies chose a mix of these instruments and the instruments used often did not strictly fall into one category. All companies investigated used some type of code of conduct. Almost all codes of conduct (with the exception of two) were signed for by supply partners. This has some consequences for the relevance of the concept of a 'code of conduct' in the original, voluntary sense. By requiring that all suppliers sign the code of conduct, these 'codes' would in fact qualify as general terms and conditions. They are a set of standardised terms, to be used repeatedly within the context of a certain type of contract. While this does not have major consequences in terms of Dutch private law – after all, title 6.5.3 of the DCC does not apply to international contracts – it does provide us with an excellent indication that the discussion concerning to what extent codes of conduct are binding is of limited importance in the supply chain.

Furthermore, these codes of conduct become contractually binding. The MNC extends an offer to its supplier, which the supplier – by signing for the code of conduct – accepts. It turns out that MNCs do not wait to see whether courts deem codes of conduct to be binding upon those who adhere to them; rather, they take matters into their own hands and ensure that COCs are binding on their supply partners through the means of contracting. Furthermore, the content of COCs does not bar them from becoming binding. In my opinion, even the content of weaker codes of conduct would meet the criterion of having sufficiently determinate terms.

Using a CSR clause in a contract was the least popular option among this sample. Apparently, CSR contracting is very much standardised (either through the use of COCs or general terms or conditions). Only 5 of the 14 companies also included some kind of ethical clause in their contracts. Usually, these were fairly general clauses that described the CSR obligations of the supply partner on an abstract level. For example, 'manufacturer is obliged to demonstrate that it is actively promoting good labour conditions for its workers'. The companies that did include CSR clauses in contracts indicated that they only did so in the case of contracts where the risk of CSR violations would be high. In such cases, a CSR clause would be inserted to draw extra attention to CSR issues. When asked why companies did not include such a clause, most answered that they felt such an ethical clause would not be necessary since the code of conduct had already been signed for and was therefore a contractual obligation in and of itself.

Patterns

Another important discovery was that a pattern could be deduced from the choices that companies made. Those companies that used CSR codes of conduct or general terms and conditions of which the content qualified as weak did not create contractual mechanisms to embed these codes of conduct. As a result, these codes would not be contractually binding for supply partners. Furthermore, the implementation of these instruments was lacking: the use of these codes was not widespread among employees dealing with supply partners and they were often overlooked in the contracting process.

Those companies that had moderate codes of conduct and general terms and conditions made some effort in respect of the content of the code, but often one or more issues concerning implementation did arise. A number of MNCs indicated that while elaborate codes were in place, employees neglected to include them in contracts in the heat of the commercial process. Another company explained that not all supply partners signed the code, but that the general terms and conditions contained a reference to the COC. The set of general terms and conditions provided on the company website did not include such a reference. Another example was a code consisting of both a company COC and a third-party, NGO COC (the second COC being much more specific and stronger), while the form that must be signed by the NGO only referred to the weak company COC. Yet other MNCs chose to include a reference to their code of conduct in their general terms and conditions. As set out above, this would be problematic if the code of conduct is then not provided to the supplier at the time of concluding the agreement. These companies would therefore need to make sure that the code of conduct is provided with the general terms and conditions (for instance, by attaching the code to the general terms and conditions). Those MNCs that used the strongest COCs from a content perspective also embedded their codes in the broadest manner from a contractual perspective. They not only requested that their suppliers sign their code of conduct, but they also frequently drafted specific general terms and conditions for suppliers that related to CSR and included CSR clauses in contracts. Finally, with the exception of one MNC, all strong codes included a perpetual clause in respect of sub-tier suppliers: any further sub-suppliers that the supplier engaged with would also need to agree to the content of the code of conduct.

Private International Law, Battle of the Forms

All general terms and conditions included a choice of law. With the exception of two sets, all chose the law of the Netherlands as the law applicable to the agreement.50 On the basis of Rome I, this will generally mean that Dutch law applies to the agreement. Assuming that Dutch law applies, it is not likely that any battle of the forms would cause any problems. All general terms and conditions explicitly rejected any other set of general terms and conditions, thereby meeting the criterion of a sufficient rejection described supra. Furthermore, COCs are almost always signed for separately by suppliers. This means that these codes do not run a great risk of becoming 'victims' of a battle of the forms. If a set of general terms and conditions loses the battle of the forms, only that set of general terms and conditions will not apply; only CSR clauses laid down in those general terms and conditions would then not apply. Only one company investigated in this research had only anchored its CSR policy through general terms and conditions without requesting that suppliers sign for it. All other companies either also requested that suppliers sign for their COCs, or made the COC applicable through a reference in the standard contract.

Other Aspects: Third Parties, Implementation

As set out in Section 5.2, all strong COCs and most moderate COCs extended obligations to sub-tier suppliers by means of a perpetual clause. While such a perpetual clause is not perfect, it is the only contractual option that MNCs have available in such a case. The options that MNCs have available in case their suppliers do not include a perpetual clause are exceptionally limited – they may claim damages from their supply partner on the basis of non-performance, but there is no way to restore a CSR contract in a clause between supplier and sub-tier suppliers or to claim damages from the sub-tier supplier on the basis of tort. All of the codes included references to the rights of workers, such as clauses on non-discrimination and freedom of association. Under certain conditions, such clauses may be considered clauses for the benefit of a third party, as set out in Section 4.2. In order for a third party to derive rights from a contract between a MNC and its supplier, this clause must be sufficiently determinate. In the case of strong codes of conduct, this is generally the case. Furthermore, the clause (the offer, as it were) should be accepted by such a third party.

Within the context of CSR contracting, the most likely category of 'third parties' to accept such a clause would be the employees of the supply partner. It is not clear whether the codes of conduct that contained clauses for the benefit of a third party are in practice always provided to the employees of suppliers, so that they can accept these clauses and derive rights under the supplier code of conduct. In the Netherlands, it has also been considered sufficient for third parties to accept clauses by means of instigating a procedure requesting that the promissor fulfils its obligations in respect of the third party.51 It is therefore not unthinkable that employees would be able to derive rights from the supplier codes of conduct. All three types of codes of conduct included the possibility to terminate the agreement. On the basis of the conducted interviews, however, it quickly became clear that all companies were reluctant to terminate relationships; they rather engaged with the supplier in order to draft a plan for improving the points that fell short from a CSR perspective.

CONCLUSION

In conclusion, codes of conduct are not used in the true sense of the term in the supply chain. Companies really attempt to obtain contractual control; not only by requiring that their supply partners sign their code of conduct, but also by anchoring the code of conduct in their general terms and conditions or in the contract. Furthermore, within the context of the supply chain and supplier codes of conduct, the discussion revolving around whether these codes are binding is virtually irrelevant; after all, nearly all companies with any kind of serious supply chain corporate social responsibility system in place ensure that these codes are contractually anchored. Moreover, companies that have weaker codes of conduct from a content perspective less frequently anchor their code contractually by means of signing codes of conduct or references in contracts or general terms and conditions. This would support the idea that multinationals which have really thought their CSR policy through would also have thought better about how to implement that policy; not only from a practical point of view but also from a contractual point of view.

The findings so far provide material for further research. All companies interviewed have shown a great interest in the question of what the consequences of their policies and contracts are in terms of extracontractual liability. All of the general terms and conditions and contracts included some kind of limitation of liability. Could such a limitation of liability also be valid in respect of claims on the basis of CSR violations by third parties? Furthermore, many of the investigated MNCs use the same instruments in all companies they operate. But the same instruments may have different consequences (in terms of validity and their binding nature) in different legal systems. Do companies need to adapt their instruments for each state they operate in? The continuation of this research project will attempt to answer these questions. The research to date nevertheless already provides MNCs with a frame of reference for evaluating their own codes of conduct. They can gain more insight into the extent to which their own instruments are binding on their supply partners, as well as exploring some of the best practices of other MNCs in the Netherlands.

NOTE:

1 R. van Tulder & A. van der Zwart, Reputaties op het spel: maatschappelijk verantwoord ondernemen in een onderhandelingssamenleving, 2003, p. 43.

2 Sociaal-Economische Raad, Duurzame Globalisering: een Wereld te Winnen, 2008, p. 30.

3 Ibid., p. 42.

4 EIRIS Foundation, A Risky Business? Managing core labour standards in company supply chains, 2009, p. 17.

5 M.T. Kamminga in J.J.A. Hamers et al., Maatschappelijk Verantwoord Ondernemen: Corporate Social Responsibility in a Transnational Perspective, 2005, p. 64.

6 M.P. Vandenbergh, 'The New Wal-Mart Effect: The Role of Private Contracting in Global Governance', 2007 UCLA Law Review, p. 919.

7 See, inter alia, 'Apple and Dell investigate Foxconn plant', The Financial Times, 26 May 2010, <http://www.ft.com/cms/s/2/8287fed0-68cd-11df-96f1-00144feab49a.html#axzz1UdGOiVK0> (last visited 10 August 2011).

8 See, inter alia, 'Shell accepts liability for two oil spills in Nigeria', The Guardian, 3 August 2011, <http://www.guardian.co.uk/environment/2011/aug/03/shell-liability-oil-spills-nigeria>(last visited 10 August 2011).

9 F. Spreckley, Social Audit - A Management Tool for Co-Operative Working, 1981.

10 European Commission, 'Corporate Social Responsibility: Encouraging best behavior', 15 June 2006, at: <http://ec.europa.eu/enterprise/library/ee_online/art11_en.htm> (last visited 16 November 2011).

11 For further reading on the moral and legal foundations of CSR, see inter alia the report by the SER, supra note 2; D. McBarnet et al., (eds.), The New Corporate Accountability: Corporate Social Responsibility and the Law, 2007, and A. Crane, The Oxford Handbook of Corporate Social Responsibility, 2008.

12 A. Kolk, & R.J.M. van Tulder, 'Child labor and multinational conduct: a comparison of international business and stakeholder codes', 2002 Journal of Business Ethics 36, p. 293.

13 Examples of exceptions being CSR reporting obligations under the corporate governance code in the Netherlands, and an obligation to create tracking systems for conflict minerals in the United States under the Conflict Minerals Act.

14 To be found at: <http://www.oecd.org/document/28/0,374

6,en_2649_34889_2397532_1_1_1_1,00.html> (last visited 4 November 2011).

15 Transparantiebenchmark, The Hague, Ministerie van Economische Zaken, 2004, p. 30.

16 See: <http://www.ketens-netwerken.nl/resources/uploads/files/documenten/WetOpenbaarheidvan productieen Ketens.pdf> (last visited 10 August 2011).

17 See: European Parliament resolution 'Towards an EU strategy on the rights of the child' 2007/2093(INI), accessible through <http://www. europarl.europa.eu/oeil/file.jsp?id=5479632> (last visited 11 November 2011).

18 See inter alia, Report by MakeITFair, Roundtable on Conflict Minerals Legislation, 26 May 2011, http://somo.nl/news-en/long-but-hopeful-path-towards-legislation-on-conflict-minerals/at_download/attachment (last visited 19 September 2011).

19 Date listed: 1 January 2011.

20 Convention C87, Freedom of Association and Protection of the Right to Organise Convention (1948), Convention C98, Right to Organize and Collective Bargaining Convention, (1949), Convention C138, the Minimum Age Convention (1973), Convention C182, Worst Forms of Child Labour (1999), Convention C29, Forced Labour Convention, (1930), Convention C105, Abolition of Forced Labour Convention, (1957), Convention C100 (Equal Remuneration, 1951) and C111 (Discrimination, 1958).

21 This in contrast to other, more 'progressive' human rights that can be brought within the umbrella of CSR, such as the right to a living wage and the right to a healthy environment (including measures to reduce CO2).

22 R. van Tulder, & A. Kolk, 'Multinationality and Corporate Ethics: Codes of Conduct in the Sporting Goods Industry', 2001 Journal of International Business Studies 32, pp. 267-283.

23 For further reading on these topics, see inter alia: I. Mamic, 'Managing Global Supply Chain: The Sports Footwear, Apparel and Retail Sectors', 2005 Journal of Business Ethics 59, pp. 81–100; A. Kolk & R.J.M. van Tulder, 'Multinationality and Corporate Ethics: Codes of Conduct in the Sporting Goods Industry', 2001 Journal of International Business Studies 32, no. 2.

24 The term contractual control was first coined by D. McBarnet & M. Kurkchiyan, 'Corporate social responsibility through contractual control? Global supply chains and "other-regulation"', in D. McBarnet et al. (eds.), The New Corporate Accountability, The new corporate accountability: corporate social responsibility and the law, 2007.

25 Van Tulder & Kolk, supra note 22.

26 Out of the 14 Dutch model agreements, 13 effectively included a choice for Dutch law.

27 Art. 9 of Rome I relates to the application of overriding mandatory provisions (respect for which is regarded as crucial by a country for safeguarding its public interests, such as its political, social or economic organization) of national law, which depends on the scope of the provision. Provisions of the law of the forum as well as of the country in which the contract is to be performed may be applied. It should be noted that there may be some overlap between these provisions and the subjects governed by the CSR contract or COC (e.g. labour standards). This article investigates matters of validity and the binding nature of these documents, as well as the consequences of these codes and contracts for liability, rather than the validity of the content of these documents under national law.

28 If parties each refer to a different set of general terms and conditions, the acceptance will be different from the offer. This is referred to as a 'battle of the forms' and this is elaborated upon in Section 4.3.

29 C. Asser et al., Mr. C. Asser's Handleiding tot de beoefening van het Nederlands burgerlijk recht: 3, 2010, no. 283. Case law e.g.: Hof Den Bosch 15 October 2002, NJ 2003, 477; Hof Leeuwarden 8 June 2010, Prg. 2010, 169.

30 HR 13 March 1981, NJ 1981, 635.

31 The next paragraphs relate only to the obligations on the basis of a contract. The content of a contract may also have consequences for the extracontractual liability of contracting parties in respect of third parties. Such liability is – unfortunately – outside the scope of this article but will be further explored in my PhD research.

32 HR 4 June 1965, NJ 1965, 381 and HR 28 June 1974, NJ 1974, 400.

33 Hof Arnhem 8 March 1985, NJ 1985, 678.

34 It should be noted that under Dutch law, performance – rather than damages – is the primary obligation in case of non-compliance with contractual obligations.

35 This title is partly based on EU Directive 93/13/EEC on Unfair Contract Terms for Consumers.

36 Which, as we will see, is highly likely.

37 See, for example, Rechtbank Rotterdam 12 March 1998, S&S 1999, 45 and Hof Arnhem 2 December 2003, LJN AO 1612.

38 S. A. Kruisinga, 'Battle of Forms', in B. Wessels et al. (eds.), Algemene voorwaarden, 2010, p. 35.

39 R.H.C. Jongeneel, 'Gebondenheid', in B. Wessels et al. (eds.), Algemene voorwaarden, 2010, p. 113.

40 Van Tulder & Van der Zwart, supra note 1, p. 108.

41 R.C.J. Galle, Ondernemen en ethiek, 2000, p. 65.

42 S.C. Eyk, The Oecd Declaration and Decisions Concerning Multinational Enterprises: An Attempt to Tame the Shrew, 1995, p. 20; M. Koelemeijer, 'Gedragscode: effectief instrument voor maatschappelijk verantwoord ondernemen?', 2004 Ondernemingsbestuur, no. 1, p. 13.

43 R.J. Hoff, De Integere Onderneming, De Bedrijfscode En Het Recht, 2006, p. 130.

44 OECD Guidelines for Multinational Enterprises, 2011, Concepts and Principles I.1.

45 M. Koelemeijer, 'Naar een Nederlandse gedragscode maatschappelijk verantwoord ondernemen?', in J.J.A. Hamers et al. (eds.), Maatschappelijk Verantwoord Ondernemen: Corporate Social Responsibility in a Transnational Perspective, 2005, p. 108.

46 See note 45 supra.

47 Van Tulder & Kolk, supra note 22.

48 Ibid.

49 As well as in respect of working hours, which lies outside the scope of this research.

50 One company chose English law. Another chose the law of the country where the relevant contracting entity was located, which would often, but not always, be Dutch law.

51 HR 19 March 1976, NJ 1976, 407.

CHAPTER 4

INTERNATIONAL FRAMEWORK AGREEMENTS. AN ANALYSIS OF THE INTERNATIONAL FRAMEWORK AGREEMENT AS AN INSTRUMENT FOR IMPROVING WORKING STANDARDS IN GLOBAL BUSINESS OPERATIONS

Aalt G. Colenbrander

Keywords: International framework agreement, workers, rights, trade unions, international labour regulation

INTRODUCTION

International Framework Agreements

As a result of globalising economies it is not unusual nowadays for companies' business organisations to be located all over the world. As there is no single regulatory body that has the authority to formulate universal rules applicable to these organisations, it is not guaranteed that they meet the human rights standards that have become common in most western jurisdictions.1 A significant issue in this regard is the protection of fundamental working standards worldwide, as many workers connected to the business organisations of internationally operating companies live and work in developing countries with an underdeveloped legal system.2 A recent example that represents possible consequences of this existing regulatory gap is the disaster in the Rana Plaza manufacturing building in Bangladesh.3

Among the instruments developed to deal with the problems described above is the international framework agreement (IFA). An IFA is an agreement concluded between (at least) a multinational company (MNC) and a global trade union (GTU), a trade union representing workers on the global level with regard to a specific sector and/or activities. 'Global framework agreement' is another term that is frequently used to designate these agreements. The primary goal of these agreements is to improve fundamental working standards in the worldwide business operations of the contracting enterprises. IFAs are different from other regulatory instruments aimed at improving the social dimension of doing business (e.g. corporate codes of conduct) in that one or more external parties (the GTU and/or its affiliates) often have an active role in the functioning of the agreement. This monitoring role can be laid down explicitly in the content of the agreement.4 Being a fairly recent phenomenon (the first IFA was concluded in 1988), the number of IFAs is constantly increasing, particularly since 2000. At this moment 107 MNCs have committed themselves to improving fundamental working standards by signing a framework agreement.5

The growing number of IFAs is, in principle, acknowledged as a positive development as it offers possibilities to increase working standards worldwide. The European Union considers supportive measures to stimulate the establishment of new framework agreements.6 This being said, several comments are in order. The number of IFAs is unevenly distributed both geographically (with most signatory MNCs based in Europe) and amongst sectors.7 In addition, the agreements vary significantly in their substantive and procedural contents. As

Citation: Aalt G. Colenbrander, International Framework Agreements. An analysis of the international framework agreement as an instrument for improving working standards in global business operations, DOI: http://doi.org/10.18352/ulr.327.

a result, no generalizable statements can be made about the actual results that an IFA achieves. This paper aims to analyse the present state of the IFA as an instrument and formulate conclusions with regard to conditions an IFA has to fulfil in order to be able to meet its objectives. It does so by comparing information available in academic literature to experience of actors dealing with IFAs in practice. The following primary research question has been established to guide this study:

Are the conditions under which the international framework agreement in academic literature is considered a suitable instrument for safeguarding fundamental working standards in the global business operations of contracting enterprises reflected in the experience of actors working with the international framework agreement in practice?

This research question may need some clarification. An instrument is considered 'suitable' when it is capable of achieving concrete and demonstrable results. The 'fundamental working standards' are embodied in the fundamental conventions of the International Labour Organisation (ILO). These conventions deal with the freedom of association and recognition of the right to collective bargaining, the elimination of forced, compulsory and child labour and the elimination of discrimination in respect of employment.8 In addition to these conventions, the 'fundamental working standards' include the duty to observe safety and health conditions and the duty to ensure fair wages and fair terms of contract (including social security and working hours).9 The term 'enterprise' is used because the global business operations are considered to include not only the activities in the legal person(s) that constitute the company, but also additional activities in the supply chain. There is no uniform definition of 'supply chain'. For the purpose of this paper, it is defined as the process in which different actors collaborate in order to retrieve natural resources or knowledge, process these resources or this knowledge into products or services, and deliver these products or services to the public.

Methodology and Reading Guidance

In order to answer the main research question described above, this paper combines information available from existing literature with empirical data derived from interviews with relevant actors, and desk research. In Section 2, existing legal and non-legal literature is examined. Factors on which the proper functioning of an IFA according to this literature depends are identified in Section 2.2. Thereafter, in Section 3, the experience of relevant actors from practice is described. In order to do so, interviews were first conducted with representatives of MNCs and GTUs. A total of four interviews took place, one with a company representative and three with representatives of GTUs. These interviews were set up in a semi-structured manner, i.e. a questionnaire was used but this was deviated from whenever it was deemed useful.11 The conversations were processed into interview reports that were verified afterwards by the interviewees.

The interview reports were categorized making use of coding, thus linking parts of the interview reports to certain predefined categories,12 in order to formulate sound conclusions. The categories that were used are the factors set out in Section 2.2. When dealing with these categories in Section 3, some overlap may inevitably occur between the information that is presented, as certain topics bear relevance to more than one category. The information collected from the interviews is supplemented by desk research,13 in which 10 MNCs were examined. These MNCs were selected to represent 5 different sectors: (1) food retail (Sodexo and Carrefour); (2) ready-made garments (H&M and Mizuno); (3) building contracting (Royal BAM and Hochtief); (4) electronics (Bosch and Siemens); and (5) tourism (Club Mediterranée and Melia). Regrettably, given the European concentration of MNCs that have concluded an IFA, it was not possible to make a geographically evenly distributed selection as well. The desk research covered the MNCs' websites and the IFAs that the MNCs concluded. The IFAs are readily accessible on the website of the GTUs. Evidently, making use of a relatively small number of MNCs cannot lead to absolute conclusions. The information gathered was used to bring theory to life and substantiate the other research results. In Section 4, the research results presented in Section 3 are tested against the conclusions found in the literature as these are described in Section 2. On the basis of this comparative synthesis, the current value of the IFA as an instrument can be assessed, and critical success factors for its function can be identified. Section 5 concludes this paper's analysis.

Using semi-structured interviews allows both researcher and response bias to occur.14 Still, this paper provides useful insights regarding the dynamics of the IFA as an instrument and the position it currently has in the range of available international instruments. By dealing with IFAs in relation both to existing literature and to the practical experience of the interviewees it is furthermore deemed a solid introduction for those getting acquainted with the subject.

LITERATURE REGARDING INTERNATIONAL FRAMEWORK AGREEMENTS

An Overview

The literature takes a mainly positive attitude towards the existence of IFAs, as a result of their potential to (at least) strengthen fundamental basic rights for workers, especially in developing countries.15 Furthermore, IFAs appear to be suitable instruments to influence the globalising business of enterprises in terms of their compliance with fundamental working standards, an area where (inter)national legislation and regulation currently fall short.16 Through the initiation of this instrument, GTUs laid down the foundation for an international dialogue between international trade unions and MNCs.17 It is emphasized, however, that the sole establishment of an IFA will not suffice; the actual achievement of positive effects is dependent on various factors. The main factors that were extracted from literature are: (1) the content of the agreement; (2) the composition of the parties to the agreement; (3) the incorporation of implementation and monitoring mechanisms; and (4) the degree to which specific attention is paid to the supply chain. These factors are elaborated below.

IFAs vary significantly in content; some are established to deal with one specific topic, e.g. a reorganisation, whereas the majority is committed to improving a broader range of fundamental working standards.18 Notwithstanding these variations, all framework agreements contain some elements of the fundamental conventions established by the ILO19 dealing with the freedom of association and recognition of the right to collective bargaining, the elimination of forced, compulsory and child labour and the elimination of discrimination in respect of employment.20

Although formally only the MNC and the GTU may sign the IFA, as regularly is the case, a wide variety of actors may be involved in the negotiations that precede the conclusion of the agreement. These actors include national trade unions, a European Works Council (EWC) whenever relevant, national works councils, the management of subsidiary companies, public institutions or persons and non-governmental organisations (NGOs).21 The extent to which these parties exercise influence during the negotiation process and will participate in upholding the regime that the IFA establishes is a relevant factor when trying to determine the effects of the agreement. Other elements that need to be considered (in addition to the substantive textual contents of the agreement) when examining the likeliness that an IFA will be able to meet its objectives are, for instance, the geographical scope of the enterprise's business, the implementation and monitoring mechanisms that are incorporated in the agreement, the de facto powers that the various parties involved are able to exercise and the ideology that encouraged the contract parties to conclude the agreement.22 These elements are of major importance for the sake of understanding the functioning and dynamics of a specific agreement.23

The incorporation of implementation and monitoring mechanisms is considered in literature the most important prerequisite for the actual functioning of an IFA; without these mechanisms the agreement is nothing more than a noncommittal promise.24 For the purpose of this paper, implementation of an IFA is defined as any act in or between companies that raises awareness regarding the existence of the framework agreement or contributes to the agreement's entering into force. The MNC and GTU can make collective efforts in this regard. Examples include publication of the agreement on the website and in the annual (sustainability) report of the MNC, distribution of flyers and posters at any location where business activities of the enterprise take place, informing subsidiary companies, companies in the supply chain, relevant national trade unions and local works councils about the IFA (e.g. in meetings organised for this purpose) and providing translations in local languages.25 Monitoring an IFA in this paper means any act related to the supervision of compliance with the substantive content of the agreement in the enterprise's business organisation. Control may be constructed in various ways, such as the establishment of external supervision (e.g. by accountancy firms), local supervision by national trade unions, the establishment of multi-stakeholder initiatives (MSIs)26 or the establishment by an MNC and a GTU of a mutual supervisory body that meets regularly and conducts inspections and field visits. GTUs prefer to be directly involved in some form of supervision, to avoid the risk of losing control over a specific agreement.27 Their resources are limited, however. Whenever a violation of the agreement's content is discovered, parties will normally try to resolve this at the local level, between the local trade union and management. In case this approach fails to lead to a successful solution, the GTU will raise the issue at the MNC's central management. Some IFAs contain the possibility to appoint a mediator to facilitate a solution. As a last resort, the GTU can exercise pressure by informing the public about the violation and ultimately terminate the IFA.28

Influencing working standards in the supply chain of MNCs is regularly mentioned as an important challenge that an IFA faces.29 In a buyer-dominated supply chain, in which many different parts of the production process are carried out by different actors,30 an MNC may not be able to inform every relevant actor about the existence of the agreement as a result of the complex network of suppliers. A supplier can furthermore be confronted with various IFAs at the same time, in case it does business with different MNCs that established an IFA. These different agreements may impose different and potentially conflicting requirements. In a producer-dominated supply chain, composed of a relatively small number of actors each of which has the capacity to implement various elements of the production process in its organisation,31 the suppliers of an MNC can maintain such strong market positions that it is difficult to influence them.32 Bearing in mind the goals for which the instrument was set up, influencing working standards in the supply chain is of major importance for the success of the IFA as an instrument, given their potential to end inhuman treatment and achieve actual change. Provided attention is paid to the supply chain during the drafting process and subsequent operation of an IFA, the impact of the agreement is therefore likely to increase.33 Notwithstanding this importance, IFAs rarely explicitly state that the agreement's content applies to the supply chain and/or define methods in which fundamental working standards will be enhanced and compliance with the IFA will be controlled in the supply chain.34

Common Threads

The literature described above allows identification of four common threads,35 which can be tested against empirical data and provide the structure of the next section.

(1) There are significant differences between IFAs regarding the scope of the substantive content.

(2) Every IFA has its own set of dynamics, depending on the parties involved in drawing up the agreement and supervising compliance with the agreement after signing.

(3) The functioning of an IFA (almost) entirely depends on the existence of implementation and monitoring mechanisms in operation.

(4) Ensuring fundamental working standards in the supply chain is one of the most important challenges IFAs face at the moment.

BEYOND THE BOOKS

This section describes the results of the interviews and desk research with respect to the four aforementioned common threads. These four common threads are used to guide this description.

Substantive Content

The interviews confirmed that IFAs, although all containing elements of the fundamental ILO conventions, vary significantly with regard to their substantive content. This is firstly explained by the fact that IFAs were initially weakly worded agreements; GTUs focused on concluding as many IFAs as possible, thereby not paying sufficient attention to the scope the agreement would cover and results it would achieve. Over the years, the focus of the trade unions shifted from quantitative to qualitative, resulting in more comprehensive agreements. Secondly, the general attitude of the MNC involved can possibly affect the content of the IFA. Certain MNCs are prepared to agree to more than is necessary, e.g. on the basis of their core values or business principles. In this sense, for example, extensive health and safety warranties can be laid down in the agreement, something that is not directly required under the fundamental ILO conventions. In line with this, a constructive and inspired attitude of top level management was mentioned as an overall key to success. Thirdly, the cultural and historical background of the country an MNC is embedded in can influence the manner in which it perceives decent work issues. This is particularly evident in the extent to which it is common to collaborate with trade unions and allow them to actively participate in the functioning of an IFA, but may also be contained in the working standards that are acknowledged to be fundamental.36 The IFAs that were studied more closely in this paper also reveal great diversity in their substantive content, although maintaining a fairly homogeneous minimum standard. The analysed agreements, save for a few exceptions, have all incorporated the fundamental ILO conventions. This is visually presented in Table 1 below.

Table 1: Stimulating the implementation of the fundamental ILO conventions

	Prevention and abolition of forced labour	Freedom of association and protection of the right to organise	Right to collective bargaining	Setting a minimum age for work conducted by children	Prevention or eradication of child labour	Equal remuneration	Prevention of discrimination
Sodexo	X	X	X	X	X	X	X
Carrefour	X	X	X	-	X	-	X
H&M	X	X	X	X	X	X	X
Mizuno	X	X	X	X	X	X	X
Royal BAM	X	X	X	X	X	X	X
Hochtief	X	X	X	-	X	-	X
Bosch	X	X	X	X	X	X	X
Siemens	X	X	X	X	X	X	X
Club Mediterranée	X	X	X	X	X	X	X
Melia	X	X	X	X	X	X	X

However, looking beyond these fundamental conventions established by the ILO, the agreements to a varying degree include the additional safeguards identified in Section 1, as can be seen in Table 2 below.

Table 2: Social and economic safeguards

	Safe and healthy working conditions	Aids prevention	Pensions, health insurance, disability insurance and other social securities	Fair pay/ compensation (living wages/fair income)	Terms of employment
Sodexo	X	-	X	-	X
Carrefour	-	-	-	-	-
H&M	X	-	X	X	X
Mizuno	-	-	-	-	X
Royal BAM	X	X	X	X	X
Hochtief	X	-	X	X	X
Bosch	X	-	X	X	X
Siemens	X	-	-	X	X
Club Mediterranée	-	-	-	-	X
Melia	X	-	-	-	-

Parties Involved

The interviews confirmed that there is a particular spectrum of actors connected to each IFA. These actors cannot be detected by solely looking at the signatory parties to the agreement; the actors responsible for the establishment, implementation and monitoring of the agreement do not always formally endorse the document. Not seeking to provide an exhaustive account of actors that may be involved, this section discusses some actors that were mentioned during the interviews.

Local trade unions (that are often affiliates of a GTU) are regularly involved in the different stages of setting up and keeping up a functioning framework agreement. In the establishment of an IFA, the local trade union in the country of the MNC's headquarters often takes part in the negotiation process. In various instances it was confirmed that the entire negotiation process was conducted by the local trade union, after which the GTU was included to enter the agreement as a signatory party. In those cases, the GTU was not involved until signing the agreement. It is believed that this is done by the local trade union to highlight its connection to the GTU and its (global) goals, as well as its resources and network. As already mentioned, the local trade unions can also play a significant role after the signing of an IFA through the implementation and monitoring of the agreement. The GTUs consider their local affiliates as a significant source of capacity. Given their presence on site, they are able to create awareness on the local level among workers about the agreement's existence and content and can monitor compliance with the agreement. An example was provided in which the local trade union is the sole actor engaged in the controlling process, presenting periodic reports to the GTU.

Whenever present, the works council and/or EWC (in the case of certain European MNCs) can play a significant role in the establishment and control of an IFA. They are regularly included as a signatory party, although certainly not always. The GTUs furthermore indicated that they closely collaborate with NGOs and other parties that may add value in certain cases (e.g. by giving advice or providing access to information and other resources). However, these parties are not usually included anywhere in the process of establishing an IFA and are therefore not a signatory party. This is because the GTUs believe that only trade unions have the right to negotiate on behalf of organised workers. Parties other than trade unions may be directly or indirectly included in the monitoring process, e.g. as a party to an MSI. The Clean Clothes Campaign, composed of two hundred different organisations, is a frequently mentioned example.37 The varying composition of signatories is apparent in the ten agreements that were studied for this paper, as presented in Table 3 below.

Table 3: Signatory parties to the selected IFAs38

	MNC	GTU	Other
Sodexo	Sodexo	The International Union of Food, Agricultural, Hotel, Restaurant, Catering, Tobacco and Allied Workers' Associations (IUF)	–
Carrefour	Carrefour	Union Network International (UNI)	–
H&M[38]	H&M AB	Union Network International (UNI) | IndustriALL Global Union	None | Industrifacket Metall
Mizuno	Mizuno Corporation	International Textile, Garment & Leather Workers' Federation (ITGLWF, now IndustriALL)	Japanese Federation of Textile, Chemical, Food, Commercial, Service and General Workers' Unions, Mizuno Workers' Union
Royal BAM	Royal BAM Group NV	Building and Woodworkers International (BWI)	–
Hochtief	Hochtief Executive Board	International Federation of Building and Wood Workers, (IFBWW, now the BWI)	German Construction Workers' Union (IG BAU), Hochtief General Works Council
Bosch	Robbert Bosch GmbH	International Metalworks' Federation (IMF, now IndustriALL) for the IMF member unions represented in the Bosch Group	European Committee of the Bosch Group (which is the Bosch Group's European Works Council)
Siemens	Siemens AG	IndustriAll Global Union	German Industrial Union of Metalworkers (IG Metall), Central Works Council of Siemens AG
Club Mediterranée	The Club Méditerranée company	The International Union of Food, Agricultural, Hotel, Restaurant, Catering, Tobacco and Allied Workers' Associations (IUF)	The European Federation of Trade Unions in the Food, Agriculture and Tourism sectors and allied branches (EFFAT)
Melia	Melia Hotels International S.A.	The International Union of Food, Agricultural, Hotel, Restaurant, Catering, Tobacco and Allied Workers' Associations (IUF)	-

Implementation and Monitoring Mechanisms

The interviews confirmed that the functioning of an IFA very strongly depends on the presence of implementation and monitoring mechanisms. One interviewee pointed out that without these mechanisms, an IFA would be a mere statement by an MNC that it accepts the fundamental working standards specified in the agreement. This would actually be inconsistent with the objective of IFAs, as it suggests that MNCs have a choice whether or not to recognize certain fundamental working standards. The existing IFAs vary when it comes to implementing such mechanisms to ensure a proper functioning of the agreement. This is reflected in the ten agreements that were studied for this paper, as presented in Table 4 below.

Table 4: Implementation and monitoring mechanisms

	Explicit implementation mechanisms	Explicit monitoring mechanisms
Sodexo	X	X
Carrefour	-	-
H&M	X	X
Mizuno	-	X
Royal BAM	X	X
Hochtief	-	X
Bosch	X	-
Siemens	X	X
Club Mediterranée	-	X
Melia	X	X

Some good practice examples were mentioned during the interviews, in which the agreement directly facilitated various activities aimed at improving and ensuring working standards in the business organisations of the enterprise involved. At the same time, some comments indicated that many of the activities are still underdeveloped, as stated not infrequently by the same person introducing a favourable effect of an IFA. It was said that, although the workers' (human) rights that IFAs aim to protect are not different, the local situations that might impede them are. Therefore the specificities of different local contexts need to be taken into account during the implementation and monitoring of an IFA, preferably through the establishment of local protocols. These local protocols can be negotiated between national trade unions and national or local managements, under supervision of the MNC. In this scenario, an IFA will have various local protocols, adapted to the various relevant local contexts. This method puts more direct pressure on the management responsible for local workplaces and factories, where IFAs can have great impact.39 While it is not possible to provide a conclusive overview of the functioning of existing implementation and monitoring mechanisms in this paper, some examples derived from the interviews are highlighted below.

The activities that were mentioned include (semi)annual meetings between the MNC and the GTU, in which the progress made under the agreement is discussed and focal points for the near future are determined. These (semi)annual meetings are believed to facilitate regular communication between MNC and trade union representatives. They fail to deal with all events in the day-to-day business of the enterprise, however. As a result, some consider IFAs to be unsuitable for ensuring enduring compliance with all norms laid down in the agreement. In this regard, contact on a more frequent basis throughout the year, in which success is measured on the basis of concrete results, is said to be much more important. Another example is field visits, in which a team representing the MNC, national union(s) and/or the GTU visits some of the MNC's workplaces (sometimes also workplaces of its suppliers). The report of these visits is sometimes published on the website of the trade union(s) and/or MNC.40 Reports submitted to the author of this paper by the interviewees revealed that these field visits were conducted by delegations representing the local and global trade union(s) as well as the MNC. The field visits aimed to uncover the local reality, e.g. paying attention to salaries, working times and conditions, health and safety issues and local trade union activity. The reliability of these field visits and other forms of local audits is disputed, as it is hard to verify whether workers conceal the truth under pressure or in fear of potential repressions.

The close involvement of its national affiliate unions gives the GTU great capacity and knowledge regarding local circumstances and customs. In some cases the local trade union is responsible for all monitoring activities of a specific IFA, regarding which it provides a periodic report to the GTU. An undesired side effect of an approach focusing on this local expertise is that it is difficult – if not impossible – for GTUs to act in regions where no national unions are present. This is the case in China and Vietnam, for example.41 In places where GTUs have local capacity, they suffer from resource problems. At this moment, the financial and human resources GTUs have access to are insufficient to proactively oversee compliance with the existing IFAs. As a result of this resource problem, monitoring is said to be a reactive process too often, instead of objective and preventive, responding to indications that the agreement may be violated somewhere. While the number of IFAs concluded is steadily growing, the capacity of GTUs and their local counterparts remains constant. The resource problem is therefore set to increase. One interviewee suggested that governments committed to improving working standards should endeavour to strengthen the position of GTUs. Parties committed to the success of IFAs are not indifferent to these observations, however. They attempt to improve the functioning of existing and future agreements. Some GTUs have established internal or public guidelines in which (minimum) standards are determined for IFAs.42 In addition to the substantive content, these guidelines also deal with practical issues. These include the implementation of the agreement (e.g. in the form of language and financial issues) and the mandatory incorporation of sufficient implementation and monitoring mechanisms in the agreement (e.g. prescribing the establishment of local protocols). These guidelines offer the opportunity to establish coherent and similar agreements, applicable in different regions and sectors. Thus, newly negotiated agreements are likely to be more comprehensive than their predecessors. Whenever this is considered possible, existing weakly worded agreements are renegotiated. Still, it was mentioned that MNCs turn out to not always be aware of the practical implications of the agreement they enter into, complicating the agreement's implementation later on. For example, an interviewee explained that one MNC appeared unpleasantly surprised when the GTU exercised a competence laid down in the IFA.

The Supply Chain Challenge

The interviewees confirmed that MNCs operating across borders have a potentially negative impact on the working environment in their supply chain. They order large quantities at sharp prices in countries where working standards are insufficiently guaranteed, for which they should know there is no capacity. As a result, the supplier will either violate decent working hours standards or hire subcontractors. In turn, these subcontractors may not observe decent working standards. Often, the supply chain becomes so complex that MNCs simply cannot be aware of what goes on in them. It was indicated that, although each sector has its peculiarities, this issue is present in all of them. At the same time, it is submitted that the presence of foreign MNCs in countries with poorly functioning regulations also entails the opportunity for these MNCs to impose their own standards on foreign suppliers. This way, MNCs can improve instead of maintain bad working standards abroad. It was stated that an MNC needs to accept that decent working standards are (most likely) not complied with throughout the supply chain. It needs to strive to change this situation and focus on what it does when supply chain issues are raised. This is what is called the 'supply chain challenge.' The interviewees mentioned some success stories in which the involvement of an MNC resulted in higher standards at the workplace.

Given its primary goal, an IFA seems a suitable instrument to promote fundamental working standards in the supply chains of MNCs operating across borders. As GTUs are vertically integrated organisations representing workers in each level of the supply chain, they attach major importance to the topic and aim to incorporate the supply chain challenge in newly negotiated agreements. Existing IFAs vary with regard to the extent in which they mention the supply chain and specific measures that apply to it.43 When an IFA states to be applicable to the supply chain, the controlling mechanisms as they are laid down in the agreement can be used to raise awareness in case of a violation of the agreement in the supply chain. In this case, the supply chain can also be addressed during periodic meetings, field visits and other monitoring mechanisms based in the IFA. Reports of field visits, as mentioned above, reveal that suppliers were indeed inspected during these visits. In other cases, the content of the IFA was processed in an MNC's suppliers' code of conduct.44 An MNC may, under certain circumstances, terminate the contract with suppliers that do not comply with this suppliers' code of conduct. Interviewees indicated that this happens quite often in practice. The legal basis for terminating the contract under those circumstances is not the IFA, however, but the suppliers' code. In addition, the suppliers' code of conduct is affected by other factors as well. Finally, the existence of an IFA sometimes allows a GTU in its mutual relationship with the MNC to raise awareness regarding specific supply chain issues, e.g. by informing them about suppliers that the MNC did not know.

Either by using the mechanisms as laid down in the IFA, by incorporating the content of the IFA in the suppliers' code of conduct, or through the mutual relationship between GTU and MNC created by the agreement, the IFA can be used as an instrument to improve working standards in the supply chain. This way, IFAs can contribute to the supply chain challenge. According to the interviewees, the problem is that this is not yet common practice.

Additional Insights

The previous sections dealt with the four common threads as identified in literature, approaching them from the perspective of relevant actors from practice. This section presents some additional insights derived from the interviews.

All interviewees stated that they were satisfied that IFAs have achieved some positive results and various success stories were shared. At the same time, they all indicated that the IFA as an instrument needs to be perceived in a broader range of instruments that organisations may apply to meet the challenges the IFA was designed for. These instruments among other things include the (suppliers') code of conduct, the multi-stakeholder dialogue, the side letter (an agreement between a trade union and an MNC dealing with a specific issue) and specific projects focusing on a single issue or nation. GTUs are party in all of these instruments and strive to use one or more of them in their relationship with an MNC. In this regard, it is important that neither IFAs nor the other initiatives mentioned in this section can be used as a justification for the absence of binding regulation on fundamental working standards; they deal with issues regulators have omitted to address until now but are no substitute for clear and enforceable rules.

The interviewees showed varying degrees of enthusiasm about the possibility of IFAs reaching their objectives in their current form, referring to the issues described above, including the frequent absence of functioning implementation and monitoring mechanisms and the complexity of supply chains. However, the agreements have often been able to create a platform for communication between a GTU and an MNC, on the basis of which concrete issues could be identified, discussed and resolved. The company representative indicated that the on-going dialogue with GTUs allows companies to benefit from the expertise and network of the GTU involved and that this gives them the possibility to compare their policy and achievements to those of similar businesses. There is a growing awareness regarding the existence of GTUs and they receive increasing response from major brands and employers' organisations. These are desirable side effects of IFAs, but may be achieved through the use of other instruments as well. The interviewees agreed: creating a functional mutual dialogue between employee representatives and company is the main objective. When an IFA appears to be the right instrument in this regard, GTUs will proceed to concluding one. Thus, even when an IFA is not functioning optimally, its existence may still indirectly have useful results.

ASSESSING THE INTERNATIONAL FRAMEWORK AGREEMENT

In general, the common threads identified in literature are confirmed by the experiences from practice discussed in the previous section: (1) IFAs indeed vary significantly regarding their substantive content, although the fundamental ILO conventions are applied as a plain minimum standard; (2) there are often multiple parties involved in the IFA-related processes, who are not always signatories to the agreement; (3) implementation and monitoring mechanisms are of vital importance for the actual functioning of an IFA; and (4) the supply chain challenge is difficult but important to pay attention to. At the same time, the interviews showed that the relevant actors are very much aware of the shortcomings of the IFA and they are proactively working to address these limitations. These efforts, which have been described, allow for the identification of circumstances that are necessary for an IFA to function as it was meant to, i.e. as a legally binding contractual arrangement between (at least) an MNC and a GTU, aimed at strengthening fundamental working standards in the worldwide business operations of the contracting enterprise. In order to achieve the intended results, an IFA firstly needs to establish proper implementation and control mechanisms. With regard to these mechanisms, attention has to be paid explicitly to practical issues, e.g. regulating what measures will be carried out, which parties are responsible for carrying out these measures and who bears financial responsibility for the functioning of the agreement. They need to be specified according to different local circumstances and sectoral particularities. A selection of possible measures that can be taken is given in Table 5 below.

Secondly, the parties to an IFA, or the parties involved in preparing an IFA, need to explore which actors can be of value and are willing to contribute to the preparation and subsequent operation of the agreement. Addressing the right parties, and thereby their resources, may improve the extent to which the IFA corresponds with reality and is able to realise concrete results. Thirdly, the supply chain of the MNC has to be explicitly included in the scope of the agreement, thus making it possible to apply the implementation and monitoring mechanisms to parties in the MNC's supply chain as well. An alternative would be to incorporate the content of the IFA in the MNC's suppliers' code of conduct. A single reference to the IFA appears sufficient in this regard. In this case, however, not the IFA but the suppliers' code of conduct will be the direct contractual basis that imposes requirements (and potentially penalties) on suppliers. Paying explicit attention to the supply chain is important, since it is otherwise unclear whether the agreement is applicable to the MNC's suppliers in the first place, and if it does apply, what the practical consequences are.

Table 5: Possible implementation and monitoring mechanisms45

Implementation mechanisms	Monitoring mechanisms
Publish IFA on website and in social report	Organise joint and/or separate monitoring activities, e.g. in the form of field visits and audits
Distribute agreement, both digitally and in print, including necessary guidelines and translations, to employees, suppliers, local and regional trade unions and other relevant stakeholders	Establish formalized and accessible complaint mechanisms, including hotlines
Provide digital and real-life training to management and suppliers at all levels	Organise periodic joint meetings to discuss the functioning of the IFA
Organise public presentations, obtain press coverage	Establish various local or national protocols to adapt the mechanisms that are in place to the specificities of each local or national situation

This being said, the research results demonstrate that even if an IFA is not a functioning contractual arrangement between the MNC and the GTU (i.e. when parties agreed to guarantee certain fundamental working standards, but no, or few, activities take place on the basis of the agreement) the existence of an IFA or IFAs in general may already generate positive side effects. The agreement can serve as a basis for a mutual dialogue between the MNC and the GTU, in which concrete problems can be identified, discussed and resolved. In this scenario, the IFA indirectly achieves concrete positive results. These results are not made possible solely by the IFA; rather, the framework agreement is a single element in the mutual relationship between the MNC and the GTU. It is important to realise that both MNC and GTU representatives consider this mutual relationship to be the primary key to success. However, it is doubtful whether these side effects connected to the existence of an IFA – on their own – can justify the existence of an agreement. It seems inappropriate to accept that a contractual arrangement may not (in its entirety) be fulfilled, only because through its existence it indirectly generates some welcome results. These results are also generated by the other instruments mentioned by the interviewees. It seems appropriate for GTUs to only pursue the establishment of new IFAs and the keeping up of existing IFAs on the condition that the agreements can realise their goals on the basis of their own substantive content. An agreement that is presented as a binding contractual arrangement that is not, or cannot, be enforced in court, is rather paradoxical; it may exert some pressure on the counterparty, but in the end is likely to leave you empty-handed.

CONCLUDING REMARKS

The IFA is a relatively new instrument, used by GTUs to respond to the impact of globalization on the business operations of companies operating worldwide. This way, they address an issue (inter)national legislators and regulators have difficulties dealing with. Although in general the emergence of IFAs is perceived as a positive development with the potential to improve fundamental working standards in global business operations, some comments are made in literature. These comments were confirmed and fleshed out by the empirical data presented in this paper. For an IFA to be able to reach its objectives, extensive attention must firstly be paid to the context in which the agreement operates, including the sectors, countries and cultures involved. Secondly, the practical issues connected to the functioning of the agreement need to be considered, including the parties involved and their responsibilities, the establishment of decent implementation and monitoring mechanisms and the allocation of financial and human resources. The supply chain of major companies includes great opportunities to improve working standards in countries with an underdeveloped legal system. This study shows that, as a side effect, the mere existence of an IFA may create a platform for negotiation between MNCs and GTUs. However, the question is whether this is appropriate and sensible.

The issues identified in literature and in this paper show that the IFA can be a compelling tool for GTUs to pursue their aims. Unfortunately, not all existing IFAs deal with these issues and some appear to achieve no direct practical impact at all.

NOTE:

1 H. Platzer & S. Rüb, 'International Framework Agreements: An Instrument for Enforcing Human Rights?' (2014), accessible at: <http://library.fes.de/pdf-files/iez/10474.pdf> (last visited 13 December 2015), pp. 2-3.

2 I. Schömann & P. Wilke, 'Towards a sustainable economy: the potential contribution of international framework agreements', in S. Vitols & N. Kluge (eds.), The sustainable company: a new approach to corporate governance (2011), p. 167.

3 'Bangladesh collapse search over; death toll 1,127', Yahoo News, 13 May 2013, accessible at: http://news.yahoo.com/bangladeshcollapse-search-over-death-toll-1-127-122554495.html (last visited 13 December 2015).

4 K. Papadakis (ed.), Shaping Global Industrial Relations: the Impact of Global Framework Agreements (2011), pp. 2-3.

5 This number is based on the information on the websites of the existing GTUs, see http://www.global-unions.org/+-frameworkagreements-+.html (last visited 13 December 2015). Some MNCs signed various IFAs, either with one GTU or with various GTUs.

6 European Commission, 'Transnational company agreements: realising the potential of social dialogue', 10.9.2012, SWD/2012/264 final, accessible at: <http://ec.europa.eu/social/main.jsp?catId=707&langId=en&intPageId=214> (last visited 19 May 2015).

7 Platzer & Rüb, supra note 1, pp. 6-7.

8 See the ILO website, accessible at: <http://www.ilo.org/global/standards/introduction-to-international-labour-standards/conventionsand-recommendations/lang--en/index.htm>(last visited 19 May 2015).

9 The ILO has also drawn up conventions with regard to these standards, which are not considered 'fundamental', however, see the ILO website, accessible at: <http://www.ilo.org/dyn/normlex/en/f?p=NORMLEXPUB:12000:0::NO:::> (last visited 2 October 2015). These standards have also been laid down in the Universal Declaration of Human Rights of the United Nations, accessible at: <http://www. un.org/en/documents/udhr/> (last visited 2 October 2015), paras. 23-24.

10 Based on a definition used in: B. Beamon, 'Supply Chain Design and Analysis: Models and Methods', (1998) 55 International Journal of Production Economics, no. 3, http://doi.org/10.1016/S0925-5273(98)00079-6, p. 281.

11 M. Saunders et al., Research Methods for Business Students (2009), pp. 320-321.

12 J. Saldana, The Coding Manual for Qualitative Researchers (2013), pp. 1-40.

13 Saunders et al., supra note 11, pp. 258-259.

14 J.A. Maxwell, Qualitative research design – an interactive approach (2013), pp. 124-125.

15 T. Müller et al., 'International Framework Agreements: Opportunities and Limitations of a New Tool of Global Trade Policy' (2008) accessible at: <http://library.fes.de/pdf-files/iez/05814.pdf> (last visited 18 September 2015), pp. 10-11.

16 A. Nollkaemper, Kern van het internationaal publiekrecht (2014), pp. 52-53.

17 A. Sobczak, 'Legal Dimensions of International Framework Agreements in the field of Corporate Social Responsibility', (2007) 62 Relations Industrielles – Industrial Relations, no. 3, http://doi.org/10.7202/016489ar, p. 479; Papadakis, supra note 4, p. 17.

18 Sobczak, supra note 17, p. 476, Schömann & Wilke, supra note 2, p. 173.

19 V. Dehnen & L. Pries, 'International Framework Agreements: A thread in the web of transnational labour regulation', (2014) 20 European Journal of Industrial Relations, no. 4, http://doi.org/10.1177/0959680113519187, p. 338.

20 ILO website, supra note 8.

21 J. Sydow et al., 'Implementation of Global Framework Agreements:towardsamulti-organizationalperspective',(2014) 20 Transfer, no. 4, http://doi.org/10.1177/1024258914546270, p. 493, Dehnen & Pries, supra note 19, pp. 339-340.

22 Dehnen & Pries, supra note 19, pp. 344-348.

23 Ibid., pp. 346-347.

24 Platzer & Rüb, supra note 1, pp. 9-10.

25 Ibid., p. 11; Sobczak, supra note 17, pp. 476-477; Müller et al., supra note 15, p. 8.

26 These MSIs can be composed of companies, GTUs and NGOs, for example. They can be made responsible for overseeing (a number of) IFA(s).

27 Müller et al., supra note 15, pp. 7-8; Platzer & Rüb, supra note 1, p. 12.

28 Platzer & Rüb, supra note 1, p. 13. To the author's knowledge, termination of an IFA has not yet occurred.

29 N. Hammer, 'International Framework Agreement in the Context of Global Production', in K. Papadakis (ed.), Cross-border Social Dialogue and Agreements: an Emerging Global Industrial Relations Framework? (2008), pp. 94-95; Sobczak, supra note 17, pp. 469-470; Schömann & Wilke, supra note 2, pp. 174-175.

30 E.g. the ready-made garments industry, see: D. Miller, 'Preparing for the long haul – negotiating international framework agreements in the global textile, garment, and footwear sector', (2004) 4 Global social policy, no. 2, http://doi.org/10.1177/1468018104045110, p. 218.

31 E.g. the automotive industry and complex electronics industry.

32 Platzer & Rüb, supra note 1, pp. 14-15.

33 Dehnen & Pries, supra note 19, p. 345.

34 Sobczak, supra note 17, pp. 470-471; I. Schömann, 'The Impact of Transnational Company Agreements on Social Dialogue and Industrial Relations', in K. Papadakis (ed.), Shaping Global Industrial Relations: the Impact of Global Framework Agreements (2011), p. 34.

35 It is submitted that other general conclusions may be based on the existing body of literature as well. Save for some additional insights, this paper is restricted to the four common threads listed in the text.

36 It is admitted that the concentration of IFAs in Europe to a certain extent mitigates the disruptive influence of culture. However, keeping in mind the further development of the IFA as an instrument, and with a view to future research projects, it is still important to consider it.

37 For more in-depth information, see their website, accessible at: <http://www.cleanclothes.org/> (last visited 2 September 2015).

38 H&M has concluded two IFAs with different GTUs.

39 The concept of establishing a local protocol is elaborated in an internal policy document, sent to the author of this paper by an interviewee.

40 See for example a report on the website of Building and Woodworker's International, accessible at: <http://www.bwint.org/default. asp?index=4638&Language=EN> (last visited 13 December 2015).

41 Miller, supra note 30, p. 227.

42 See for example IndustriALL, 'IndustriALL Global Union's Guidelines for Global Framework Agreements', accessible at: http://www. industriall-union.org/sites/default/files/uploads/documents/GFAs/industriall_gfa_guidelines_final_version_exco_12-2014_english.pdf (last visited 13 December 2015). These guidelines are clearly reflected in the IFA concluded between IndustriALL and H&M on 3 November 2015.

43 The ten IFAs that were studied in the context of this paper,

if they include the supply chain in the agreement, apply a variety of ways to do so. For example, the IFA concluded by Siemens states: 'The principles of this agreement are reflected in the Siemens Code of Conduct for Suppliers. Thus Siemens also actively endeavors to have these principles incorporated into the business policy of its suppliers.' The IFA concluded by Royal BAM states that the company will 'refrain from using the services of those trading partners, subcontractors and suppliers which do not respect the criteria listed above'.

44 For more about the functioning of suppliers' codes of conduct, see L. Vytopil, 'Contractual Control and Labour-Related CSR Norms in the Supply Chain: Dutch Best Practices', (2012) 8 Utrecht Law Review, no. 1, http://doi.org/10.18352/ulr.186, pp. 155-169.

45 For a more comprehensive overview of possible measures, see: Sydow et al., supra note 21, p. 496.

CHAPTER 5

AMBIGUOUS LAW: THE RIGHT TO BARGAIN FOR JOB SECURITY IN COLLECTIVE AGREEMENTS

Elizabeth Shi

INTRODUCTION

It is the duty of a democratic parliament to enact statute which is clear, unambiguous, readily applicable and unproblematic so that it can be understood and followed without difficulty.[1] As legal philosopher Wesley Hohfeld sagaciously observed '[c]hameleon-hued words are a peril both to clear thought and to lucid expression.'[2]

This article will argue that the right to bargain for job security in collective agreements in the Fair Work Act 2009 (Cth) ('Fair Work Act 2009') is not clear, unambiguous, readily applicable and unproblematic. The law is unclear because it lacks detail and specificity, both in the provisions themselves and in the explanation of the law provided by the Parliament.

Prior to the Fair Work Act 2009, the Workplace Relations Amendment (Work Choices) Act 2005 (Cth) ('Work Choices') prohibited specific matters from being included in employment agreement negotiations and outcomes. These 'prohibited content' rules included restrictions on the engagement of independent contractors and labour-hire workers and requirements relating to the conditions of their engagement.[3] These restrictions and requirements were described as 'job security clauses'. Under the 'prohibited content' rules, if a trade union chose to pursue claims for job security clauses, then the trade union would lose their right to take protected industrial action.[4] If an employer chose to agree to job security clauses, it would face potential legal action.[5] The prohibited content laws were unambiguous and clear. The Fair Work Act 2009 has now abolished the 'prohibited content' rules, so job security clauses are no longer prohibited in enterprise agreements certified under the Act. However, Parliament did not explain its intentions in regulating job security clauses.

This article will argue that the precedents dealing with 'permitted matters' are unclear and inconsistent. The Explanatory Memorandum provides only limited guidance on which job security clauses fall into the definition of 'permitted matters'.[6]

Further, this article will argue that when making workplace determinations, the Fair Work Act 2009 requires the Fair Work Commission ('FWC') to take account of 'the interests of employees and employers who will be covered by the determination',[7] but the meaning of this is ambiguous. The article will argue that it is unclear whether employees' job security is an interest that should be taken into account, and if so, how much weight should be placed on this interest. The explanatory memorandum provides no guidance on this question either.[8] The interpretations in Transport Workers' Union of Australia v Qantas Airways Ltd[9] ('Qantas Workplace Determination') will be discussed and used to illustrate the lack of clarity. [10]

Both 'permitted matters' and 'interests of employees and employers' will be considered in this article because both provisions have a direct impact on job security clauses. For example, if a job security clause falls within 'permitted matters', then it is permissible for employees to take industrial action to bargain for the clause. If the 'interests of employees and employers' includes job security interests then arguably the FWC must do more than just pay lip service to job security interests in deciding on job security clauses.

It is conceded at the outset that Parliament did intend to grant FWC wide discretion.[11] Despite this, it will be argued

Citation: Elizabeth Shi, Ambiguous Law: The Right to Bargain for Job Security in Collective Agreements, DOI: http://dx.doi.org/10.15209/vulj.v4i1.45.

that the jurisprudence on these provisions is inconsistent and unpredictable, and therefore further legislative clarification is necessary.

THE DEFINITION OF JOB SECURITY AND JOB SECURITY CLAUSES

At the core of this article is the concept of job security. The word 'security' is defined in the Macquarie Dictionary as free from or not exposed to danger, safe, free from care, and without anxiety.[12] According to Standing, 'security' means a sense of being in control over one's development and activities.[13]

This article defines 'job security' as a state where an employee's 'reasonable and probable expectation of continued employment' are being met; that is, the absence of fear of loss of employment. In the English case of Allen v Flood, Hawkin J explained this concept:

The daily labourer, whose tested character for steadiness, honesty, and industry has induced his master, as a matter of course, through a long series of years, week by week to renew or continue his employment finds in this the foundation for his 'reasonable and probable expectation' that he may rely on continual employment in the future.[14]

Generally speaking, when politicians, law makers, trade unions, and the media talk about 'job security', they are talking about meeting this expectation of continued employment.[15] For the purposes of this article, a job security clause is defined as any intervention that restricts managerial decision making with regards to contracting out.[16] Contracting out means hiring contractors who are not parties to a collective agreement to perform similar jobs to workers who are parties to a collective agreement.

A job security clause includes any clause that restricts contracting out, for example, a clause which states that contracting out is only permitted if internal employees are not interested in the jobs.

A job security clause also includes any clause that makes contracting out less attractive for an employer. For example, a clause which stipulates the employer must hire outside contractors on the same rates and conditions as the internal employees. Such a clause is commonly referred to as a 'site rates clause'.[17] The intention of the site rates clause is to make it less attractive for the employer to use outside labour, and to increase job security for direct employees.

Any clause that prohibits contracting out all together is also a job security clause. Such clauses are less common than the clauses which restrict or remove the incentive for contracting out.

Any clause that prohibits or restricts forced redundancies as a result of contracting out is also a job security clause.

By its very definition, job security clauses can be construed as an interference of managerial prerogatives. Once a job security clause is agreed to or arbitrated into an agreement, employers will not have complete freedom to do whatever they want in relation to hiring outside contractors. As will be discussed below, the view taken by FWC in the Qantas Workplace Determination was that key job security clauses were interfering with managerial prerogatives.

PROHIBITED CONTENT PROVISIONS IN THE WORKPLACE RELATIONS ACT

Prior to the Fair Work Act 2009, Work Choices legislation prohibited an extensive list of matters from being included in employment agreements. The majority of these prohibited content related to employee and union rights and benefits.[18] With regards to job security clauses, reg 8.5 of Workplace Relations Regulation 2006 (Cth) stipulated that following job security clauses were prohibited content:

A term of a workplace agreement is prohibited content to the extent that it deals with the following:

...

- restrictions on the engagement of independent contractors and requirements relating to the conditions of their engagement;
- restrictions on the engagement of labour hire workers, and requirements relating to the conditions of their engagement, imposed on an entity or person for whom the labour hire worker performs work under a contract with a labour hire agency

The prohibitions applied to both employees and employers. If a trade union chose to pursue claims for job security clauses, then the trade union would lose their right to take protected industrial action.[19] If an employer chose to agree to job security clauses, it would face potential legal action.[20] The prohibited content restrictions led many unions to attempt to insert the prohibited terms into common law contracts or side agreements to operate alongside the statutory collective agreements.[21] This side-stepping strategy was only successful if the employer was willing to agree to the side agreements.

JOB SECURITY CLAUSES AND PERMITTED MATTERS PROVISIONS IN THE FAIR WORK ACT

As will be discussed below, in the Qantas Workplace Determination the FWC rejected job security clauses because it was of the view that they interfered with managerial prerogatives. Work Choices legislation prohibited certain job security clauses from enterprise agreements.[22] The prohibitions were clear-cut and unequivocal. The Fair Work Act 2009 has now abolished the

'prohibited content' rules. Instead it confined the content of agreements to 'permitted matters'[23] and deemed certain matters 'unlawful terms'[24].

Section 172(1) stated that the enterprise agreements can be made about the following 'permitted matters':

Matters pertaining to the relationship between an employer that will be covered by the agreement and that employer's employees who will be covered by the agreement;

Matters pertaining to the relationship between the employer or employers, and the employee organisation or employee organisations, that will be covered by the agreement;

Deductions from wages for any purpose authorised by an employee who will be covered by the agreement;

How the agreement will operate.

Employers have frequently argued that the job security

clauses were not matters pertaining to the relationship between an employer or employer and employees and therefore were not permitted matters. For example it has been argued that the site rates clause was not a matter pertaining to the relationship between an employer and employees, because the clause did not govern the wages and conditions of employees.[25] It only governed the wages and conditions of contractors.[26]

What, then, was the meaning of 'matters pertaining to the relationship between an employer or employer and employees' ('matters pertaining')? The Explanatory Memoranda answered this question only to some extent by providing that certain clauses were not matters pertaining, while certain other clauses were matters pertaining. The guidance provided was only partial and left many grey areas.

The Explanatory Memoranda stated that clauses that contain a general prohibition on the employer engaging labour hire employees or contractor were not matters pertaining to the relationship between an employer and employees, nor were clauses that contain a general prohibition on the employer employing casual employees.[27]

Further, the explanatory memorandum stated:

It is intended that the following terms would be within the scope of permitted matters for the purpose of paragraph 172(1)(a): ... Terms relating to conditions or requirements about employing casual employees or engaging labour hire or contractors if those terms sufficiently relate to employees' job security – e.g. a term which provided that contractors must not be engaged on terms and conditions that would undercut the enterprise agreement.[28]

It remains unclear what constitutes something which 'sufficiently related to' employees' job security, other than the example given. A term which provided that contractors must not be engaged on terms and conditions that would undercut the enterprise agreement is basically a site rates clause. Therefore explanatory memorandum stipulates that a site rates clause was a 'permitted matter'. Accordingly, site rates clause had been accepted as permitted content in a number of cases, including Liquor Hospitality and Miscellaneous Union v Coca-Cola Amatil[29] and Flinders Operating Services Pty Ltd v Australian Municipal, Administrative, Clerical Services Union (Flinders).[30]

Whilst the explanatory memorandum provided guidance on specific clauses such as site rates clauses, it did not provide guidance on many other types of job security clauses. Whilst it is true that there is indeed a substantial jurisprudence about matters pertaining,[31] many parts of this jurisprudence are uncertain, incoherent and inconsistent.[32] The following section demonstrates the uncertain, incoherent and inconsistent case law concerning job security clauses.

INCONSISTENTCIES IN CASES INTERPRETING 'PERMITTED MATTERS'

As discussed above, many parts of the jurisprudence of 'permitted matters' are uncertain, incoherent and inconsistent. Cases which concern almost identical job security clauses have often received very different treatments in different cases. The following two cases illustrate the inconsistencies.[33]

In Flinders [34], the Australian Municipal Administrative Clerical and Services Union wanted to insert the following clauses which limited the circumstances in which supplementary labour may be used:

The Company may from time to time use supplementary labour for the absence of direct employees on extended leave, temporary vacancies and peak workloads in areas normally staffed by direct employees.

Direct employees will be given the option of working overtime and/or being called back to work before external personnel are engaged.[35]

Under these clauses, the employer could not use supplementary labour in circumstances other than absence, temporary vacancies or peak workloads, nor could it use supplementary labour without offering overtime or offering calling back direct employees first. The employer, Alinda Energy, refused to agree to these two clauses, as well as to other job security clauses proposed.[36] The union then gave the employer formal notice to take industrial action. The employer then applied to FWC in order to stop the industrial action, arguing, among other things, that the above clauses were not permitted matters because they did not pertain to the relationship between the employer and employees.[37] The employer argued that the clauses impermissibly restricted the employer's ability to engage outside labour to meet its operational needs.

Deputy President Bartel rejected the employer's argument. DP Bartel held that the clauses were permitted matters, because while these provisions may be construed as a partial restriction on the use of external employees, the overall intent is to maximise permanent employment.[38] DP Bartel compared these clauses with a clause in Re Schefenacker Vision Systems Australia Pty Ltd, AWU, AMWU Certified Agreement ('Schefenacker') which stipulated that the maximum level of labour hire workers to be 20% of total employees.[39] In Schefenacker, the Full Bench ruled a 20% cap was a permitted matter.[40] DP Bartel concluded that a 20% cap was arguably more restrictive than the clauses in Flinders, and therefore the clauses in Flinders should be construed as permitted matters.

The reasoning in Flinders appears quite logical. However a very similar clause was held not to be permitted content in the case of Australian Postal Corporation v Communicationa, Electrical, Electronic, Energy, Information, Postal, Plumbing and Allied Services Union of Australia [41] ('Australian Postal Corporation').

In Australian Postal Corporation, the trade union attempted to bargain for the following clause: 'Australia Post must advertise every position internally and to only contract out a position if it is not wanted by an Australia Post employee.'[42]

This clause was very similar to the clauses in Flinders which required the employer to offer overtime to existing employees, and to only hire from outside in circumstances of extended leave, peak vacancy and extended workloads.

Australia Post argued that this clause was not a permitted matter, as it did not pertain to the relationship between the employer and employees.[43] The Full Bench, consisting of Senior Deputy President Acton, Deputy President Hamilton and Commissioner Blair, agreed with Australia Post.[44] The Full Bench cited French J's judgment in Wesfarmers Premier Coal Ltd v Automotive, Food, Metals, Engineering, Printing and Kindred Industries Union (No 2)[45]('Wesfarmers'). In that case, French J found that 'provisions restricting or qualifying the employer's right to use independent contractors' are not matters pertaining to the employment relationship.

Surprisingly, the Full Bench made absolutely no mention of that fact the Explanatory Memorandum to the Fair Work Act 2009 expressly stated that clauses relating to conditions or requirements about employing casual employees or engaging labour hire or contractors are matters pertaining to the relationship between an employer and employees, if those clauses sufficiently relate to employees' job security.[46] The Full Bench failed to give any consideration to the question of whether the clause in question fitted into this category. Instead, the Full Bench relied heavily on the precedent set in Wesfarmers. Wesfarmers might be relevant but it was a case decided under the previous legislation, not the Fair Work Act 2009.

UNCLEAR PROVISION OF 'THE INTERESTS OF EMPLOYERS AND EMPLOYEES'

The previous section has shown that parts of the jurisprudence of 'permitted matters' are unclear and inconsistent. This section will argue that the requirement to take into account 'the interests of employers and employees' when deciding on workplace determinations is also unclear. In particular, it is unclear whether employees' job security is an interest that should be taken into account, and if so, how much weight should be placed on this interest. The explanatory memorandum does not provide guidance on this question.[47]

It must be pointed out that the context in which workplace determinations are made are different from the cases where appropriate parameters of workplace bargaining are determined, such as Flinders and Australian Postal Corporation discussed in section V of this article. There has been the longstanding legal principle in workplace determinations that any substantial interference with managerial prerogatives requires careful consideration.[48]

Despite this longstanding legal principle, s 275(c) provides that FWC must take into account interest of both employers and employees. However, the precise meaning of 'the interests of employers and employees' was not defined in the explanatory memoranda.[49] Therefore the courts and FWC were given wide discretion in the interpretation.

In addition, the courts and FWC must also consider the following matters in deciding which terms to include in a workplace determination (broadly referred to as 'merit grounds'):

Section 275

- the public interest;
- how productivity might be improved in the enterprise or enterprises concerned;
- the extent to which the conduct of the bargaining representatives was reasonable;
- the extent to which the bargaining representatives have complied with the good faith bargaining requirements;
- incentives to continue bargaining at a later time.

'INTERESTS OF EMPLOYERS AND EMPLOYEES' IN THE QANTAS WORKPLACE DETERMINATION

In the Qantas Workplace Determination,[50] the Full Bench of FWC had to apply s 275 and take account of the merit grounds in reaching its conclusion. As argued below, although the Full Bench paid lip service to employees' 'legitimate concerns as to their job security',[51] it made a determination which effectively ignored these concerns.

The Transport Workers' Union failed to persuade the Full Bench on two major job security clauses: the site rates clause and the 20% cap clause. Both of these major job security clauses had an immediate effect on the labour costs incurred by Qantas. The clauses the Union did persuade the Full Bench to accept had no effect on the labour costs incurred by Qantas: the no forced redundancies clause and the consultation and paid time off for Union representatives.

Site Rates Clause

The Transport Workers' Union sought a site rates clause, which stipulated that if, after consultation, Qantas decides to use supplementary labour and/or outsider hire, Qantas will ensure that they will receive the same rates and conditions as the direct employees.[52] During the industrial dispute, the union told Qantas and the public that the site rates clause was the 'number one issue' for its members.[53] The union argued that it wanted the site rates clause in place because it wanted to ensure that the workplace determination will not be undermined or avoided by contracting out and the engagement of contractors.[54] It wanted to increase job security for the direct employees and to make contracting out less attractive for Qantas.

Qantas objected to this clause on merit grounds. Qantas argued that it was already paying its contractors lower rates than its direct employees. Qantas also argued that such a clause was unprecedented both in Qantas and in the airline industry, interfered in the 'heartland of managerial discretion', and will lead to an increase in costs, undermine competitiveness, and was 'inimical to improving productivity'.[55]

The Full Bench viewed the site rates clause as a clause which dealt with contractors and labour hire employees, and not with Qantas's direct employees. Because the determination was for Qantas and Qantas's direct employees, the Full Bench held that it was inappropriate for the Workplace Determination to directly or indirectly govern the terms and conditions of employment of employees not covered by it.[56] The Full Bench also observed that the use of contractors and labour hire employees was a widespread operational strategy in the airline industry and it allowed airlines to achieve operational flexibility and reduce costs.[57] Granting the site rate clause would overturn the current Qantas approach in using contractors and lead to immediate and significant increases in labour costs.[58] It also took into account Qantas's strong opposition and its expressed need to reduce costs in a difficult market environment. It concluded the site rates failed on the grounds of merit and because of its negative impact on efficiency and productivity.[59]

What was noticeably missing in the Full Bench's reasoning was any genuine considerations of job security. As discussed above, s 275(c) required the Full Bench to take into account the interests of employers and employees.[60]The Full Bench paid lip service to job security by acknowledging that 'in the competitive environment and in the face of organisational restructure, the employees also have legitimate concerns as to their job security' and that 'ultimately it is in the interests of both Qantas and its employees that Qantas operates a viable and competitive business and is able to retain, attract and reward skilled and motivated employees.'[61] However, the Full Bench's actual reasoning on the site rates clause seemed to ignore employees' legitimate concerns as to their job security. The site rates clause was intended to bolster the employees' job security. In its reasons for rejecting the site rates clause, the Full Bench gave priority to Qantas's need to reduce costs over considerations of job security.

Further, the Full Bench's reasoning favoured the 'current Qantas approach' and what is 'widespread' in the airline industry. Whilst these considerations were certainly relevant, the Full Bench did not explain why these considerations should be given more weight than considerations of job security.

20% Cap on Supplementary labour and outside Hire

In addition to the sites rates clause, another job security clause the union wanted was a clause which required the total number of supplementary labour and outside hire to be no more than 20% of the total number of directly hired employees at any given time.[62]

This clause, in conjunction with the site rates clause was intended to limit the use of supplementary labour. TWU opposed the extent to which Qantas engaged labour hire and supplementary employees and argued that Qantas should not be permitted to allow the number of direct Qantas employees to dwindle by attrition.[63]

Qantas contended that this clause should fail on both merit grounds and on jurisdictional grounds. It argued that a percentage cap did not deal with a permitted matter and thus failed on jurisdictional grounds.[64] It also argued against the percentage cap on merit grounds: that it had no precedence within Qantas or the airline industry, it will increase costs and reduce flexibility and did not enhance productivity.[65]

The Full Bench held that this claim failed on merit.[66] It ruled that using contractors and outside hire has been a long standing practice and it has not been shown that current Qantas employees have been adversely affected by this practice.[67] It went on to say:

> To interfere with management's decisions on such a matter would require clear and strong evidence of unfairness. No such case has been established with respect to current employees or otherwise. In the light of this conclusion it is not necessary that we determine whether there is jurisdiction to insert the clause. Even if there is jurisdiction to grant such a clause we would dismiss it on the grounds of merit.[68]

What the Full Bench meant by 'clear and strong evidence of unfairness' was ambiguous. The Full Bench did not explain why the fact full time employees were dwindling by attrition was not 'evidence of unfairness'. A higher and higher percentage of Qantas workers were becoming contractors engaged on worse terms than the direct employees. This was detrimental to the employees' interests. Similar to its reasoning on the site rates clause, the Full Bench's reasoning on the 20% cap clause again effectively ignored employees' legitimate concerns. It again favoured the 'current Qantas approach' and what was 'widespread' in the airline industry over the interests of the employees.

No Forced Redundancies Clause

Unlike the previous two clauses, TWU was able to persuade the Full Bench on a clause that stated that there will be no compulsory redundancies as a consequence of the utilisation of supplementary labour and outside hire.[69]

Qantas opposed the insertion of the clause into the collective agreement but did agree to issue a side letter with slightly altered wording.[70] The Full Bench ruled that the commitment Qantas was willing to give should be included into the collective agreement.[71] The Full Bench reasoned that although there has been no history of compulsory redundancies as a result of hiring contractors and no plans for this to occur in the near future, the extensive use of contractors did raise legitimate concerns about the impact of these changes on job security.[72]

The difference between this clause and the two rejected clauses listed above seems to be the fact there would be no immediate increase in labour cost for Qantas in order to obey this clause. In addition, Qantas had already agreed to the clause anyway in a side letter.

Consultation and Paid Time Off for Representatives

The union also succeeded in obtaining a clause which required Qantas to weigh up all alternative options before making arrangements to contract out, as well as a comprehensive consultation process and a reasonable time frame for consideration with all Qantas employees affected by such an option.[73] It also required Qantas to provide reasonable resources and paid time off for union nominees and union members to attend meetings to respond to the business case for contracting out and prepare specific in-house bids.[74]

Once again, this clause did not lead to an immediate increase in costs for the employer, because Qantas had provided resources and paid time off in the past. There would be no change to existing practice.

FWC's Consideration of 'Interests of Employers and Employees' in Qantas

The Full Bench of FWC rejected the site rates clause and the 20% cap clause, but accepted the no forced redundancies clause and the consultation and time off clause. The key difference between them was the fact that the site rates clause and the 20% cap clause led to a direct and immediate increase in the cost of labour for Qantas and departed from existing practice.

By giving such weighty consideration to the cost of labour and existing practice, the Full Bench effectively ignored the employees' interests in ensuring job security. The site rates clause and 20% cap clause would have increased the employees' job security.

As discussed in Part VI above, FWC had broad discretion to interpret the merit grounds section.[75] It chose to interpret the section in a way which did not give any weight to the employees' interests in ensuring job security. It is unclear how much later decisions will rely on the Qantas Workplace Determination, because the Full Bench did emphasise the specific difficulties faced by the aviation industry.[76] This might mean that if a future dispute arose in an industry which was more robust and less affected by the economic downturn than the aviation industry, the outcome could be more favourable for job security.[77]

CONCLUSION

This article has argued that 'permitted matters' law is unclear and inconsistently interpreted. Cases which concern almost identical job security clauses have received different treatments.

This article has also argued that the 'interests of employers and employees' is not clearly defined, thus granting FWC very wide discretion when arbitrating job security clauses in workplace determinations.

Certainly, granting FWC a very wide discretion was a conscious decision by Parliament, but the lack of clarity in the legislation, coupled with the abolition of 'prohibited content' has resulted in unpredictable legal outcomes for Australian employers and employees. Historically the tribunal has been reluctant to arbitrate outcomes that interfere with managerial prerogatives. By their very nature, all job security clauses could be construed as interfering with managerial prerogatives, so why not prohibit job security clauses altogether in workplace determinations? This would be a much clearer approach. The previous law of 'prohibited content' did exactly that. It would save a lot of time and resources for employees and trade unions who are attempting to argue for job security clauses to be included into a workplace determination and lead to a more efficient legal process.

It is time for Parliament to follow the advice given by legal philosopher Wesley Hohfeld and take action to clarify this area of law.[78]

Footnotes:

1. Tom Campbell, The Legal Theory of Ethical Positivism (Dartmouth, 1996) ch 6.
2. Wesley Newcomb Hohfeld, 'Some Fundamental Legal Conceptions as Applied in Judicial Reasoning' (1913) 23 Yale Law Journal 16, 28..
3. BWorkplace Relations Regulation 2006 (Cth) regs 8.5(1)(h)–8.5(1)(i). For a general discussion of agreement-making under Work Choices, see Christopher Jon Arup et al, 'Assessing the Impact of Employment Legislation: The Coalition Government's Labour Law Program 1997-2008 and the Challenge of Research' (Research Report, Workplace and Corporate Law Research Group and Australian Centre for Research in Employment and Work, Monash University, 2009); Carolyn Sutherland, 'Making the 'BOOT' Fit: Reforms to Agreement-Making from Work Choices to Fair Work' cited in Anthony Forsyth and Andrew Stewart (eds), Fair Work: The New Workplace Laws and the Work Choices Legacy (Federation Press, 2009) 99.
4. Workplace Relations Act 1996 (Cth) s 365.
5. Ibid ss 357, 365.
6. Explanatory Memoranda, Fair Work Bill 2008 (Cth) 110 [672].
7. Fair Work Act 2009 (Cth) s 275(c).
8. Explanatory Memoranda, Fair Work Bill 2008 (Cth) 177 [1118].
9. [2012] FWAFB 6612 (8 August 2012) [41].
10. Ibid.
11. Breen Creighton and Andrew Stewart have commented that the Rudd government's aim was to avoid micro-regulation by conferring broad functions and appropriate discretion on Fair Work Commission. See Breen Creighton and Andrew Stewart, Labour Law (Federation Press, 5th ed, 2010) 48; Explanatory Memoranda, Fair Work Bill 2008 (Cth) 1 [4].
12. Arthur Delbridge et al (eds), The Macquarie Dictionary Federation Edition (1997) 1706.
13. See Guy Standing, Global Labour Flexibility Seeking Distributive Justice (Basingstoke, 1999) 52.
14. [1898] AC 1, 16.
15. 15 See Peter Reith and Department of Employment, Workplace Relations and Small Business (Cth), Job security in Australia (Office of the Minister for Employment, Workplace Relations and Small Business, 2000); Australian Council of Trade Unions, 'Australian Workers Want Better Job Security, Not a Return to Work Choices-Style Policies' (Media Release, 17 July 2011); Amy Coderoy, 'Job Preservation a Concern for Nation of Insecure Workers', The Sydney Morning Herald (Sydney), 28 September 2011; John Gennard, Job Security and Industrial Relations (Paris Organisation for Economic Co-operation and Development, 1979); Di Yerbury, 'Redundancy: The Response of Australian Industrial Law' (Working Paper No 82-002, Australian Graduate School of Management, 1982); Di Yerbury and Robert Clark 'Redundancy and the Law: the Position in mid-1983' (1983) 25 Journal of Industrial Relations 353; Stephen Deery 'Trade Unions, Technological Change and Redundancy Protection in Australia' (1982) 24(2) Journal of Industrial Relations 155.
16. There are many cases involving job security clauses, both in the context of unions seeking to take protected industrial actions to obtain the clauses and in workplace determinations. See for example, Liquor Hospitality and Miscellaneous Union v Coca-Cola Amatil [2009] FWA 920 (3 November 2009); Flinders Operating Services Pty Ltd v Australian Municipal, Administrative, Clerical Services Union [2011] FWA 4506 (14 July 2011); Re Schefenacker Vision Systems Australia Pty Ltd, AWU, AMWU Certified Agreement (2005) 142 IR 289; Australian Postal Corporation v Communicationa, Electrical, Electronic, Energy, Information, Postal, Plumbing and Allied Services Union of Australia [2009]FWAFB 599 (12 October 2009).
17. Site rates clause was the number one issue for the unions in the Qantas dispute.; see Transport Workers' Union of Australia v Qantas Airways Ltd [2012] FWAFB 6612 (8 August 2012).
18. Sutherland, above n 3, 99, 109.

19. Workplace Relations Act 1996 (Cth) s 365.

20. Ibid ss 357, 365.

21. Andrew Stewart and Joellen Riley, 'Working Around Work Choices: Collective Bargaining and the Common Law' (2007) 31 Melbourne University Law Review 903.

22. Workplace Relations Regulation 2006 (Cth) regs 8.5(1)(h)-8.5(1)(i). For a general discussion of agreement-making under Work Choices, see Sutherland, above n 3, 99.

23. Fair Work Act 2009 (Cth) s 172(1).

24. Ibid s 194; Unlawful Content includes discriminatory terms, objectionable terms, unfair termination term, a term modifying unfair dismissal protection, a term inconsistent to industrial action laws, a term that interferes right of entry laws, a term which modifies State or Territory OHS rights.

25. A site rates clause is a clause which stipulates the employer must hire outside contractors on the same rates and conditions as the internal employees; see Transport Workers' Union of Australia v Qantas Airways Ltd (2012) FWAFB 6612 (8 August 2012).

26. Liquor Hospitality and Miscellaneous Union v Coca-Cola Amatil [2009] FWA 920 (3 November 2009); Flinders Operating Services Pty Ltd v Australian Municipal, Administrative, Clerical Services Union [2011] FWA 4506 (14 July 2011).

27. Explanatory Memoranda, Fair Work Bill 2008 (Cth) 108 [673].

28. Ibid 108 [672], emphasis added.

29. [2009] FWA 920 (3 November 2009).

30. Flinders Operating Services Pty Ltd v Australian Municipal, Adminitsrative, Clerical Services Union [2011] FWA 4506 (14 July 2011).

31. Explanatory Memoranda, Fair Work Bill 2008 (Cth) 107 [670]. The law of 'matters pertaining to the relationship between an employer or employers and employees' is of long standing. Similar provisions had existed in both the Industrial Relations Act 1988 (Cth) and the Workplace Relations Act 1996 (Cth) before 27 March 2006. After 27 March 2006, a clause that was not about such matters was prohibited content.

32. Andrew Stewart made these observations in 2009. See 'FWA Tackles Content Rules on Contracting and Labour Hire ', Workplace Express, 5 November 2009 www.workplaceexpress.com.au. For discussions of matters pertaining cases and legislation, see also Esther Stern, 'Industrial Disputes and the Jurisdiction of the Federal Industrial Tribunal: An Analysis of Recent Developments' (1990) 3 Australian Journal of Labour Law 130; J T Ludeke, 'Whatever Happened to the Prerogatives of Management?' (1992) 66 Australian Law Journal 11; Marilyn Pittard, 'Agreement Straying Beyond Employment Matters: The Impact of the Agreement Validation Matters Legislation' (2005) 18 Australian Journal of Labour Law 71.

33. Both of these cases concerned the employees' right to take protected industrial action. It is well-settled case law that industrial action may not be taken in support of claims which are not permitted content in an agreement. This doctrine arose out of the High Court decision of Electrolux Home Products Pty Ltd v The Australian Workers' Union and Others (2004) 221 CLR 309 and this case was confirmed as good law in the Explanatory Memorandum of the Fair Work Act 2009. In addition, s 409 of Fair Work Act 2009 also prevents employees and their bargaining representatives from organising or taking protected industrial action if their claims are not for permitted matters.

34. [2001] FWA4506 (14 July 2011).

35. Ibid 80.

36. Ibid 60.

37. Ibid 60.

38. Ibid 80.

39. Re Schefenacker Vision Systems Australia Pty Ltd, AWU, AMWU Certified Agreement (2005) 142 IR 289.

40. Ibid [73].

41. [2009] FWAFB 599 (12 October 2009).

42. Ibid [49].

43. Ibid [33].

44. Ibid [62].

45. [2004] FCA 1737 (23 December 2004).

46. Explanatory Memoranda, Fair Work Bill 2008 (Cth) 108 [672].

47. Ibid 177 [1118].

48. Re Cram; Ex parte NSW Colliery Proprietors' Association Ltd (1987) 163 CLR 117, 136-7.

49. Explanatory Memoranda, Fair Work Bill 2008 (Cth) 177 [1118].

50. Fair Work Act 2009 (Cth) pts 2-5 describes the circumstances in which FWA has the power to make Workplace Determinations. These circumstances include bargaining related workplace determinations, low-paid workplace determinations and industrial action related workplace determinations. Workplace determination must occur after a termination of industrial dispute instrument has been made on the grounds either of significant economic harm to the negotiating parties or of actual or threatened harm to the broader economy or community and a post-industrial action negotiation period expires. This was the trigger for the FWA arbitration in Transport Workers' Union of Australia v Qantas Airways Ltd [2012] FWAFB 6612 (8 August 2012) [41].

51. Transport Workers' Union of Australia v Qantas Airways Ltd [2012] FWAFB 6612 (8 August 2012) [41].

52. Ibid [63].

53. See 'Site Rates Key to Qantas Dispute: TWU', Workplace Express, 22 March 2012www.workplaceexpress.com.au ; TWU's priorities are also stated in several media releases online, March 2012, see TWU

website www.twu.com.au.

54. Transport Workers' Union of Australia v Qantas Airways Ltd [2012] FWAFB 6612 (8 August 2012) [64].

55. Ibid [65].

56. Ibid.

57. Ibid.

58. Ibid

59. Ibid.

60. The Full Bench also cited Automotive, Food, Metals, Engineering, Printing and Kindred Indistries Union v Curragh Queensland Mining Ltd (Australian Indistrial Relations Commission, Q4464, C2758, 983/98, 11 August 1998, in holding that the 'interests of employers and employees' in s 275(c) calls for an appropriate balance between the legitimate expectations of the employers and employees.

61. Transport Workers' Union of Australia v Qantas Airways Ltd [2012] FWAFB 6612 (8 August 2012) [41].

62. Ibid [78]. A percentage cap clause has been accepted by previous courts and tribunals as 'permitted matter' and a 'matter pertaining to relationship of employers and employees'. See for example, Re Schefenacker Vision Systems Australia Pty Ltd, AWU, AMWU Certified Agreement (2005) 142 IR 289.

63. Transport Workers' Union of Australia v Qantas Airways Ltd [2012] FWAFB 6612 (8 August 2012) [82].

64. Ibid [80].

65. Ibid [81].

66. Ibid [82].

67. Ibid

68. Ibid

69. Ibid [74].

70. Ibid [76].

71. Ibid [77].

72. Ibid.

73. Ibid [72].

74. Ibid.

75. The broad discretion given to FWA was not unique to the merit grounds section. See Creighton and Stewart, above n 11, 48.

76. bid 95.

77. Other commentators have also commented on the Qantas dispute and the status of the aviation industry. See Anthony Forsyth and Andrew Stewart, 'Of Kamikazes and Mad Men: the Fallout from the Qantas Industrial Dispute' (2013) 36 Melbourne University Law Review 785, 808; Joellen Riley, 'A Safe Touch-Down for Qantas?' (2012) 25 Australian Journal of Labour Law 76; Sue Bussel and John Farrow, 'Continuity and Change: The Fair Work Act in Aviation' (2011) 53 Journal of Industrial Relations 392.

78. Hohfeld, above n 2, 28.

CHAPTER 6 THE PROTECTION OF THE FUNDAMENTAL RIGHT TO STRIKE

Albertine Veldman

Keywords: Fundamental rights protection, the right to strike, internal market, economic freedoms, international labour law standards, incoherence of legal systems

INTRODUCTION

With the entry into force of the Treaty of Lisbon, the protection of fundamental rights within the European Union is increasingly gaining momentum. Article 6 TEU not only endows the Charter of Fundamental Rights of the EU – already proclaimed at the Nice summit in 2000 – with a binding legal nature, but, moreover, states that 'the Union shall accede to the European Convention for the Protection of Human Rights and Fundamental Freedoms' (hereafter the ECHR). This strengthening of European fundamental rights protection is, of course, to be welcomed. Still, at the same time it raises questions of legal coherency. The legal orders of the EU and the Council of Europe differ in nature and so can the protection of fundamental rights within these orders. This already holds true before the accession of the EU to the ECHR will materialise, as the Union at present must respect fundamental rights as guaranteed by the ECHR and as they result from the constitutional traditions common to the Member States, as general principles of the Union's law.1 Indeed, the jurisprudence of the European Court of Justice (ECJ) in the past shows ample examples of the application of fundamental rights that are (also) recognised under the European Convention.

This contribution will focus on the coherency aspects of especially social fundamental rights, more particularly the right to strike, also addressed as 'the right to collective action' because there are more types of actions which are feasible to defend the social and economic interests of workers than solely regular work stoppages. When debating the upcoming accession of the EU to the ECHR, social rights including the right to collection action warrant special attention for several reasons. Firstly, the application of social fundamental rights can highlight, or be a test case for, the upcoming complexities when the European Court of Human Rights (ECtHR) is to adjudicate on EU actions in this field. It is here where the divergent nature of the EU legal order, when it concerns fundamental rights protection, becomes most obvious. Unlike the ECtHR, the ECJ, when applying social fundamental rights, has to give due regard to the economic freedoms of establishment and to provide services and goods, being fundamental principles of the Union's legal order. As the well-known Viking and Laval case law has shown,2 this requires the balancing of fundamental workers' rights against economic market interests, which is unprecedented in international social law, but appears inherent in an European legal order in which the creation and safeguarding of a common market lies at its heart.

Secondly, there is more to the balancing of fundamental social rights and economic freedoms than differing adjudication methodologies of European courts alone. At the end of the day, the politically preferred social economic model of the EU may be at stake. Internationally recognised minimum labour standards all go back to the fundamental principle, adopted in the Constitution of the International Labour Organisation (ILO), that 'labour is not a commodity'. This entails that labour is not like an apple or a television set, an inanimate product that can be negotiated for the highest profit or the lowest price. Work is part of everyone's daily life and is crucial to a person's dignity, well-being and development as a human being. Can minimum labour conditions within the context of the EU internal market nevertheless be subjected to cross-border economic competition, as this was at stake in the above-

Citation: Albertine Veldman, The Protection of the Fundamental Right to Strike, DOI: http://doi.org/10.18352/ulr.216.

mentioned Viking and Laval cases? If so, would, or should, it be up to a ECtHR to decide on that in the future? A third and final reason for concentrating on the fundamental right to strike in the light of the aforementioned accession of the EU to the ECHR is the remarkable contrast in the evolving case law in this field of the ECJ and the ECtHR. Almost at the same time when the ECJ delivered its rulings in Viking and Laval, holding that the exercise of the fundamental right to collective action must meet the justification test of the economic freedoms of establishment and providing services, the ECtHR delivered its benchmark rulings in Demir & Baykara and Enerji Yapi-Yol Sen. In these judgments it gave full protection to the right to collective bargaining and collective action under Article 11 ECHR (freedom of association, including the right to form and join trade unions) with extensive reference to the standards of the ILO and the European Social Charter (ESC), as interpreted by their, respective, international supervisory committees. The rulings constituted ground-breaking decisions, considering that, up until then, the ECtHR had for a time held that the right to collective bargaining and the right to strike were not 'essential means' in order for a Member State to uphold the right of trade unions to represent the interests of their members under Article 11.

In the following, the different aspects of legal coherency with regard to the application of the right to strike by both European courts will be discussed more thoroughly. This is done by, firstly, examining the way the ECJ addresses the collision of the social fundamental right to strike and the economic freedoms on the basis of its relevant case law. This analysis includes the legal methodology applied and the possible implications thereof for national trade unions and current national systems of industrial relations (Section 2). Hereafter, the developments in the right to strike in the case law of the ECtHR are addressed (Section 3). This section will, furthermore, contain a brief outline of some of the relevant jurisprudence of the International Labour Organisation and the European Social Charter, this being embedded by the Court in the right to strike under Article 11 ECHR. Section 4 contains a comparative analysis of the approach of both European courts and discusses the apparent incoherencies. In the final section some conclusions are drawn from this, as well as some possible solutions to the problems that are presumed to arise. In this, the role of the EU Charter, the judicial method of balancing applied by the ECJ and the possible role of the European legislator will be taken into account (Section 5).

THE PROTECTION OF THE RIGHT TO STRIKE BY THE ECJ

The decisions of the ECJ in the Viking and Laval cases are well known and have been discussed intensively.3 Below, the merits of the case law are, therefore, just briefly outlined, thereby concentrating on some of the main points to be raised from the perspective of the clash between fundamental social rights and economic freedoms within the framework of Union law. Although the cases are often summarized in one breath, being both about the right to strike and decided upon with an interval of just one week, it is nevertheless important to separate them from one another in the current context. In adjudicating fundamental workers' rights, Laval shows even more than Viking the impact of the specific nature of the EU legal order, compared to the purely human rights-oriented order of the Convention, due to the fact that the specific workers' interests at stake in this case are partially harmonized in view of internal market aims by way of an EU directive.

The Viking Case

The Facts

Viking, a ferry operator incorporated under Finnish law, sought to reflag its vessel by registering it in Estonia. This was due to the higher wages applicable under a collective bargaining agreement, governed by Finnish law, with the Finnish Seamen's Union (hereinafter: 'the FSU'). Based on the 'Flag of Convenience' policy of the International Transport Workers' Federation (hereinafter: 'the ITF'),4 the FSU requested that the ITF, whose headquarters was in London, send out a circular asking its affiliates to refrain from entering into negotiations with Viking, which it duly did. Following the expiry of the applicable collective labour agreement, the FSU threatened strike action against Viking in order to deter Viking from its plans to reflag its vessel. Viking applied to the English court for an injunction to stop the trade unions' actions, on the grounds that it infringed Article 43 EC on the freedom of establishment (now Article 49 TFEU).

The Ruling

The ECJ, in addressing the questions raised by the English Court of Appeal, began by considering the applicability of Article 43 to the unions. The Court did not consider trade unions to be public bodies, but it held that the free movement provisions 'do not apply only to the actions of public authorities but extend also to rules of any other nature aimed at regulating in a collective manner gainful employment, self-employment and the provision of services'.5 The Court further held that collective bargaining and collective action were inextricably linked, hence also collective action fell within the scope of Article 43.6 In respect of whether the collective action at issue constituted a restriction within the meaning of article 43 EC, the ECJ concluded that the FSU's action 'has the effect of making less attractive, or even pointless (...) Viking's exercise of its right to freedom of establishment' because Viking would enjoy less favourable treatment than other economic operators established in the host state.7 It was also held that ITF's campaign against flags of convenience 'must be considered to be at least liable to restrict Viking's exercise of its right of freedom of establishment'.

Turning, finally, to the question of justification, the Court already recognised the fundamental nature of the right to collective action, referring to the ESC, ILO Convention No. 87 on Freedom of Association and the Right to Organize and to Article 28 of the EU Charter.9 Still, the exercise of a fundamental right must be reconciled with the requirements of the Treaty. The Community not only has an economic, but also a social purpose and social policy interests must be balanced with the free movement rules. It turns out that 'balancing' implies that the respective collective action must meet the justification test for the restriction of free movement, including its proportionality test. Still, the ECJ accepted that the right to take collective action for the protection of workers is, in principle, a legitimate interest which can justify a restriction of the freedom of establishment.10 Leaving it up to the national court to apply the justification test to the facts of the case, it continued, however, to give very narrow guidance on this. Factors to be considered were if the collective action indeed served the protection of workers, meaning there was a serious threat to jobs or conditions of employment at issue,11 whether the collective action was suitable for ensuring the achievement of the objective pursued,12 and if the union had exhausted other, less restrictive, means available to resolve the dispute before initiating a strike.13

The Laval Case

The Facts

Central to the dispute in Laval is again the issue of social dumping. Having won a public tender in Sweden to renovate a school, the Latvia-based construction company Laval posted workers to Sweden. Estimates suggest that these posted workers earned around 40% less than their Swedish counterparts. Concerned that the posting of cheaper labour to Sweden would undermine the labour standards of Swedish construction workers, the trade union opened negotiations with Laval with the aim of extending the applicable collective agreement to the posted workers, allowing the union to negotiate minimum wages for them. The negotiations failed and the union, supported by the electricians' union, began a blockade of Laval's building sites. In response, Laval called on the Swedish Labour Court to rule that the action was unlawful because of an infringement of the free movement of services, and to be compensated by the unions for the losses it had suffered.

The Ruling

Responding to the questions raised by the Swedish court, the ECJ partly reasoned along the same lines as in Viking. It considered the right to collective action to be a fundamental right that, however, had to be reconciled with Article 49 EC (now 56 TFEU). The latter also applies to private unions because 'compliance with Article 49 EC is also required in the case of rules which are not public in nature but which are designed to regulate, collectively, the provision of services'.14 Again starting out from the perspective of the economic freedom that may be restricted 'only if (the restriction) pursues a legitimate objective compatible with the Treaty and is justified by overriding reasons of public interest',15 the Court accepted that 'the right to take collective action for the protection of the workers of the host state against possible social dumping may constitute an overriding reason of public interest'.16 However, dealing with the merits of the case itself, the Court did not find the unions' action to be justified. It is here that the Posted Workers Directive17 came into play. Although not applicable in the present case because directives lack horizontal effect, the Court slipped it into its proportionality test.

The said Directive basically strikes a balance between workers' protection and the free movement of services by compelling the host Member State to apply a mandatory minimum set of employment conditions according to its national law, including a minimum wage, to posted workers from other Member States. This has to be accomplished by national laws, generally applicable collective agreements or, where such mechanisms are lacking, by other ways that ensure the equal treatment of foreign and national firms. Because of the Scandinavian system of industrial relations, in which trade unions enjoy a large autonomy to regulate labour, Sweden has no legislation on a minimum wage, expecting the relevant trade union to negotiate a minimum wage for each work place with the employer. The ECJ, however, took exception to this system of 'case-by-case' negotiations because it lacked transparency for foreign firms, unduly restricting their trade prospects.18 Moreover, it perceived that the content of the collective agreement sought by the union would also be an infringement of the Directive, since the union was seeking negotiations on additional subjects that went beyond the minimum terms and conditions envisaged in Article 3(1).19

Assessment of the Case Law With Regard To the Balancing Of Social Rights and Free Movement Rights

Implications of the Balance Struck

The strike action, central to the Laval decision, appears not to be so much balanced against the fundamental freedom to provide services, but rather to be assessed in isolation as an (unlawful) technique under the Posted Workers Directive.20 While it is not the objective of this Directive to reconcile the exercise of the fundamental right to collective action with fundamental economic freedoms, the Union even lacking competence in the field due to Article 153(5) TFEU, the Directive can still be regarded as a 'legislative balance' struck between the freedom to provide services and the social policy goal of workers' protection. As interpreted by the ECJ, though, the weight seems to shift to the side of its internal market aims. This was to be underlined in the later Rüffert case, which ruled out the adoption in the local government's tender specifications of a so-called social clause ensuring the observance of the applicable collective labour agreement, because the collective agreement was not universally applicable.21 Despite the fact that the Posted Workers Directive compels the Member State to ensure a nucleus of minimum employment conditions is applied to posted workers and states in Article 3(7), this shall not prevent the application of more favourable employment conditions to workers, the Court, nevertheless, held in Laval that the minimum employment conditions of Article 3(1) to be applied by the host state also constituted the maximum.

According to the Court, Article 3(7) merely covered the situation in which a firm signed 'of its own accord' a collective agreement in the host state providing for more favourable terms and conditions.22 This suggests that trade unions do have the freedom to engage in collective bargaining on terms of employment beyond the nucleus of Article 3(1) of the Directive, but not to back it up with the threat of industrial action in case of foreign-based contractors.23 Such an industrial action would surely be unjustified since the collective agreement sought would be concluded on a case-by-case basis. Here it appears that the Court envisages that collective bargaining can be isolated from collective action.24 However, without 'equality of arms' for both sides of industry the system of voluntary collective bargaining would simply not work. According to the views of the ILO, collective action is the corollary of collective bargaining and, therefore, is indispensably connected to the freedom of association and the right to collective bargaining. Remarkably, the ECJ held in Viking that collective bargaining and collective action are inextricably linked, however, using the argument to bring collective action within the scope of Article 49 TFEU (supra, Section 2.1).

Implications of the horizontal effect of the free movement provisions

By doing so, the provisions on the free movement of establishment and services were accorded horizontal effect. However, appointing private unions to be addressees of the public interest law provisions guaranteeing free movement, comes at a price.25 On the one hand, trade unions are conceived as being semi-public organizations deemed capable of 'regulating, collectively, the provision of services';26 on the other hand, they cannot invoke the exceptions laid down in the Treaty or in the Posted Workers Directive in respect of public policy considerations. According to the ECJ in Laval: '[trade unions] not being bodies governed by public law (...) cannot avail themselves of that provision by citing grounds of public policy'.27 Bestowing (semi-)public responsibilities on trade unions while at the same time conceiving them as ordinary private persons, also does not seem to sit very well with the fact that the social partners, according to the Treaty, may implement directives and, at the European level, are awarded a regulatory role in social policy matters with priority over the Commission and Parliament.28

Oscillating methods for Scrutinizing Proportionality

More generally, in the application of the balancing test by the ECJ trade unions apparently enjoy far less leeway when compared to the margin of discretion allowed for Member States to protect fundamental rights.29 This is even, or perhaps more, so when these rights have but a particularly national constitutional dimension like in Omega or Sayn-Wittgenstein. 30 Still, in Viking and Laval the ECJ took no note of the particularity of national social systems and the, sometimes also constitutionally-based, national traditions of industrial relations, especially those in which the attainment of national social policy goals may fall within the autonomous reign of the social partners. Furthermore, as Barnard points out, the case law makes clear that the protection of the fundamental right to strike as such cannot justify the restriction on free movement, but requires the exercise of the fundamental right to pursue a wider legitimate aim, i.e. the protection of workers, and be suitable to that end.31 Moreover, the aim of workers' protection is not one to be accepted lightly but requires a 'serious threat' to the jobs or employment conditions at issue. To conclude, national courts must assess whether other possible means have been exhausted, thereby implying that the exercise of a fundamental social right may only be a last resort

In the case that the fundamental right to be protected is exercised by private interest groups, analogous to Viking and Laval, the differences in the methodology applied by the ECJ seem even more striking. When compared to the Schmidberger case dealing with a road blockade by environmental groups in Austria restricting the free movement of goods,32 the ECJ assessed proportionality in that case by a far more 'marginal' test. The Austrian Government, in authorizing the protest action, was not compelled to scrutinize whether the particular exercise of the freedom of assembly or of expression by the social interest groups served a wider legitimate aim such as environmental protection and whether the environment was indeed seriously threatened. Neither was the State compelled to assess if the particular protest action was suitable to achieve that environmental aim and if other, less restrictive means had been exhausted by the demonstrators before initiating the road blockade. In contrast, it was found adequate that 'citizens were (...) manifesting in public an opinion which they considered to be of importance to society',33 while for the means applied to be proportionate it sufficed that the road blockade was a single occasion during a limited period and accompanied by public alerts to limit its implications.34

Implications for the National Systems of Industrial Relations and the National Unions

The intrusiveness of the assessment required by national courts into trade union autonomy may place considerable restraints on the exercise of the fundamental right to take collective action in cross-border industrial disputes. Because of this, and the fact that universally applicable legislation is required under the Posted Workers Directive depending on the particularities of the national collective bargaining system, the course taken by the ECJ 'may be seen as threatening not only autonomous collective bargaining structures in the Member States, but also the flexibility inherent in the European Social Model and, in particular, the Open Method of Coordination'.35 Following the decisions by the ECJ, the European Trade Union Confederation uttered a strong protest on the first count, stating that 'an intolerable uncertainty (was created) for unions involved in virtually any case of industrial action over migration and free movement'.36

The restraints on autonomous collective bargaining and collective action are aggravated by the fact that trade unions may be faced with claims for damages by the employer if it were to transpire that their action was unjustified under European law, as was experienced by the Swedish unions in Laval. 37 The notorious English BALPA case, involving a cross-border relocation of labour at British Airways, shows that the possible amount of damages to be paid can easily bankrupt an union, forcing it in the end to abstain from taking the industrial action it anticipated.38 Moreover, a cap on the amount of damages to be generally retrieved from trade unions, common in some Member States in order to prevent this effect, could well be incompatible with the established principle of EU law requiring national remedies for the breach of Union law to be effective and equivalent to remedies in domestic law. A national cap on the amount of damages in case of a breach of the free movement provisions will probably not apply to nonunion actors.

THE PROTECTION OF THE RIGHT TO STRIKE BY THE ECTHR

When adopting its human rights instruments, the Council of Europe drew a strong distinction between civil and political human rights, contained in the European Convention (1950) and watched over by an international court, and the social and economic rights laid down in the European Social Charter (1961)39 and accompanied by a 'light' regime of supervisory committees and, later on, an optional collective complaint procedure (1995). The social rights of especially collective bargaining and collective action have never really fitted the general distinction made, encompassing 'freedoms' that, like the 'classical' human rights, are not 'programmatic' in nature but require predominantly abstention by the State. Still, according to the long-standing case law of the ECtHR, established in the 1970s and reiterated as recently as 2002, 40 collective bargaining and strike action were not rights which were guaranteed as such by the European Convention. The Court did hold Article 11 ECHR (i.a. the right to form and join trade unions) to safeguard the freedom to protect the occupational interests of workers by trade union action; however, the choice of means to be used by the State in order that the trade union 'should be heard' fell within the Member State's margin of appreciation.41 'Whilst concluding collective agreements (or initiating strike action) is one of these means, there are others'.42 This view was to be changed into its opposite by Demir and Baykara, followed up by Enerji Yapi-Yol Sen.43

The cases of Demir & Baykara and Enerji Yapi-Yol Sen

Demir & Baykara

The Demir & Baykara case concerned the legal status and collective bargaining rights of a Turkish civil servants' union. When the trade union brought legal action to enforce the collective agreement it had concluded with a local municipal council, it was eventually successful. This ruling, however, was ultimately quashed by the Court of Cassation on the ground that collective bargaining by public servants required specific domestic legislation, which was absent. As a consequence the trade union was denied legal personality and, hence, the collective agreement which had been concluded was deemed null and void. After an unanimous chamber of the ECtHR held that the applicants' rights had been violated under Article 11,44 the case was referred, at the request of Turkey, to the Grand Chamber. This Court, also unanimously, held that there had been a violation of Article 11 on account of (a) the interference with the right to form a trade union and (b) the annulment ex tunc of the collective agreement entered into by the trade union following collective bargaining with the employer

The Court's Grand Chamber placed the international instruments related to freedom of association and collective bargaining at the centre of its analysis.45 For this purpose, it reflected, first, on its approach to international law more generally. More specifically, it stated that the analysis of the 'evolving norms of national and international law' is an essential feature of interpreting the ECHR as a 'living' document.46 In this regard, the Court did not consider it necessary that (all) the international instruments referred to had been ratified by Turkey. 'It will be sufficient (...) that the instruments denote a continuous evolution in the norms and principles applied in international law or in the domestic law of the majority of Member States (...) and show, in a precise area, that there is common ground in mo-dern societies'.47 Subsequently, the Court applied this reasoning to its analysis of the trade union's rights under Article 11. Importantly, the Court relied on international instruments when examining whether the right to collective bargaining actually fell within the scope of the right to organize. As has been mentioned before, up until then the Court had refused to consider the right to collective bargaining to be an essential element of Article 11. The Court now stated, however, that the list of essential elements also had to be interpreted in the light of present-day conditions, and in accordance with developments in international law, so as to reflect the increasingly high standard being required in the area of the protection of human rights.48

The Court then turned to analysing the relevant international law framework. Here, it focused on ILO Convention No. 98 and ILO Convention No. 151 on Labour Relations in the Public Service. Whilst noting that, in accordance with Article 6 of ILO Convention No. 98, public servants were not covered by that instrument, it pointed to the ILO Committee of Experts' settled position that this exception must be restricted to those officials whose activities are specific to the administration of the state, like for instance (some) members of the police force or members of the armed forces.49 After referring to Article 6(2) ESC as interpreted by the European Committee of Social Rights (ECSR), the EU Charter and state practice,50 the Court, on these grounds, reached the conclusion that the right to bargain collectively had, in principle, become one of the essential elements of Article 11(1), extending also to civil servants except for very specific cases, a category to which the applicants, however, did not belong.51

The Court also explicitly used ILO instruments, besides a more general reference to 'regional instruments' and 'European practice' in order to establish the substance of the right to collective bargaining under Article 11. Again following an examination of ILO Convention No. 98 and the reports of the ILO Committee of Experts,52 it held that the Turkish Government omitted to show how the interference was 'necessary in a democratic society',53 or corresponded to 'a pressing social need',54 under the allowed restrictions grounds of Article 11(2).

Enerji Yapi-Yol Sen

Only a few months later, this new approach was confirmed in the case Enerji Yapi-Yol Sen. 55 The case concerned the right to strike of, again, a Turkish public service trade union, as public sector employees were prohibited from taking part in a national one-day demonstration to secure the right to collective bargaining. In this judgment the Court drew on the fundamental considerations developed in Demir & Baykara, albeit in a more succinct form. The right to collective action was not explicitly considered to be 'essential' (though 'important') to secure freedom of association and the right to organize. Instead, the Court relied on the interpretations of ILO Convention No. 87 by the ILO supervisory bodies, according to which the right to strike is an intrinsic corollary of workers' freedom of association.56With reference to Demir & Baykara and after recalling that the ESC also recognises the right to strike as a means of ensuring the effective exercise of the right to collective bargaining, the Court concluded that the right to collective action was protected by Article 11. As to its content, acknowledging the right to strike was not absolute, the Court found that the Government had not demonstrated 'the need in a democratic society for the impugned restriction', due to its blanket ban on strike action for all public servants.57

Assessment of the Case Law's Impact

The impact of the cases can hardly be over-estimated. In the present context, however, the implications of the case law of the ECtHR may be confined to a threefold assessment. Firstly, the European protection of fundamental social rights is, of course, significantly enhanced, due to the fact that 'the ECtHR (i) repudiated its earlier decisions on the question of trade union rights, (ii) embraced collective bargaining as an essential right protected by Article 11, and in doing so (iii) introduced a body of reasoning that should apply with equal force to other forms of trade union activity, notably the right to take collective action'.58 The latter is supported by the later rulings in Özcan and Kaya and Seyhan, concerned with disciplinary action for taking part in protest strikes.59 Although concerned principally with the question of the individual sanction, that could only be an issue if the strike action itself was protected under the Convention.

Secondly, because of the use of a dynamic and intertexual interpretation method of Article 11 ECHR, the Court embedded the international labour law standards of the ILO and the ESC and the jurisprudence of its supervisory committees into that right.60 Thereby, the body of principles and decisions which has evolved in international law on the social rights of collective bargaining and collective action is now indirectly subjected to a new, and more effective, international enforcement mechanism. While the findings and decisions of the ESC and ILO committees, although granted much authority, are formally non-binding,61 the European Convention has its international Court attached, taking legally binding decisions. Thirdly, as a consequence of the former, this opens up the possibility for trade unions and individual trade union members to have an alleged infringement of their social rights to be adjudicated upon by, ultimately, the ECtHR, also in those Member States, like for instance the UK, that did not accept the collective complaint procedure under the ESC. More importantly, adjudication by the ECtHR could possibly distress the decisions of the EU institutions after the accession of the EU to the ECHR, due to the apparent conflict between the line of reasoning of the ECtHR and the ECJ in respect of trade union rights, to be discussed more carefully in the next section. Some commentators already speculate about the 'mouth-watering possibility of a high noon conflict between the two', appealing to trade unions and trade unionists to bring claims to Strasbourg.62 In this, they might not have to await actual accession to the ECHR when alleging that a particular decision of a national court giving effect to Viking and Laval constitutes a breach of the Convention.63

COMPARATIVE ANALYSIS

In the following a comparative analysis will be made of the general methods of adjudication applied by both European courts in respect of the protection of the fundamental right to strike. The comparison does not see to the particularities of the case law discussed, as the underlying facts differ, but focuses on the body of norms, principles and interpretation methods flowing from these benchmark cases, which will generally apply to the courts' assessment of the lawfulness of strike action in Europe. Cases brought before the ECJ will, of course, be confined to strike actions involving industrial disputes on the migration or relocation of labour in order to have an cross-border element, but this does not interfere as such with the competence of the ECtHR. This Court can assess whether a Member State, which after its accession to the Convention will include the EU, has complied with the fundamental right to strike as protected by Article 11 ECHR, irrespective of the nature of the industrial dispute that caused the (anticipated) particular strike action. Even before the actual accession of the EU, as already indicated in the former section, national Member States might be faced with a dual set of international obligations when a strike action in their territory restricts fundamental economic freedoms. National Member States are under the obligation to give effect to Union law but at the same time are not absolved from their Convention responsibility in the areas covered.64 It is from these perspectives that the comparison is drawn.

From the assessments of the case law of the ECJ and the ECtHR, delivered in Sections 2 and 3, it can be concluded that possible legal incompatibilities might arise from the way in which the fundamental right to strike is applied and protected by the respective European courts in the case of cross-border strike actions.65 These legal incoherencies are mainly manifested in respect of (i) the general legal methodology applied, (ii) the nature of the restriction grounds allowed for, (iii) the proportionality required, and (iv) the perception of the relationship between the rights of collective bargaining and collective action. These points will be addressed below.

General Legal Methodology Applied

Under the systems of the European Convention and the TFEU the respective legal methodologies applied for assessing the lawfulness of (cross-border) strike actions seem hard to reconcile. The methods applied by the ECtHR and the ECJ start out from opposite directions. Strike action being a fundamental right protected under the Convention implies that any state intervention, including by its judiciary, must meet the restriction grounds provided for by Article 11(2). An injunction by a national court to stop a particular trade union's action will, therefore, require that this restriction is 'prescribed by law and is necessary in a democratic society in the interests of national security or public safety, for the prevention of disorder or crime, for the protection of health or morals or for the protection of the rights and freedoms of others'.

Because of the fundamental nature of the economic freedoms, the EU law system, on the other hand, only allows for a strike action that infringes these principles if the trade union's action 'pursues a legitimate objective compatible with the Treaty and is justified by overriding reasons of public interest'.66 So, where the ECtHR is compelled to scrutinize the lawfulness of the particular restriction or even a ban on the fundamental right to strike, the ECJ must assess the lawfulness of resorting to the fundamental right to strike when it considers the particular strike action to be an infringement of a fundamental economic freedom. The chances of the outcome of such differing starting points in legal reasoning being contradictory seem fairly great due to the fact that both legal systems embrace a strict interpretation of the limitations allowed for in regard of the question asked.

The Systems for a Limitation of the Exercise of Fundamental Rights

In respect of the nature of the restriction grounds allowed for when fundamental rights are concerned, it is recalled that under EU law trade unions cannot avail themselves of the exception grounds laid down in the TFEU (or in the Posted Workers Directive) in respect of public policy considerations (supra, Section 2.3). Still, the right to take collective action for the protection of workers can be an (unwritten) justification ground according to the ECJ, albeit the national court has to assure itself of a sufficient cause for taking collective action in the given case (supra, Section 2.1). As stated before, the exercise of a fundamental social right as such is not a sufficient ground for justification, but taking strike action can, nevertheless, fit the EU system of limitations on free movement depending on the circumstances of the case.

Taking the different starting point of the ECtHR, it is, however, doubtful if the exercise of an economic freedom can also fit the system of limitations of the ECHR. The grounds mentioned in Article 11(2) do not envisage economic interests to be a 'pressing social need'. Moreover, especially in case of the fundamental right to strike, it is exactly the negative economic consequences for the employer that is perceived to be the 'firing power' of the weapon of collection action, counterbalancing the employer's position who only has to lean back to prevent collective bargaining in the interests of workers. Because of this, the chances seem also remote that the protection of the employer's interests of establishment or to provide services can be conceived as being necessary 'for the protection of the rights and freedoms of others' under Article 11(2) ECHR. According to the ECSR's settled position on the interpretation of Article 31 ESC,67 which is equivalent to Article 11(2) ECHR, the employer involved in the industrial dispute cannot be regarded as a third party. After all, unlike third parties the employer is in a position to protect his interests by settling the dispute with the trade union.

Under ILO law, which so far has provided strong guidance for the ECtHR when interpreting trade union rights, there is even less room to manoeuvre, in order to include economic freedoms in the established system of lawful restriction grounds. Following ILO Convention No. 87, as interpreted by the Committee of Experts and the Committee on the Freedom of Association, the prohibition of strikes could only be acceptable in case of 'essential services' in the strict sense of that term, i.e. services whose interruption could endanger the life, personal safety or health of the whole, or part of the population.68 In its 2010 Report the Committee of Experts, reflecting on the impact of the ECJ's case law on the effective exercise of the right to strike in the British BALPA case (supra, Section 2.3), stated in so many words: '(...) the doctrine that is being articulated in these ECJ judgements is likely to have a significant restrictive effect on the exercise of the right to strike in practice in a manner contrary to the Convention'.69

Concept of Proportionality

The ECJ's proportionality test in order to balance the opposing rights of workers and employers appears difficult to reconcile with the norms and principles on strike action applied in international law and in the domestic law of the majority of Member States. Because these norms and principles are taken into account by the ECtHR when interpreting Article 11 of the Convention, one may assume that problems of incoherency will arise once the EU accedes to the ECHR. Although the concept of proportionality generally applied by the ECJ seems flexible and allows for a lenient as well as a strict interpretation (supra, Section 2.3), the guidance provided in Viking to access proportionality in case of trade union action turns out to be very strict. This holds especially true for the assessment of a sufficient cause for strike action ('serious threat to jobs or employment conditions'), as well as the exhaustion of all other means to resolve the dispute.

Of course, by its very nature strike action will be a last resort when all negotiations have failed or were refused. One has to assume that trade unions will not take such decisions without due consideration. After all, a strike action may also harm the occupational interests of the workers (no pay; the economic welfare of the company guarantees the jobs at the end of the day). Nevertheless, according to international labour law standards Member States can set some requirements by law in respect of the legitimacy of a strike action. This covers, for instance, the need to give prior notice when a strike is called, allowing the employer to resume negotiations or take precautionary measures, or requirements as to the number of workers who have to agree to a strike.70 Examinations by the judiciary of a sufficient cause for the action or of the possibilities for further negotiations prove, however, to be problematic because they could amount to unlawful state interference with the right to collective action itself.

Deciding on whether workers' interests are indeed sufficiently harmed or whether there is still room for negotiations implies that national courts have to become substantially involved in the industrial dispute. This leaves ample room for interpretation by national courts and, possibly, the influence of political sentiments. As Brian Bercusson pointed out: 'Any test based on proportionality in assessing the legitimacy of collective action is generally avoided in the industrial relations morals of Member States for the very reason that it is essential to maintain the impartiality of the state in economic conflicts'.71 The ECSR, reporting on the ultimum remedium requirement in Dutch law, remarked: 'The fact that a national judge may determine whether recourse to strikes is 'premature' is not considered (...) to be in conformity with Article 6(4) ESC, as this allows the judge to exercise one of the trade unions' key prerogatives'.72 Again commenting on the UK's BALPA case, the ILO Committee of Experts simply stated: 'The Committee observes that when elaborating its position in relation to the permissible restrictions that may be placed upon the right to strike, it has never included the need to assess the proportionality of interests bearing in mind a notion of freedom of establishment or freedom to provide services. (...) The Committee is of the opinion that there is no basis for revising its position in this regard.'73

The Relationship between the Right to Collective Bargaining and the Right to Collective Action

The perception of the relationship between the rights to collective bargaining and to collective action in EU law and international law has already been discussed (supra, Section 2.3). The issue relates to strikes in respect of social dumping.

In Laval the ECJ placed an outright ban on collective action following caseby-case collective bargaining with foreign-based employers, due to the constraints of the Posted Workers Directive. Since the ECJ, however, does allow for collective bargaining beyond the terms of the Directive with foreign-based contractors on condition that such a firm signs an agreement of its own accord, the right to collective action is isolated from the right to collective bargaining. The latter is contrary to international labour law standards, by which collective action is perceived as the intrinsic corollary of the freedoms of collective bargaining and association. The ECtHR, in its interpretation of Article 11 of the Convention, confirmed as much in Enerji.74 Bearing in mind the significance of the uniform application of human rights, it seems difficult to imagine that the ECtHR would put this principle aside in respect of foreign-based contractors only. Indeed, within a Member State the trade unions would undeniably enjoy the fundamental right to collective action in order to back up a collective bargaining process on posted workers' employment conditions.

Conclusions and the Way Forward

Since the Demir and Enerji cases, by which the socio-economic rights of collective bargaining and strike were incorporated into the 'classical' human rights catalogue of the ECHR, it seems that the ECtHR and the ECJ are likely to head for a clash in respect of the protection of the fundamental right to strike, once the EU accedes to the ECHR. The legal systems of the ECHR and the TFEU are difficult to reconcile in this regard. From the disparities that are outlined in the former section two main reasons for legal incoherency in this field can be distilled. Firstly, the methodologies applied to reconcile the opposite interests of workers and employers in the EU internal market start out from different directions. As is broadly discussed above, the ECtHR starts out from the possible infringement of the fundamental right to strike, whereas the ECJ starts out from the possible infringement of a fundamental economic freedom. Secondly, and more importantly perhaps, within a human rights law system, especially one that embeds the international labour law standards that show common ground in modern societies, economic freedoms of establishment or to provide services or goods are only to conceived of, in the end, as business interests that cannot as such outweigh fundamental trade unions' rights. On the other hand, it is easy to understand why within the EU legal order these same economic freedoms are deemed 'fundamental', given that the creation and safeguarding of an European internal market is one of its principal aims. It is also from this perspective that it is suggested that the particular strict approach taken by the ECJ in Viking and Laval can perhaps be explained by the fact that trade unions could easily engage in protectionism leading to retaliatory measures and eventually to the fragmentation of the internal market.75 Still, because of the multilevel nature of the EU legal order the problem appears to be more complex than that.

It could also be said that the unions in cross-border disputes are striving for a level playing field in the internal market in respect of workers' protection. Cross-border business should adhere to local labour standards so as not to undermine the employment conditions of the workers already present. It turns out that the EU system does offer such a protection system in respect of the European labour market because free-movement workers are entitled to equal treatment with home-state workers. But when posted workers are concerned or in the case of downward pressure on home state labour standards because of the relocation of labour to other Member States, an effective level playing field is lacking. This brings us to the heart of the matter. The lack of a true European system of industrial relations alleviating economic competition on labour conditions comparable to those on the national level results predominantly from the fact that the Member States want to preserve national sovereignty over their social systems. It is not without reason that the subjects of wages and strike action are explicitly excluded from the Union's competences in the Treaty. Nevertheless, the ECJ brought the subject of strikes in by the backdoor, requiring the exercise of the right to strike to comply with the Treaty.

Although the conflict concerning the right to strike arises between two autonomous, yet different European legal orders, it appears the issue underlying this conflict stems basically from controversies over competences in the social field within the Union's multilevel order. This could perhaps give some indication of the ways out of the impasse. To start with, it seems unlikely that the ECtHR could bridge the gap on the basis of its current interpretation of the Convention. Even when this Court would not exclude the Union's economic freedoms from the list of lawful restriction grounds under Article 11(2) ECHR, there is still the problem of disparities in the protection of human rights. Single Member States cannot allow economic reasons to prevail over fundamental trade unions' rights in case of an 'internal' strike action, whereas the EU could do so in case of a cross-border strike. When the dispute is to be resolved within the Union's legal order itself, the first option could be an adjustment in the case law of the ECJ. One could argue that the now binding EU Charter on Fundamental Rights might have changed the relevant legal landscape. Article 28 of the Charter does contain the rights to collective bargaining and to collective action. Nevertheless, taking into account the scope of the guaranteed rights, according to Article 52, it is doubtful the Charter will shed any new light on the matter: rights shall be exercised under the conditions and within the limits defined by the Treaties.76 With the Charter having probably no profound impact on conflicts between fundamental rights or freedoms, this leaves just a change in the current position of the ECJ. Still, a retreat by this Court, for instance by giving the exercise of trade unions' rights immunity with regard to the free movement provisions, seems difficult to envisage.77 The ECJ will want to have some means of control, especially in the case of a misuse of the strike weapon, when it comes to such fundamental EU principles. Adjustments are perhaps more feasible with regard to the strictness of the proportionality test applied, in order to bring it more into line with the restriction grounds accepted under ILO law and the ESC. Whether this is likely to happen, however, remains to be seen. These internationally accepted restriction grounds, like demanding a cooling-off period or the continuation of minimum services,78 exclude the possibility of any balancing of rights or interests of those involved in the dispute.

The second way out would be the political one. An attempt has recently been made with the proposal for a so-called Monti II Council Regulation.79 Invited by the Council to bring clarity in the exercise of the freedom of establishment and the freedom to provide services alongside fundamental social rights, the text proposed by the Commission was, however, not very promising. On the one hand, the proposal provided in respect of its scope that 'this regulation shall not affect in any way the exercise of fundamental rights as recognized in the Member States, including the right or freedom to strike (...)'.80 On the other hand, the proposal laid down the balancing rule of Viking and Laval, which does potentially limit the exercise of the freedom to strike at the national level in the case of an industrial dispute involving a cross-border element. Nevertheless, according to the regulation, not only strike actions should respect the economic freedoms but, conversely, the exercise of free movement should also respect fundamental rights.81 How this 'double test' could be applied in practice seemed difficult to visualize. For the part that the proposed balancing test coincided with the Viking and Laval rulings, it was in conflict with the indicated scope of the regulation.82 Moreover, there was the question of the legislative competence of the Union in view of Article 153(5) TFEU. In the end overall dissatisfaction with the proposed regulation caused a third of the national parliaments to draw their first 'yellow card',83 a procedure on the principle of subsidiarity made possible by the Lisbon Treaty.84 On 11 September 2012 the Commission decided to withdraw its proposal.

Because the legal coherency problems discussed hide a long-term political struggle over the lines that run between the EU single market and the social dimension at the national level, one may conclude that a regulatory solution is not within reach. Hence, the chances of the ECJ and the ECtHR having their 'high noon conflict' in the end do not seem that remote. Although it may take a while before the EU actually accedes to the ECHR, there are certainly interesting times ahead.

Note:

1 Art. 6(3) TEU.

2 Case C-438/05, International Transport Workers' Federation v Viking Line, 11 december 2007, [2007] ECR I-10779; Case C-341/05, Laval un Partneri Ltd v Svenska Byggnadsarbetareförbundet, 18 december 2007, [2007] ECR I-11767.

3 The list is far too long to be cited here. To name some (rather randomly chosen) English language submissions, i.a., A. Davies, 'One Step Forward, Two Steps Back? The Viking and Laval Cases in the ECJ', 2008 Industrial Law Journal 37, no. 2, pp. 127-148; A. Hinarejos, 'Laval and Viking: The Right to Collective Action versus EU Fundamental Freedoms', 2008 Human Rights Law Review 8, no. 4, pp. 714-729; P. Syrpis & T. Novitz, 'Economic and social rights in conflict: Political and judicial approaches to their reconciliation', 2008 European Law Review 33, no. 3, pp. 411-426.

4 The ITF has a long-standing and well-known campaign against the use of 'flags of convenience', meaning the use of the flag of one country where lower labour standards apply by a beneficial owner situated in another country.

5 Viking, supra note 2, Para. 33.

6 Ibid., Para. 36-37.

7 Ibid., Para. 72.

8 Ibid., Para. 73.

9 Ibid., Para. 43.

10 Ibid., Para. 77.

11 Ibid., Para. 81.

12 Ibid., Para. 84.

13 Ibid., Paras. 86-87.

14 Laval, supra note 2, Para. 98.

15 Ibid., Para. 101.

16 Ibid., Para. 103.

17 Directive 1996/71/EC.

18 Laval, supra note 2, Paras. 69-70, 100.

19 Ibid., Paras. 70 and 79.

20 Cf. A. Van Hoek & M. Houwerzijl, 'Loonconcurrentie als motor van de interne markt? Deel I', 2008 Nederlands tijdschrift voor Europees recht, no. 7/8, pp. 190-205.

21 Case C-346/06, [2008] ECR I-01989. See, i.a., A. Van Hoek & M. Houwerzijl, 'Loonconcurrentie als motor van de interne markt? Deel II',

2008 Nederlands tijdschrift voor Europees recht, no. 12, pp. 337-346; A. Bücker & W. Warneck (eds.), Reconciling Fundamental Social Rights and Economic Freedoms after Viking, Laval and Rüffert, 2011.

22 See Laval, supra note 2, Para. 81.

23 Cf. Davies 2008, supra note 3, p. 129.

24 Ibid.

25 Cf. Davies 2008, supra note 3, p. 130.

26 See Laval, supra note 2, Para. 98. Compare also Viking, supra note 2, Para. 33.

27 See Laval, supra note 2, Para. 84.

28 Resp. Art. 153(3) and Arts. 154-155 TFEU.

29 Cf. Case C-112/00, Schmidberger, [2003] ECR I-5659; Case C-36/02, Omega, [2004] ECR I-9609; Case C-208/09, Sayn-Wittgenstein, [2010] ECR I-13693.

30 For an extensive analysis of this aspect, see S.A. de Vries, 'Balancing Fundamental Rights with Economic Freedoms According to the European Court of Justice', 2013 Utrecht Law Review 9, no. 1, pp. 169-192.

31 C. Barnard, 'EU "Social" Policy: From Employment Law to Labour Market Reform', in P. Craig & G. De Búrca, The Evolution of EU Law, 2011, p. 371.

32 Case C-112/00, Schmidberger, [2003] ECR I-5659.

33 Ibid., Para. 86.

34 Ibid., Paras. 85 and 87.

35 R. Zahn, 'The Viking and Laval Cases in the Context of European Enlargement', 2008 Web Journal of Current Legal Issues, no. 3, at <www.webjcli.ncl.ac.uk/2008/issue3/zahn3.html>.

36 Resolution adopted by the Executive Committee of the ETUC at its meeting of 4 March 2008 in Brussels, EC.179, see at <www.etuc.org>.

37 See J. Malmberg, 'Trade union liability for "EU-unlawful" collective action', 2012 European Labour law Journal 3, no. 1, pp. 5-18, who offers a critical assessment of the aftermath of the Laval case in Sweden.

38 For a detailed description of the (discontinued) litigation

in the English Balpa case, see K.D. Ewing & J. Hendy, 'The Dramatic Implications of Demir and Baykara', 2010 Industrial Law Journal 39, no. 1, pp. 44-46.

39 The ESC was revised in 1996, but the revised charter has not been ratified by all EU Member States.

40 UNISON v the United Kingdom, [2002] Appl. No. 53574/99, ECHR 2002-I.

41 National Union of Belgian Police v Belgium, [1975] Series A, No. 1, Para. 38; Swedisch Engine Drivers' Union v Sweden, [1976] Series A, No. 20, Para. 40; Schmidt and Dahlström v Sweden, [1976] Series A, No. 21, Para. 36.

42 Ibid.

43 Demir and Baykara v Turkey, ECtHR (Grand Chamber) 12 November 2008, Appl. No. 34503/97; Enerji Yapi-Yol Sen v Turkey, ECtHR 21 April 2009, Appl. No. 68959/01.

44 ECtHR 21 November 2006, Appl. No. 34503/97.

45 Demir and Baykara v Turkey, supra note 43; the summary draws on the discussion paper by F.C. Ebert & M. Oelz, Bridging the gap between labour rights and human rights: The role of the ILO in regional human rights courts, 2012, Geneva: International Institute for Labour Studies (see at <www.ilo.org>).

46 See Demir, supra note 43, Para. 68.

47 Ibid., Para. 86.

48 Ibid., Para. 146.

49 Ibid., Paras. 147-148.

50 Ibid., Paras. 149-151.

51 Ibid., Para. 154.

52 Ibid., Para. 166

53 Ibid., Para. 163.

54 Ibid., Para. 164.

55 See Enerji, supra note 43.

56 Ibid., Para 24.

57 Ibid., Para 32.

58 Ewing & Hendy, supra note 38, p. 4.

59 Saime Özcan v Turkey, Appl. No. 22943/04 (15 September 2009); Kaya and Seyhan v Turkey, Appl. No. 30946/04 (15 September 2009)

60 Cf. D. Harris et al., Law of the European Convention on Human Rights, 2009; T. Novitz, 'Protection of Workers under Regional Human Rights Systems: An Assessment of Evolving and Divergent Practices', in C. Fenwick & T. Novitz (eds.), Human Rights at Work. Perspectives on Law and Regulation, 2010, pp. 409-438; Ebert & Oelz, supra note 45, p. 13. See also Ólafson v Iceland, ECtHR 27 April 2010, Appl. No. 20161/06 for an example of an extensive analysis by the Court of international labour principles in respect of Article 11 ECHR, directly based on the Digest of the Freedom of Association Committee of the Governing Body of the ILO and on the conclusions of the European Committee of Social Rights.

61 Cf. for a critical assessment of, for instance, the complaints procedure of the ESC, R. Churchill & U. Khaliq, 'The Collective Complaints System of the European Social Charter: An effective Mechanism for Ensuring Compliance with Economic and Social rights?', 2004 European Journal of International Law, no. 3, pp. 417-456

62 Ewing & Hendy, supra note 38, p. 4 and pp. 41-42.

63 In Bosphorus Airways v Ireland, Appl. No. 45036/98 (20 June 2006), the ECtHR held that measures taken by a Member State to give effect to Community law did not absolve it from its Convention responsibility in the areas covered. Still, it also held the protection of fundamental rights by Community law to be equivalent to that of the Convention system. With the upcoming accession of the EU to the ECHR, though, understanding the latter stance as irrefutable would make such an accession meaningless.

64 Ibid.

65 E.g. S. Laulom, 'Les Arrêts Viking et Laval: Et après?', 2010 Droit Ouvrier, no. 578, pp. 570-575.

66 Laval, supra note 2, Para. 101.

67 Article G in the revised European Social Charter (1996).

68 I.a. 1996 Digest, Para. 544; and 326th Report, Case No. 2135, Para. 267; 307th Report, Case No. 1898, Para. 323; 309th Report, Case No. 1865, Para. 145; 321st Report, Case No. 2066, Para. 336; 336th Report, Case No. 2383, Para. 767.

69 ILC, 99th Session (2010), Report of the Committee of Experts on the Application of Conventions and Recommendations, Report III [1A], 2010, p. 209.

70 Cf. J. Servais, International labour law, 2011, pp. 121 et seq.

71 Assessment of the Opinions of the Advocates General in Laval and Viking and Six Alternative Solutions, advice to the ETUC, 2007, p. 304.

Available at <www.etuc.org/a/4295>.

72 Conclusions XVII-1, Netherlands, p. 319; Digest of the case law of the ECSR, 2008, p. 55.

73 See note 69, supra.

74 See note 43, supra, Para. 24.

75 E.g. De Vries, supra note 30.

76 Article 52(2) of the Charter.

77 In Albany (C-67/96, [1999] ECR I-05751) the Court granted collective agreements such an immunity in respect of EU competition rules, see A. Jaspers & K. Mortelmans, 'Cao's en mededingingsrecht', 2000 Sociaal Maandblad Arbeid, no. 7/8, pp. 324-339. However, an analogous application of this case law was already turned down by the Court in Viking.

78 Cf. Servais, supra note 70.

79 COM(2012) 130.

80 Article 1(2) of the proposed regulation.

81 Article 2 of the proposed regulation.

82 Cf. F. Dorssemont, 'De ontwerp-Verordening Monti II, oude wijn (azijn) in nieuwe zakken?', 2012 Arbeidsrechtelijke Annotaties 11, no. 2, pp. 3-35.

83 See for the objections made and the national parliaments involved: Dossier No. APP/2012/0064 at <www.ipex.eu>.

84 Protocol No. 2.

CHAPTER 7

STUCK IN THE TERMINAL WITH THE GATES FIRMLY SHUT: SUSPENSION AND TERMINATION OF INDUSTRIAL ACTION AFTER QANTAS

Dr Graham Smith and Leigh Howard

THE HISTORY OF INDUSTRIAL ACTION AND TRIBUNAL INTERVENTION

New Beginnings

Until Paul Keating's reforms (the Industrial Relations Reform Act 1993 (Cth)), Federal industrial legislation (and also generally state industrial legislation) was dominated by an award system, which set wages and conditions for employees in a centralised way. The Federal industrial tribunal (known as the Australian Conciliation and Arbitration Commission until 1 March 1989, and subsequently, the Australian Industrial Relations Commission (AIRC) until 1 July 2009) achieved this through a combination of compulsory arbitration underpinned by conciliation.6 A central feature was that any legislative regulation of industrial action was largely non-existent, and industrial action was treated as a de jure civil wrong.7

The major change arising from Keating's reforms was the introduction of 'certified agreements', a vehicle for setting employee conditions at the enterprise-level. Part-and-parcel with this reform was the legalisation of industrial action by making industrial action taken in support of enterprise bargaining immune from civil suit (hence the notion 'protected industrial action'). The reforms provided for the initiation of 'bargaining periods' by unions, and during the bargaining period, protected action taken by a union in support of enterprise bargaining claims would be immune from civil suit.8 A precondition to taking protected action was that 72 hours notice of the protected action had to be given to the employer and the union parties had to have first tried to reach an agreement with the employer.9 Importantly, the AIRC was given the power to suspend or terminate the bargaining period. The grounds upon which the AIRC could suspend or terminate the bargaining period were limited compared to provisions in later legislation. The AIRC had to be satisfied that:

(a) a negotiating party that has organised or is organising, or has taken, industrial action to support or advance claims that are the subject of the industrial dispute:

(i) is not genuinely trying to reach an agreement with the other negotiating parties in settlement of the industrial dispute; or

(ii) has failed to comply with any directions by the Commission relating to negotiating in good faith; or

(b) industrial action that is being taken to support or advance claims that are the subject of the industrial dispute is threatening:

(i) to endanger the life, the personal safety or health, or the welfare, of the population or of part of it; or

(ii) to cause significant damage to the Australian economy or an important part of it; or

(c) if the bargaining period relates to employees employed in a part of a single business, or at a single place of work in a single business, and the initiating party is not complying with an award or order, or a direction of the

---

Citation: Dr Graham Smith and Leigh Howard, Stuck in the Terminal with the Gates Firmly Shut: Suspension and Termination of Industrial Action after Qantas, DOI: http://dx.doi.org/10.15209/vulj.v2i1.12.

Commission, in relation to another part of the single business or another place of work in the single business.10

If a bargaining period was terminated under this section, then the AIRC could, after exercising conciliation powers, arbitrate the outcome.11 In other words, the AIRC was given a power to determine the terms of the enterprise agreement, and the arbitrated outcome was referred to as an award (in reality it was not an award but an arbitrated enterprise agreement).12 In addition, suspending or terminating the bargaining period meant that the industrial action ceased to be protected. The sanctions for taking unprotected action were to be found outside the confines of the Federal industrial legislation. The union parties and the employees became susceptible to common law legal action by the employer, under what are generally referred to as the industrial torts.13

The Workplace Relations Act Reforms

The election of John Howard's coalition saw the passage of the Workplace Relations Act 1996 (Cth) (_WR Act‘). In many ways, changes created by the WR Act were evolutionary rather than revolutionary. The WR Act did introduce provisions allowing the AIRC to order a 'secret ballot' to establish whether employees wanted to take protected action.14 But otherwise, the provisions relating to initiation of bargaining periods and allowing for protected action were at least conceptually the same.

The AIRC's jurisdiction to suspend or terminate a bargaining period was slightly altered. Most significant was a new ground that allowed suspension or termination if protected action was being taken against an employer to advance claims in respect of employees who were not members of the union or eligible to be members of the union.15 The grounds for suspension or termination if life, safety, health was threatened, or if significant economic damage was threatened, were substantially replicated within s 170MW(3) of the WR Act. Significantly, the High Court in Coal and Allied Operations Pty Ltd v AIRC examined the scheme as it stood under the WR Act, and made the following comments about some of the statutory language that would be replicated in later legislation:

The nature of the threat as to which a decision-maker must be satisfied under s 170MW(3) of the Act involves a measure of subjectivity or value judgment. A decision under that sub-section would involve appealable error if, for example, regard was had to irrelevant material, relevant material was disregarded, or, although there was some factual material by reference to which the decision-maker might be satisfied, he or she mistook those facts. If the Full Court intended to suggest otherwise, it was wrong. More to the point, however, is that a decision under s 170MW(3)(b) that industrial action is _threatening ... to cause significant damage to the Australian economy or an important part of it‘ is not simply a matter of impression or value judgment. The presence of the words _significant‘ and _important‘ in s 170MW(3)(b) indicate that the decision-maker must have some basis for his or her satisfaction over and above generalised predictions as to the likely consequences of the industrial action in question.16

The WorkChoices Reforms

By enacting the Workplace Relations Amendment (Work Choices) Act 2005 (Cth) ('WorkChoices'), the Howard government removed a number of powers that had traditionally been given to Federal industrial tribunals. For example, even the power to scrutinise and approve enterprise agreements was removed from the AIRC and given to a new entity (the Office of the Employment Advocate).17 That said, changes in relation to the taking of protected action and the powers of the AIRC to suspend or terminate were again evolutionary rather than revolutionary.18 One important change was the removal of protection for industrial action taken in support of 'pattern bargaining' claims19 (i.e. bargaining claims across two or more agreements to obtain common wages and conditions across two or more enterprises).20

Two new grounds for suspending or terminating a bargaining period were given to the AIRC. Negotiating parties were now able to obtain a 'cooling-off'. The AIRC was required to suspend if it considered suspension was appropriate, having regard to whether suspending the bargaining period would be beneficial in assisting to resolve matters at issue. The AIRC was also required to consider whether suspending the bargaining period would be contrary to the public interest or inconsistent with the objects of the Workplace Relations Act. 21 The second new ground was directed at significant harm to a third party, or in other words, a party that that was not a negotiating party. If third party harm was established, the AIRC was required to suspend (but could not terminate) for a period not exceeding three months. Again, the AIRC had to take into account a public interest test. Factors that the AIRC was required to consider before suspension on this ground included:

(a) if the [third party] was an employee - the extent to which the industrial action affected the interest of the person as an employee;

(b) the extent to which the [third party] was particularly vulnerable to the effects of the industrial action;

(c) the extent to which the action threatened to:

damage the ongoing viability of a business carried on by the [third party]; or

disrupt the supply of goods or services to a business carried out by a [third party]; or

reduce the [third party's] capacity to fulfil a contractual obligation; or

cause other economic loss to the [third party].22

The third party harm ground recognized that protected action, whilst justified as a tool for creating pressure to reach agreement, could cause other persons significant damage. The Minister for Workplace Relations was given standing to apply under this ground in order to facilitate such applications.23 The Minister was also empowered to terminate the bargaining period upon their own motion if satisfied that the protected action was adversely affecting the parties and a threat to health, safety or welfare of the population, or a threat of significant damage to the economy, existed.24

The Fair Work Act Reforms

The election of the Rudd government, on the back of a fierce campaign to abolish the controversial aspects of WorkChoices, resulted in passage of the Fair Work Act 2009 (Cth) ('FW Act‘).

Instead of working within existing legislation and institutions, the Rudd government consolidated and revamped the existing framework, and established the supposed 'one-stop-shop', FWA.25

Insofar as the law regarding the powers to suspend or terminate, one new ground was created to cater specifically for the bargaining parties. FWA was given the discretion to suspend or terminate if a protected action was causing or threatening to cause significant economic harm to both the employees and employer.26 The other grounds established through the successive reforms were maintained, although the machinery behind them was slightly altered. A wider range of options for affected parties to pursue suspension or termination has resulted.

THE SCHEME IN THE FAIR WORK ACT

Changes made to suspension and termination of industrial action by the Fair Work Act 2009 (Cth) is best understood when considered against the scheme underpinning them. That scheme commences in section 3, which sets out a number of objects of the legislation including:

(f) achieving productivity and fairness through an emphasis on enterprise-level bargaining underpinned by simple good faith bargaining obligations and clear rules governing industrial action.27

Part 3-3 of the Fair Work Act gives effect to this object allowing employees and unions to organise and engage in protected action in support of claims for improvements in wages and conditions. As the explanatory memorandum explains:

The bill recognises that employees have a right to take protected industrial action during bargaining. These measures recognise that, while protected industrial action is legitimate during bargaining for an enterprise agreement, there may be cases where the impact of that action on the parties or on third parties is so severe that it is in the public interest, or even potentially the interests of those engaging in the action, that the industrial action cease — at least temporarily. It is not intended that these mechanisms be capable of being triggered where the industrial action is merely causing an inconvenience. Nor is it intended that these mechanisms be used generally to prevent legitimate protected industrial action in the course of bargaining.

Implicit in the structure of the FW Act is recognition that the right to strike is the primary bargaining tool open to employees and their unions. This reflects the obligations Australia has entered into under International Labour Organisation treaties,29 but also is a long-standing principle of labour law aptly articulated by Sir Otto Kahn Freund, who argued that the right to strike counters the power imbalance in the employee-employer relationship:

[T]he relation between an employer and an isolated employee or worker is typically a relation between a bearer of power and one who is not a bearer of power. In its inception it is an act of submission, in its operation it is a condition of subordination, however much the submission and the subordination may be concealed by that indispensable figment of the legal mind known as the 'contract of employment.' The main object of labour law has always been, and we venture to say will always be, to be a countervailing force to counteract the inequality of bargaining power which is inherent and must be inherent in the employment relationship.30

The FW Act continues to restrict protected action to certain times or circumstances, but has eliminated the concept of a 'bargaining period' and replaced it with the right to take protected action after the expiry date of an existing enterprise agreement.31 A ballot is still required to approve the taking of protected action.32 Notably, the only form of protected action allowed by employers is a limited form of lockout, termed an 'employer response action'. The employer can only lawfully lockout its employees in response to protected action organised or engaged in by employees and their unions.33

SUSPENDING OR TERMINATING PROTECTED ACTION UNDER THE FW ACT: AVENUES, OUTCOMES AND GROUNDS

Under the FW Act, termination and suspension of protected action has become a prescriptive and complex area of labour law. In order to demystify it, it is useful to categorise the key requirements into categories; being 'avenues' (pathways that can lead to the protected action ceasing), 'outcomes' (how the protected action can cease) and 'grounds' (circumstances that give rise to the jurisdiction to cease the protected action). Under the scheme, avenues and outcomes differ depending upon each ground.

There are five 'avenues' through which protected action could be suspended or terminated under part 3-3 of the FW Act. They are:

(a) upon an application to FWA by the parties (i.e. the employer or trade union);

(b) upon an application to FWA by a third party;

(c) on FWA's own initiative;

(d) upon application to FWA by the Federal Minister for Workplace Relations or a state/territory minister with responsibility for workplace relations; or

(e) by a ministerial declaration by the Federal Minister for Workplace Relations (without application to FWA).

There are three 'outcomes'. Protected action can be terminated, and the right to protected action ceases. FWA is then able to arbitrate the dispute (termed a 'workplace determination') if the parties fail to negotiate an agreement after a 21 day period (extendable to 42 days).34 Secondly, it can be suspended for a defined period of time that FWA determines as appropriate.35 Thirdly, FWA can order a cooling-off if satisfied that it would assist the parties in resolving the dispute at hand. Only one extension of the period of suspension or cooling-off is available.36 Importantly, if one of these outcomes is ordered, it applies to all the protected action on foot in the dispute, not just the protected action that is threatened or being taken and is the subject of the application.37

The three outcomes, through the five avenues, can only be triggered if certain 'grounds' are occurring or are likely to occur. There are six separate grounds. The grounds have mostly been adapted from the successive reforms to industrial legislation described above, in that they focus on harm to health and welfare of persons and/or the economy. However they have been slightly expanded in each case. In its short history, FWA has been required to adjudicate upon each ground brought under almost every avenue. A summary of each ground, along with the major cases that have been brought under them, is offered below.

Ground 1: Significant Economic Harm to the Employer and Employees (s 423)

Under s 423, FWA has discretion to suspend or terminate protected action should it be causing 'significant economic harm' to the employer and employees. Applications may be made under all avenues, except by application from a third party. FWA must be satisfied that:

- the protected action is causing, or threatening to cause, significant economic harm to the employer and employees;38
- the protected action must be occurring and have occurred for a protracted period of time;39
- the dispute that is subject of the protected action will not be resolved for a protracted period of time;40 and
- if the significant economic harm has not yet eventuated, the risk of it occurring must be imminent.41

If the protected action is a retaliation in response to other protected action (for example, a lockout in response to employee protected action), then FWA will only consider the harm that is borne by the employees in such action.42 In determining what constitutes 'significant economic harm', the factors that FWA is to have regard to include the following:

(4) the source, nature and degree of harm suffered or likely to be suffered;

(a) the likelihood that the harm will continue to be caused;

(b) the capacity of the person (i.e. employee or employer) to bear the harm;

(c) the views of the person and the bargaining representatives for the agreement;

(d) whether the bargaining representatives have met the good faith bargaining requirements during negotiations;

(e) whether the bargaining representatives have not contravened any bargaining orders in relation to the agreement;

(f) the objective of promoting and facilitating bargaining for the agreement; and

(g) if FWA is considering terminating the protected action (rather than suspend it):

(i) whether the bargaining representatives genuinely are unable to reach agreement on the terms that should be included in the agreement; and

(ii) whether there is no reasonable prospect of agreement being reached.43

At the time of writing, s 423 had been considered five times by FWA, 44 and in all but one case the application has failed. This can be explained by the fact that employees will usually collectively endorse the protected action, despite any suffering that may be inflicted, and will campaign against such an order.45 In those circumstances, and noting that employee harm is a prerequisite to an order even when employer harm is evident, it is difficult to establish that protected action is causing significant economic harm upon employees. In Schweppes, the only successful case to date, this issue was overcome when a number of employees wrote to FWA (on an anonymous basis) to ask that the protected action stop. Based on the contents of those letters, Kaufman SDP summonsed the parties to FWA, and requested submissions as to whether he ought to terminate the protected action on his own motion. After an affidavit was filed confirming the thrust of those letters, Kaufman SDP terminated the protected action after a lockout that had lasted 58 days.46

Ground 2: Endangering the Life, Safety or Well-being of the Population (s 424(1)(c))

Under s 424(1)(c), FWA must suspend or terminate protected action if satisfied that the action is or is going to endanger life, personal safety, health or welfare of the population or part of it. Applications may be made under all avenues, except by application from a third party. The concepts of 'endanger', 'life', 'health', 'safety' and 'welfare' are not defined in the FW Act, and the Explanatory Memorandum is of little assistance. The concepts take their ordinary English meaning. At the time of writing, FWA has been called upon to interpret s 424(1)(c) twelve times, and six applications have resulted in either suspension or termination.47 Cases to date have concerned service providers of essential goods such as health care and utilities, and accordingly, FWA has taken a more sensitive and interventionist approach. FWA has not looked favourably upon a failure to customise protected action in order to limit any potential harm that may be caused to life, safety or wellbeing.

Ground 3: Significant Harm to a Third Party (s 426)

Under s 426, FWA has power to suspend, but not terminate, protected action should it be causing significant harm to a person that is not the employer, employees or bargaining representative. Only two avenues, being upon application by a third party or application by the Minister, are available under this ground. Whilst the inquiry is directed at 'significant harm', and not 'significant economic harm' (as in s 423), FWA has equated the tests to be of the same nature.49 To gain such an order FWA must be satisfied of the following:

(a) the protected action must be causing significant economic harm to a third party;50

(b) the protected action must be 'adversely affecting' either the employer or the employees; 51 and

(c) protected action must be on foot (rather than merely threatening, pending or probable).52

FWA must also be satisfied that the suspension is 'appropriate', by taking into account:

(a) whether the suspension would be contrary to the public interest or the objectives behind the FW Act; and

(b) any other matter that FWA considers relevant.53

In assessing significant harm, FWA is again entitled to take account of any matter it considers relevant, but can consider the extent that the protected action threatens to:

(a) damage the ongoing viability of the third party's enterprise;

(b) disrupt the supply of goods or services to the third party;

(c) reduce the third party's capacity to fulfil a contractual obligation; and

(d) cause any other economic loss caused to the person.54

This ground has only been determined once, unsuccessfully, in CFMEU v Woodside Burrup. 55 In Woodside, a Full Bench of FWA confirmed how the suspension and termination provisions generally operate in light of the legislative intention behind the FW Act, and has proved to be the most significant decision concerning suspension or termination of protected action to date. In an expansive interpretation, the Full Bench concluded that 'substantial harm to third parties is a common consequence of effective industrial action,'56 and went on to hold:

[T]he word 'significant' indicates harm that is exceptional in its character or magnitude when viewed against the sort of harm that might ordinarily be expected to flow from industrial action in a similar context. In this way, an order will only be available under s 426 in very rare cases ... Unless the harm is out of the ordinary then suspension would be contrary to the legislative intention that suspension should not be able to used generally to prevent legitimate protected industrial action in the course of bargaining. 57

The Full Bench reasoned that the basis for such a high threshold was justified once the right to strike, as enshrined in international law and reflected in the FW Act's extrinsic materials, was duly considered and applied.58 Arguably, this reasoning goes further than that articulated by the High Court in Coal and Allied Operations Pty Ltd v AIRC, extracted above. The reasoning in Woodside has been influential in subsequent decisions and partly explains the number of failed applications across each ground.

Ground 4: If FWA Considers that a Cooling-Off is Appropriate (s 425)

Under s 425, FWA must suspend protected action for a cooling-off period if FWA is satisfied it is appropriate. Only one avenue, being an application by the bargaining representatives, is available. In determining such an application, FWA is to take into account:

(a) whether the suspension would be beneficial to the bargaining representatives in assisting in the resolution of outstanding matters;

(b) the duration of the protected action;

(c) whether the suspension would be contrary to the public interest or inconsistent with the objects of the FW Act; and

(d) any other matters that FWA considers relevant.

At the time of writing, six applications for a cooling-off have been made before FWA, and only one has been granted.59 The general trend of FWA decisions under s 425 has been to refuse a cooling-off 'unless there was a finding that a cooling-off period would assist in the resolution' of an agreement.60 However, and taking the holdings of Woodside to their full extent, it could be argued that the existence of the possibility of protected action 'has the effect of reducing the differences between the parties and making agreement more likely.'61 So construed, it seems that cooling-off will only be ordered by FWA if there is a real and probable prospect that such an order would shepherd the parties to agreement.

Ground 5: Significant Damage to the Australian Economy or an Important Part of it (s 424(1)(d))

Under s 424(1)(d), FWA must suspend or terminate protected action if satisfied that the action is or is going to cause significant damage to the Australian economy or an important part of it. Again all avenues may be used under s 424(1)(d), except upon application by a third party. The terms 'significant damage' and 'important part [of the Australian economy]' are not defined and thus take their ordinary meaning. Applications under s 424(1)(d) have been brought before FWA three times, and two have been successful.62 Cases brought under this ground commonly involve economic forecasting as to how protected action will impact on parts of the Australian economy, and are thus necessarily imprecise.63 Whilst the Qantas dispute could have been brought under any number of different grounds, it was pleaded under s 424(1)(d). This was due to the fact that the Federal minister had to act immediately, and evidence of damage to the Australian economy was readily available by calling senior public officials with expertise in affected sectors of the economy.

Ground 6: If the Federal Minister is Satisfied that a Threat to Health, Safety, Welfare or Economic Damage Exists (s 431)

The final ground for intervention is through a declaration published by the Federal minister under s 431, which is effected if the minister is satisfied that:

(a) the protected action is being engaged in, or is threatened, impending or probable; and

(b) the protected action is threatening, or would threaten:

(i) to endanger the life, the personal safety or health, or the welfare, of the population or a part of it; or

(ii) to cause significant damage to the Australian economy or an important part of it.64

A declaration can only terminate and not suspend protected action. The Federal minister must publish the declaration in the Government Gazette and make all bargaining representatives aware of the declaration as soon as practicable.65 The FW Act does not provide a mechanism to review a declaration; however, judicial review would be available.

Such a declaration has not yet been made, and the Gillard government came under some criticism for refraining from issuing a declaration during the Qantas dispute.66 However, a declaration made under s 431 is an administrative process, subject to the principles of procedural fairness and natural justice. If it is assumed that the government was notified of the lockout around the same time the public was, the urgent application to FWA would have produced a quicker outcome. That said, the Qantas dispute shows that it is highly unlikely that a declaration will ever be made under the Gillard government.

THE QANTAS DISPUTE

On Saturday, 29 October 2011 Qantas issued a media release announcing that from 8:00 pm on Monday, 31 October 2011, it would lockout, in effect, all of its licensed engineers, ramp staff and baggage handlers and Australian and international pilots. The media release went on to state that aircraft currently in the air would complete their sectors but that there would be no further Qantas domestic departures or international departures anywhere in the world. Qantas stated that the lockout would continue until the relevant unions (the Australian Licensed Aircraft Engineers Association (ALAEA), the Transport Workers Union (TWU) and the Australian and International Pilots Union (AIPA)) drop their _extreme demands that have made it impossible for agreements to be reached'.67 These demands had persisted despite 14 months of negotiations, including 99 bargaining meetings and at least 18 formal mediations/conciliations before FWA.68 The lockout was an 'employer response action' legally brought under the FW Act. For legal purposes, it was 'in response' to protected action being taken by all three unions; being one hour stoppages proposed by the ALAEA, the various work bans and stoppages proposed by the TWU, and the wearing of red ties and the making of bargaining related in-flight announcements by the AIPA. 69 In reality, the lockout was a response to a 'slowbake' tactic engineered by the ALAEA and TWU. The tactic was to notify Qantas of a pending stoppage, and after Qantas had cancelled flights and rearranged schedules, cancel the stoppage.70 This tactic ensured employee wages were preserved but the damage done to Qantas remained. The cost this inflicted upon Qantas had had reached $68 million and approximately $15 million per week in loss of revenue. Approximately 7,000 passengers had been affected and 600 flights had been cancelled.71

Practitioners and HR professionals in aviation will be attuned to the crucial importance labour cost commands in the industry. As Doganis observes:

> because the unit price of labour differs significantly between airlines – even neighbouring airlines on the same continent – labour cost is a major factor in differentiating costs between competing airlines. In short, reducing labour costs is critical because they are the highest single cost and because they are a major cost differentiator between airlines.72

Sue Bussell, Group General Manager of Industrial Relations for Qantas, has stated that labour cost:

> rather than any particular ideological or political perspective, drives Qantas' industrial relations policy as the airline addresses how to best operate under the rules that apply on any given day. Our objective is to maintain a competitive advantage and to provide a sustainable rate of return to fund investment, maintain job security and reward investors.73

The protected action taken by the union parties leading up to the proposed lockout was primarily in pursuit of the aforementioned job security. According to Qantas, it was pursued by the three unions' in a number of ways:

1. In relation to the ALAEA, that:

a. Qantas build a fully tooled and staffed heavy maintenance facility;

b. third party labour providers be controlled and restricted;

c. Qantas' access to productivity improvements, including those conferred by technology andregulatory changes, be restricted;

d. other unions' members in competition with the ALAEA be excluded from undertaking certain functions;

2. In relation to the TWU, that:

a. third party labour providers be controlled and restricted;

3. In relation to AIPA, that:

a. terms and conditions of employment of employees who work for other companies (whether associated entities of Qantas or not) be regulated by Qantas; and

b. terms and conditions of other Qantas employees, including those who reside overseas, be overridden or supplemented by the agreement at hand.74

Considering the wide scope of these claims, their likely negative impact on Qantas 'flexibility and profitability, as well as the questionable legality of some of them,75 it is unsurprising that Qantas vigorously opposed their inclusion in the agreements throughout the 14 months of negotiations. Viewed in this context, it is tolerably clear that Qantas had resigned to the fact that negotiations had failed. It instigated the lockout in order to have it terminated. This in turn would trigger FWA's jurisdiction to arbitrate each enterprise agreement and end the costly industrial tactics inflicted by the ALAEA and the TWU.

THE HEARING BEFORE FWA

Qantas' lockout, and its obvious consequences for the economy, forced the hand of the Federal minister to intervene in dramatic circumstances in the evening of Saturday, 29 October 2011. FWA listed the matter before a Full Bench (Giudice J, Watson SDP and Roe C) for 10:00 pm that night, and initial arguments were heard until 2:00 am the following morning. The matter resumed on 2:00 pm that afternoon and judgment was handed down at 2:00 am on Monday, 31 October 2011. The minister and the four respondents (i.e. Qantas and the three unions) were joined by the Victorian, New South Wales and Queensland governments, as well as the Australian Council of Trade Unions (ACTU), who all intervened to make submissions.

The minister lead evidence from Mike Mrdak, Secretary, Department of Infrastructure and Transport and Drew Clarke, Secretary, Department of Resources, Energy and Tourism to establish the extent the extent to which the Australian economy would suffer damage if the lockout proceeded. Collectively, the Secretaries testified that:

(a) Qantas accounts for 65 per cent of domestic aviation capacity, 20 per cent international capacity and 80 per cent of airfreight delivery services;

(b) the aviation sector directly employs 50,000 Australians and the downstream effects of employment in the aviation industry represents up to half a million Australians employed in tourism and other sectors;

(c) in-bound tourists contribute $24 billion to the Australian economy per annum;

(d) any reduction in aviation capacity has immediate and severe impacts on all sectors of the economy; and

(e) if the proposed lockout was not put to an end within 24 hours, the tourism sector and the wider economy would suffer because of reduced international and domestic bookings.

This evidence, not unexpectedly, went unchallenged.76

The significance of the damage to the Australian economy was not in dispute. What was in dispute was whether FWA should terminate and trigger its jurisdiction to arbitrate, or suspend and keep negotiations open ended. Set out below are summaries of the arguments advanced by each party as recorded on transcript.77

Arguments of the Federal Minister: Terminate, or in the Alternative, Suspend for a 120 Day Period

The Federal minister argued that FWA must terminate rather than suspend the protected action in light of the uncertainty that the unions‘ protected action was causing and the lockout would make worse. The temporary nature of suspension would only preserve uncertainty and further escalate it as time passed. Upon the expiry of a suspension, the economy would face the same danger if the unions took further protected action and Qantas responded with another lockout. Thus, if FWA was not satisfied that it should terminate, the Federal minister submitted that it should suspend for a 120 day period.

Arguments of the State Ministers: Terminate

The Victorian, New South Wales and Queensland ministers made submissions in support the Federal minister‘s application (although the Victorian and New South Wales ministers did not support the alternative application for suspension). The state ministers did not call evidence, but added that:

(a) the unions had not provided any evidence that they were willing to withdraw or modify their claims, and as such, extending a negotiation period via suspension would have no effect;

(b) a termination would give effect to the FW Act‘s objective to promote productivity and economic growth by ensuring that Qantas flights would not be grounded by a second lockout; and

(c) the grounding of the Qantas fleet had potential to devastate remote areas of the economy, such as Mt Isa, where Qantas is the only aviation provider.

Qantas: Terminate

Qantas chose not to make any submission concerning the damage caused by the lockout, but instead lead evidence from an economist and three Qantas managers which sought to establish that:

(a) the agreement content sought by the three unions was not viable;

(b) all three unions had refused to resile from their claims for a prolonged period of time, and as such, there was no prospect of reaching an agreement with any of the unions;

(c) the lockout was issued to quell safety concerns that the Civil Aviation and Safety Authority had expressed in regards to the impact of the unions‘ protected action; and

(d) the unions‘ protected action had caused a collapse in forward bookings in recent months, and as such, Qantas was required to take preventative action.

In light of this evidence, Qantas vigorously opposed a suspension of all protected action and argued that termination was the appropriate order. At a late stage of the hearing, Qantas foreshadowed the possibility of Qantas reissuing a lockout after a period of suspension, and advised that a suspension would not necessarily mean that the Qantas fleet was to resume operation.

ACTU, TWU, ALAEA and AIPA: Suspension for a Period of 90 or 120 Days

The ACTU and the three union parties all accepted that Qantas‘ proposed lockout was going to cause significant damage to the economy. While arguments slightly differed, all pressed for a suspension for a period of 90 or 120 days. Arguments in advance of that position included:

(a) Qantas‘ lockout was capricious and disproportionate to the action that had been taken by the unions, and as such, terminating their right to take protected action would be unfair;

(b) the 21 day negotiating period that arises from a termination order is not sufficient time for the unions to reach agreement with Qantas; and

(c) due to the dramatic developments, the unions would reconsider and amend their demands.

THE FINDINGS

FWA’s decision to publish reasons when handing down judgment, rather than making an order and publishing reasons later, meant the reasoning and legal analysis in the decision is minimalist. The reasoning within the decision may not be of significant precedential value for the future, but that said, the inferences drawn from it will. Firstly, the Full Bench concluded that it was ‘unlikely’ that the protected action that had been taken by the three unions, even taken together, was threatening to cause significant damage to the tourism and aviation industries.78 Qantas’ losses of $68 million and $15 million per week in revenue, together with the cancellation of 600 flights affecting 7,000 passengers, did not amount to damage of the requisite significance. Thus, a suspension based on the unions’ protected action alone would not have succeeded. In terms resonating with Woodside, the Full Bench opined:

> There is a need to balance this issue against the fact that protected industrial action is permissible under our system and has been now for many years and has been taken relatively frequently in the airline industry with successive bargaining rounds. It is also important that encouragement of enterprise bargaining is also part of the system. In that respect, what we have heard indicates there are still prospects for a satisfactory negotiated outcome in all three cases. The prospect of a negotiated resolution in relation to the three proposed enterprise agreements still remains.

It was Qantas’ lockout, and its effect on consumers of airline passenger and cargo services, that satisfied the Full Bench that significant damage was being threatened in the tourism industry, the aviation industry and industry more generally.79 FWA’s jurisdiction to suspend or terminate pursuant to section 424(1)(d) was therefore enlivened, and in coming to their decision to terminate, the Full Bench held: It is apparent that a suspension of all action on an interim or short term basis is not appropriate and in the end no party supported that course. Some of the principal issues in the negotiations have so far proved very difficult to resolve. Other matters may be easier to resolve. On the evidence there is significant uncertainty arising from the protected action initially of the unions but in particular arising from the lockout and the grounding of the airline. We should do what we can to avoid significant damage to the tourism industry.

...

We have decided that in the particular circumstances of this case, which on the evidence include the particular vulnerability of the tourism industry to uncertainty, suspension will not provide sufficient protection against the risk of significant damage to the tourism industry and aviation in particular. Suspension is necessarily temporary - it leaves open the possibility there may be a further lockout with its attendant risks for the relevant part of the economy. That is, a risk the situation we are now dealing with will recur.80

THE AFTERMATH

By obtaining the termination, Qantas was able to bring an end to the protracted negotiations and trigger arbitration of the agreements. In the weeks following, Qantas and the ALAEA were able to come to terms. The ALAEA-Qantas deal was treated as a consent based workplace determination before the Full Bench, and was the first workplace determination ever made under the Fair Work Act 2009 (Cth). 81 Predictably, the ALAEA did not achieve many of the bargaining objectives outlined above.82 The workplace determination more or less replicates the previous Qantas-ALAEA agreement, with the job security clause remaining the same. The ALAEA was however able to negotiate a significant increase of redundancy pay.83 TWU and AIPA were unable to come to a like agreement. FWA began arbitrating the Qantas-TWU agreement in March 2012 and the Qantas-AIPA agreement in April 2012.84 AIPA also appealed the decision to terminate, which was heard on an urgent basis by a Full Federal Court (Lander, Buchanan and Perram JJ). AIPA argued that Qantas' lockout was unlawful industrial action in as far as it was responding to AIPA. This was because Qantas' lockout was really a response to the industrial tactics taken by the TWU and ALAEA; it was not in response to the wearing of red ties and the bargaining related in-flight announcements by AIPA members. Taken in isolation, the lockout was entirely disproportionate to AIPA's industrial action. AIPA argued that it therefore followed that it was not 'as a response' as required by the FW Act.

This argument was categorically rejected by the Court in three separate judgments. For example, Perram J accepted the 'rhetorical force in the proposition that the lockout of the pilots could not sensibly be seen to have been done in response to [AIPA's] industrial action'85 but nonetheless concluded that a lockout:

does not have to be reasonable, proportionate or rational. Indeed, it would be a response under s 411 even if Qantas' motives were shown to be, as in the case of the pilots they probably were, opportunistic. Further, s 411 neither requires that the response action be taken solely in response to the industrial action of the party with whom the proposed enterprise agreement may be made nor that it be predominantly or even substantially in response to the employee claim action. All that is required is that it is a response. The threshold is low ... an opportunistic response is a response none the less.86

CONSIDERATION OF THE POLICY DEBATE

The Qantas case has prompted debate as to whether the Fair Work Act 2009 (Cth) is effective in assisting parties during protracted industrial disputes. A diverse range of views have been shared, including a call for a complete overhaul modelled on the interest-arbitration systems in North America.87 Former ACTU Secretary, Jeff Lawrence, has adopted a more constrained but similar opinion:

Fundamentally we think that the whole question of arbitration really needs to be revisited....We've got the ability to get arbitration where an employer takes an extreme step like Qantas and threatens to lockout people. But the ability for workers to get arbitration is really quite confined.88

Recently retired Chief Executive of the Australian Industry Group, Heather Ridout, has retorted by declaring:

We would be vehemently opposed to reintroducing arbitration in bargaining between employers and unions of course in the old days, the unions would rock up with an ambit claim. They'd pull on industrial action. We'd have a big stoush. Then we'd end up in arbitration and they'd get half too much, and then that would flow on to the rest of the economy. So it is much better that employers and employees can work out their own agreements under the rules.89

As the juxtaposition of the both views demonstrates, any policy response arising out of Qantas will be controversial. In the view of the authors', Qantas may demonstrate a case for improvement, but wide scale reform is unnecessary. If anything, Qantas demonstrates the need for legislative change to make it easier for an affected party to apply for suspension or cooling-off of protected action. The grounds for suspension and termination, as outlined above, set too high a bar for temporary respite for employers (and arguably third parties) from protected action. The Fair Work Act 2009 (Cth), as it presently stands, fails to adequately recognise the facilitative role FWA can play during suspension of industrial action. Parties all too often become deadlocked during damaging industrial action, and continuation of it often entrenches that deadlock. Suspension provides an opportunity to re-evaluate those positions without loss of face. It can increase the likelihood of resolution and agreement without necessarily diminishing the fairness and equity of the outcome. For this reason, it is regrettable that policy-makers have failed to distinguish suspension from termination and make use of this fact. However, this could be easily achieved with minor amendment to the cooling-off provisions in s 425. Ancillary provisions mandating and enhancing FWA conciliation powers during a coolingoff may be appropriate in this context.

The issues are finely balanced, in a policy sense. Australia is obliged to, and will, continue to observe its obligations entered into under international treaties concerning freedom of association and industrial action, and the right to strike in certain circumstances will remain in Australia's industrial legislation for many years to come. But there is no policy reason why suspension of protected action should be available only 'in very rare cases' and unless harm is 'out of the ordinary.'90

As with all civil rights, the right to strike is not absolute; it may be limited to the extent as can be demonstrably justified, taking into account the rights and liberties of others. From a fair and holistic standpoint, the economic viability of enterprises that employ people ought not be of lesser importance than the right to strike. So construed, it is the authors' view that there is scope for making suspension and cooling-off periods more accessible in order to prevent more protracted and economically damaging disputes of the kind endured in Qantas. 91 These policy choices, as represented in the legislation, have now been in evolution since 1993. The balance is a fine one, but wide-scale revision against the evolution of these provisions is unnecessary. Slight amendments, perhaps to the cooling-off ground outlined in s 425, is all that may be required to strike the right balance. At the time of writing, a review panel appointed by the Gillard Government (consisting of Emeritus Professor Ron McCallum, former Federal Court Justice Michael Moore and Reserve Bank Board Member John Edwards) is due to report on the operation of the Fair Work Act 2009 (Cth), including the provisions that have been considered by the authors in this article.92 It remains to be seen if further legislative changes will emerge from that review.

Notes:

1 Simon Lauder, _Unions Say Qantas Grounding was Premeditated', ABC News (online), 30 October 2011 <http://www.abc.net.au/news/2011-10-30/unions-say-qantas-grounding-was-premeditated/3608726>.

2 Senate Rural Affairs and Transport Legislation Committee, Parliament of Australia, Inquiry into the Air Navigation and Civil Aviation Amendment (Aircraft Crew) Bill 2011andQantas Sale Amendment (Still Call Australia Home) Bill 2011 (2010) 8-10.

3 ABC, 'Interview with Bill Shorten', Insiders, 30 October 2011(Bill Shorten), available at <http://www.abc.net.au/insiders/content/2011/s3351474.htm>.

4 See Australian Labor Party, Platform (as enacted at the 46th ALP National Conference, Sydney, 4 December 2011), ch 5.

5 Re Minister For Tertiary Education, Skills, Jobs and Workplace Relations [2011] FWAFB 7444 (31 October 2011) ('Qantas').

6 See generally Malcolm Rimmer, 'Unions and Arbitration' in Joe Isaac and Stuart MacIntyre (eds), The New Province for Law and Order: 100 Years of Australian Industrial Conciliation and Arbitration (Cambridge University Press, 2004); Bill Harley, 'Managing Industrial Conflict' in Joe Isaac and Stuart MacIntyre, The New Province for Law and Order:100 Years of Industrial Conciliation and Arbitration (Cambridge University Press, 2004).

7 See generally Bill Harley, above n 6,338-45.

8 Industrial Relations Act 1988 (Cth) (as enacted at 18 February 1994) s 170PM.

9 Ibid ss 170PH(1)-PI(1).

10 Ibid s 170PO (emphasis added).

11 Ibid s 170PP(2).

12 Industrial Relations Act 1988 (Cth) (as enacted at 18 February 1994) s 170PP(3).

13 'Industrial torts' are actions that grant relief for the wrongful infliction of economic loss in an industrial context. The most commonly litigated industrial tort is interference with contract. See generally Breen Creighton and Andrew Stewart, Labour Law (Federation Press, 5th ed, 2010) 797 - 806; Shae McCrystal, The Right to Strike in Australia (Federation Press, 2010) 93-108.

14 See Workplace Relations Act 1996 (Vic) (as enacted at 20 January 1997) pt VI div 4.

15 Workplace Relations Act 1996 (Vic) (as enacted at 20 January 1997) s 170MW(4).

16 Coal and Allied Operations Pty Ltd v Australian Industrial Relations Commission (2000) 203 CLR 194, 208 [28] per Gleeson CJ, Gaudron and Hayne JJ (emphasis added).

17 WorkChoices (the Workplace Relations Act as enacted at 27 March 2006) pt 8 div 5.

18 See generally Greg McCarry 'Industrial Actions under the Workplace Relations Act 1996 (Cth)' (1997) 10 Australian Journal of Labour Law 133; Shae McCrystal, 'Smothering the Right to Strike: Work Choices and Industrial Action' (2006) 19 Australian Journal of Labour Law 198.

19 WorkChoices (the Workplace Relations Act as enacted at 27 March 2006) pt 9 div 3 subdiv B.

20 Ibid s 421.

21 Ibid s 432

22 Ibid s 433.

23 Ibid s 433(1)(b)(ii)

24 Ibid s 498. Note that under s 30J of the Crimes Act 1914 (Cth), the Federal Government can issue a proclamation that prohibits industrial action in connection with the transport of goods, the conveyance of passengers, or the provision of any Commonwealth public service. Any person that engages, incites or encourages such industrial action after a proclamation is guilty of an offence punishable by a maximum of 1 year imprisonment. Section 30J has not been utilised since its inception in 1926.

25 See generally Andrew Stewart, _Fair Work Australia: The Commission Reborn?' (2011) 53(5) Journal of Industrial Relations 563.

26 Fair Work Act 2009 (Cth) s 423.

27 Fair Work Act 2009 (Cth) s 3(f).

28 Explanatory Memorandum, Fair Work Bill 2008 (Cth) cl 267-68.

29 Freedom of Association and Protection of the Right to Organise Convention (ILO No. 87), open for signature 31 August 1948, 68 UNTS 17 (entered into force 4 July 1950); Right to Organise and Collective Bargaining Convention (ILO No. 98), opened for signature 18 August 1949, 96 UNTS 257 (entered into force 18 July 1951). Both treaties were ratified by the Whitlam government on 28 February 1973.

30 Otto Kahn-Freund, Labour and the Law (Stevens and Sons, 2nd ed, 1977) 6.

31 Fair Work Act 2009 (Cth) s 417(1). Conceptually this has always been the case since the WR Act was enacted.

32 Ibid s 409(3).

33 Construction, Forestry, Mining and Energy Union v

Woodside Burrup Pty Ltd (2010) 198 IR 360, 370 [27]; Shae McCrystal, 'The Fair Work Act 2009 (Cth) and the Right to Strike' (2009) 23(1) Australian Journal of Labour Law 3.

34 Fair Work Act 2009 (Cth) s 266.

35 Ibid ss 423–27.

36 Ibid s 428.

37 National Tertiary Education Union v University of South Australia (2010) 194 IR 30, 33 [11].

38 Fair Work Act 2009 (Cth) s 423(2).

39 Ibid s 423(6)(a).

40 Ibid s 423(6)(b).

41 Ibid s 423(5).

42 Ibid s 423(3).

43 Fair Work Act 2009 (Cth) s 423(4)

44 Successful cases: Schweppes Australia Pty Ltd v United Voice (B2012/461, Kaufman SDP, 10 February 2012, decision delivered on transcript) (_Schweppes'). Unsuccessful cases: Prysmian Power Cables and Systems Australia v National Union of Workers [2010] FWA 9402 (7 December 2010); Nyrstar Port Pirie v Construction, Forestry, Mining and Energy Union [2009] FWA 1148(16 November 2009) and Schweppes Australia Pty Ltd v United Voice [2011] FWA 9329 (29 December 2011); POAGS Pty Ltd v Maritime Union of Australia [2012] FWA 114(9 January 2012).

45 See, eg, Prysmian Power Cables and Systems Australia v National Union of Workers [2010] FWA 9402 (7 December 2010) [47], [92] where a unanimous resolution was passed by employees requesting the tribunal not to order a termination of the protected action. Cargill C concluded that the resolution indicated that the protected action did not meet the requisite magnitude to be significant for employees.

46 Schweppes, Transcript, PN5-15, 503-530.

47 Successful cases: Ambulance Victoria v Liquor, Hospitality and Miscellaneous Union (2009) 187 IR 119; National Tertiary Education Union v University of South Australia (2010) 194 IR 30; Re Pelican Point Power Limited [2010] FWA 8666 (10 November 2010); State of Victoria v Community and Public Sector Union [2011] FWA 9245 (23 December 2011); Victorian Hospitals' Industrial Association v Australian Nursing Federation [2011] FWAFB 8165 (15 December 2011). Unsuccessful cases: Tyco Australia Pty Ltd v Communications, Electrical, Electronic, Energy, Information, Postal, Plumbing and Allied Services Union of Australia [2011] FWAFB 1598 (24 March 2011); Minda Inc v Liquor, hospitality and Miscellaneous Union [2010] FWA 3753 (14 May 2010); Minda Inc v Liquor, Hospitality and Miscellaneous Union [2010] FWA 3217 (27 April 2010); Geo Group Australia Pty Ltd v United Voice [2011] FWA 9025 (22 December 2011); St John Ambulance Australia (NT) Inc v United Voice [2011] FWA 4782 (21 July 2011); Toyota Motor Corp Australia Ltd v Automotive, Food, Metals, Engineering, Printing and Kindred Industries Union [2011] FWA 6268 (12 September 2011); G4S Custodial Services Pty Ltd v Health Services Union of Australia [2011] FWA 5902 (1 September 2011)

48 See University of South Australia v National Tertiary Education Union [2009] FWA 1535 (4 December 2009) [39] where O'Callaghan SDP was implicitly critical of the NTEU's refusal to modify a ban on marking student assessments to accommodate graduating students.

49 The test under the Fair Work Act 2009 (Cth) s 423, while setting out a greater number of factors, does not direct that FWA consider only the listed factors. As such, it can be inferred that FWA has discretion to consider anything additionally relevant, akin to the test in s 426. See Prysmian Power Cables and Systems Australia v National Union of Workers [2010] FWA 9402 (7 December 2010) [84] per Cargill C.

50 Fair Work Act 2009 (Cth) s 426(3).

51 Fair Work Act 2009 (Cth)s 426(2).

52 Fair Work Act 2009 (Cth) s 426(1).

53 Fair Work Act 2009 (Cth)s 426(5).

54 Fair Work Act 2009 (Cth)s 426(4).

55 (2010) 198 IR 360 (_Woodside').

56 Woodside' 375 [44].

57 Woodside' 375 [44] (emphasis added).

58 Woodside' 372 75 [37]-[44].

59 Successful cases: Nyrstar Port Pirie v Construction, Forestry, Mining and Energy Union [2009] FWA 1144 (17 November 2011). Unsuccessful cases: Tas Paper Pty Ltd v Automotive, Food, Metals, Engineering, Printing and Kindred Industries Union [2009] FWA 1872 (22 December 2009); Transit Australia Pty Ltd v Transport workers Union of Australia [2011] FWA 5006 (29 July 2011); Mammoet Australia Pty Ltd v Construction, Forestry, Mining and Energy Union [2010] 4389 (14 June 2010); Patrick Stevedores Holdings Pty Ltd v Maritime Union of Australia [2011] FWA 3059 (18 May 2011); Communications, Electrical, Electronic, Energy, Information, Postal, Plumbing and Allied Services Union of Australia v Carter Holt Harvey Wood Products Australia Pty Ltd [2011] FWA 101 (11 January 2011).

60 Mammoet Australia Pty Ltd v Construction, Forestry, Mining and Energy Union [2010] FWA 4389 (14 June 2010) [27] per McCarthy DP; applied in Communications, Electrical, Electronic, Energy, Information, Postal, Plumbing and Allied Services Union of Australia v Carter Holt Harvey Wood Products Australia Pty Ltd [2011] FWA 101 (11 January 2011) [6] per Blair C.

61 Mammoet Australia Pty Ltd v Construction, Forestry, Mining and Energy Union [2010] FWA 4389 (14 June 2010) [31] per McCarthy DP.

62 Successful cases: Qantas [2011] FWAFB 7444 (31 October 2011); Sucrogen Australia Pty Ltd v Australian Workers Union [2010] FWA 6192 (27 August 2010). Unsuccessful cases: Toyota Motor Corporation Australia Ltd v Automotive, Food, Metals, Engineering, Printing and Kindred Industries Union [2011] FWA 6268 (12 September 2011).

63 Cf Sucrogen Australia v Australian Workers Union [2010] FWA 6192 (27 August 2010), where industrial action was suspended to prevent a sugar harvest from being compromised, with Toyota Motor Corporation Australia Ltd v AMWU [2011] FWA 6268, where a suspension order was refused despite protected action potentially delaying a refit of plant and equipment. The delay in the latter case eventuated in a stand down: Automotive, Food, Metals, Engineering, Printing and Kindred Industries Union v Toyota Boshoku Australia Pty Ltd

[2012] FWA 1135 (8 February 2012).

64 Fair Work Act 2009 (Cth) s 431(1).

65 Ibid s 432. While unclear, it seems that publication in the Government Gazette is not a precondition for the declaration to take effect. The declaration takes effect on the day that it is 'made', rather than published: FW Act s 431(2).

66 Eric Abetz, _Qantas Evidence is Clear: Government Could Have Acted But Didn't' (Media Release, 4 November 2011).

67 Qantas, _Qantas Responds to Industrial Action' (Media Release, 29 October 2011).

68 Qantas [2011] FWAFB 7444 (31 October 2011) [4] – [6].

69 Minister's Form F37 Application in Qantas [2011] FWAFB 7444 (31 October 2011) attachment 1.

70 Such a tactic is permissible under the Fair Work Act 2009 (Cth): see Re Boral Resources (NSW) Pty Ltd (2010) 193 IR 286.

71 Qantas, above n 68.

72 Rigas Doganis, The Airline Business (Routledge, 2nd ed, 2006) 119, cited in Sue Bussell and John Farrow, 'Continuity and Change: The Fair Work Act in Aviation' (2011) 24(3) Journal of Industrial Relations 392, 393.

73 Bussell and Farrow, above n 72, 393.

74 Qantas, Qantas Group Submission to the Review of the Fair Work Act (17 February 2012) Fair Work Act Review, .

75 As 'permitted matters' allowed to be included in agreements under the FW Act: see s. 172(1)(a). The legality of the unions' claims is outside the scope of this paper. See generally Australian Industry Group v ADJ Contracting Pty Ltd [2011] FWAFB 6684 (13 October 2011), which is subject of a Full Federal Court appeal at the time of writing

76 Qantas [2011] FWAFB 7444 (31 October 2011) [9].

77 Transcript of Proceedings, Qantas (FWA, B2011/3816, Giudice J, Watson SDP and Roe C, 29-30, October 2011).

78 Qantas,[2011] FWAFB 7444 (31 October 2011) [10].

79 Ibid [10].

80 Ibid [12] - [13], [15].

81 Australian Licenced Aircraft Engineers Association v Qantas Airways Limited [2012] FWAFB 236 (23 January 2012).

82 Cf Australian Licenced Aircraft Engineers Association v Qantas Airways Limited [2012] FWAFB 236 (23 January 2012) [11], [17] for a comparison between the claims that remained outstanding after the lockout and what was eventually agreed.

83 See also Joellen Riley, 'A Safe Touch-down for Qantas?' (2012) 25 Australian Journal of Labour Law 76.

84 Workplace Express, 'Qantas-TWU Arbitration to Begin in March, Pilots in April, as ALAEA Asks Members to Consider Status Quo on Job Security', Workplace Express (online), 25 November 2011.

85 Australian and International Pilots Association v Fair Work Australia [2012] FCAFC 65 (10 May 2012) [156].

86 Ibid [157]. Other more technical legal issues dealt with in this case warrant more detailed analysis than is possible in this article.

87 Alex Bukarica and Andrew Dallas, Good Faith Bargaining Under the Fair Work Act 2009 (Federation Press, 2012) 131-50; Anthony Forsyth, 'Qantas Case Shows the Need for Interest Arbitration', The Conversation (online), 28 November 2011 .

88 Mark Skulley 'Unions Want Stronger Hand', Australian Financial Review (Australia), 14 November 2011, 3.

89 Heather Ridout, 'Taking Charge of Our Future' (Speech delivered at the National Press Club, Canberra, 30 November 2011); as cited in Rae Cooper, 'Testing Fair Work: Australian Industrial Relations in 2011' (2012) 54(3) Journal of Industrial Relations 267, 270.

90 Woodside (2010) 198 IR 360, 375 [44].

91 For a contrasting viewpoint (albeit in a differing context) see McCrystal, above n 13, 251-56, 277-82.

92 Bill Shorten, 'Fair Work Act Review Announced' (Media Release, 20 December 2011). See generally Fair Work Act Review, available at <http://www.deewr.gov.au/WorkplaceRelations/Policies/FairWorkActReview/Pages/Home.aspx>.

CHAPTER 8

INTERNATIONAL REGULATIONS CONCERNING GENDER DISCRIMINATION IN PROFESSIONAL LIFE

Patrycja Zwiech

Keywords: Gender science, gender discrimination, gender equality, legal regulations

INTRODUCTION

Equality of all citizens is a fundamental principle obeyed by democratic societies. Equal job and power opportunities policy is still one of the main pillars of international law. It is considered the main requirement of democracy. International community takes action aimed at developing legal and institutional infrastructure which allows obeying gender equality rules as well as protecting against discrimination, sexual discrimination in particular. The United Nations, International Labour Organization and the European Union have developed guidelines for combating discrimination against women on labour market.

The paper is aimed at presenting legal regulations imposed by International Labour Organization, the United Nations and the European Union, and regarding gender equality in professional life. It seems vital to pay special attention to issues relating to discrimination against women particularly as the aforementioned regulations are complicated, and although the situation of women and men on labour market differs to a great extent. Research on gender discrimination suggests that the situation of women on labour market is worse and there are many factors determining such a state of affairs (Balcerzak-Paradowska, 2001 and 2003; Dijkstra and Plantega 2003; Gawrycka, Wasilczuk, and Zwiech, 2007; Kalinowska-Nawrotek, 2005; Kryńska, 2001; Titkow, 2003; Zwiech, 2008 and 2003; World Bank, 2004; National Labour Inspectorate, 2005).

Women earn less and occupy lower positions in organizational hierarchy, are less often marked for professional training and face greater difficulties in gaining employment in the majority of the Member States, hence also in Poland.

REGULATIONS REGARDING DISCRIMINATION AGAINST WOMEN ON LABOR MARKET - IMPOSED BY INTERNATIONAL LABOR ORGANIZATION

First regulations regarding female work were imposed by International Association for Labour Legislation. The Association was established after the Paris Conference in 1900. It was a precursor of International Labour Organization, headquartered in Basel, which took on the translation and publication of labour legislation in particular countries. Furthermore, it organized a conference in Brno in 1906. Two conventions were established during the conference. The former regarded the reduction of white phosphorus use (toxic substance for the production of matches at that time), whereas the latter imposed a ban on night work for women.

International Convention banning Night Work for Women in Industry signed in Brno on 26 September 1906 was the first document that attempted to regulate female work. Once these two conventions had been adopted, a new chapter in the history of international relations began. The Association started to prepare regulations banning night work for young people and implementing a maximum ten-hour working day for juveniles

Citation: Patrycja Zwiech, International Regulations Concerning Gender Discrimination In Professional Life, ISSN 1804-0519.

and women. However, an outbreak of war in 1914 disallowed the implementation of the conventions.

International Labour Organization (ILO) was established in 1919 to make governments, entrepreneurs and trade unions take joint action aimed at social justice and improving the living conditions all over world1. Regulations regarding female work are still one of priorities to ILO. During the first session in 1919, ILO adopted normalizations concerning female work. Out of six conventions ratified then, two concerned women's labour: Convention nr 3 of 29 October 1919 on employing women before and after childbirth and Convention nr 4 of 29 October 1919 on night work for women (later amended by Convention nr 103 of 28 June 1952). Other conventions signed by ILO with reference to female work were: Convention nr 41 of 4 June 1934 on night work for women, amended by Convention nr 89 of 17 June 1948, Convention nr 171 of 16 June 1990, and Convention nr 45 of 04 June 1935 on underground work for women.

However, issues relating to discrimination against women on labour market were addressed by International Labour Organization only in 1951. On 29 June 1951 it adopted Convention nr 100 on equal remuneration for male and female workers for work of equal value. Subsequent Conventions ratified by ILO also referred to discrimination against women, e.g. Convention nr 111 of 25 June 1958 on discrimination in the field of employment and occupation, and Convention nr 156 of 23 June 1981 on equality of opportunity and treatment for male and female workers with family responsibilities.

Legal Regulations Imposed By the United Nations With Reference To Discrimination against Women

The United Nations was the first international organization to raise issues relating to discrimination against women. It was in 1948 that the UN addressed the matter in Universal Declaration of Human Rights. Article 2 and Article 16(1) of the Declaration referred to the equality of women and men.

The UN discussed discrimination against women in International Covenant on Civil and Political Rights of 19 December 1966 in Article 26, and stated that "the law shall prohibit any discrimination (...) on any ground such as race, colour, sex, language, religion, political or other opinion, national or social origin, property, birth or other status."

The Convention on the Elimination of All Forms of Discrimination Against Women of 18 December 1979 was a significant breakthrough and defined the essence of this discrimination. The Convention obliged particular states to pursue policy aimed at combating gender discrimination in every sphere of life and provide women with conditions for full development and promotion in every sphere of social, economic, political and public life. The Convention on the Elimination of Discrimination Against Women in the scope of employment puts an emphasis on the following rights that women should retain (Article 11):

- right to permanent employment and equal working conditions (working time, form of employment); right to equal job opportunities and criteria for selection;
- right to choose profession and job, to be promoted and have access to training;
- right to equal remuneration for work of equal value;
- right to social security;
- right to health care and safe working conditions.

Another regulation implemented by the UN on 20 December 1993 was Declaration on the Elimination of Violence against Women. Nevertheless, it should be noticed that this was declaration and not convention. While convention obliges particular countries to take actions and does not allow any exceptions, declaration does not have such legal force. The latter ought to be treated as a recommendation, thus actions contradictory to the convention do not lead to negative legal and international consequences. However, in this document the UN has explicitly stated that male domination and discrimination against women cannot be denied and should be combated in order to encourage full development.

In 1982, the UN established the Committee on the Elimination of Discrimination against Women (CEDAW), which was a major step in fighting the phenomenon. During the period 1986-2008, the Committee put forward 26 recommendations on the situation of women. As for professional life, the recommendations concerned equal access to employment and equal remuneration (Recommendation nr 13 of 1989), unpaid women working in family enterprises (nr 16 of 1991), migration of female workers (nr 26 of 2008). On the other hand, taken social policy into account, the recommendations referred to violence against women (nr 12 of 1989 and nr 19 of 1992), equality in marriage (nr 21 of 1994), gender equality in the public and political life (nr 23 of 1997), or equal access to health care (nr 14 of 1990, nr 15 of 1990, nr 18 of 1991, nr 24 of 1999) and education (nr 3 of 1987).

Regulations Imposed By the European Union on Discrimination against Women in Professional Life

The European Union has provided the Member States with structural and institutional basis for pursuing equal opportunities policy (Dijkstra and Plantega, 2003, p.137). The policy involves:

- making various spheres of social life and external environment available to everyone;
- taking needs expressed by every individual into account;
- making every individual participate in social life;
- implementing a number of regulations, as well as equal rights and obligations to be met by everyone as rightful citizens.

The European Union has introduced directives, recommendations and programs of actions aimed at combating discrimination against women. Each of them differs as far as obligatoriness level is concerned. Directives oblige the States to introduce changes into national legislation by given deadlines. Recommendations and programmes are not obligatory. They are designed to make the Member States follow proper policy.

Founding Treaties of the Community (Treaty of Rome - Article 119, Treaty of Amsterdam - Article 141) include regulations on equal treatment of women and men in the field of employment. Furthermore, Treaty of Amsterdam (Article 13) bans discrimination. So far the European Union has adopted a great number of directives on equal opportunities for women and men in professional life.

The first Council Directive on equal treatment of women and men was adopted in 1975. Directive 75/117/EEC of 10 February 1975 referred to the approximation of the laws of the Member States relating to the application of the principle of equal pay for men and women. This directive obliges the States to provide women and men with equal remuneration for work of equal value. Another Council Directive (76/207/EEC of 9 February 1976) required the implementation of the principle of equal treatment for men and women as regards access to employment, vocational training and promotion, and working conditions. The Directive in question was amended in September 2002. It is now catalogued as 2002/73/EC and refers to sexual harassment as an act of sexual discrimination.

Council Directive 79/7/EEC of 19 December 1978 on the progressive implementation of the principle of equal treatment for men and women in matters of social security refers to the statutory schemes which provide protection against the risks of sickness, invalidity, old age, accidents at work, occupational diseases and unemployment, and in social assistance. Council Directive 86/378/EEC of 24 July 1986 has implemented the principle of equal treatment for men and women in occupational social security schemes, and particularly with reference to social security legislation that has not been referred to in the previous Directive and to employees or selfemployed persons working in particular branches of industry or labour market sectors. Council Directive 96/97/EC of 20 December 1996 amended the aforementioned Directive. Council Directive 86/613/EEC of 11 December 1986 on the application of the principle of equal treatment between men and women engaged in an activity, including agriculture, in a self-employed capacity, and on the protection of self-employed women during pregnancy and motherhood. It extends the principle of equal treatment to women in self-employment or working with their husbands.

Council Directive 92/85/EEC of 19 October 1992 on the introduction of measures encouraged improvements in the safety and health at work of pregnant workers and workers who have recently given birth or are breastfeeding. Council Directive 96/34/EC of 3 June 1996 offers men the possibility of taking parental leave. Council Directive 97/75/EC of 15 December 1997 amended the aforementioned Directive and extended it to the United Kingdom of Great Britain and Northern Ireland.

Council Directive 97/80/EC of 15 December 1997 (on the burden of proof in cases of discrimination based on sex) burdens a defendant with a necessity to prove that no discrimination has occurred. Council Directive 98/52/EC of 13 July 1998 amended the aforementioned Directive and extended it to the United Kingdom of Great Britain and Northern Ireland. Council Directive 2000/78/EC of 27 November 2000 has established a general framework for equal treatment in employment and occupation. Council Directive 2004/113/EC of 13 December 2004 has implemented the principle of equal treatment between men and women in the access to and supply of goods and services. And last but not least, Council Directive 2006/54/EC of 5 July 2006 required the implementation of the principle of equal opportunities and equal treatment of men and women in matters of employment and occupation, and required transparency in legal acts so that all the regulations established in this scope were included in one text. Therefore, on 15 August 2009 Directives 75/117/EEC, 76/207/EEC, 2002/73/EC, 86/378/EEC, 96/97/EC, 97/80/EC, 98/52/EC were annulled and Directive 2006/54/EC was implemented.

The aforementioned Directives require the Member States to pursue equality policy and pay special attention to the creation of systemic solutions that allow combating discrimination against women. The Directives under discussion highlight the need for expert organs dealing with the popularization of equal treatment, monitoring equality policy and helping lay discrimination claims. Recommendations and declarations are flexible instruments that require the Member States to take specific measures within their structures. It is worth mentioning the following recommendations on equalizing the opportunities for women and men, namely Council Recommendation 84/635/EEC of 13 December 1984 on the promotion of positive action for women, Council Resolution 84/C 161/02 of 7 June 1984 on action to combat unemployment amongst women, Commission Recommendation 92/131/EEC of 27 November 1991 on the protection of the dignity of women and men at work, Council Recommendation 96/694/EC of 2 December 1996 on the balanced participation of women and men in the decision-making process, and Council Resolution 95/C 296/06 of 5 October 1995 on the image of women and men portrayed in advertising and the media.

Programmes of action are also a fundamental element of equal opportunities policy pursued by the EU. So far five programmes have been implemented during the following periods: 1982-1985, 1986- 1990, 1991-1995, 1996-2000, 2001-2006. Gender equality is currently addressed as part of the 6th Framework Programme 2006-2010. The first programme of action dealt with legal barriers to equal opportunities for women and men as well as placed an emphasis on extending individual rights enjoyed by women. The second programme recommended that women should continually educate themselves, depart from traditional decisions about education, and men ought to participate in housework to a larger extent. It also addressed issues relating to parental leave. The third programme discussed women's situation with reference to general labour market policy. It indicated the necessity to develop instruments helping reconcile career with household duties. The fourth programme was a continuation of integration approach. It was aimed at promoting equal opportunities while formulating, implementing and monitoring all the policies, measures and actions taken by society at a national, regional and national levels. This program raised issues relating to gender equality in decision-making process. The fifth program referred to actions aimed at shaping social awareness and combating xenophobia and intolerance.

Taken the programme currently implemented by the European Parliament into account, the popularization of gender equality has two aspects as gender issues should be addressed as part of various political strategies, and at the same time supported with the use of special measures. The programme addresses the following questions: violence against women and human trafficking, respect for women's rights as part of the European Neighbourhood Policy, development of plans for employment and social integration to be implemented at a national level to help women enter labour market and enjoy the same rights as men. Finally, to enforce the rule "equal remuneration for work of equal value". Furthermore, actions should be aimed at the development of women's entrepreneurship, shaping the policy aimed at reconciling private and professional life, greater participation of women in decision-making process and political life, opportunities for women to undertake scientific and research work, positive image and achievements of women portrayed in the media, and finally eliminating gender stereotypes, particularly with reference to labour market.

CONCLUSION

Issues relating to discrimination against women on labour market have been addressed by international institutions for over 60 years. The first organization that raised the matter was the UN (in 1948). International Labour Organization addressed the issue in 1951. The European Union has been continually introducing legal regulations regarding equal treatment of women and men in professional life. Therefore, anti-discrimination legislation is being developed. Despite the regulations, the situations of female and male employees still differ considerably. That is why the EU has been implementing not only legal regulations, but also plans of action aimed at eliminating discrimination against women, enforcing the regulations in social life and developing social awareness.

REFERENCES

1. Balcerzak-Paradowska, B. (Ed.), 2001. Kobiety i mężczyźni na rynku pracy. Rzeczywistość lat 1990-1999, IPISS, Warszawa.
2. Balcerzak-Paradowska, B. (Ed.), 2003. Praca kobiet w sektorze prywatnym. Szanse i bariery, IPISS, Warszawa.
3. Dijkstra, A., Plantega J. (Eds.), 2003. Ekonomia i płeć. Pozycja zawodowa kobiet w Unii Europejskiej, Gdańskie Wydawnictwo Psychologiczne, Gdańsk.
4. Gawrycka, M., Wasilczuk, J., Zwiech, P., 2007. Szklany sufit i ruchome schody - kobiety na rynku pracy, CeDeWu sp. z o.o., Warszawa.
5. Kalinowska-Nawrotek, B., 2005. Dyskryminacja kobiet na polskim rynku pracy, Wydawnictwo AE w Poznaniu, Poznań.
6. Kryńska E., 2001. Dylematy polskiego rynku pracy, IPISS, Warszawa.
7. Raport Banku Światowego, 2004. "Płeć a możliwości ekonomiczne w Polsce: Czy kobiety straciły na transformacji?", Biuro Banku Światowego w Polsce, No.29205, Warszawa.
8. Raport Państwowej Inspekcji Pracy, 2005. "Równe traktowanie kobiet i mężczyzn w stosunkach pracy. Mobbing w środowisku pracy," Warszawa.
9. Titkow, A. (Ed.), 2003. Szklany sufit. Bariery i ograniczenia karier kobiet, ISP, Warszawa.
10. Zwiech, P., 2008. "Dyskryminacja zatrudnieniowa kobiet w Unii Europejskiej, USA i Japonii," in: Noga, M., Stawicka, M. (Eds.), Globalizacja a konkurencyjność w gospodarce światowej, CeDeWu Sp. z o.o., Warszawa, pp.317-28.
11. Zwiech, P., 2003. "Dyskryminacja kobiet na polskim rynku pracy," in: Kopycińska, D. (Ed.), Kapitał ludzki w gospodarce, PTE, Szczecin, pp.135-46.

CHAPTER 9

THE MULTIPLICITY OF REGULATORY RESPONSES TO REMEDY THE GENDER IMBALANCE ON COMPANY BOARDS

Linda Senden

Keywords: Gender equality, company boards, soft law, quota laws, effectiveness

INTRODUCTION

From the very foundation of the European Economic Community, now the European Union, the principle of equality and of equal treatment of men and women is one of the legal cornerstones of its underlying system of core values, yet the unequal representation of women in political and economic decision-making is still a huge problem throughout the EU. While women make up at least half of the population, their share in the exercise of political and economic power has remained at a very low level even in the 21st century. Focussing in this contribution on economic decision-making and in particular on the representation of women on company boards, the following figures are telling. The EU average for women in such top management positions of large listed company boards1 is still at the very low figure of 17.8 %, while there are significant cross-country differences, the lowest figure concerning Malta (2.1%) and the highest being that in Finland (29.8%),2 other countries ranging in between such as Greece (8.4%), Belgium (16.7%) and Germany (21.5%). The non-EU country Norway shows the highest figure: 42%. At CEO level, the figures are even far lower; less than three out of the hundreds of the largest listed companies in Europe are women.3 From a special Eurobarometer poll conducted in 2011, there appears to be quite a large societal consensus in Europe that this is indeed problematic and that women, given their equal competence, should be equally represented in company leadership positions.4 As will be discussed in more detail, three different normative justifications can be distinguished for holding this view and for taking action: there is the economic, business case argument; the private, individual fairness, equal opportunities and equal qualifications argument; and the general societal, public interest and fundamental rights rationale.5 Yet, there are quite diverging views as to the methods and instruments to be applied for achieving a (more) balanced representation of women and men. According to the mentioned Eurobarometer poll, only 8% of European citizens deem that no action is needed because a balance is not needed, while 15% do not know what action should be taken. Some 31% percent have a preference for self-regulation, 26% for binding legal measures and 20% for voluntary measures such as non-binding Corporate Governance Codes and Charters.6 Such variation is in fact also visible in the national legal and regulatory systems of the Union's Member States, reflecting the non-alignment or disagreement as to the ways in which this problem should be dealt with (if at all) and by whom; by companies themselves, by the public regulator or jointly. But clearly, the introduction in Norway in 2006 of a hard law quota regime for bringing about gender balance in the boardroom has triggered the debate in quite a number of EU Member States and has led to important legislative changes in some of them. On the EU level as well, the European Commission has been shifting its soft law approach to a hard law approach, by putting forward a proposal for a directive on this topic in 2012,7 leading to a – still ongoing – vibrant and heated discussion.

In this article the variation in regulatory and enforcement regimes, strategies and styles will be charted that have

Citation: Linda Senden, The Multiplicity of Regulatory Responses to Remedy the Gender Imbalance on Company Boards, DOI: http://doi.org/10.18352/ulr.300.

developed throughout Europe with a view to tackling the problem of the under-representation of women on company boards and to bring about actual change. Specifically, this comparative analysis seeks to offer insights into the following issues: how do public and private regulators and regulation interact with each other in this regard or what kind of co-regulation and/or co-enforcement regimes can one identify; what are relevant factors or principles that determine the chosen strategy and types of instruments; what are important conditions or factors for ensuring that the chosen instruments will be effective in the light of the goal to be achieved; what lessons can one draw when it comes to the (non-) effectiveness of the privatization of both regulation and enforcement in this area, also for policymakers? Can one single out certain factors for determining the optimal mix of regulation and enforcement arrangements for realizing the goal of a more balanced gender representation? With a view to this, the article proceeds as follows. First, the multitude of regulatory responses will be presented, thus depicting the variety of possible approaches to addressing one and the same problem (Section 2). In the following section, the reasons that may explain this multitude of approaches will be discussed (Section 3) and next their (potential) effectiveness will be compared and a linkage will be made in this respect with the monitoring, enforcement and sanctioning mechanisms that have been put into place, relying on already available studies (Section 4). We will end the contribution with some conclusions and by identifying lessons that can be learned from the analysis (Section 5).

THE MULTITUDE OF REGULATORY RESPONSES

Regulatory approaches to remedying the gender imbalance on company boards vary widely throughout the European Union (and beyond), ranging from no regulatory action whatsoever in still quite a number of Member States to hard quota legislation in others and softer – both public and private – regimes somewhere in between these two extremes. These regimes come in quite different forms as will be seen. Furthermore, it must also be noted that in some Member States self- or co-regulatory approaches and public law approaches may be both put into place, as a result of in particular the distinction that is being made between private companies and state-owned companies.

No Specific Regulatory Action

National law may allow for positive action measures, but specific measures for promoting women on company boards may not have been (so far) adopted. This holds true for many of the more recently acceded countries to the EU, where the legislator has not put any provisions or preference measures of any kind, including quota rules, into place with a view to promoting the number of women on company boards. This is the case for Bulgaria, Croatia, the Czech republic, Cyprus, Latvia, Lithuania, Malta and Slovakia. But also in some of the older Member States, such as Luxembourg and Portugal, no such measures have been taken either. In such countries, one can thus merely rely on the general gender equality law provisions. In some countries, like Estonia, the law limits itself to some general, declaratory provisions setting out the objective to promote the gender balance in personnel policy in both the public and private sector, but without as such imposing a legally binding obligation.8 Croatian law only imposes a duty on private companies to respect the prohibition of sex discrimination and it is questionable to what extent it even allows such companies to autonomously adopt measures involving sex-related preferences or quotas, as the Croatian Sex Equality Act requires positive action measures to be first defined by statutory law. State-controlled companies are also not subject to a requirement to adopt any positive action measures of any kind, but must produce periodical equality action plans.9

Self-Regulation

In some countries, business organizations have taken initiatives for promoting gender diversity in boardrooms. In the absence of binding public regulation, as is not only the case in the aforementioned countries but also for instance in Poland, Sweden and the United Kingdom, such initiatives are the closest thing to persuading corporations to pay some attention to the issue of women in the boardroom. Most often, this occurs through rules or recommendations included in corporate governance codes. However, the norms that these codes contain regarding gender diversity are usually phrased quite openly, without any hard rules or standards being imposed. This holds true for the British Corporate Governance Code, but also the Polish Code of Best Practice for WSE Listed Companies issued by the Warsaw Stock Exchange provides an example of this, recommending that shareholders and companies should ensure 'a balanced proportion of women and men' in management and supervisory positions, without elucidating what 'balanced' exactly means. It also requires companies to give information on an annual basis about the participation of women and men on the Management Board and on the Supervisory Board of the company in the last two years.10 Only since 2012 do these recommendations fall under the 'comply or explain' mechanism.11

Besides these corporate governance codes, which mostly only apply to stock listed companies, companies may also adopt other, more individually customized measures. These concern certificate and pledge programmes, and mentoring and education programmes. The Dutch 'Talent to the Top' programme is an example of this, providing a platform where companies can make a public pledge in which they commit themselves to promoting gender diversity. This is very much voluntary and its focus is on stimulating companies to work on an effective gender diversity policy. To date, 239 Dutch corporations have made this pledge.12 There is no sanction in this system other than the fact that companies are put on the initiative's website with their pledge, and thus can be held accountable for it by the public. An example of a large-scale mentorship programme is the United Kingdom FTSE 100 Cross-Company Mentoring Executive Programme, which is executed by the Mentoring Foundation. This Foundation offers mentoring and related services to high-potential women within the 100 highestvalue stock companies on the London Stock Exchange. The programme brings together these women and Chief Executives and Chairmen in order to help women progress and also to teach those Chairmen and Chief Executives about women leadership. Since 2003, 136 mentoring pairs have been established.13 Besides this, the United Kingdom also has the 30 percent club, which is a private initiative taken by investors to achieve 30% women on FTSE 100 boards by 2015. This group does not support mandatory quotas, and refers on its website to the experience in Norway where still only 3% of CEOs are female according to statistics on their website, in spite of the quota for board members there, thus arguing that the 'trickle down' effect of mandatory measures is virtually non-existent.14 In Hungary, some large private companies have introduced equality plans as part of their corporate policy, one of which also includes goals for female board membership; in 2011 Hungarian Telecom (under the German Telecom plan) adopted the goal of increasing the number of women in board positions to 30% by 2015.15

Conditioned Self-Regulation or Co-Regulation

In a number of countries, it has not been fully left to industry how to deal with the problem of female under-representation on company boards in their corporate governance codes or otherwise, but the legislator or public regulator has set certain goals, norms or conditions for this. This is the case for instance in Germany, where in 2001 the Federal Government and the principal business associations concluded an agreement to promote the equality of women and men in the private sector, including the increase of women in decision-making positions. If successfully implemented, the Federal Government has promised not to introduce gender equality legislation unless it is obliged to do so under EU law.16 This led inter alia to the introduction of a gender diversity provision in the German Corporate Governance Code, established by a semi-public committee, reading as follows: 'When filling managerial positions in the enterprise the Management Board shall take diversity into consideration and, in particular, aim for an appropriate consideration of women.'17 A similar provision applies to supervisory boards. But here again, one must note that nowhere in the Code is it explained what 'appropriate' entails or how the company should prove that it has complied with this rule. According to the original German wording (soll), this rule is not even binding. Perhaps not so surprisingly then, no significant changes came about until in 2011 most of the German stock listed companies (the DAX 30) set concrete targets, ranging from 20% to 30%.18 In the subsequent three years this has led to an increase of 11% to about 22% female representation on the boards of these companies. There is also a legal 'comply-or-explain' duty contained in the German Stock Corporation Act (Section 161) which requires companies to report on the implementation of the Code's standards in their annual reports.19 In fact, most corporate governance codes rely on the 'complyor-explain' mechanism, in which the explanation for a deviation from the code should be accounted for in the company's annual report. The listing rules of the country where the code applies thus normally serve as its backbone, and reporting duties thus can often be traced back to public law statutes, such as the Civil Code.20

While the issue of quotas was discussed at a political level pursuant to their introduction in Norway in 2006 (see Section 2.5 below), Finland – aligning itself more with the Swedish approach – opted in 2008 for a self-regulatory approach through the Corporate Governance Code to be implemented in 2010. The Code provides that 'both genders shall be represented on the board', as such not necessarily recommending an equal distribution of board seats among the sexes. The Swedish Code on Corporate Governance applies to both listed private and public limited-liability companies and contains a – voluntary – rule that 'the company is to strive for equal gender distribution on the board', but there is also an obligation to justify the final proposal on the board's composition. The Swedish Corporate Governance Board monitors compliance with the Code and there is a legal duty to provide an audit report, including on the Code. As regards state-owned companies there are also the 'general owner policies', which have long aspired to gender equal boards, meaning there should be 40% of each sex.

Co-regulatory regimes may also take other forms, such as the Charter for more women in the management of companies which the Danish Minister for Gender Equality launched in 2008. The Charter was drawn up jointly with public and private sector companies and applies to both types of companies.

Companies that sign the Charter undertake to prepare a plan or strategy to attract more women into management positions and to set goals and/or target figures for the proportion of women at selected executive levels to be achieved within a fixed period of time. In 2011, 109 companies/authorities had signed the Charter, of which only 16 were private ones but they include Denmark's largest companies. The Charter takes account of corporate diversity and does not seek to impose a 'one size fits all' model but rather the identification and sharing of good and best practices.21 Participating companies are under a duty to report on the actions they have taken.

Soft Public Law and Target Regimes

The extent to which obligations have been imposed by way of public law to bring about a gender balance on company boards varies considerably in terms of scope and precision and thereby in terms of the discretion they leave to companies. Some of these public law regimes may in fact be very soft. The Hungarian Equality Act thus merely imposes a duty to adopt an equal opportunity plan, and this only for public employers. A failure to adopt such a plan is subject to a fine by the Equal Treatment Authority, but there is no scrutiny of its content and, generally speaking, such plans only contain soft provisions not conferring any rights on employees. In Portugal, the Fourth National Plan for Gender Equality covering 2011-2013 also aims to implement equality plans for companies in the public sector. In Ireland, some collaborative schemes have been designed for the implementation of positive action measures, such as the National Women's Strategy that seeks to increase the number of women on company boards by maintaining a database for competent women and by providing training.22 Under Finnish law as well, an obligation was introduced in 2005 for both public and private companies with at least 30 employees to produce an annual gender equality plan, which entails a relatively detailed planning obligation of measures and follow-up actions to promote gender equality. Yet, the means to be used are left to the employers themselves. Upon the proposal of the Ombudsman for Equality, the Equality Board may impose a fine upon an employer failing in its equality planning duty within a certain deadline,23 but the Parliamentary Committee has also noted that the Equality Ombudsman Office should have more resources to monitor equality planning and that there may be a need to reinforce the equality planning duty by imposing more precise, mandatory provisions.24 Denmark has recently hardened its approach somewhat, moving beyond the general provision in its Gender

Equality Act that merely stipulated that boards of state-owned companies 'should have an equal gender balance'. By two laws of December 2012 the Gender Equality Act and the Companies Act were thus modified so as to include an obligation for both private and public enterprises (which covers the 1,100 largest Danish companies) to set concrete – realistic and ambitious – targets for enhancing the number of the under-represented sex on the companies' main governing body and to develop a recruitment policy with a view to their realization. It also entails a comply-or-explain approach, forcing companies to state in their annual reports how they have implemented this policy and, where appropriate, to explain why the objective was not realized. If it fails to report on this, a fine may be imposed.25 There are also initiatives by public authorities that seek to set some concrete quantitative targets, yet they are (very) soft in terms of their legally binding nature and the sanctioning in case of nonachievement and non-compliance. An example is the European Commission launching in March 2011 a voluntary pledge for companies to achieve 30% female representation on company boards by 2015 and 40% by 2020. However, this programme failed, as only 24 companies had signed the pledge a year after its announcement.26 This has incited the Commission to come up with a proposal for a directive on the issue. Spain provides another example, introducing a law in 2007 that recommends that big companies ensure a representation of at least 40% of each gender on company boards before 2015.27 However, there are no sanctions attached to this rule, only a duty for companies to state the gender composition of their board of directors in their annual reports.28 Yet, the Government may take the performance of companies concerning this requirement into account in the issuing of the equality label and when deciding on public subsidies and state administration contracts.29 The Netherlands initiated a similar measure a year earlier, when it amended its Civil Code in such a way that it now obliges privately and publicly-held limited companies and private limited companies to strive for a 30% representation of each sex on their boards.30 This rule only applies to large corporations and companies which fulfil two of the following criteria will be exempted from it: the value of their assets is no more than EUR 17,500, their net annual turnover is no more than EUR 35,000 and they do not have more than an annual average of 250 employees. If a company does not achieve the balanced representation of at least 30% of each sex, it has to explain this in its annual report and what methods it has used to achieve a balanced representation and how it will achieve this goal in the future.31 However, no sanctions for not following the norm are laid down. Moreover, the measure is only temporary and will expire on 1 January 2016 regardless of the results achieved.32 In Ireland, the Labour Coalition Government set an aspirational target in 2011 of 40% of each gender for all state boards. Yet, this target does not have any legal standing and does not appear even to extend to state-owned commercial companies. The only specific legislative provision that can be found is the one in the Irish Broadcasting Act 2009, which requires public service broadcasting corporations to have a 12-person board comprising at least 5 men and 5 women.33

Some states have framed the target in a more open way, such as is the case for state-owned companies in Finland; according to the Finnish Equality Act (in Section 4a(2)) their boards must be comprised of 'an equitable proportion of both women and men, unless there are special reasons to the contrary'. 'Whenever possible', both a woman and a man should be proposed for every membership position.34 The Equality programmes of 2004-2007 and 2008-2011 crystalized this even further, setting a target for state-owned companies to realize 40% women on boards, thereby raising the target that had been set in the 1990s at 30%.35 Nominations that have been made in contravention of the Act on Equality may be overturned by the administrative courts. In Sweden, a proposal was put forward in 2006 to introduce in the Companies Act a 40% quota rule for each sex on the boards of state-owned public and private limited-liability companies, providing for a fine of EUR 15,000 in the case of non-compliance.36 Yet, this proposal was never adopted, but debates on the necessity of legislation in this area still emerge (see Section 4).

Hard Public Law and Quota Regimes

In other countries, governments have moved towards more stringent approaches and have established mandatory quota regimes, yet these regimes may not apply to public and private companies in the same way. The first country in Europe to introduce such a quota was Norway in 2006, and requires a representation of 40% of both genders on company boards, but only of public limited companies, intermunicipal companies and state-owned companies.37 The regime is (very) strict concerning compliance and enforcement: existing companies not complying with the rule may be liquidated after a court ruling on the matter.38 In order for this court ruling to follow, a company must have failed to notify the Registrar of Business Enterprises that it complies with the quota requirement. The company then receives up to two warnings, after which the company can be dissolved. Companies registering as a public limited company may be denied registration by the Registrar of Business Enterprises if they do not comply with the quota law.39 Interestingly, this law would not have become mandatory if all companies would have complied with it before July 2005. However, when it appeared that most companies had not complied with the rule by this time, the Norwegian Government gave companies another two years (from 2006 onwards) to comply, after which the sanctions stated above would follow. Companies registering from 2006 onwards had to comply with the quota immediately.40 The law was extended in order to apply to cooperative companies with more than 1,000 members in 2008 and to private limited companies where municipalities own two-thirds or more of the shares in 2010, both with a two-year transition period. Overall, compliance with this mandatory quota has been good, with almost all companies complying within the two-year transition period.41

Other countries in Europe have followed suit, most notably France, Belgium and Italy. In France, a quota law passed in 2011, which states that listed companies or non-listed companies (with revenues or total assets of over EUR 50 million or employing at least 500 persons for the last three years) should have a proportion of men or women that is at least 40%.42 The law, which applies to both private and stateowned companies, specifies that companies have six years from the implementation of the law onwards to reach this quota, although companies trading on a regulated market are obliged to reach a target of 20% by the end of three years after the implementation of the law. Moreover, companies with no female board members should fill any seat which becomes available within three years after the implementation of the law with a female candidate. The sanction for not complying with this law is the nullity of the appointment of any director which does not comply with the quota requirement.43

In Belgium, mandatory quota rules were established by the Law of 28 July 2011, after a fierce and intense political debate. As regards certain economic public undertakings,44 this law requires that 'at least a third of the members of the board of directors appointed by the Belgian State or by a company controlled by the Belgian State shall be of a different gender from the other members'.45 A similar provision has been inserted in the Code of Company Law for listed companies.46 In the case of noncompliance and the number of directors of a different gender does not meet the minimum laid down, the next director appointed shall belong to this gender failing which the appointment shall be invalid. For ensuring compliance with the one-third quota provision by listed companies, the Law provides for yet an additional rule stipulating that 'the next general meeting after the entry into force of this provision must form a board of directors complying with the quota of at least one-third, failing which all the benefits [financial or otherwise – LS] of the members of the board of directors of the company concerned, in connection with the performance of their mandate, will be suspended'.47 A transitional period during which the target should be realized has been allowed for both existing and newly established listed companies.

The Italian Act No. 120/2011 modified the Merchant Banking Code so as to provide for the obligation that company statutes must ensure that directors and auditors of one sex cannot be elected in a proportion greater than two-thirds compared to directors and auditors of the opposite sex. This rule is to be enforced for three periods of tenure for directors and auditors and this 33% rule must be ensured by 2015.48 The obligation applies to the appointment of managing directors and auditors of both listed companies and state subsidiaries.49 The Consob (the National Securities and Exchange Commission) has been made responsible for monitoring compliance and can issue a warning that the quota system must be applied within four months and, in the case of non-compliance, impose a fine of EUR 100,000 up to EUR 1 million (EUR 20,000 up to EUR 200,000 for auditors), together with a second warning that the quota must be achieved within three months. In the case of a failure to do so, this may result in the dissolution of the company board.50

Greek law also contains a binding quota rule, where it specifies that if the state or legal persons governed by public law appoint or designate members of boards of legal persons governed by public or private law, 'the number of members thus appointed or designated shall consist of at least one third of persons of each sex, provided that the appointees are more than one'.51 Decisions which contravene this rule are liable to annulment by the competent administrative court. In Slovenia, the Government adopted in 2004 the Regulation on criteria for respecting the principle of gender-balanced representation which provides that nominations or appointments of government representatives in public enterprises, including supervisory and executive boards, must comprise at least 40% of either sex.52

EXPLAINING THE – DIVERSITY OF – APPROACHES

The above analysis reveals a huge diversity in many aspects of the regulatory and enforcement approaches that have been and are still very much at the development stage in this area. Besides the differences in terms of the public and/or private nature and voluntary or binding nature of the regimes established, there is considerable variation as to the size and type of companies actually covered by them (private, listed and/or state companies); their duration (temporary or permanent); the level of ambition and targets that are actually being set; the time-limits for realising these targets; their implementation and monitoring mechanisms; and the – harshness of the – means and sanctions to punish non-compliance. The issue that then needs to be addressed in view of this is what factors can possibly explain this diversity in approaches and the choice for a particular course of action. In particular, how do the different approaches link with the various normative justifications for a – more – balanced representation of women and men on company boards and what other factors are at play in the establishment of the different regulatory and enforcement regimes?

As mentioned briefly in the introduction, three main normative justifications can be identified for taking regulatory action to tackle the gender imbalance on company boards. The economic, business case argument underscores the business need for (more) gender-balanced boards, submitting that this will lead to improved performance by companies53 and to an enhanced quality of decision-making, that it will entail an improved quality of corporate governance and ethics, a better utilization of the talent pool, be a driving force for innovation and will also better mirror the market as women take most decisions on household spending.54 The absence of women at the top of corporations also does not square well with companies seeking to show that they are taking their social responsibility seriously and that they engage in modern stakeholder management.55 The individual, equal opportunities justification relies on the argument that addressing the power imbalance between women and men on company boards is simply a matter of individual fairness; women, who have equal qualifications, should have the same opportunities as men to be part of bodies – even if they are private bodies – that yield economic power and that affect the economic, financial and social life of all citizens. The societal, public interest and fundamental rights argument underscores the importance of a balanced representation from the more general perspective of ensuring social justice and democratic legitimacy, which are part of the core values underlying the EU as a political and economic system and which in legal terms translates into the principle of equality and of equal opportunities.56

A first observation in this regard is that in a number of Member States where no – specific – regulatory action whatsoever has been taken, the problem is apparently not (yet) considered to be sufficiently important to be at all tackled. Clearly, in those countries none of the identified normative justifications is seen as a sufficient or convincing driver – not in itself, nor in conjunction – to take any action, not by the public regulator or by industry. In these countries, there may be a mere reliance on the operationalization or enforcement of the general principle of equality and of equal opportunities and there is no movement (as yet) towards the development of a more proactive approach to overcome persisting inequalities in this domain.57 Where specific action has been taken or is being considered, the above normative justifications play varying roles. Self-regulatory approaches may be induced first and foremost by the business case rationale and developed in particular as part of corporate social responsibility policy, as reflected in corporate governance codes. This is quite explicit, for example, in the recommendation of the Polish Warsaw Stock Exchange Management Board which links the balanced participation of men and women to the strengthening of the creativeness and innovativeness of companies' economic activities. The Swedish Corporate Governance Board has pointed to the necessity for companies to behave in a responsible and sustainable way, which is said to include gender equality, with a view to earning the trust of the general public. But it has also noted the increasing emphasis that shareholders are putting on gender equality.58 The other two rationales appear more prominently in the discussion on and the establishment of hard quota rules. The Norwegian quota model thus finds its primary justification not in the business case rationale, but in the argument that 'reaching balanced participation is a question of democracy' and 'the Government regards the legislation on women in boards as an important step towards equality between the sexes, a fairer society and a more even distribution of power, and as an important factor in the creation of wealth in society'.59 But interestingly, it is actually through amendments to company law that the quota rules were imposed and not through equality law.

Also in a number of other Member States, politicians have started to give more weight to equal opportunities, individual fairness and social justice considerations, as a result of which political pressure and support has accrued for more stringent, legally binding measures because of insufficient progress. In some states this has led to the establishment of either soft targets or hard quota rules. Such developments may have come about only after intense and polarised debates, as the Belgian case illustrates. In Belgium there has thus been fundamental political disagreement on the hard quota law that was proposed. Whilst there was a certain acceptance that the Government could impose such a quota on state companies, it was fiercely contested by some political parties as regards private sector companies. They were proponents of a more liberal view of society and that this matter should be dealt with through corporate policy and by voluntary means, following the recommendations of the Code of Corporate Governance.60 The battle was won by those who were of the opinion that such a hard legislative approach is justified because progress has so far been much too slow, that voluntary approaches have not proven to be sufficiently effective and that companies have an important societal responsibility in this matter not only as regards their shareholders but also other stakeholders; more women on boards allows for a broader representation of the views and interests of all stakeholders which will lead to more optimal decision-making.61

In other countries, like Denmark, one witnesses different, 'softer' or more intermediate outcomes of such political and societal discussions and the political rejection of mandatory quota rules, yet supporting the introduction of soft targets and a comply-or-explain approach. More generally, co-regulatory regimes or conditioned self-regulation, as contained in certain corporate governance codes and charters, reflect a certain degree of awareness and a sense of urgency on the part of the Government to put pressure on the private sector to enhance individual fairness and social justice in this regard, while still leaving it very much to industry itself as to how to actually deal with the problem. The Swedish approach fits in with this; the Swedish Government's gender equality policy aims to 'ensure [that] power and resources are distributed fairly between the sexes, and to create the conditions that give women and men the same power and opportunities'. Its soft approach regarding a balanced representation of women and men on company boards is clearly also grounded on these rationales. While Swedish business, as represented by the Swedish Corporate Governance Board, is supportive of this goal as well from the perspective of enhancing gender equality and corporate social responsibility, it is very much opposed to a legislative quota or a quota rule in the corporate governance code because of the restriction on proprietary rights that this is considered to entail. It also deems that such a general rule would disregard legitimate differences that may exist between companies.62

At a more fundamental level, other factors can and must be identified that have a certain bearing on the regulatory and enforcement choices made and which can also explain cross-country divergences to a certain extent. These relate in the first place to the type of political and welfare system prevailing in a Member State and to cultural differences. The different political, socio-economic and cultural context within which companies and employees operate not only has consequences for the scope of the problem of under-representation as such, but also for the type of regulatory solutions and instruments that are resorted to for resolving it. Thus, a higher level of the masculinity of society is considered to have a negative impact on the participation of women on boards.63 Furthermore, one can see a correlation in a country like the UK, typified as a liberal welfare system,64 and the self-regulatory approach which still prevails there. The top-down imposition by public law of hard quota rules does not square well with such a system, as it sees the encouragement of the market as the major role of the state and hence such rules as being too restrictive on business freedom. Yet, self-regulatory action is deemed to fit in with the development of a corporate social responsibility policy. Only if self-regulation will not produce the expected results may a hard law approach be considered. So, self-regulation is opted for under the 'threat' of public regulation or it operates in the shadow of the law.

By contrast, social-democrat countries strive for the highest welfare standards for everybody and the Government may interfere in the market and introduce binding regulations with a view to realising this. The Nordic countries fit within this category, but while there are significant similarities between the social, political and economic structure of these countries65 and they all strive for the establishment of an egalitarian society, Sweden, Denmark and Finland have devised a mixed and soft public law approach whereas Norway has developed a very hard law quota approach. In the literature, the difference between the Swedish and Norwegian approach has been related to two main reasons,66 the first being the varieties of capitalism being in place even within the Scandinavian model. In Norway, the capacity of the state to interfere in business life has thus been considered larger because the state was a dominant capitalist itself when compared to Sweden, where a strong and traditionally socially responsible business life enjoyed more autonomy than its Norwegian counterpart. It has thus been argued that it has been more difficult for the Swedish Government to interfere in business life. As the Swedish Corporate Governance Board itself put it, self-regulation is a model that has served Sweden well for decades and introducing 'legislation on the composition of company boards would be a dangerous departure from the Swedish model'.67 Secondly, it has been related to different cultures concerning gender equality and the attitudes towards state intervention. In Norway, there was already an established gender quota tradition since 1981 and also rather positive attitudes towards state intervention. This has been said to lead to a different discursive climate in gender equality matters, which was quite positive in Norway in accepting women as a group being different from men as a group and rather hostile in Sweden. Swedish feminists have been found to be more active and conflict-oriented, thereby creating a polarized gender equality discussion.68 Moreover, it has been found that the previous resistance among business leaders in Norway to appoint women to their boards has now disappeared as a result of the quota law and that it is 'back to business as usual'.69

In countries that are usually typified as conservative-corporatist welfare regimes, like France, Germany and Italy, governments interfere more readily with market mechanisms and introduce social policies as the state is considered to have a redistributive role as well.70 When it comes to the Central Eastern European (CEE) countries, so far these are quite difficult to classify because of their still rather recent transition from a communist to a capitalist system, yet it is clear that they cannot be fitted into a homogenous or unitary 'post-communist' welfare model, given the great welfare diversity in these countries.71 But interestingly, in recent research the Slovenian welfare regime has been typified as a social corporatist regime that comes close to that of Western countries and even as a 'Scandinavian island' in the CEE.72 This may explain why in Slovenia, and not in any other CEE country, some kind of quota rule for a balanced representation on company boards has been established (see Section 3). While the above differences are clearly relevant aspects to take into account, it must also be acknowledged that there is still an ongoing academic debate as to how significant the link is between the wider social, political and economic context and the level of women's representation on corporate boards.73 Terjesen and Singh have thus argued, based on a 43-country study, that there is a strong link and that higher levels of women on corporate boards correlate with higher levels of women in management jobs and with lower levels of gender inequalities in pay.74 Yet, other studies come to less positive conclusions. Storvik and Teigen thus found that while the proportion of women on corporate boards has risen, this has not been the case for the number of female chairpersons of boards or of women in other top management positions (see also Section 4).75

Another factor which the diversity of approaches can to some extent be related to concerns the different regulatory and legal systems and traditions of the Member States. It has thus become clear that in some Member States there is less legal – constitutional – room for the establishment of quota rules, even through self-regulation. It has thus appeared that in some countries positive action may only come about after rather stringent legal procedures or positive action are simply not part of the legal and political tradition and have therefore never been applied. In other countries, legislative and even constitutional checks and changes – such as has been the case in France – may be required before any quota rules may be adopted. In Germany, the debate on the possible introduction of quota rules by legislation is also being blighted by doubts as to the constitutionality thereof. In particular, it is doubtful whether such rules would be in conformity with the way in which the freedom of property, the freedom of association and the principle of equality are understood under the German Constitution.76 In Finland, the currently applicable constitutional provision would only allow for a soft quota system.77 It has also been seen that in Norway the introduction of such rules was less controversial (at least when compared to other Member States) given that quota rules were not alien to the existing legal system and were already practised in other areas, so their constitutionality was beyond doubt.

More generally and as an extension to the above observations, the preference – and pressure – from both political parties and business to stick to soft private or public regimes rather than introducing (binding) quota rules is clearly also induced by a different balancing of two conflicting fundamental, human rights; equality versus ownership and corporate freedom, which is seen as a cornerstone of the market economy. Not only in Sweden, but also in other states the balance is tilted towards the latter, relying on arguments such as that quota rules ignore the functioning logic of the business environment; that there is more need to deregulate than to regulate business in the light of global competition; that a labour law view cannot be applied to a corporate structure that is determined by ownership; that quota rules should only be used when the business sector has shown an unwillingness to change; and that the effectiveness of a binding target figure is not demonstrated. Such arguments have clearly come to the fore in the debates on the European Commission's proposal for a directive.78 At the same time, the non- or too limited effectiveness of voluntary commitments appears to be a strong trigger for the debate on and louder calls for quota rules, either soft or hard, and thus to slowly tilt the balance in the other direction. This can be seen, for instance, in Germany.79 This brings us to the question as to how the different regulatory and enforcement regimes compare in terms of effectiveness.

COMPARING THEIR EFFECTIVENESS

How are effectiveness and regulatory approaches, including their implementation, monitoring and sanctioning mechanisms, related to one another? This assessment will depend on what one sees as the ultimate goal to be achieved: equality in terms of outcome or rather the creation of equal opportunities? The former takes the main policy goal to be to ensure a balanced representation of women and men on company boards and the actual result is then what counts. By considering the current figures and the speed of change in relation to the regimes that were developed at a certain point in time in a number of countries, one can then assess whether such regimes have been effective or not. An equal opportunities approach is more oriented towards offering the same possibilities to have access to a corporate board function for both men and women and is less focused on the realization of a specific outcome. One can say that the hard quota law regimes are more top-down outcome-oriented and that self-regulatory and co-regulatory approaches are more bottom-up opportunities-oriented. From the perspective of realizing equality of outcome, the hardest regulatory and enforcement regimes, with the most stringent and binding targets or quotas, indeed appear to be the most effective ones. A recent report that was produced at the request of the European Parliament and that reviewed the evidence on the effectiveness of legal instruments as compared with voluntary regimes, thus concluded that 'legal instruments to enforce quotas are an effective and fast means of achieving change.80 The use of voluntary regimes has led to some increase in the proportion of women on corporate boards, but the effects are significantly smaller and slower. The only instance of achieving 40% of each gender was through the use of legal instruments to enforce quotas.'81 The authors also underscore the variation in the legal mechanisms for the implementation of quotas and that 'it may be that these make considerable difference to the effectiveness of the law.' The fact that in Norway the quota rules were introduced in company law rather than equality law has thus enabled the imposition of the very strong sanction of the dissolution of non-compliant companies. If sanctions are limited to the imposition of a fine, the issuance of warnings or, even less, the willingness to comply could be very different.82 Furthermore, as an extension to what has already been observed in Section 3, whether a certain regulatory and enforcement approach will be successful will also depend on the extent to which this approach fits in with already existing (legal) culture; or, what works well in one state will not necessarily be effective in another. The Norwegian case also illustrates this; the quota approach was already well engrained and the hard sanction for its non-realization – warnings, fines, the delisting of a company from the Stock Exchange in case of persistent non-compliance – as such was met with (relatively) limited resistance, while precisely the sanctioning mechanism led to quite some opposition or even hostile positions concerning quota regimes in other countries.

Other studies have also come to the conclusion that in Norway quick and true progress was only achieved after the implementation of a quota law coupled with strong sanctions, while the preceding voluntary initiatives were deemed not to bring about much progress.83 Yet, the Norwegian success has not only been related to the – harshness of the – quota regime, but also to voluntary measures that were coupled with it, especially professional training programmes for qualified female candidates and stakeholder cooperation with a view to creating support systems. The availability of female role models has also been identified as a relevant factor.84 Such an approach concurs with the views in the literature that a regulatory strategy relying on a mix of instruments will most often work better with a view to realizing specific policy goals and be more effective if it also includes a broader range of participants that are capable of implementing them.85 Soft and hard law measures may thus rather be seen as complementing each other than as alternatives to one another.86

Yet, it appears that countries that have adopted soft regimes have realised positive results as well, so factors other than a legal binding character and strict sanctions are at play and have a bearing on the outcome effectiveness of regulatory regimes. Noteworthy is thus the progress that has been realised in Finland, which shows a 10% increase in the female board membership of private companies in a fouryear period; from 12% in 2008 to 22% in 2012. This positive result has been explained by the underlying strategy being based on the following elements: the Government leading by example by setting the target at a minimum of 40% women on boards of state-owned companies and the realization of this figure; the establishment of a corporate governance code including the recommendation that both sexes should be represented on the board; conducting and publishing studies supporting the business case; but in particular also an active and positive role by the media, putting pressure on companies to make the necessary changes and to avoid negative publicity. So, it has been a combination of political pressure, intensive public debate and substantive argumentation that has contributed to making this progress and in lending credibility to the self-regulatory approach. Yet, the figures also reveal that the biggest companies have witnessed the highest increase and that the smallest companies have lagged behind. For bigger companies the cost of public reputation being affected or lost in the case of non-compliance is clearly higher than for smaller companies. It has been argued that the comply-or-explain principle as contained in the Corporate Governance Code 'works effectively in those cases where companies' public reputation in the eyes of the investors, shareholders and public is on line: consumer business gets easily damaged through the bad publicity, and the importance of the public image management goes for any large cap company.'87

However, it has also been established that progress is significantly less and slower in the case of sticking to soft, voluntary measures and that it may grind to a halt at some point in time. Soft law recommendations contained in Corporate Governance Codes have thus been found to have had some effect in Norway, Spain and Finland, but no major impact in others.88 The situation in Sweden and the UK would indeed seem to underscore such a finding, at least as regards listed private companies, as both countries have initially realised some progress following the adoption of a voluntary regime but are now no longer showing any significant improvements. In Sweden, one must also note a rather huge gap between state-owned and private listed companies; as a result of the 'general owner policies' concerning state-owned companies (see Section 2), the goal of 40% female representation on boards had already been realised in 2003 and as of 2008 it stood at 49%, compared to 19% in private companies.89 Since 2008, the overall figure has however halted at about 26%.

So, even if some countries have (initially) realized relatively high increases in the number of women on corporate boards with the mere establishment of soft, voluntary rules and with the state leading by example, it can be doubted whether the soft approach will be sufficient to realize the desired outcome.90 Very recently, the Swedish Corporate Governance Board itself explicitly acknowledged that 'the development towards equal gender distribution has proceeded too slowly, and that a number of nomination committees have not taken the requirement to report on their work regarding diversity and gender balance seriously'.91 Specific problems to be solved are 'the reluctance to work methodically with the issue and report properly on how it is being addressed'. It has thus considered it necessary to establish clearer principles, to tighten the regulation and to develop supporting activities. The regulatory requirements for nomination committees led by shareholders now include the obligation to analyse the board evaluation in a gender balance perspective, to explain and justify the candidates they propose for board positions in the light of the Corporate Governance Code's requirement to seek an equal gender distribution and to make it an agenda item for the shareholders' meeting to report on how they have worked to achieve an equal gender distribution on the board. Some[92] see these steps as an attempt to prevent the Swedish legislator from moving towards the adoption of quota rules as some politicians advocate.[93] On a more general note, the reluctance on the part of industry to truly address the problem may also have to do with the fact that there is no conclusive scientific evidence supporting the business case for more women on boards.[94] If the industry is not convinced of the need to bring about change from this perspective and does not commit itself to the goals of equal opportunities and social justice, this will work against the credibility and thereby the effectiveness of a self-regulatory approach.

In other cases self-regulatory codes contain (very) little promise as to the impact they can actually have and the contribution they can make to achieving the desired result, by not setting any specific or hard goals for companies to achieve and by not providing for any sanctions (besides giving an explanation) when companies deviate from the recommendation of a gender-balanced representation. In addition, as the Polish case illustrates, specific criteria as to how the explanation for deviant company policies should be published may be lacking and it is also unclear who is actually in charge of checking these explanations, as neither the Code nor the website of the Warsaw Stock Exchange point to any supervisory authority. Statistics on compliance with codes are also difficult to find. Clearly, besides the substantive vagueness of the target itself, the implementation, monitoring and enforcement mechanisms provided – or rather the lack thereof – may thus be important reasons why there is no significant progress in certain states. But it must also be noted that the application and monitoring of Corporate Governance Codes has been found to be generally problematic.[95] In particular, it has been concluded that while the comply-orexplain approach which the European Commission formally adopted in 2006 enjoys wide acceptance by the corporate community, its practical implementation still suffers from certain deficiencies, mainly as regards the level and quality of information on deviations by companies, which is deemed unsatisfactory. Furthermore, there is also a low level of shareholder monitoring.[96]

The above should not lead one to conclude that the voluntary, self-regulatory approaches and measures are devoid of any relevance; they can make important contributions to raising awareness among the public, employees and company management of the need to change organizational practices and also to consensus-building on further measures that are needed to address power imbalances between men and women at the level of company boards.[97] Furthermore, relevant factors for ensuring that initiatives bring about (cultural) change in a company's organizational structure and in promoting company acceptance thereof have been found to be flexibility (such as sensitivity to company size); professionalism in the organisation of the initiatives; a positive framing thereof rather than in terms of punishment; clear monitoring and evaluation criteria; publicity; and binding commitments with the engagement of management.[98]

On a final note, so far it has not been possible to establish that the imposition of the quota system in Norway has led to an increase in other, lower, middle and top management positions.[99] As Armstrong and Walby conclude, the increase in the number of women on corporate boards has thus not been part of a general change in the position of women in senior management.[100] In that sense, the expected 'trickle down' effect of the quota regime has not materialized and one could thus maintain that while it has proven effective in terms of realizing the desired numerical outcome, it has apparently not contributed significantly in enhancing equal opportunities for women in management positions more generally. To bring about such a change, it can be said to be essential for both self- and co-regulatory approaches and command-and-control approaches to be coupled with the further development of supporting measures and corporate best practices for enhancing gender diversity in management positions. Best practices that have been deemed most important in this regard relate to the creation of transparency by implementing gender diversity key performance indicators; the adoption and implementation of measures that facilitate the work-life balance; the adaptation of the human resources process so as to make sure that this does not work against women's career advancement; and to help women in mastering dominant company codes and to nurture their ambition through network-building and mentoring.[101]

CONCLUSIONS AND LESSONS

The EU Member States show a huge variety in regulatory, monitoring and enforcement regimes and strategies when it comes to addressing the problem of the power imbalance that persists between men and women in economic decision-making, specifically as this manifests itself in women's under-representation on company boards. What emerges in particular from the analysis is that in an increasing number of states self- and co-regulatory regimes have proven to be stepping-stones for the establishment or consideration of command-and-control approaches in the form of hard law quota regimes, an important reason for this being the insufficient level of progress the former manage to bring about. Norway has played a trendsetting role in this regard, but the quota approaches in other countries have been tailor-made when it comes to their level of bindingness and compliance and enforcement mechanisms. Yet, what these states have in common is that they have all recognized the need to move beyond the mere establishment of the formal right to equal treatment and equal opportunities and beyond the mere reliance on industry, with a view to overcoming persisting gender inequalities in the boardroom. Hence, they have introduced proactive legislation.[102] In doing so, these states have given more weight to considerations of individual fairness and social justice – and thus that women should have an equal share in the exercise not only of political but also of economic power and decision-making – than to business and shareholders' freedom, especially where these quota rules also apply to private companies. The shareholders' interest in economic profit making, efficiency and value creation[103] has as such been offset or balanced with another important societal interest and fundamental right. In other states, this balancing act has been seen to lead to different outcomes that are more to the benefit of corporate freedom. This national diversity and different balancing of the interests and fundamental rights involved also explains the different levels of support for the Commission's proposal for a directive on promoting gender balance on corporate boards and the difficulties there are in reaching a political agreement thereon. There are also some important lessons that can be drawn from the analysis. First of all, it has appeared that for any regulatory and enforcement approach to be successful, it needs to fit in with – legal – culture and have broad societal, public and shareholder and stakeholder support. Yet, it has also appeared that culture is not a static phenomenon in this regard. More in particular, as a result of changing societal views over time, political and public pressure may accrue and lead to changes in – even constitutional – law so as to be able to move from a laissez-faire industry approach to a more forceful command-and-control approach to bring about the desired balanced representation. Secondly, as selfand co-regulatory approaches lack, almost by definition, strong enforcement mechanisms and sanctions for non-compliance, their credibility and effectiveness depends on other factors. These have been seen to include, in particular, intensive public debate, and thus a strong role for the media, as well as a strong role for the state and public companies, which are to lead by example. As such, these factors can be a strong incentive for bringing about the required corporate changes in attitude and a commitment to gender equality issues and therewith for the further development of CSR policies, also from the point of view of otherwise suffering from a loss of reputation. Finally, in view of the regulatory and enforcement developments as witnessed in an increasing number of states, self- and co-regulatory approaches may on the one hand be seen as insufficient steps to bring about the full equality strived after, but on the other hand as rather indispensable steps towards creating a basis of support for this policy goal and for the adoption of a more forceful legal approach by which to realize it. Self- and co-regulation can thus indeed be seen as important mechanisms for creating more industry, political and public awareness of the problem itself and for rethinking appropriate and effectives responses thereto. In the end, such responses often entail a mixed toolbox of instruments, the exact contents of which may however depend on context, time and place. ¶

NOTES:

1 It must be noted that figures may be considerably lower when including also non-listed companies.

2 See European Commission, Improving the gender balance in company boards, June 2014, , last visited 24 November 2014.

3 European Commission, Gender balance on corporate boards. Europe is cracking the glass ceiling, March 2014, , last visited 24 November 2014.

4 See the Special Eurobarometer 376 on Women in decision-making positions held in September 2011 in the EU, (last visited 24 November 2014) view, p. 11; almost 9 out of 10 respondents hold this view.

5 Cf. also the Special Eurobarometer, supra note 4, pp. 13-14.

6 Ibid., pp. 15-17.

7 COM(2012) 614 final.

8 Art. 11(1) of the Gender Equality Act, as represented by A. Albi & A. Laas, 'Estonia', in G. Selanec & L. Senden, Positive Action Measures to Ensure Full Equality in Practice between Men and Women, including on Company Boards, Publication of the European Network of Legal Experts in the Field of Gender Equality, 2013, p. 72, available at: , last visited 24 November 2014.

9 G. Selanec, 'Croatia', in Selanec & Senden 2013, supra note 8, pp. 54-55.

10 Warsaw Stock Exchange, Code of Best Practices for WSE Listed Companies, Art. 9, Art. 2 sub. a.

11 Provision No. 1 point 2a of Chapter II of Good Practices as amended by resolution No. 20/1287/2011 of 19 October 2011. See , last visited 24 November 2014.

12 See: (last visited 24 November 2014) and D.M. Branson, 'Initiatives to Place Women on Corporate Boards of Directors—A Global Snapshot', 2012 The Journal of Corporation Law 37, no. 4, p. 806.

13 See: , last visited 24 November 2014.

14 See: , last visited 24 November 2014.

15 C. Kollonay Lehoczky, 'Hungary', in Selanec & Senden 2013, supra note 8, p. 107.

16 B. Rudolf & U. Lembke, 'Germany', in Selanec & Senden 2013, supra note 8, pp. 91-92. See also more generally, B. Waas, 'Gender Quota in Company Boards: Germany', in M. de Vos & Ph. Culliford (eds.), Gender Quotas for Company Boards, 2014, p. 131.

17 German Corporate Governance Code, May 2013, Art. 4.1.5.

18 See Waas 2014, supra note 16, p. 132.

19 See on this also K. Langenbucher, Legal aspects of gender balance on corporate boards in Germany, Note for the European Parliament, March 2013, p. 30.

20 See for instance Art. 2:391(5) of the Dutch Civil Code. In an algemene maatregel van bestuur (order in council), the Dutch Corporate Governance Code has been indicated as the Code of Conduct to which Article 2:391 refers, and which is thus a required section of the annual report for listed companies.

21 R. Nielsen, 'Denmark', in Selanec & Senden 2013, supra note 8, pp. 65-66.

22 F. Meenan, 'Ireland', in Selanec & Senden 2013, supra note 8, p. 118.

23 Section 21(4) of the Act on Equality in conjunction with Section 6a, as represented by K. Nousiainen in Selanec & Senden 2013, supra note 8, pp. 77-80.

24 Ibid., p. 83.

25 Act. No. 1288 of 19 December 2012 amending the Gender Equality Act and Act No. 1383 of 23 December 2012 amending the Companies Act and certain other laws. Further on this, R. Nielsen, 'Denmark', 2013 European Gender Equality Law Review, no. 1, pp. 61-63.

26 European Commission Press Release, Women on Boards: Commission Proposes 40% Objective, 2012. See also <http://ec.europa.eu/commission_2010-2014/reding/multimedia/news/2012/03/20120305_en.htm>, last visited 26 November 2014.

27 Art. 75 of Law 3/2007.

28 Royal Legislative Decree 1/2010, of 2 July, on the Law on Capital Companies, states that the report that accompanies the annual accounts shall include information on the gender distribution of the staff of such a company, breaking down the categories and levels, which shall include top executives and board members.

29 B. Valdés de la Vega, 'Spain', in Selanec & Senden 2013, supra note 8, p. 207.

30 Staatsblad 2011, 275; Wet van 6 juni 2011 tot wijziging van boek 2 van het Burgerlijk Wetboek in verband met de aanpassing van regels over bestuur en toezicht in naamloze en besloten vennootschappen.

31 See Art. 2:391(7) Civil Code.

32 See Art. VII of the Law amending the Civil Code and more in detail C. Remery, The Dutch Solution: No Quota but Legal Targets, in De Vos & Culliford 2014, supra note 16, pp. 159-170.

33 F. Meenan, 'Ireland', in Selanec & Senden 2013, supra note 8, p. 116.

34 Sections 4a(2) and 3 of the Act on Equality, as represented in Selanec & Senden, supra note 8, p. 78.

35 A. Kovalainen & L. Hart, Role of self-regulation in listed companies recruitment of women into top positions in Finland, in De Vos & Culliford 2014, supra note 16, p. 112.

36 A. Numhauser-Henning, 'Sweden', in Selanec & Senden 2013, supra note 8, p. 218.

37 See the Norwegian Public Limited Liability Companies Act, in Section 6-11a.

38 Norwegian Public Limited Liability Companies Act, Section 16-15, Subsection 2.

39 Norwegian Register of Business Enterprises Act, Section 5-2.

40 The Ministry of Children, Equality and Social Inclusion, Press Release No. 05116: Rules regarding gender balance within boards of Public Limited Companies, 8 December 2005.

41 P. Hastings, Breaking the Glass Ceiling: Women in the Boardroom, 2013, third edition, p. 96.

42 Law 2011-103 of 27 January 2011, Journal Officiel, 28 January 2011.

43 See in more detail on the French law, B. Gresy, 'France: The Measures of Positive Discrimination within the Boards of Directors of Undertakings', in De Vos & Culliford 2014,supra note 16, pp. 123-130; and A. Masselot & A. Maymont, 'Balanced Representation between Men and Women in Business Law: The French 'Quota' System to the Test of EU Legislation', Centre for European Law and Legal Studies Online Paper Series (University of Leeds) Volume 3, 2014, issue 2, available at: , last visited 26 November 2014.

44 These include Belgacom, SNCB Holding Infrabel, Societe nationale des Chemins de fer belges, bpost, Belgocontrol and the National Lottery.

45 Arts. 2 and 5 of the Law of 28 July 2011, as presented in Ph. Lambrecht, 'The Law of 28 July 2011 to guarantee the presence of women on the decision-making bodies of autonomous public undertakings, listed companies and the National Lottery', in De Vos & Culliford 2014, supra note 16, p. 101.

46 Art. 4 of the Law of 28 July 2011 inserting a new Art. 518a in the Code of Company Law. See in more detail Lambrecht 2014, supra note 45.

47 Lambrecht 2014, supra note 45, p. 105.

48 S. Renga, 'Italy', in Selanec & Senden 2013, supra note 8, p. 125.

49 Ibid., p. 127.

50 Ibid., p. 125.

51 Art. 6(1) of Act 2839/2000, as represented in S. Koukoulis-Spiliotopoulos, 'Greece', in Selanec & Senden 2013, supra note 8, p. 101.

52 T. Koderman Sever, 'Slovenia', in Selanec & Senden 2013, supra note 8, pp. 200-201.

53 Even if one must note that causation, positive or negative, has so far not been unequivocally proven. See also on this L. Senden & M. Visser, 'Balancing a Tightrope: The EU Directive on Improving the Gender Balance among Non-Executive Directors of Boards of Listed Companies', 2013 European Gender Equality Law Review, no. 1, p. 21.

54 See e.g. 'Women in Mature Economies Control Household Spending' (<www.marketingcharts.com/topics/asia-pacific/women-inmature-economies-control-household-spending-12931>), last visited 26 November 2014.

55 Senden & Visser, supra note 53.

56 See on this in more detail A. Buijze, I. de Koning & L.A.J. Senden, 'Efficiency or justice? Correcting for power imbalances under EU telecommunications, air transport and gender equality law', to be published by Intersentia in 2015, now on file with the author.

57 Cf. L. Warth, 'Gender Equality and the Corporate Sector', UNECE Discussion Paper Series, No. 2009.4, p. 16.

58 The Swedish Corporate Governance Board, 'Questions and answers regarding the Swedish Corporate Governance Board's efforts to improve gender balance on the boards of listed companies', document dating from 30 May 2014, available at: , last visited 26 November 2014.

59 The website of the Norwegian Ministry for Children, Equality and Social Inclusion as quoted by G. Selanec, 'Executive Summary', in Selanec & Senden 2013, supra note 8, p. 26.

60 See extensively on this debate, Lambrecht 2014, supra note 45.

61 See the proposal for the Law: Kamerstukken 2010 – 2011, no. 53 - 211/2, 4, 5 -7 and also Advies nr. 108 van 12 mei 2006 van het bureau van de raad voor de gelijke kansen van mannen en vrouwen met betrekking tot quota in raden van bestuur, approved on 13 October 2006, available at: , last visited 27 November 2014.

62 Swedish Corporate Governance Board 2014, supra note 58, p. 3.

63 A. Carrasco et al., 'Appointing women to boards: Is there a cultural bias?', Journal of Business Ethics, April 2014, DOI 10.1007/s10551- 014-2166-z.

64 According to G. Esping-Anderson, The Three Worlds of Welfare Capitalism, 1990.

65 J. Armstrong & S. Walby, Gender Quotas in Management Boards, 2012, PE 462.429, p. 12, available at: , last visited 27 November 2014.

66 V. Heidenreich, 'Why Gender Quotas in Company Boards in Norway – and not in Sweden?', in F. Engelstad & M. Teigen, Firms, Boards and Gender Quotas: Comparative Perspectives, 2012, pp. 147-183.

67 Swedish Corporate Governance Board 2014, supra note 58, p. 4. 68 In this sense Heidenreich 2012, supra note 66. 69 M. Teigen, 'Gender Quotas for Corporate Boards in Norway: Innovative Gender Equality Policy', in C. Fagan, et al. (eds.), Women on Corporate Boards and in Top Management: European Trends and Policy, 2012.

70 Cf. Esping-Anderson 1990, supra note 64, p. 28.

71 It must be noted that the Esping-Andersen categorization fallsshort in respect of the CEE countriesfor the simple reason that they did not take these countries into account. More recent studies have distinguished three types of systems in relation to the CEE countries: neoliberal; dual welfare; and social corporatist welfare regimes. See in particular N. Lendvai, 'EU Integration and Post-Communist Welfare: Catch-up Convergence before and after the Economic Crisis', in Converging Europe: Transformation of Social Policy in the Enlarged European Union and in Turkey, 2011, pp. 181-207; M. Potucek, 'Metamorphoses of Welfare States in Central and Eastern Europe', in M. Seeleib-Kaiser (ed.), Welfare State Transformations Comparative Perspectives, 2008, pp. 79-96. I thank Ivana Palinkas for bringing this point to my attention.

72 In this sense Lendvai 2011, supra note 71.

73 Armstrong & Walby 2012, supra note 65, p. 11.

74 S. Terjesen & V. Singh, 'Female presence on corporate boards: a multi-country study on environmental context', 2008 Journal of Business Ethics 83, no. 1, pp. 55-63.

75 A. Storvik & M. Teigen, Women on board: the Norwegian experience, Friedrich Ebert Stiftung, International Policy Analysis, 2010, p. 8. The proportion of female chairpersons rose from 3% in 2002 to only 5% in 2009; only 2% of CEOs are women and only 10% of top management of the largest companies are female.

76 See on this Waas 2014, supra note 16.

77 See K. Nousiainen, 'Finland', in Selanec & Senden 2013, supra note 8, p.

78. 78 See for an overview of the concerns that have been uttered by national parliaments concerning this proposal.

79 See for Germany e.g. the Berlin Declaration, an initiative of MPs of six major political parties and of six leading women's organizations, calling for binding legislation for ensuring a minimum of 30% women on the supervisory boards of listed, public companies; see , last visited 27 November 2014; and also the First Report on Gender Equality of 16 June 2011, presented by the German Federal Government, , last visited 27 November 2014.

80 With reference to Storvik & Teigen 2010, supra note 75 and M. Hoel, 'The quota story: five years of change in Norway', in S. Vinnicombe et al. (eds.) Women on Corporate Boards of Directors: International Research and Practice, 2008.

81 Armstrong & Walby 2012, supra note 65.

82 Ibid.

83 See J.A. Rasmussen & M. Huse, 'Corporate governance in Norway: women and employee-elected board members', in C.A. Mallin (ed.), Handbook on International Corporate Governance. Country Analyses, Second Edition, 2011; M. Teigen, 'Gender Quotas on Corporate Boards', in K. Niskanen (ed.), Gender and Power in the Nordic Countries – with a focus on politics and business, 2011, available at: , last visited 27 November 2014.

84 See the Working Paper 'The Quota-instrument: different approaches across Europe', European Commission's Network to Promote Women in Decision-Making in Politics and the Economy, 2011, p 11, available at: , last visited 27 November 2014.

85 N. Gunningham & P. Grabosky, Smart Regulation. Designing Environmental Policy, 1998, pp. 14-15.

86 Cf. also Warth 2009, supra note 57.

87 Kovalainen & Hart 2014, supra note 35, pp. 115-116 and 119.

88 Armstrong & Walby 2012, supra note 65. The other countries included in their study are Slovenia, France, Sweden, the UK and Hungary.

89 A. Numhauser-Henning, 'Sweden', in Selanec & Senden 2013, supra note 8, p. 213.

90 'Slow pace of board room equality 'deplorable'', The Local, 4 June 2014, , last visited 27 November 2014.

91 Swedish Corporate Governance Board 2014, supra note 58.

92 See the document mentioned in note 58, supra.

93 'Swedish minister open to boardroom quotas', The Local, 24 June 2013, , last visited 27 November 2014.

94 See e.g. R. Adams & D. Ferreira, 'Women in the Boardroom and their Impact on Governance and Performance', 2008, available at: , last visited 27 November 2014; and Women Matter, Women at the top of corporations: Making it happen, McKinsey & Company report, pp. 6-8, available at: , last visited 27 November 2014.

95 European Commission in its Green Paper on the EU Corporate Governance Framework (European Commission, COM(2011) 164 final).

96 RiskMetrics Group, Study on Monitoring and Enforcement Practices in Corporate Governance in the Member States, 2009, p. 188, available at: , last visited 27 November 2014.

97 Cf. Warth 2009, supra note 57.

98 Armstrong & Walby 2012, supra note 65, p. 13.

99 But this also holds true for self-regulatory regimes such as the Finnish one; the number of women in top management positions has shown only a minor increase since the Corporate Governance Code was changed in 2008 (from 16% in 2008 to 17% in 2011).

100 Armstrong & Walby 2012, supra note 65, p. 12.

101 McKinsey&Company, which has based the identification of these best practices on interviews with 12 companies that have realized noteworthy progress when it comes to women's representation in the boardroom and in top management positions. See its report 'Women Matter – Gender diversity, a corporate performance driver', 2007, available at: , last visited 4 December 2014.

CHAPTER 10

GENUINE OCCUPATIONAL REQUIREMENT IN THE GERMAN FIRE SERVICE: CASE C-229/08, COLIN WOLF V. STADT FRANKFURT AM MAIN, JUDGEMENT OF THE EUROPEAN COURT OF JUSTICE (GRAND CHAMBER) OF 12 JANUARY 2010

Sarah Speekenbrink

Keywords: European Council, Article 13 EC Treaty, ECJ, Directive 2000/78/EC, Age Discrimination, Genuine Occupational Requirement

INTRODUCTION

In 2000, the European Council used its competence under Article 13 EC Treaty and adopted Directive 2000/78/EC.1 This Directive provides a legal framework for combating discrimination in employment on grounds of religion or belief, disability, age and sexual orientation. Since its adoption the European Court of Justice (ECJ) has received numerous preliminary referrals, mostly dealing with age discrimination. Within this context, the case of Colin Wolf is important because so far it is the only age discrimination case dealing with Article 4(1) of the Directive: the genuine occupation requirement (GOR) exception.

BACKGROUND AND MAIN LEGAL QUESTION

Mr. Wolf (31 years old) applied for an intermediate career post in the fire service in Frankfurt, Germany. The City of Frankfurt refused to consider his application because he was older than the age limit of 30 year. According to a German national provision only persons under 31 years of age can be recruited to intermediate career posts in the fire service. The German government submits that these posts entail exceptionally high physical demands on certain operations. Persons past the age of 45 to 50 are not able to perform these heavy tasks. Consequently, the age at which a person is recruited determines the length of time within which the person will be able to fulfill the highly demanding tasks. To ensure the operational capacity and proper functioning of the fire service a maximum age limit of 30 year was introduced. Wolf disagreed with the refusal and started domestic procedures claiming he had been discriminated against on the ground of age. The Administrative Court Frankfurt am Main was uncertain about the compatibility of the German provision with Directive 2000/78/EC. Therefore, the Court referred the case to the ECJ for a preliminary ruling under Article 234 EC Treaty. The main legal question that is dealt with in this case is whether the national provision that sets the maximum age for recruitment to intermediate career posts in the fire service at 30 years is unjustified discrimination.

THE JUDGEMENT

Directive 2000/78/EC provides more than one justification or exception to discrimination.2 The German Court aligned its preliminary questions to Article 6(1) of the Directive which

Citation: Speekenbrink, S., (2010). Genuine Occupational Requirement in the German Fire Service: Case C-229/08, Colin Wolf v. Stadt Frankfurt am Main, judgement of the European Court of Justice (Grand Chamber) of 12 January 2010. Utrecht Journal of International and European Law. 26(71), pp.26–28. DOI: http://doi.org/10.5334/ujiel.ad.

provides an objective justification clause specifically for age discrimination. However, interestingly, the ECJ found Article 4(1), providing a GOR exception for all grounds, was to be assessed.3 This means that the ECJ assessed whether physical fitness is a characteristic related to age, whether it constitutes a genuine and determining occupational requirement and, further, whether the aim pursued by the provision was legitimate and the requirement proportionate.4 The ECJ stated that the activities that come with the job, such as fighting fires, rescuing persons and protecting the environment, are characterised by their physical nature. The possession of particularly high physical capacities may therefore be regarded as a GOR.5 Crucial in this judgement is the demonstration of a link between the need to possess high physical capacities and the age of a person. The German government produced scientific data which shows that respiratory capacity, musculature and endurance diminish along with age. From these data the ECJ drew the conclusion that only few officials over the age of 45 have sufficient physical capacity to perform the fire-fighting part of their job. Moreover, there are no officials at the age of 50 that have the capacity of rescuing persons.6 Finally, the ECJ found the age limit of 30 was appropriate and necessary to ensure the efficient functioning of the professional fire service.7 In conclusion, the ECJ ruled that a national provision such as that at issue is in conformity with the GOR exception of Article 4(1).

COMMENT

The GOR exception was created to prevent the prohibition of discrimination from making it difficult or impossible to carry on those occupational activities for which a person's sex, race, religion, disability, age or sexual orientation is an indispensable prerequisite.9 In general, the ECJ has emphasised that the exception must be interpreted strictly since it is a derogation from an individual right laid down in a directive.10 Nevertheless, in the case of Colin Wolf the ECJ interpreted the GOR exception in a much broader manner. On the one hand, this is understandable considering the factor that the work field (fire brigade) is an emergency service. It is emphasized in Directive 2000/78/EC that although the GOR exception only applies in very limited circumstances (recital 23), the Directive does not require emergency services to recruit persons who do not have the necessary capacities to carry out a range of activities (recital 18). On the other hand, the German provision is not directed at persons who do not fulfil the physical fitness requirement at the moment of the application. Instead it applies to all persons older than 30 years regardless of whether they possess the necessary physical capacities. All persons above 30 years are declined on the basis of the assumption that these persons will not posses the necessary physical capacities (maximum) 15 to 20 years from the moment of the application. There will certainly be persons who at the age of 45 have the necessary capacities; similarly there will be persons at the age of 40 who will not. Furthermore, in 15 to 20 years time the techniques in activities like fire fighting may have changed in such a way that the present standard of physical capacities is outdated. For example, Advocate General Bot raised the fact that the protective clothing alone weighs approximately 30 kilograms.11 With technologies advancing at high speed it is unlikely that 15 to 20 years from now the clothing will weigh the same. Additionally, there is an assumption that a person under the age of 31 can fulfil the GOR in the future. But, being under the age of 31 is not a guarantee that persons work a minimum number of years in the fire service. For example, persons can get disabled due to the dangerous tasks in the fire service or persons can decide to change careers. In conclusion, it is in my opinion reasonable that the GOR exception is interpreted more broadly in cases dealing with employment in the armed forces and the police, prison or emergency services. However, in the case of Colin Wolf the ECJ goes too far by upholding a rule that excludes all persons older than 30 years even though they fulfil the occupational requirement of possessing high physical capacities.

NOTES:

1 Directive 2000/78/EC establishing a general framework for equal treatment in employment and occupation, O.J 2000, L 303/16.

2 Directive 2000/78/EC provides exceptions to age discrimination in Arts. 2(2)(b), 2(5), 4(1) and 6.

3 Case C-229/08 Colin Wolf v Stadt Frankfurt am Main (ECJ 12 January 2010), paras. 31 and 32.

4 Colin Wolf v Stadt Frankfurt am Main (n 3), para. 36.

5 Colin Wolf (n 3), para. 40.

6 Colin Wolf (n 3), para. 41.

7 Colin Wolf (n 3), para. 43.

8 Colin Wolf (n 3), para. 46.

9 A.G. General Mancini in case C-248/83, Commission v. Germany, [1985] ECR 1459, para. 7.

10 Case C-222/84, Johnston v. Chief Constable of the Royal Ulster Constabulary, [1986] ECR 1651, para. 36; case C-273/97, Sirdar v. The Army Board and Secretary of State for Defence, [1999] ECR I-7403, para. 23 and case C-285/98, Kreil v. Bundesrepublik Deutschland, [2000] ECR I-00069, para. 20.

11 A.G. Bot in Colin Wolf (n 3), para. 28.

CHAPTER 11

TRACING THE SCOPE OF RELIGIOUS EXEMPTIONS UNDER NATIONAL AND EU LAW: SECTION 37(1) OF THE IRISH EMPLOYMENT EQUALITY ACTS 1998–2011 AND IRELAND'S OBLIGATIONS UNDER THE EU FRAMEWORK DIRECTIVE ON EMPLOYMENT AND OCCUPATION, DIRECTIVE 2000/78/EC

Amy Dunne

Keywords: EU employment equality, Irish Employment Acts, Directive 2000/78/EC, Religious exemptions, Organisations

INTRODUCTION

It is contended that a hidden intolerance2 is latent in the overly broad exemptions reserved to religious organisations under Irish employment equality legislation, which serves to insulate these organisations from the generally applicable EU grounds of non-discrimination. The overly broad interpretation of the religious exemptions provided for in the EU Framework Directive on Employment and Occupation3 is partly attributed to the seemingly wide latitude within the Directive afforded to national practices and constitutional principles. It will be argued in this submission that the Irish Government has exhausted this latitude far beyond its reasonable construction. Further, it is questioned whether the exhaustion of this latitude – in the form of overly broad exemptions afforded to religious organisations – is readily reconcilable with the State's own self-professed commitment to equality and freedom of religion in its constitutional provisions and case-law. At a more basic level, this paper seeks to establish that the Irish legislator has failed to comply with even the unambiguous obligations of the Employment Equality Directive. This is evident in circumstances in which derogations from the Employment Equality Directive are expressly prohibited on the basis of national practice or constitutional provisions. It will be seen in this regard that nuances apparent from the explicit text of the Employment Equality Directive have failed to be incorporated into the Irish Employment Equality Acts. Conversely, in other instances, derogations have been granted to religious organisations contrary to the explicit obligations of the Directive. Without the incorporation of these delimiting nuances, the Irish Employment Equality Acts when applied serve to rescind the protections afforded to Irish citizens falling within the other grounds of non-discrimination of the Employment Equality Directive. The incongruity between the Employment Equality Directive and the Irish Equality Acts, aside from circumstances in which the Directive permits a consideration of national practices and constitutional provisions, culminates in a contravention of the EU obligations prescribed upon the Irish State and serves to defeat the spirit of

Citation: Dunne, A., (2015). Tracing the Scope of Religious Exemptions under National and EU Law: Section 37(1) of the Irish Employment Equality Acts 1998–2011 and Ireland's Obligations Under the EU Framework Directive on Employment and Occupation, Directive 2000/78/EC. Utrecht Journal of International and European Law. 31(81), pp.33–45. DOI: http://doi.org/10.5334/ujiel.dh.

the Employment Equality Directive overall. The starting point for this submission is the initiatives undertaken by one of the Irish houses of Parliament, Seanad Éireann, to reform the system of legislative exemptions for religious institutions as stipulated by section 37(1) of the Employment Equality Acts.4Reforms to section 37(1) have been proposed in the Employment Equality (Amendment) Bill 20125 and under a second, Employment Equality (Amendment) (No. 2) Bill 2013.6The religious exemptions provided for in section 37(1) of the Irish Equality Acts and the proposed legislative amendments will be analysed in the context of the obligations of the Irish State under EU law in the Employment Equality Directive, which establishes a general framework for equal treatment in employment and occupation. Through following the legislative evolution of the Irish Equality Acts, it is submitted that it is the enlarged scope of the religious exemption, as opposed to the existence of an exemption in Irish employment equality, which hinders the effective transposition of the Employment Equality Directive.

At this juncture, it is acknowledged that the Irish State has a long tradition in the provision of religious exemptions to religious belief systems in order to preserve the "life and reality"7 of these beliefs systems. Therefore, it must be understood that the Employment Equality Directive cannot be credited with introducing these novel conceptions of religious exemptions into Irish law. In fact, Article 44 of the Irish Constitution, Bunreacht na hÉireann, which guarantees the freedom of religion, was included in the 1937 constitutional text to facilitate religious pluralism in furtherance of the State's obligations under the Anglo-Irish Treaty of 1921. It was thought that Article 44 would avoid "the establishment or the preference for any religious denomination which would have the undesirable consequence of a bigger breach between North and South".8 The discrepancies between the Employment Equality Directive and the Irish Equality Acts therefore do not hinge on the provision of a religious exemption but rather on the difference in the scope of the religious exemption afforded to religious organisations under each respective body of legislation. Therefore, in the analysis hereunder, as per Sandberg and Doe, the consideration is "not whether there ought to be a religious exemption but rather [what is] the scope of the exemption".9

The present analysis has been sparked by the traction gained by the civil rights movement of the LGBT community in Ireland and the social evolution in Irish society to renounce the systemic exclusion of the LGBT community from public life generally. Following on from the introduction of a statutory civil partnership registration scheme for same-sex couples in January 2011 under the Civil Partnership and Certain Rights and Obligations of Cohabitants Act 2010, calls for the amendment of section 37(1) of the Irish Employment Acts came to the fore. In the intervening period, the Gender Recognition Bill 2014 was passed in Seanad Éireann on the 11th March 2015.10 This Bill seeks to grant formal legal status to transgender Irish citizens. It is noted that at present Ireland is the only EU Member State that does not permit legal recognition of its transgender citizens.11At the time of writing, the Irish public are due to vote in the constitutional referendum of the 22nd May 2015 on the Thirty-Fourth Amendment of the Constitution on Marriage Equality to Article 41 of the Constitution. It will be decided whether the additional wording; "marriage may be contracted in accordance with law by two persons without distinction as to their sex"12 will be added as Article 41.4, and by consequence whether LGBT citizens may contract marriage and avail of the accompanying constitutional protections in that regard. These LGBT civil rights developments have therefore motivated a renewed discussion of the religious exemption afforded to religious organisations under Irish law, which curtail the employment equality rights of Irish LGBT citizens.

It is noted that calls for the amendment of section 31(1) have also arisen from other civil rights groups and international organisations. Atheist civil groups in Ireland have protested against the continued application of the religious exemptions in their current conception as they serve to accord a more favourable and protected status to traditional belief systems as opposed to non-belief system.13 Ireland has also been subject to international pressure calling for the reform of section 37(1). Most recently, the UN Human Rights Committee criticized section 37(1) at Ireland's fourth periodic examination in July 2014, during which it was recommended that this section "at a minimum, [...] be repealed to prohibit discrimination against persons in relation to one or more of the nine grounds covered under the legislation. [...] It should be replaced by new wording that complies with Article 4 of the European Union Framework Directive".14

The LGBT civil rights movement has in its activism highlighted the clash between two protected grounds of non-discrimination in Irish legislation: the religion or belief ground and the sexual orientation ground. However, it is necessary to see this in the context that clashes between fundamental rights and equality rights are germane to the European continent as a whole and do not relate exclusively to these selected grounds. In fact, the propensity for clashes to occur between any and each of the protected grounds has increased given that "the catalogue of legally protected fundamental rights has grown incessantly".15 However, clashes between the non-discrimination grounds of religion and sexual orientation have given rise to particularised tensions. It is further acknowledged that there is the potential for clashes of fundamental rights and equality rights to be exaggerated for ideological purposes. Therefore, in order to escape a highly normative and politicized discussion, this analysis does not hang on the crux of the ideological clash between these particular non-discrimination grounds. Rather, emphasis is placed on the scope of the exemptions afforded to religious organisations and the equity of the balance that should be achieved between competing rights. As to methodology, the paradoxical relationship between religious exemptions, which may serve to foster both tolerance for the manifestation of religious belief and simultaneously foster intolerance for the lifestyle of those individuals falling within the protected categories of non-discrimination, is set out hereunder. Thereafter, a consideration of the legislative evolution of the Irish Equality Acts is undertaken. Firstly, the fissure between the current Irish Equality Acts and the Employment Equality Directive is identified. Secondly, it will be analysed whether the first or second amendment Bills contribute to breaching this gap in line with the State's obligations under EU law. Finally, comments are made as to the consequences of the continued misapplication of the Employment Equality Directive in Irish law and a limited discussion of the latitude afforded to constitutional provisions and nationals practices is entertained before concluding remarks are set out.

PART A

Religious Exemptions

Religious exemptions in pluralist democracies, although a "challenge to the existing anti-discrimination paradigm",16 are indispensable to the preservation of religious plurality. Tolerance, particularly when plurality means that society will comprise of persons unable to comply with certain laws for religious reasons, is expressed through the granting of exemptions from laws which would force a practitioner to violate their mandated beliefs. Providing for plurality of belief but denying practitioners the ability to fulfil the mandates of their beliefs would constitute an empty tolerance. The exemption approach accords legitimacy to beliefs and by consequence facilitates the flourishing of differentiated and unique value systems and in particular, minority belief systems. Compliance with generally applicable non-discrimination law in these circumstances constitutes a limitation on the freedom of religious organisations to segregate themselves from non-members in order to maintain their integrity.

However, proper appreciation must be taken of the anomaly religious exemptions create: a practitioner's right to violate a law that both practitioners of different belief systems and non-practitioners alike, must obey.17 In this model, differentiated practitioners and non-practitioners alike are subject to legislative burdens, i.e. their rights may have to be limited in order to accommodate the religious mandates of practitioners.18 Any limitations on the rights of others to accommodate religious belief are subject to scrutiny under concepts of proportionality. Therefore, when an exemption is sought from an equally protected ground of non-discrimination, without objective justification, the limits of tolerance are reached. More precisely, the limits of tolerance are reached where an exemption is sought from a protected ground of non-discrimination where the genuine occupational requirement is not satisfied. It will be submitted that a religious exemption promotes tolerance where it is broad enough to facilitate the flourishing of a diversity of majority and minority religions and belief systems but yet still requires practitioners and non-practitioners alike to adhere strictly to the generally applicable grounds of non-discrimination in the absence of the application of the genuine occupational requirement.

Religious Exemptions under the EU Employment Equality Directive

The Employment Equality Directive requires Member States to provide for employment equality on the grounds of disability, religion or belief, age and sexual orientation. However, Article 4(1) of the Employment Equality Directive permits Member States to make provision for occupational requirements. Under this provision, employers may give effect to a difference in treatment based on a characteristic related to disability, religion, age and sexual orientation where "by reason of the nature of the particular occupational activities concerned or of the context in which they are carried out, such a characteristic constitutes a genuine and determining occupational requirement, provided that the objective is legitimate and the requirement is proportionate".19 In other words, Article 4(1) permits a limitation on rights where there is a genuine occupational requirement.

A second, circumlocutory and conditional, exemption from the grounds of non-discrimination applies specifically to religious employers, churches and other public or private organisations whose ethos is based on religion or belief. The religious exemption provided for in Article 4(2) is in essence a restatement of the genuine occupational requirement in Article 4(1), addressing the particular circumstance whereby a religious organisation may accord preferential treatment to co-religionists where that religion or belief is a "genuine, legitimate and justified occupational requirement" and where such preferential treatment satisfies the extensive conditionality of the provision. The lengthy Article 4(2) provides that

"Member States may maintain national legislation in force at the date of adoption of this Directive or provide for future legislation incorporating national practices existing at the date of adoption of this Directive pursuant to which, in the case of occupational activities within churches and other public or private organisations the ethos of which is based on religion or belief, a difference of treatment based on a person's religion or belief shall not constitute discrimination where, by reason of the nature of these activities or of the context in which they are carried out, a person's religion or belief constitute a genuine, legitimate and justified occupational requirement, having regard to the organisation's ethos. This difference of treatment shall be implemented taking account of Member States' constitutional provisions and principles, as well as the general principles of Community law, and should not justify discrimination on another ground.

Provided that its provisions are otherwise complied with, this Directive shall thus not prejudice the right of churches and other public or private organisations, the ethos of which is based on religion or belief, acting in conformity with national constitutions and laws, to require individuals working for them to act in good faith and with loyalty to the organisation's ethos."

Ahdar and Leigh note that the presence of no fewer than six qualifying terms in Article 4(2) is indicative of "the extreme sensitivity surrounding the exception".20 This religious exemption is limited by the requirements that the difference in treatment relates solely to the "reason of the nature of these activities or of the context in which they are carried out", constituting a "genuine, legitimate and justified occupation requirement" and which "should not justify discrimination on another ground."21

The interpretation of the latitude afforded to national practices and constitutional provisions under Article 4(2), in the absence of any Court of Justice of the European Union ruling, has been shrouded in ambiguity. However, given that the Directive is a set of minimum requirements,22 the Employment Equality Directive unambiguously and expressly sets out that a religious exemption from the other generally applicable grounds of non-discrimination may not be granted at the national level. This prohibition applies irrespective of national practices and constitutional provisions. Exemptions under Article 4(2) are therefore subject to the absolute condition that the employment practices of such organisations "should not justify discrimination on another ground." It is submitted that any ambiguity surrounding this prohibition is contrived in situations where "national practices", "constitutional provisions and principles" are advanced as obstacles to the application of non-discrimination to the pursuits of religious organisations. In particular, the contrivance of this ambiguity may be fuelled by the political stakes involved in enforcing compliance with generally applicable non-discrimination legislation by religious organisations.

This interpretation has also been adopted by other authors. For example, Ahdar and Leigh construe Article 4(2) to mean that "the language appears to leave open the possibility that a state could allow a religious body to argue that a life-style condition related to its doctrines means that it should be exempted, despite its effect on practicing homosexuals and lesbians".23 It is submitted that this is a misconstruction of the scope of the religious exemption on two bases. Firstly, as *supra*, it is an unqualified condition that the exemption "should not justify discrimination on another ground". Secondly, it cannot be said that an exemption is allowable "despite its effect" on the established grounds of non-discrimination as such is contrary to the concept of indirect discrimination. An interpretation in this manner would render the concept of indirect discrimination null. The concept of indirect discrimination aims to combat apparently neutral provisions, criteria or practices which would put persons having a particular racial or ethnic origin, religion or belief, sex, disability, age or sexual orientation at a particular disadvantage compared with other people. It is precisely this effect which is to be taken into account when balancing the application of competing rights. In summation, the Employment Equality Directive represents a set of minimum requirements, an exemption accorded from which cannot serve to rescind the protections afforded to other grounds of non-discrimination. In permitting the scope of the religious exemption to extend also to the other protected grounds of non-discrimination, established protections for the individuals falling within these protected categories are rescinded. Where the mandates of religious organisations clash with the other protected grounds of non-discrimination, the provision for religious exemption may not be construed so broadly as to in fact be used to support discriminatory practice dealt by religious organisations. Individuals identifying within the protected category of non-discrimination on the grounds of sexual orientation therefore may not be subject to differential treatment on this ground where religion or belief is not a genuine occupational requirement. Hereunder, the exemptions for religious organisations as set out under the Irish Equality Acts are contrasted with Article 4(1) of the Employment Equality Directive.

Religious Exemptions under the Irish Equality Acts 1998–2011

Under Irish employment law, section 37(1) of the Irish Equality Acts legislates for an exemption from the generally applicable grounds of non-discrimination in order to preserve religious ethos. Whereas the Employment Equality Directive applies to "occupational activities within churches and other public or private organisations", the Irish legislation is addressed to the arguably more narrowly defined category of "religious, education or medical institution(s)". Section 37(1) in its current conception states that

"A religious, education or medical institution which is under the direction or control of a body established for religious purposes or whose objectives include the provision of services in an environment which promotes certain religious values shall not be taken to discriminate [...] if

i. it gives more favourable treatment, on the religion ground, to an employee or a prospective employee over that person where it is reasonable to do so in order to maintain the religious ethos of the institution, or
ii. it takes action which is reasonably necessary to prevent an employee or a prospective employee from undermining the religious ethos of the institution."

Significant divergence between Article 4(2) of the Employment Equality Directive and section 37(1) of the Irish Equality Acts can be identified. The provisions of Article 4(2) of the Employment Equality Directive are narrower than section 37(1) in two significant respects. Firstly, the Directive requires that it has to be shown that by virtue of the nature or context in which they are carried out, the employee's religion or belief constitutes a genuine, legitimate and justified occupational requirement with regard to the employer's ethos. Thus, as per Bolger, it is "necessary to show that a person's religion is a determining factor in her actual ability to discharge the duties of her job, rather than simply showing the employers perception that such religion or belief is fitting in light of the organisation's ethos".24 Secondly, the standard applicable to secure a religious exemption differs between the EU and Irish level. It is acknowledged that the Irish legislation does require religious employers apply a semblance of the genuine occupational requirement test, which considers whether the employee needs to practice a specific religion in order to undertake the role within the ethos of the organisation. However, the legislative text merely indicates that an employer may secure the exemption where "it is reasonable to do so in order to maintain the religious ethos of the institution". This standard is far less rigorous than that elucidated in the EU Employment Equality Directive which requires that religiosity be a genuine occupational requirement of the role in question. Therefore, within section 37(1), religiosity serves a blanket exemption that insulates organisations identifying as having a religious ethos from non-discrimination law where there is a mere reasonable link between preferential treatment and religiosity. In applying treatment blanket exemption, it can be argued that adequate appreciation is not taken on a case-by-case basis of situations where there is no clear link between religiosity and the employee's role within the organisation. Further, it is not convincing that this reasonable link standard would motivate enquiries into alternatives for the redistribution or reorganisation of the responsibilities of that role where the role only partially requires religiosity in order to be to effectively carried out. Finally, this blanket exemption fails to appreciate that employees may keep their own values without simultaneously detracting from the ethos of the organisation as well as fulfil the role and "act in good faith and with loyalty",25 without identifying with the religion or belief in question.

In connection with these two delineated discrepancies between the religious exemption under the Employment Equality Directive and section 37(1) of the Irish Equality Acts, section 37(1)(b) is discussed. Section 37(1)(b) states that a religious organisation shall not be taken to discrimination where:

"it takes action which is reasonably necessary to prevent an employee or a prospective employee from undermining the religious ethos of the institution."

Section 37(1)(b) is identified as a threat to the effective enforcement of the grounds of non-discrimination. Whereas Article 4(2) allows religious organisations to place a positive obligation on "individuals working for them to act in good faith and with loyalty to the organisation's ethos", section 37(1)(b) provides the capacity to religious organisations to take action against employees which will not be reprimanded as discriminatory action.

In its present conception, 37(1)(b) has been described as a "mandate to discriminate"26and may serve to reinforce prejudices and fear of reprisal amongst the LGBT community. As per Angela Kerins, Chairperson of the Irish Equality Authority, "it is clear that this clause has reinforced fears of discrimination against lesbian, gay and bisexual workers in religious-run institutions, for example in schools and hospitals and makes it even more difficult for such workers to be open about their sexuality".27 The reflection of the duty to act in good faith and with loyalty of Article 4(2) in section 37(1) creates an inverse power in religious employers to act in a discriminatory manner and to be extrapolated from liability for this discrimination.

In implementing the Employment Equality Directive, section 37(1) fails to incorporate the qualifying nuances of Article 4(2). In so doing, minimum non-discrimination requirements are rendered negligible and the current protections afforded to those falling within the protected grounds of non-discrimination are rescinded. Section 37(1), therefore, represents a modest interpretation of the obligations Article 4(2) requires of the implementing Member State.

In the second part of this submission, this discourse will consider the provisions of first and second Amendment Bills in legislative evolution of the Irish Equality Acts in order to determine whether they serve to bring the Irish legislation more in line with obligations under EU law incumbent on the Irish State.

PART B

First Amendment Bill

The first Amendment Bill of May 2012 took tentative steps towards requiring that religious organisations submit to the grounds of non-discrimination legislated for in the Irish Equality Acts; and by consequence, towards ensuring that the Irish State conform with its obligations under EU law. At this juncture, it is noted that the protected grounds of non-discrimination differ as between the Employment Equality Directive and the Irish Equality Acts. The Employment Equality Directive legislates against discrimination on the grounds of religion or belief, disability, age or sexual orientation. Additionally, it is noted that the EU has also passed Directives implementing the principle of equal treatment between persons irrespective of racial or ethnic origin28 and in the access to and supply of goods and services on the basis of sex.29 By comparison, Irish legislation provides nine grounds of discrimination, amongst which superfluous to EU law are the "family status ground", "civil status ground" and the "traveller community ground".

Section 3 of the first Amendment Bill proposed to amend section 37 through the insertion of the following subsection immediately after subsection (6):

"Nothing in subsection (1) may be relied upon by an institution referred to in subsection (1) to justify or permit discrimination or to allow any action to be taken against any employee or potential employee on the basis of that employee's or potential employee's civil status or sexual orientation."30

On one hand, this proposed insertion would have served to subject religious organisations to the non-discrimination grounds of "civil status" and "sexual orientation" and contribute to alleviating the typified intolerances between religion and sexual orientation. However, on the other hand, the scope of the exemptions afforded to religious organisations under the first Amendment Bill is still overly broad and religious organisations would still not be subject to all grounds of non-discrimination in the Employment Equality Directive, namely the gender ground, race ground, age ground, disability ground, membership of the traveller community ground and, of particular relevance to a discussion concerning the civil rights movement for the LGBT community, the family status ground. Similarly, although section 37(1)(b) as a "mandate to discriminate"31 against individuals on the civil status or sexual orientation ground, it is mitigated; religious organisations under section 37(1)(a) are still afforded the opportunity to accord preferential treatment to employees or prospective employees on religious ground without being subject to the stringent test of genuine, legitimate and justified occupational requirement. Therefore, in its application, the first Amendment Bill may still have circumvented the prescriptions of the Employment Equality Directive in the absence of a stringent genuine occupation requirement and through allowing religious organisations to still evade the application of the other grounds of non-discrimination.

Second Amendment Bill

The first Amendment Bill was defeated in the Seanad Éireann; mostly due to constitutional concerns32 at the second stage on 2nd May 2012.33 The, then, Minister for Justice and Equality, Deputy Alan Shatter, elucidated those constitutional concerns as rooted in the balance struck by the Irish courts between the rights of religious organisations to manage their internal affairs and the rights of other Irish citizens to equality before the law and to earn a livelihood. These concerns are addressed limitedly at the conclusion of this submission.

Following the defeat of the first Amendment Bill, a second private members bill34 was introduced proposing amendments to section 37(1).35 The second Amendment Bill of the 8th March 2013 proposed that section 37(1) remain in place for wholly autonomous religious institutions whereas medical and educational institutions in receipt of public funds may only impose more favourable treatment on their employees where this preferential treatment does not contravene any of the protected grounds of non-discrimination grounds set out in the Employment Equality Directive. The Bill proposed to amend section 37(1) by inserting section 3 of the Bill which states

"(1) (a) Subject to paragraph (b) below, a religious, educational or medical institution which is under the direction or control of a body established for religious purposes or whose objectives include the provision of services in an environment which promotes certain religious values shall not be taken to discriminate against a person for the purposes of this Part or Part II if—

1. *it gives more favourable treatment, on the religion ground, to an employee or a prospective employee over that person where it is reasonable to do so in order to maintain the religious ethos of the institution, or*

2. *it takes action which is reasonably necessary to prevent an employee or a prospective employee from undermining the religious ethos of the institution.*

(b) Notwithstanding paragraph (a), where an educational 5 or medical institution of the type mentioned in that paragraph is maintained or assisted by recurrent grants provided out of public funds—

1. *More favourable treatment of the type referred to in subparagraph (i) of that paragraph shall be 10 taken to be discrimination unless—*

    1. *the treatment does not constitute discrimination on any of the other discriminatory grounds, and*

    2. *by reason of the nature of the institution's activities or the context in which they are carried out, the religion or belief of the employee or prospective employee constitutes a genuine, legitimate and justified occupational requirement having regard to the institution's ethos;*

2. *action of the type referred to in subparagraph (ii) of that paragraph shall be taken to be discrimination unless, by reason of the nature of the employment concerned or the context in which it is carried out, the action taken is objectively justified by a legitimate aim and the means of achieving the aim are appropriate and necessary."*

Encouragingly, it is seen that the second Amendment Bill adopts the genuine occupational requirement test as mandated expressly by Article 4(2) of the Employment Equality Directive in respect of publicly funded organisations. Further, it is seen that as per the Directive, public religious organisations are subject to all grounds of the generally applicable non-discrimination legislation. However, effectively these amendments create a situation whereby the inadequate provisions of the first Amendment Bill, although applicable only to private institutions, subsist sidelong the provisions of the second Amendment Bill, which would implement the full conditionality of Article 4(2) but only with respect to publicly funded religious organisations.

The approach of the second Amendment Bill creates a two-tier system of exemptions. The first tier of exemptions permits private religious organisations to continue to avail of overly broad exemptions and to elude the application of the stringent genuine occupational requirement test. Further, section 37(1)(b) as a mandate to discriminate is reincarnated as section 37(1)(a)(ii). The second tier of exemptions, which satisfy Article 4(2) of the Employment Equality Directive, are applicable to publicly funded religious institutions. Section 37(1)(b) allows for more favourable treatment to be accorded to an employee on the religion ground where it does not constitute discrimination on another ground and where it is strictly related to the genuine occupational requirement. This two-tiered system of exemptions cannot be understood to fulfil the Irish State's obligations under the Employment Equality Directive. It is noted in this respect that Article 4(2) does not distinguish between private and public institutions – "in the case of occupational activities within churches and other public or private organisations". Therefore, the two-tiered approach of the second Amendment Bill, which addresses different standards of compliance to different categories of Irish citizens, may continue to leave the state exposed to a breach of its Article 4(2) obligations. By virtue of this distinction, the protections afforded to the LGBT community under the employment legislation are still rescinded in practice. This is a particularly cogent concern as organisations with a religious ethos are demonstrated to be dominant in the provisions of services in the field of education and medicine. It is not proven empirically in this discussion whether that is the case; rather it is advanced that where EU non-discrimination protections are secured partially, the protection for the whole class of individuals is nominal.

The second Amendment Bill was presented on the 8th of March 2013 and proceeded to the Second Stage on the 13th and advanced to the Committee stage as of the 9th of April 2014. Amongst the Committee Stage amendments proposed it is seen that section 6(2)(e) is submitted to be revised making reference to "religion and belief", and not merely "the religion ground". The Government at the time proposed that the amendments be signed into law before end of 2014; which has not yet transpired at the time of writing.

Oversight of the Implementation of the Employment Equality Directive by European Commission

The discrepancy between the Employment Equality Directive and Irish Equality Acts have come under scrutiny by the European Commission, the executive branch of the European Union empowered to monitor the application of Union law. In the Commission's 2006 report on religion and belief discrimination in employment, it was noted that that section 37(1)(b) does not conform with Article 4(2) of the Employment Equality Directive given that the exemption thereunder is broader in scope and "does not provide the religion or belief must be relevant to the particular job in question, nor does it limit the exception to discrimination based on the grounds of religion or belief so that it cannot be used to justify discrimination on another ground".36

That the Irish Equality Acts maintain in force lesser protections than those granted to EU citizens under the Employment Equality Directive is a deleterious position which would leave the State open to infringement proceedings taken by the European Commission under Article 258 TFEU. Article 258 TFEU provides that

"If the Commission considers that a Member State has failed to fulfil an obligation under the Treaties, it shall deliver a reasoned opinion on the matter after giving the State concerned the opportunity to submit its observations. If the State concerned does not comply with the opinion within the period laid down by the Commission, the latter may bring the matter before the Court of Justice of the European Union."

However, it should be noted at the outset that the invocation of Article 258 TFEU by the Commission is a politically sensitive procedure and by consequence, the Commission's dealings with Member States thereunder are politically charged rather than legal in character. For this reason, resolution of the inconsistency may be sought through dialogue exchanged with the Commission rather than through the hefty court procedure. In this regard, the Commission, under Article 258 TFEU, issued a reasoned opinion to the Irish State on the 31st January 2008 regarding its concerns with the transposition of the Employment Equality Directive into Irish law; one concern of which related to the exemptions for religious institutions which were seen to be overly broad in their ambit.37The Department of Justice and Equality responded to this reasoned opinion by letter of 8th April "providing additional explanations on several topics, including the one concerning the protection against discrimination based on religion".38 Unfortunately, these explanations regarding the maintenance of discriminatory provisions in Irish statutory law which were provided by the Irish Department of Justice and Equality to the European Commission have not been made available to the public. However, in the Commission's responses to the queries of the European Parliament concerning these discussions with the Irish Department of Justice and Equality, there is evidence for the proposition that the Irish State relied upon the balance struck in the Irish Constitution between competing rights and the role of the Irish judiciary in evaluating conflicts on a case by case basis. Thereafter, it was announced that the Commission would not pursue infringement proceedings at this juncture as it was "satisfied with the measures that have been taken and has, therefore, decided not to pursue the infringement procedure at this point".39 In the European Parliament in June 2014, the Commission was called to answer a written question on the closure of infringement proceedings against Ireland concerning non-conformity of Irish transposing legislation with Employment Equality Directive on the 6th May 2008 and in particular, the "the compatibility of Article 4(2) of the Directive and Section 37(1) of the Employment Equality Acts".40 The Commission indicated that it had considered the issue in detail and

"is of the view that the implementation of the Directive in Ireland provides for the necessary balancing of rights on a case by case basis. The Commission has not received any complaints concerning individual cases of discrimination which would indicate that this is not the case. It would be for the national court in any particular given case to decide what was 'reasonable' or what was 'reasonably necessary'".41

Therefore, it appears that the Commission did not see cause to take reprisal against the Irish Equality Acts as currently in force based on its exchanges with the Irish State. It is submitted that this course of action is partly attributed to the fact that the Commission has erroneously identified "reasonably necessary" in the Irish Equality Acts as conforming to the stringent genuine occupational requirement test. It is seen that over-reliance is placed on the ability of Irish LGBT citizens to litigate their rights before the Irish courts. It is advanced that the judicial protection afforded to the provisions of the Employment Equality Directive in Irish law is negligible. Further, as will be discussed briefly below, it is seen that the balance struck by the Irish courts system has been conceptually broader than that envisaged under the Employment Equality Directive. Nevertheless, as heretofore mentioned, non-reprisal of the Commission does not mean that the Irish Equality Acts are deemed to conform with the Employment Equality Directive for all time and the issue may be revisited depending on further amendments. Should the second Amendment Bill proceed to be signed into law, the author submits that the discrepancies between section 37(1) and Article 4(2) will be enhanced and the two-tier application of religious exemptions in Irish Equality Acts will evince the flawed nature of the transposition of the Employment Equality Directive on a greater number of technicalities than under the current Irish Equality Acts. In this situation, the Commission may be motivated to revisit the implementation of the Employment Equality Directive into Irish law.

Constitutional Principles and Provisions

Section 37(1) has been deemed to pass constitutional muster in the Irish Supreme Court in *In Re Article 26 and the Employment Equality Bill 1996*;42 in which it was pronounced that

"it would therefore appear that it is constitutionally permissible to make distinctions or discriminations on grounds of religious profession belief or status insofar – but only insofar – as this may be necessary to give life and reality to the guarantee of the free profession and practice of religion contained in the Constitution".43

In the judgement, Hamilton CJ considered that "the use of the words "reasonable" and "reasonably necessary" implies that the test is to be an objective one and that the matter is to be resolved on a case to case basis".44 Further, it is advanced in the same breath that "the final decision on this question as well as the final decision on what is reasonable or reasonably necessary to protect the ethos will rest with the court and the court in making its overall decision will be conscious of the need to reconcile the various constitutional rights involved".45 It is clearly seen that the Commission's comments on closure of the Article 258 TFEU procedure are borrowed directly from Irish constitutional precedent; no doubt as result of correspondence with the Irish Ministry for Justice and Equality. The ratio of Hamiliton CJ in *In Re Article 26 and the Employment Equality Bill 1996*is advanced as the proper balance struck by the Irish judiciary between the rights of religious organisations to manage their own affairs and maintain institutions for religious and charitable purposes and the rights of other citizens to equality before the law and to earn their livelihood under the Irish Constitution. This balance is different than that enunciated by Article 4(2) of the Employment Equality Directive and has so far served to operate as a shield to critics of the transposition of the Directive. The balance struck under *In Re Article 26 and the Employment Equality Bill 1996* as set out above has on a case-by-case basis served to protect that which is conducive to religiosity and not merely objectively justified. This is elucidated in the jurisprudence of *DPP v Draper*46 in which McCarthy J stated that religious exemptions "may be justified where the effect of the legislative restriction is not to inhibit religious practices, but merely to render their exercise inconvenient or disadvantageous".47 In this example, the overly broad nature of this constitutional balance as compared to the balance struck under Article 4(2) is clearly evinced. At the very minimum, the author queries the Commission's judgement, in holding this balance as legitimate, to discharge the obligations of the Irish State under the Employment Equality Directive. The Irish legislation is further reliant on individuals enforcing their rights in the Irish constitutional courts in order to secure the protections of the EU Employment Equality Directive; something, which is questionable under a consideration of judicial protection as mentioned above. In circumstances where the broad scope of section 37(1) favours religious practitioners, this would signify that persons falling within the affected categories of non-discrimination do not have equal access to employment protections. Finally, albeit in the absence of any precedent or interpretation of Article 4(2) by the Court of Justice of the European Union, it is advanced by the author that there is no indication in Article 4(2) that the discretion to maintain in place "national practices", "constitutional provisions and principles" is not similarly subject to the generally EU applicable grounds of non-discrimination. In fact, if it were not, it would constitute an illogical construction of Union legislation which seeks to introduce minimum standards in the protection of employment equality rights across the EU. The introduction of such minimum standards would be untenable if each Member State could secure varied exemptions in accordance with their constitutional provisions and national practices.

Leaving aside an analysis of the Irish constitutional principles and case-law advanced as an obstacle to the correct transposition of the Employment Equality Directive in Irish legislation, it is submitted the current legislation in force is not itself easily reconciled with the Irish State's own profound commitments to equality both in the Constitution and in legislation.48 Further, the introduction of a distinction between public and private religious organisations constitute an illogicality within Ireland's own constitutional history. It is noted that the Fifth Amendment Act of the Constitution in 1972 removed an article from the Constitution which served to create a hierarchy of religion within the State and which came to be viewed as potentially discriminatory. 49 This amendment was signed into law in 1973 by, then, President de Valera, who had originally drafted the Article 44 freedom of religion guarantee.50 The reintroduction of a distinction between private and public religious organisations goes further than that necessary to preserve the autonomy of internal management of religious organisations51 and recreates a hierarchy between variant belief systems. It is submitted that second the Amendment Bill constitutes a regression in the development of the Irish State's freedom of religion guarantee.

Far from becoming ensnared in a constitutional discussion which is not practicable in this submission, this discussion is concluded with three observations. The first of which is to acknowledge that the constitutional balance with respect to religious exemptions is broader in scope than the balance struck by the Employment Equality Directive because it serves to protect that which is conducive and not merely essential to religiosity. Secondly, it is remembered that a constitutional referendum is imminent in May 2015 which, if passed, may have far reaching consequences for the LGBT civil rights movement and motivate the re-weighting of this constitutional balance amongst other developments in Irish society in recent years, requiring the Irish courts to "re-evaluat[e] the concept of law in a culturally diverse, plural society".52 Finally, it is queried in an open-ended manner whether the mystique surrounding Irish constitutional provisions has been the main reason for the refraction of the EU employment equality guarantees of the Irish LGBT community at national level. It would seem that the Commission is reluctant to wade into the Irish constitutional provisions and case law and critically examine the balance struck by the Irish courts between these competing rights. It is submitted that if this critical examination was undertaken, the Commission may be motivated to pursue its reasoned opinion further.

CONCLUSIONS

Within this submission, the author has sought to demonstrate through comparative analysis that the Irish State maintains in force a religious exemption broader than the scope of the religious exemptions set out in the Employment Equality Directive. Further, it has been submitted that the proposed legislative amendments instigated by the Irish government would not serve to rectify the enforcement gap. In fact, with regard to the propositions of the second Amendment Bill, it is submitted that, if passed, the disparity between the Employment Equality Directive and the Irish Equality Acts will be evinced even more strongly.53 The propositions of the second Amendment Bill would serve to create a hierarchy between religion and belief systems and non-belief systems in contradiction with the Irish State's own constitutional commitment to freedom of religion. It is also submitted that the second Amendment Bill further illuminates the points of contention between the EU Employment Directive and the Irish Equality Acts which may serve as a basis for the Commission to conduct renewed enquiries into Irish equality legislation. Overall, this submission argues that the Irish government should amend its employment equality legislation to ensure that the religious exemptions therein are limited by the strict conditionality of Article 4(2) and the imperative to satisfy the exigencies of the genuine occupational requirement test. By virtue of the provision of an overly broad religious exemption in section 37(1), a hidden intolerance towards the Irish LGBT community has been permitted to fester. The subsistence of this intolerance in Irish legislation has in fact served to rescind the protections granted to these individuals under EU employment law. Beyer's maxim eloquently elucidates the crossroads at which the Irish State finds itself: "tolerance is the non-tolerance of the intolerance".54 Where the Irish State fails to implement the stringent provisions of the Employment Equality Directive, it is advanced that the State itself becomes complicit in perpetuating intolerance. The Irish State is therefore recommended to amend the scope of section 37(1) to fully comply with the textual nuances of Article 4(2) in order to strike a functionally tolerant, and not just superficially tolerant, balance between religious tolerance and generally applicable civil non-discrimination law.

Competing Interests

The author declares that they have no competing interests.

NOTES

[1]Johan de Tavernier, 'Tolerance, Pluralism and Truth' in Didier Pollefeyt (ed), *Incredible Forgiveness: Christian Ethics Between Fanaticism and Reconciliation* (Peeters Publishers 2004) 118.

[2]Council Directive 2000/78/EC of 27 November 2000

establishing a general framework for equal treatment in employment and occupation [2000] OJ L303/16 ("Employment Equality Directive").

[3]Employment Equality Act 1998 ("Irish Equality Acts") s 37(1) which came into force on 18 October 1999.

[4]Employment Equality (Amendment) Seanad Bill (2012) 11 ("first Amendment Bill").

[5]Employment Equality (Amendment) (No. 2) Seanad Bill (2013) 23 ("second Amendment Bill").

[6]*McGrath and Ó Ruairc v Trustees of Maynooth College* [1979] ILRM 166, [1979] 187. Henchy J, (Griffin, Kenny and Parke JJ concurring) notes: "The constitutional provision invoked here [Article 44.2.3°] must be construed in terms of its purpose. In proscribing disabilities and discriminations at the hands of the State on the grounds of religious profession, belief or status, the primary aim of the constitutional guarantee is to give vitality, independence and freedom to religion. To construe the provision literally, without due regard to its underlying objective, would lead to a sapping and debilitation of the freedom and independence given by the Constitution to the doctrinal and organisational requirements and proscriptions which are inherent in all organised religions".

[7]Carmen Garcimartín, 'Ireland' in Javier Martínez-Torrón and Cole Durham Jr (eds),*Religion and the Secular State: Interim National Reports* (Brigham Young University 2010), 403.

[8]Russell Sandberg and Norman Doe, 'Religious Exemptions in Discrimination Law' (2007) 66(2) Cambridge Law Journal 302.

[9]Gender Recognition Seanad Bill (2014) 116.

[10]International Service for Human Rights, 'Ireland: Ensure Legal Recognition of Transgender People' *ISHR* (Geneva, 23 February 2015) ‹http://www.ishr.ch/news/ireland-ensure-legal-recognition-transgender-people› accessed 1 August 2015.

[11]Minister Frances Fitzgerald TD, 'Government Announces Wording for Marriage Equality Referendum' *Department of Justice and Equality* (Dublin, 21 January 2015) ‹http://www.justice.ie/en/JELR/Pages/PR15000009› accessed 1 August 2015; Thirty-Fourth Amendment of the Constitution (Marriage Equality) Bill (2015) 5. This Implementation Bill was passed on the 27th of March and was accepted by 29 votes to 3 in Seanad Éireann.

[12]Atheist Ireland, 'Atheist Ireland Submission to UN Committee on Economic, Social and Cultural Rights' (26 September 2014) ‹http://atheist.ie/2014/09/atheist-ireland-submission-to-un-committee-on-economic-social-and-cultural-rights/› accessed 1 August 2015.

[13]UN Human Rights Council Legacy Steering Group, 'International Covenant on Civil & Political Rights (ICCPR) Fourth Periodic Examination of Ireland: Submission to the Seanad Public Consultation Committee', (21 March 2014) 9; The Irish Council for Civil Liberties, 'A Roundup of Coverage of Ireland's ICCPR Examination 14–25 July 2014' ‹http://iccl.ie/a-roundup-of-coverage-of-ireland's-iccpr-examination-14--25-july-2014.html› accessed 1 August 2015; Kitty Holland, 'UN Asks How State Will Protect Non-Christian Children' *Irish Times* (15 July 2014);. Human Rights Committee, 'Concluding Observations on the Fourth Periodic Report of Ireland' *IHREC* (24 July 2014) ‹http://www.ihrec.ie/publications/list/un-hrc-concluding-observations-on-ireland-and-iccp/› accessed 1 August 2015.

[14]Emmanuelle Bribosia and Isabelle Rorive, 'In Search of a Balance between the Right to Equality and Other Fundamental Rights' (DG for Employment, Social Affairs and Equal Opportunities, February 2010) 14.

[15]Sandra Fredman, 'Disability Equality: A Challenge to the Existing Anti-Discrimination Paradigm?' in Anna Lawson and Caroline Gooding (eds), *Disability Rights in Europe: From Theory to Practice* (Hart Publishing 2005) 199.

[16]Mark Rienzi, 'The Case for Religious Exemptions – Whether Religion is Special or Not?' (2014) 127(5) Harvard Law Review 1396.

[17]ibid 109.

[18]Article 4(1), Employment Equality Directive (n 2).

[19]Rex Ahdar and Ian Leigh, *Religious Freedom in the Liberal State* (2nd edn, Oxford University Press 2013) 370.

[20]Article 4(2), Employment Equality Directive (n 2).

[21]Employment Equality Directive (n 2) Recital 28 reads "[t] his Directive lays down minimum requirements, thus giving the Member States the option of introducing or maintaining more favourable provisions. The implementation of this Directive should not serve to justify any regression in relation to the situation which already prevails in each Member State." Article 8 states: "1. Member States may introduce or maintain provisions which are more favourable to the protection of the principle of equal treatment than those laid down in this Directive. 2. The implementation of this Directive shall under no circumstances constitute grounds for a reduction in the level of protection against discrimination already afforded by Member States in the fields covered by this Directive".

[22]ibid.

[23]Margaret Bolger, 'Discrimination on Grounds of Religion: Theory and Practice' (The European Network Against Racism Conference, 23 October 2003) 13.

[24]Article 4(2), Employment Equality Directive (n 2).

[25]House of the Oireachtas, 'Employment Equality (Amendment) Bill 2012: Second Stage' (2 May 2012) 215(3) Seanad Éireann Debate, Senator Ivana Bacik at para 162 ‹http://debates.oireachtas.ie/seanad/2012/05/02/00007.asp› accessed 1 August 2015.

[26]Irish Equality Authority, 'Equality Authority welcomes Minister Quinn's announcement on Lesbian, Gay and Bisexual teachers' (11 April 2012) 5 ‹http://www.ihrec.ie/download/pdf/equality_news_summer_2012.pdf› accessed 1 August 2015.

[27]Council Directive 2000/43/EC of 29 June 2000 implementing the principle of equal treatment between persons irrespective of racial or ethnic origin [2000] OJ L180/22.

[28]Council Directive 2004/113/EC of 13 December 2004 implementing the principle of equal treatment between men and women in the access to and supply of goods and services [2004] OJ L 373/37.

[29]First Amendment Bill (n 4).

[30]House of the Oireachtas (n 25), Senator Ivana Bacik at para 162.

[31]ibid, Minister for Justice and Equality (Deputy Alan Shatter) paras 152–154.

[32]ibid para 162.

[33]Second Amendment Bill (n 5).

[34]ibid 3.

[35]Lucy Vickers, 'Religion and Belief Discrimination in Employment – The EU law' (DG for Employment, Social Affairs and Equal Opportunities, November 2006) 29.

[36]European Commission, 'Employment Directive (2000/78/EC): List of Member States to Which a Reasoned Opinion or Letter of Formal Notice Will Be Sent' (MEMO/08/68, 31 January 2008) ‹http://europa.eu/rapid/press-release_MEMO-08–68_en.htm?locale=en› accessed 1 August 2015. Reasoned opinion sent to Ireland for the following reasons: "Incorrect definition of indirect discrimination, discrimination based on beliefs is not prohibited, exclusion of protection against discrimination for certain "private" types of employment, interested bodies do not have the right to participate in legal proceedings on behalf of victims of discrimination, limit to damages payable to victims of discrimination, the exception from the ban on discrimination on grounds of religion is too broad".

[37]European Commission, 'Closure of the Infringement Procedure on the Transposition in Ireland of Directive 2000/78/EC' (Press Release IP/08/703, 6 May 2008) ‹http://europa.eu/rapid/press-release_IP-08–703_en.htm› accessed 1 August 2015.

[38]European Commission, 'MEMO/08/68' (n 36) (emphasis added).

[39]Answer of Mrs. Reding on behalf of the Commission to Written Question E-004412/2014 by Emer Costello (S&D) to the Commission 'Section 37.1 of the Irish Employment Equality Act and Directive 2000/78/EC' [2014] OJ C337.

[40]ibid.

[41]*Re Article 26 and the Employment Equality Bill 1996* [1997] 2 IR 321 (SC).

[42]ibid 358.

[43]ibid 359.

[44]ibid.

[45]*The People (DPP) v Draper* (Irish Times, 24 March 1988).

[46]Eoin Daly, 'Re-Evaluating the Purpose of Church State Separation in the Irish Constitution: The Endowment Clause as a Protection of Religious Freedom and Equality' (2008) 8(2) Judicial Studies Institute Journal 32.

[47]Article 40.1° reads"[a]ll citizens shall, as human persons, be held equal before the law".

[48]Article 44.2° and 44.3° formally read as follows: "2°. The State recognises the special position of the Holy Catholic Apostolic and Roman Church as the guardian of the Faith professed by the great majority of the citizens. 3°. The State also recognises the Church of Ireland, the Presbyterian Church in Ireland, the Methodist Church in Ireland, the Religious Society of Friends in Ireland, as well as the Jewish Congregations and the other religious denominations existing in Ireland at the date of the coming into operation this Constitution."

[49]ibid.

[50]Mauro Gatti, 'Autonomy of Religious Organisations in the European Convention of Human Rights and European Union Law' in Lucia S Rossi and Giacomo Di Federico (eds),*Fundamental Rights in Europe and China: Regional Identities and Universalism* (Editoriale Scientifica 2013) 132–153.

[51]Prakash Shah, *Legal Pluralism in Conflict: Coping with Cultural Diversity in Law* (Glass House Press 2005) 1.

[52]In this regard, it is noted that in the Commission's reasoned opinion of 31 January 2008 references the grievance that "exclusion of protection against discrimination for certain "private" types of employment." See (n 36).

[53]Hendrick JM Beyer, *Tolerantie en Fanatisme: Een Studie over Verdraagzaamheid* (Van Loghum Slaterus 1948) 153.

CHAPTER 12 REGULATION OF DOMESTIC SERVICE

Manuel Abrantes

Keywords: Domestic service, law, gender, ethnicity, international Labor Organization

PALAVRAS CHAVE

I n June 2011, the International Labor Organization (ILO) adopted a convention concerning domestic workers. This offered a privileged moment to examine historical developments and lingering constraints on change toward social recognition and equity. Recent research has paid considerable attention to the global and local dynamics of domestic labor. While the importance of laws on the working and living conditions of domestic workers is a recurrent claim in such research, the legal configuration of this activity sector is seldom assessed in a detailed or critical manner. Analysis is frequently confined to the most recent reforms. As a result, the important contribution of historical research is confronted with the unclear position of domestic labor between household and labor dynamics.

This article addresses advancements in the regulation of domestic service at both national and international levels, focusing on the contexts of Portugal and the ILO. Analysis is primarily based on the documental analysis of institutional materials. Valuable insights have been drawn from open-ended interviews with domestic workers, labor and employer representatives, and local activists. This article begins by bringing together a handful of theoretical contributions that help in the understanding of lawmaking as a sociopolitical negotiation. It then focuses on the empirical examination of developments in the regulation of domestic service in Portugal. It draws as far back as the implementation of the Civil Code of 1867 to grasp the transformation in rights and meanings. The third section of the article discusses the laws currently in place and the implications of the recent international convention on domestic workers. A lingering question is to what extent exceptional legislation on particular employment sectors responds to their structural singularities, or, on the contrary, excludes them from general mobilization and the accomplishments of the working class.

Drops in Freedom, Care Chains, and Globalization

The role of law in regulating and mediating social inequality has been the subject of longstanding debates. The work of Karl Marx is particularly sensitive to norms on the minimum age of workers, daily working hours, and land expropriation, describing their establishment in a polity dominated by capitalist agents in which the elected parliament at best administers "freedom drop by drop" (Marx 2010, 183). Research on contemporary dynamics of domestic service exposes the tenacity of some elements in this view. Despite notable achievements, underage labor is still a key problem to be addressed (ILO 2010). Daily working hours remain a major controversy both in lawmaking and in everyday practice, especially for live-in domestic workers, and growing transnational dynamics are far from making a radical leap toward freedom or interethnic solidarity (Anderson 2000; Parreñas 2001; Sassen 2007; Lutz 2008; Canevaro 2009).

In this sense, paid domestic labor offers a strategic site to examine the ambiguous process through which state law draws its legitimacy from an outspoken opposition to traditional power inequality based on social status ("all are equal before the law"), while it legitimates difference and prejudice inherited from that very same source of power. The historical closeness between domestic labor and serfdom, to begin with, revives the classic questioning of the construction of wage labor as opposed to slavery (Weber 1978). Comparative historical research documents tensions in the position of domestic service between a life-stage occupation and a lifelong occupation following the dawn of industrial societies (Fauve-Chamoux and Wall 2005). Shifts toward a greater degree of commodification require both the acknowledgment of domestic service as an occupation and the break with specific forms of

Citation: Manuel Abrantes, Regulation of Domestic Service, http://dx.doi.org/10.7440/res45.2013.09.

paternalism permeating it. Beyond changes in the volume of domestic service over time, changes in a work process are at stake (Sager 2007). The potential of lawmaking to mold the complex nexus of commodification and social denigration of the occupation cannot be underestimated (Cooper 2005).

According to Pierre Guibentif (2009), two key legislative enterprises played a leading role in the consolidation of modern capitalism: constitutionalism and codification.

Civil codes adopted in several states of Western Europe following France in 1804 are especially important, insofar as they were created upon principles of positivistic policy, professional technicality, and national interest (Weber 1978). The historian Antônio Manuel Hespanha (2003) corroborates that the production of civil and other codes is nothing short of a landmark in the transition from common law into rationalist law, and therefore, in the advent of liberalism. He argues that there is a significant ambivalence in this endeavor. While it promotes the sys-tematization and understanding of the law among citizens, thereby favoring popular control over it, it is also grounded in the notion of a "juridical monument" aiming to be as permanent and consensual as possible, that is, to resist parliamentary action. In her examination of the first civil code in Portugal adopted in 1867, Teresa Beleza (2002) emphasizes its role in legitimating patriarchal rule. Women were granted an indirect relationship to the state mediated by their fathers, husbands, or older sons. She also stresses that legislation does not merely adjust to existing social inequality in a given historical moment; rather, it builds and shapes inequality. The study of legislation, which has been modified in later periods, is therefore key to understanding today's juridical discourse and practice (Beleza 2000).

The consideration of gender asymmetry has relevant implications for the subject under analysis. Historical research exposes significant links between the commod-ification of labor under capitalist industrialization and the ideology of separate spheres of production and reproduction, which prescribed the public agency of men and the invisible domesticity of women (Braudel 1969; Pinto 2007). Activities understood as domestic work have been largely "coded as feminine" (McDowell 2000, 506).[1] It is noteworthy that the gender distribution of paid household labor was more balanced in the past, although segmentation was apparent in the predominance of men in the most prestigious positions (Sarti 2005). This does not mean that the underprivileged position of domestic workers in labor law is unrelated to its extensive feminization; rather, the opposite is true. Barbara Ehrenreich and Arlie Russell Hochschild address recent developments as they refer to the "new emotional imperialism" (Ehrenreich and Russell 2002, 27). They focus on the international migration system of care labor, which has recently emerged as Western societies demand low wage workers, overwhelmingly women, to look after children and frail adults. Through the money they earn abroad, migrant women often support families and communities back home, in particular their own children and elderly relatives. The elaboration on global care chains and emotional labor thus notably frames domestic service within the dynamics of contemporary capitalism and globalization rather than traditional society.

Portugal has registered a rapid increase in immigration since the mid-1970s and severe ethnic segmentation in the labor market (Baganha 1998; Gôis and Marques 2009; Casaca and Peixoto 2010). The concentration of immigrant women in domestic service illustrates how newly arrived ethnic minorities occupy jobs abandoned by local workers due to their negative social standing. An extensive private demand for childcare and eldercare underpins the latest upsurge of domestic service (Guerreiro 2000; Wall and Nunes 2010). A recent survey on paid domestic workers in this country shows that violations of legal rights by employers abound, especially concerning social security contributions, holiday pay and benefits, concession of maternity leave, and payment of health costs in case of workplace accidents (Guibentif 2011). A large fraction of domestic service remains in the informal sector. In addition, the relative novelty of democratic politics in Portugal, where an authoritarian regime was in office from 1928 to 1974, suggests affinity with developments in other countries in Southern Europe and Latin America (Valenzuela and Mora 2009; Goldsmit *et al.* 2010). Although legal reforms have been pursued to approximate domestic service to general wage labor standards, the resilience of exceptional treatment and limited legal compliance remains at the forefront of concerns regarding domestic service.

While national politics are criticized for being too distant from citizens to allow full democratic participation, supranational authorities with different purposes have emerged as key sites in the readjustment of power (Hespanha 2003; Sassen 2007). Alain Supiot (2006) highlights the normative political orientations followed by organizations such as the European Union or the World Bank, which promote an uncritical understanding of adaptable labor markets as the desirable or only possible future. In contrast, the ILO has recognized the need to combine market liberalization and regulation since its creation in 1919. Denouncing abuse in under-regulated employment sectors remains a political trademark of this organization, and it played a significant role in the process leading to the adoption of the Domestic Workers Convention in 2011 (ILO 2010).

Effective regulation on paid domestic labor has been troubled by "variation between countries and variation between economic sectors in the same country in terms of what is socially and legally constructed as acceptable employment practice" (Anderson 2006, 25). The overarching perspective of Boaventura de Sousa Santos (2006) on globalization offers an important contribution to framing the subject at hand. In the author's view, there are two distinct spheres of production. The hegemonic camp pushes for neoliberal economy, weak state, liberal democracy with an absolute priority of civic and political rights over social and economic rights, and the primacy of the rule of law and the judicial system conceived as independent and universal mechanisms. On the other hand, the counter-hegemonic or subordinate production of globalization builds on "the aspiration by oppressed groups to organize their resistance on the same scale and through the same type of coalitions used by the oppressors to victimize them, that is, the global scale and local/global coalitions" (Santos 2006, 398). Examining the struggle for the rights of migrant domestic workers within two nongovernmental organizations in the United Kingdom, Bridget Anderson (2010) shows how radical undertakings can be captured gradually by the logic and practices of state sovereignty. Based on research in the Netherlands, Sarah van Walsum (2011) shows how the regulation of migrant domestic work challenges stationary views on the public-private divide, the limits of the labor contract, and the borders of the nation-state. These authors favor a notion of regularization and legalization of work not as ends in themselves, but as means to strengthen—or else weaken—the position of the workers at stake.

Exclusion and Approximation (1867-2012)

Consisting of a total of 2,497 articles, the Portuguese Civil Code of 1867 covers a broad range of subjects including citizenship rights and duties, ownership, family, trade, and employment. One particular chapter concerns the regulation of labor. This chapter is divided into eight sections, the first one of which is limited to the provision of domestic service. Domestic service, like liberal professions and apprenticeship arrangements, is separated from standard wage labor, which is dealt with in a section of its own applying to all occupations without specific regulation.

The focus of legislators on paid domestic labor suggests an acknowledgment of this issue not only as complex or delicate, but also as a matter of public order. The civil code establishes that domestic service can only be considered as such if it is *rewarded* and performed on a *temporary* basis. Any commitment for life is deemed invalid for legal purposes, which means both parties are free to abandon it without any cost or obligation. Interestingly, this provision is not attached to any other occupation in the Civil Code of 1867, and one of its clear goals is to distinguish domestic service from serfdom or slavery (Ferreira 1870). Further rules regarding the beginning and end of the labor relationship, as well as the set of duties and rights of both parties, are specified. The selection of words is noteworthy. The person who purchases domestic services is referred to as *amo* (master), whereas in the section of the civil code concerning standard wage labor, the word *servido* (served person) is used instead. The person who is recruited to work is called *serviçal* (servant) in both sections. This detail is interesting because it reflects a distinction not between domestic workers and regular wage earners, but between employers. This is a distinction in nature: the master—not the employer—may own more than the worker's labor. What employers buy from domestic workers, Anderson (2000) argues, may be their very personhood more than their labor power, thus challenging the postulate of modern political philosophy that all individuals possess their own body and mind—a key element in the achievement of rights for women and ethnic minorities throughout the twentieth century.

The Civil Code of 1867 also states that whenever domestic servants have not been recruited to perform a particular task, the labor relationship binds them to perform any service compatible with their physical ability. Local customs are mentioned in several articles as providing acceptable standards. While this is not particular to legislation on domestic service, it does add some peculiar elements to it. For instance, the civil code states that in the absence of an explicit agreement on remuneration, pay shall be based on local customs considering the servant's sex, age, and duty. If the servant suffers from a health problem, the master is responsible for arranging medical support and deducting its costs from the remuneration, if the master is not willing to pay for it out of "generosity" (Civil Code 1867, Art. 1384/3). Regarding inheritances, in case the master decides to leave some of his inheritance to a servant, this must not be deducted from the remuneration and dismissal compensation (15 extra days) that the master's heirs are bound to pay the servant. Concerning age, minors are allowed to perform domestic services, although in that case an agreement must be reached between the master and the minor's legal guardian. Among the employer's duties, it is stated that if the servant is underage, the master is obliged to correct his or her mistakes "as a legal guardian would" (Civil Code 1867, Art. 1384/1).

This piece of legislation offers two distinct contributions. First, it attempts to acknowledge some rights and benefits in domestic service. Second, it clearly asserts the singularity of domestic service within existing occupations and the paternalistic characteristics of this type of labor relationship. The troubled disentanglement between paid labor on the basis of an employment contract and unpaid labor on the basis of family obligations is especially apparent. Besides the aforementioned selection of words, the duties of the "master" and his authority to command go well beyond the regulation on standard wage labor. Such development is closely related to the legal construction of the inviolability of the home, which owes less to modern day constitutional rights on individual freedom and privacy than to the autonomy of the domestic sphere—as a peripheral power—toward the central power of the state (Hespanha 2003, 22). In fact, individual rights are often sacrificed within the very context of the patriarchal household. It is necessary to point out that the protection of domestic workers in the Civil Code of 1867 is minimal, as just causes for dismissal include broadly applicable notions of inability to work, bad behavior, and breaking or stealing the master's belongings. This source of employment insecurity, as shown later on in this article, remains in place until today, and is important in maintaining asymmetry in the relationship between workers and their employers.

Since the last decades of the nineteenth century, a wide array of legislation on labor issues has been adopted in Portugal. This includes the condition of minors and women as workers, the rights of workers to association and representation, the responsibility of employers regarding health and safety at work, the legal procedures to deal with disagreements between employers and workers, and the regulation of labor inspection. Some of these decrees contained an article excluding particular categories of workers, most often those employed in agricultural, maritime or domestic services. The underlying claim was, and still is, that the special conditions in which these occupations are performed warrant exceptional regulation. Labor inspection conflicts with the ambiguous notion of the inviolability of private households (Anderson 2010). A second problem is that domestic workers are required to work, or stay in the workplace, longer than standard wage earners. Notably, when the maximum number of working hours was established in Portugal in 1919 (8 hours per day and 48 hours per week, at that time), the decree explicitly mentioned that it did not apply to rural workers, hotel and restaurant workers, and domestic servants (Decree No. 5516, May 10, 1919).[2]

Introduced by an authoritarian government, the general labor law of 1933 *(Estatuto do Trabalho Nacional,* Law-Decree 23048, 23 September, 1933) imposed dramatic changes on the system of industrial relations. Collective organization was severely restricted; among other things, workers and companies were required to maintain a "social peace spirit" and forbidden to "suspend or disturb" any economic activity "with the purpose of getting different working conditions or other benefits." The law on the standard rules for employment contracts in 1937 added important provisions (Law No. 1952, March 10, 1937). By the time the civil code was revised in 1966, provisions on employment were limited to the definition of basic concepts, all further issues being dispatched to specific labor legislation. Absent from both the new civil code and standard labor law, domestic service was still regulated by the Civil Code of 1867.

The fall of the dictatorship in 1974 opened new possibilities for collective action and bargaining. Domestic service, however, was not to be merged into general labor law. When a minimum monthly wage was introduced in 1974, agricultural and domestic workers were again excluded. A minimum wage for domestic workers was only implemented in 1978. This value was increased several times in the following two decades, although it would remain below the general minimum wage until 2004 when they were finally merged.[3]

A law on domestic service was finally adopted in 1980. It resulted from the initiative of a recently created domestic service workers' union. While this initiative was acknowledged as a legitimate claim, the law was introduced by a governmental decree under the protest of competing parties that demanded a wider debate in parliament and due consultation with labor representatives. The main criticisms about the document concerned the excessive number of maximum working hours, the weekly period of rest and holiday allowances below standard labor law, and the inaccurate definitions of domestic work.[4]

Table 1. Chronology of Selected Legislation on Domestic Service in Portugal

Year	Document	Relevance
1867	Civil Code (Arts. 1370-1390)	First regulation of the domestic service relationship
1980	Law-Decree Nr. 508/80, 21 October	Extended regulation of the domestic service relationship
1978	Law-Decree 113/78, 29 May (Art. 1/1a)	Establishment of a minimum wage for domestic service workers (updated on a yearly basis)
1982	Regulatory Decree 43/82, 22 July	Inclusion of domestic service employment in the social security system
1992	Law-Decree Nr. 235/92, 24 October	Revised regulation of the domestic service relationship
1996	Law-Decree Nr. 88/96, 3 July (Art. 1/1)	Extension of the regulation on Christmas allowance to cover domestic service employment
2004	Law-Decree Nr. 19/04, 20 January (Art. 2)	Extension of the regulation on minimum wage to cover domestic service employment

The very preamble of the decree is dubious as it states that it is "an imperative of social justice to cover the activity sector of domestic services with updated and more complete, though necessarily specific, legislation." Its 24 articles cover the various possible arrangements between employer and worker regarding time, holidays and remuneration, the valid procedures to begin and terminate the labor relationship, and the minimum age of workers. The decree has three distinct aspects. First, not only is the domestic workers' minimum wage set separately from and below the standard minimum wage, but the provision of housing and food by the employer can also comprise a part of the remuneration. Second, there is no fixed maximum working time. Live-in workers are entitled to rest and eating breaks of at least two hours per day, and are entitled to rest at night for eight consecutive hours. These breaks from work "are granted without detriment to the tasks of oversight or assistance to the household," and the night rest "should not be interrupted except for serious non-regular or imperative reasons." Last, valid reasons for both parties to terminate the labor relationship include a significant change in the conditions that motivated the relationship, failure to fulfill the basic duties established in the same law, breach of confidentiality over sensitive matters, and lack of good manners. The employer is also entitled to terminate the relationship if the worker brings other people such as relatives or friends into the house without the employer's knowledge, maintains habits or behaviors that do not suit the regular operation of the household, or carelessly uses equipment owned by the employer.

The law on domestic service was revised in 1992, resulting in the version currently in force (Table 2). A number of important changes were introduced. To start with, the article on working time was substantially modified. For the first time, it was established that the "normal period of weekly work" for domestic workers must not exceed 44 hours. In the case of domestic workers who reside in the employer's premises, however, this maximum number of hours refers to time spent in "effective work." Sufficient room is left for live-in domestic workers to be available 24 hours per day as there is no specific definition of effective work. For instance, it is unclear whether surveillance tasks are considered effective work. If surveillance tasks are not considered effective work, it is unclear whether the worker is free to exit the house and return only when the next period of effective work begins. Both institutional documents and policymakers remained unanimously elliptical in this respect.

Three additional issues were introduced in 1992. First, the domestic service law mandated that the Christmas allowance to which domestic workers are entitled should not be below 50% of their monthly pay. However, a general law on the Christmas allowance was adopted in 1996, mandating that all workers, including domestic workers, are entitled to an allowance of 100% of their monthly pay, to be paid until the 15th of December every year. Second, a complete list of rules on health and safety at the workplace was incorporated. These include the employer's duty to inform the worker about the operation of equipment and maintenance products used in the household, to repair damaged or dangerous materials, and, in the case of in-house domestic workers, to provide housing and food in conditions that are not harmful to the worker's health and hygiene. More important, the employer must obtain insurance from a company or organization legally entitled to do so, to cover any damage resulting from accidents at work. After legislation was approved at the European Union level, more complete legislation on accidents and illness at work was adopted covering all workers, including those employed in domestic service. Third, an article defining what constitutes abandonment of the labor relationship by the worker and what procedures must be followed in that case was introduced.

Although a national labor code eventually came into force in 2003, domestic service is still regulated by the law on domestic service. This is also true for economic activities such as entertainment, navy and harbors, railway transportation, agriculture, sports, and public administration. The current legal configuration retains the distinction between domestic service and standard wage labor made in the Civil Code of 1867, while a gradual advancement in rights has taken place.

Table 2. Selected Topics in the Regulation of Domestic Service in Portugal by December 2012

Topic		Regime
Written employment contract		Unrequired*
Working time	Maximum	44 hours of "effective work" per week
	Rest / breaks	Unspecified meal breaks during the day + 8 hours at night "without detriment to the tasks of oversight or assistance to the household"
	Holidays	22 paid days per year
Remuneration	Minimum	485,00 Euros per month, or 2,80 Euros per hour
	In kinds	Up to 50% of the above amount
	Mandatory allowances	1 extra month pay by summer vacation; 1 extra month pay by Christmas
Social security contributions	By the employer	Mandatory
	By the employee	Mandatory
Retirement pension		Yes (particular forms of calculation)
Health benefits	Insurance by the employer	Mandatory
	Maternity	Yes
	Illness	Yes
Unemployment	Insurance	Partial**
	Compensation	One month pay for every year of service completed
Education		Protected for workers younger than 18 only

Unsolved Practicalities and the International Convention

Following the guidelines of the ILO's double discussion procedure, final versions of the Domestic Workers Convention and Recommendation were adopted in 2011 (ILO 2011a, 2011b). Since then, a trade union confederation and several nongovernmental organizations representing women and migrants in Portugal have urged the government to take action toward ratifying the convention. One of their claims is that national regulation is in agreement with the standards set in the convention; therefore, ratification shall not require any legislative innovation. This may be understood as a strategic step to depoliticize and thereby ease the ratification.

A thoughtful observation of the convention requires addressing various unsolved practicalities in the regulation of paid domestic labor in Portugal. Far from being negligible, these issues may be too significant to be dealt with as simple administrative adjustments. For the purpose of clarity, they can be organized into nine distinct yet interrelated matters.

Social Protection

The access of domestic workers to social protection remains regulated by a special scheme. Workers who are employed full-time by one sole entity on a monthly basis are in a different situation than workers under part-time arrangements. The former are able to enroll in two distinct programs: 1) a program with the same rules and benefits that apply to standard wage earners, including unemployment benefits; and 2) a program based on a lower tributary rate (28.3% against 34.75%, at the time of writing) and a standard remuneration that can be below the worker's actual pay. The latter has been implemented with a pecuniary protective aim, as a portion of the pay is not taxed by social security. The first significant distinction is that workers under part-time arrangements can only access program 2. Even among workers who are employed full-time by one sole entity, enrollment in program 1 is only accessible if they are under 57 years old and if they sign an agreement term with their employer for this particular purpose. Considering that the National Constitution (Art. 59/1b) includes the right of all workers to "material assistance when they are involuntarily in unemployment," there seems to be an odd variety of caveats in the case of domestic workers. Although this article of the Constitution prohibits discrimination based on age, sex, race (ethnicity), citizenship, place of origin, religion, and political or ideological conviction, it does not mention occupation. Encased in a lower level of benefits, domestic workers can be described as sub-workers in the social security system. In the meantime, Article 14 of the ILO Domestic Workers Convention is not without ambig-uousness itself as it requires states to "ensure that domestic workers enjoy conditions that are not less favourable than those applicable to workers generally in respect of social security protection", although measures to that end may be "applied progressively" and "with due regard for the specific characteristics of domestic work". Still, it is increasingly difficult to argue from either a critical or a normative perspective that the specific characteristics of domestic work justify social protection below general standards in the labour market.

Indistinction between Live-In and Live-Out Domestic Workers

The law examined earlier applies to both live-in and live-out domestic workers, resorting to the concept of "effective work" and the underlying fiction that live-in domestic workers perform it for a maximum of 44 hours per week, to cover up the large gray area of negotiation between employer and worker. Article 10 in the international convention refers to periods during which workers "are not free to dispose of their time as they please and remain at the disposal of the household in order to respond to possible calls," a notion that is absent from national law. Indistinction between live-in and live-out workers therefore translates into the underprivileged situation of the former, as they remain legally vulnerable to the imposition of overtime.

Dismissal

The pursuit of fair terms of employment requires a reconsideration of the norms that regulate the termination of the relationship. Just cause for dismissal by the employer is defined in a manner that is both broad and detailed. It comprises disobedience, lack of interest, mishandling of material items or confidential matters, abnormal reduction in productivity, lack of good manners, and behaving in a way that does not suit the regular operation of the household, among other things. Though more limited, just cause for dismissal by the worker also includes some of these considerations, including the ones on behavior. The relationship can also be terminated due to the employer's inability to maintain it, economic insufficiency, or substantial transformation in the circumstances under which the worker was recruited. While the convention does not elaborate on this topic, it is plausible that all measures aiming to reduce workers' vulnerability depend on addressing and reformulating the terms of employment termination.

Written Contracts

Article 7 of the convention states that measures shall be taken to ensure that "domestic workers are informed of their terms and conditions of employment in an appropriate, verifiable and easily understandable manner and preferably, where possible, through written contracts." Although absent from the law on domestic service in Portugal, written contracts are deemed compulsory in the general labor code if the relationship involves foreign workers, short-term employment, part-time employment, intermittent employment, or temporary employment. The fact that a contract of employment with full legal rights is presumed to be in place whenever a contract has not been signed may explain why this is not a common claim made by national labor unions at the moment. However, the wide legal scope for unilateral decision by the employer of a domestic worker exposed to the three issues discussed earlier throws a different light on the subject. The value of written contracts has been highlighted in one of the latest campaigns developed in Portugal for the rights of domestic workers, in a joint initiative by activists and scholars. The general informative brochure for domestic workers and employers produced by this campaign even includes a template for written contracts (GAMI 2012).

Education

Since the first version of the law adopted in 1980, domestic workers in Portugal have been required to be at least 16 years old. Education is not mentioned in the law. However, the labor code comprises a number of provisions protecting workers under the age of 18, including one on education; these apply to domestic workers as well. Aside from several provisions against child labor, the international convention requires ratifying member states to ensure that employers of domestic workers under the age of 18 do not "deprive them of compulsory education, or interfere with opportunities to participate in further education or vocational training" (Art. 4). It is crucial to address the domestic workers' right to education and attendance of courses considering present day compulsory schooling, which includes workers above 18. The importance of this issue is underlined by the lower level of schooling of many women employed in domestic service, especially natives (Guibentif 2011). Several countries in Latin America have exemplary protective clauses in this regard (Loyo and Velásquez 2009).

Living Conditions for Live-In Domestic Workers

The insufficient acknowledgment of live-in domestic workers in national law translates into the absence of objective standards for their living conditions. The only requirement is that housing and food must be provided "in conditions that safeguard the hygiene and health of workers." This is all the more problematic as general provisions on housing provided by employers to standard wage earners, such as posted or temporarily delocalized workers, tend to be equally laconic. The contribution of the convention is not straightforward either. While its reference to "decent living conditions" maintains the subject in the muddy waters of customs, the notion of "respect" for "privacy" mentioned in Article 6 may be a more fruitful ground for collective parties to build their claims.

Freedom

Article 9 of the convention protects the freedom of domestic workers to reach an agreement with their employer on whether to reside in the household, to be away from the house and household members during periods of daily, weekly, or annual leave, and to keep in their possession travel and identity documents. Clearly intertwined with some of the points discussed earlier, these three provisions are absent from the law on domestic service employment in Portugal. If this sector is to be maintained under particular regulation, such regulation should address the objective sources of vulnerability that public intervention and academic research have repeatedly uncovered. This article of the convention is especially relevant because basic human rights in the employment context are often taboo in political debate; it is presumed that both parties comply with them and all workers know about them. The fact that authoritative documents such as the National Constitution assert or implicitly require respect for these rights means that labor legislation does not need to be concerned with them. Yet this produces practical results only insofar as the concrete manifestations of such rights in particular contexts are recognized and protected.

Intermediation

Two distinct matters arise under intermediation. First, trafficking or smuggling of people is to be restrained. Again, provisions and measures are left outside the realm of domestic employment regulation, since migration and criminal laws are expected to deal with this issue, even if domestic service bears close historical links to forced labor. Far from being a matter of the past, these links have suffered new impulses under globalizing neoliberalism (Ehrenreich and Russell 2002; Peixoto 2009). Second, intermediation can also refer to lawful private companies that provide domestic services. Intervention in this regard is not only about ensuring compliance with basic human rights, but also about defining the conditions under which private agencies that recruit or place domestic workers operate. A major risk is that workers employed through agencies are not covered by either domestic service employment law or general labor law, as they become subcontracted service providers, or self-employed workers, following one of the most typical routes to precariousness in contemporary labor markets. This configuration is possible, though illegal, as independent work requires a degree of freedom and autonomy that domestic workers hardly enjoy. It is more properly understood as a way to circumvent employment rights and standards. Nevertheless, it may prosper unless domestic service regulation addresses it in proper terms.

Labor Inspection

The statutes of labor inspection in Portugal explicitly state that, whenever the workplace is a private residence, the rules of domiciliary visit set through penal regulation apply (Law-Decree 102/2000, June 2, 2000). This means a warrant for that purpose must be obtained from judicial authority. The "private workplace" is hereby protected. There is a further difficulty in the case of domestic workers. As they are often sole employees, the intervention of labor inspection is likely to contribute to the deterioration of their relationship with the employer. Although this problem in labor relations is not limited to domestic service, the vulnerability of certain employment sectors demands an explicit and straightforward strategy.

CONCLUSION

To a large extent, these nine unsolved practicalities represent the distance that still separates—albeit to a lesser degree than in 1867—domestic service from general labor law. Some of these issues can only be addressed if their roles in structuring paid domestic labor are explicitly acknowledged. Dismissal procedures and the case of live-in domestic workers are the most critical matters; addressing them may lead to a dramatic readjustment of power in this activity sector, and progressive propositions are bound to be accused of prompting unemployment and disfavoring domestic workers for their excessive aspirations. In addition, the enactment of full rights to social security and labor inspection requires changes in neighboring legal provisions, pushing the struggle beyond the law on domestic service employment. While the historical approach offers important contributions in clarifying particularities in the regulation of the sector, further study is required to examine relevant links with regulation in areas such as migration and gender equality (Va-lenzuela and Mora 2009, 294-7).

An additional issue concerns the recent changes in general law. As employment rights are pressed for reduction under neoliberal responses to economic recession (Supiot 2010), approximation may be accomplished less by the inclusion of domestic workers under labor standards of the overall workforce than by the reduction of those labor standards. This discussion echoes Ulrich Beck's (2000) claim of the process of "Brazilianization" of the West. He argues that, despite the general notion that Europe is setting the standards for the other parts of the world, the opposite may be taking place in the sphere of employment. Based on the historical examination in this article, one may wonder if, despite the general notion that standard wage labor is setting the standards for domestic service employment, a "domestic-workifi-cation" of the labor market is actually underway. At the same time, the market dynamics are likely to maintain considerable pressure to exclude domestic workers from the regulation in place, especially through the legal configuration and rhetoric of the self-employed worker.

A notable feature in the examined regulatory processes is that domestic workers and their representatives have been absent from them. Looking into the mid-twentieth century, Inês Brasão (2012) shows how the ethics of domestic service in Portugal have been historically and socially constructed by masters or employers. The analysis in this article suggests that the same assertion can be extended to cover the implementation of the Civil Code of 1867, and more surprisingly, the period following the implementation of democracy in the 1970s. New social tensions regarding the paternalistic foundations of this type of labor relationship and acts of disorganized resistance from domestic workers were accompanied by reluctant legal advancements. From an historical point of view, the juridical condition of domestic workers exposes their slippery position between paid labor on the basis of an employment contract and unpaid labor on the basis of gender, class and ethnic roles. Considering research in other locations, this study corroborates the notion of heterogeneity across countries and a common disadvantage of domestic service workers vis-à-vis the local legal framework applying to standard wage earners (ILO 2010; Loyo and Velásquez 2009).

The recent international convention is a significant tool to contest the underprivileged position of domestic workers in labor regulation. Domestic workers are now incorporated into the ILO's broader agenda for decent work. Yet, a distinct sort of decency remains at stake— one that is markedly evident in legal documents from earlier days. It is closely linked to public order, to social values and customs, and to the implicit indecency of "lower level" citizens and workers claiming for equality. It is still, in the end, a matter of decency.

REFERENCES

1. Anderson, Bridget. 2000. *Doing the Dirty Work? The Global Politics of Domestic Labour.* London: Zed Books.
2. Anderson, Bridget. 2006. *A very Private Business: Migration and Domestic Work.* Working Paper of COMPAS - Centre on Migration, Policy and Society, 28. Oxford: University of Oxford.
3. Anderson, Bridget. 2010. Mobilizing Migrants, Making Citizens: Migrant Domestic Workers as Political Agents. *Ethnic and Racial Studies* 33, no. 1: 60-74.

4. Baganha, Maria Ioannis. 1998. Immigrant Involvement in the Informal Economy: The Portuguese Case. *Journal of Ethnic and Migration Studies* 24, no. 2: 367-385.

5. Beck, Ulrich. 2000. *The Brave New World ofWork.* New York: Polity Press.

6. Beleza, Teresa. 2000. Género e direito: da igualdade ao "direito das mulheres". *Themis* 1, no. 2: 35-66.

7. Beleza, Teresa. 2002. "Clitemnestra por uma noite": a condição jurídica das mulheres portuguesas no século XX. In *Panorama da cultura portuguesa no século XX, Vol.I,* ed. Fernando Pernes, 121-150. Oporto: Fundação Serralves.

8. Brasão, Inês. 2012. O tempo das criadas: a condição servil em Portugal (1940-1970). Lisboa: Tinta da China.

9. Braudel, Fernand. 1969. *Écritssurlhistoire.* Paris: Flammarion.

10. Canevaro, Santiago. 2009. Empleadas domésticas y empleadoras en la configuración del trabajo doméstico en la Ciudad de Buenos Aires: entre la administración del tiempo, la organización del espacio y la gestión de las «maneras de hacer». *Campos* 10, no. 1: 63-86.

11. Casaca, Sara Falcão and João Peixoto. 2010. Flessibilità e segmentazione del mercato del lavoro in Portogallo: genere e immigrazione. *Sociologia del Lavoro* 117: 116-133.

12. Cooper, Sheila McIsaac. 2005. Service to Servitude? The Decline and Demise of Life-cycle Service in England. *The History of the Family* 10, no. 4: 367-386.

13. Ehrenreich, Barbara and Arlie Russell eds. 2002. *Global Woman. Nannies, Maids, and Sex Workers in the New Economy.*New York: Owl Books.

14. Fauve-Chamoux, Antoinette and Richard Wall. 2005. Domestic Servants in Comparative Perspective. *The History of the Family* 10, no. 4: 345-354.

15. Ferreira,JoséDias. 1870. *Códigocivilportuguezannotado, Vol. III.* Lisbon: Imprensa Nacional.

16. GAMI - Grupo de Apoio às Mulheres Imigrantes. 2012. *Direitos e deveres no trabalho doméstico.* Lisbon: GAMI.

17. Goldsmit Connelly, Mary Rosaria, Rosario Baptista, Ariel Ferrari and María Celia Vence (Coords.). 2010. *Hacia un fortalecimiento de derechos laborales en el trabajo de hogar: algunas experiencias de América Latina.* Montevideo: Friedrich Ebert Stiftung.

18. Góis, Pedro and José Carlos Marques. 2009. Portugal as a Semi-peripheral Country in the Global Migration System.*International Migration* 47, no. 3: 21-50.

19. Guerreiro, Maria das Dores. 2000. *Employment, Family and Community Activities: A New Balance for Women and Men.*European Foundation for the Improvement of Living and Working Conditions,http://www.eurofound.europa.eu/pubdocs/2000/112/en/1/ef00112en.pdf (retrieved 11 June 2012).

20. Guibentif, Pierre. 2009. Teorias sociológicas comparadas e aplicadas. Bourdieu, Foucault, Habermas e Luhmann face ao direito. *Novatio Iuris* 3: 9-33.

21. Guibentif, Pierre. 2011. *Rights Perceived and Practiced: Results of a Survey Carried out in Portugal as Part of the Project "Domestic work and domestic workers: interdisciplinary and comparative perspectives".* Working Paper of Dinamia'CETTUL: Centre for Socioeconomic Change and Territorial Studies, 2011/01, ISCTE. Lisbon: Lisbon University Institute.

22. Hespanha, Antônio Manuel. 2003. *Cultura jurídica europeia. Síntese de um milênio.* Mem Martins: Publicações Europa-América.

23. International Labour Office (ILO). 2011a. *Domestic Workers Convention, 2011* (C189). ILO, http://www.ilo.org/ dyn/normlex/en/f?p=1000:12100:0::NO::P12100_ILO_ CODE:C189 (retrieved 9 October 2012)

24. International Labour Office (ILO). 2011b. *Domestic Workers Recommendation, 2011* (R201). ILO, http://www.ilo.org/ dyn/normlex/en/f?p=1000:12100:0::NO::P12100_IN-STRUMENT_ID:2551502 (retrieved 9 October 2012).

25. International Labour Office (ILO). 2010. *Decent work for domestic workers, report IV(i), International Labour Conference, 99th session.* Geneva: ILO.

26. Loyo, María Gabriela and Mario D. Velásquez. 2009. Aspectos jurídicos y económicos del trabajo doméstico remunerado en América Latina. In *Trabajo doméstico: un largo camino hacia el trabajo decente,* eds. María Elena Valenzuela and Claudia Mora, 21-70. Santiago: ILO.

27. Lutz, Helma (Ed.). 2008. *Migration and domestic work: a European perspective on a global theme.* Aldershot: Ashgate.

28. Marx, Karl. 2010 [1867]. *Capital. A Critique ofPolitical Economy, Vol. I.* Moscow: Progress Publishers.

29. McDowell, Linda. 2000. Feminists rethink the economic: the economics of gender / the gender of economics. In *The Oxford handbook of economic geography,* eds. Gordon Clark, Maryann Feldman and Meric Gertler, 497-517. New York: Oxford University Press.

30. Parreñas, Rhacel Salazar. 2001. *Servants ofGlobalization. Women, Migration, and Domestic Work.* Stanford: Stanford University Press.

31. Peixoto, João. 2009. New migrations in Portugal: Labour Markets, Smuggling and Gender Segmentation. *International Migration* 47, no. 3: 185-2010.

32. Pinto, Teresa. 2007. Industrialização e domesticidade no século XIX: a edificação de um novo modelo social de género. In*Género, diversidade e cidadania, ed.* Fernanda Hen-riques, 155-168. Lisbon: Colibri.

33. Sager, Eric W. 2007. The Transformation of the Canadian Domestic Servant, 1871-1931. *Social Science History* 31, no. 4: 509-537.

34. Santos, Boaventura de Sousa. 2006. Globalizations. *Theory, Culture & Society* 23, no. 2-3: 393-399.

35. Sarti, Raffaella. 2005. Domestic Service and European Identity. In Proceedings of the Servant Project, Vol. V, eds. Suzy Pasleau and Isabelle Schopp, 195-284. Liège:

Editions de l'Université de Liège.

36. Sassen, Saskia. 2007. *A Sociology of Globalization.* New York: W. W. Norton & Company.

37. Supiot, Alain. 2006. Law and Labour. *New Left Review* 39: 109-122.

38. Supiot, Alain. 2010. A Legal Perspective on the Economic Crisis. *International Labour Review* 149, no. 2: 151-62.

39. Valenzuela, María Elena and Claudia Mora. 2009. Esfuerzos concertados para la revaloración del trabajo doméstico remunerado en América Latina. In *Trabajo doméstico: un largo camino hacia el trabajo decente,* eds. María Elena Valenzuela and Claudia Mora, 285304. Santiago: ILO.

40. Wall, Karin, and Cátia Nunes. 2010. Immigration, Welfare and Care in Portugal: Mapping the New Plurality of Female Migration Trajectories. *Social Policy and Society* 9, no. 3: 397-408.

41. Walsum, Sarah van. 2011. Regulating Migrant Domestic Work in the Netherlands: Opportunities and Pitfalls. *Canadian Journal ofWomen and the Law* 23, no. 1: 141-165.

42. Weber, Max. 1978 [1911-13]. Economy and Law (the Sociology of Law). In *Economy and Society, Vol. 2,* Max Weber, 641900. Berkeley: University of California Press.

CHAPTER 13

EXECUTIVE RULE-MAKING AND THE SECOND DIRECTIVE ON INSTITUTIONS FOR OCCUPATIONAL RETIREMENT PROVISION

Ton van den Brink, Hans van Meerten

Keywords: Legislation, delegation, implementation, better law making, IORP, EU agencies

INTRODUCTION

General

The Treaty of Lisbon has introduced a new system of legislation and executive rule-making in the European Union (EU).1 Executive rule-making falls into two categories: delegation (Article 290 TFEU) and implementation (Article 291 TFEU). The new system attracted a fair degree of scholarly attention prior to and in the initial years after the entry into force of the Lisbon Treaty. This has included analyses of the problems that the new system brings about, as well as of issues that the new system has not resolved. These issues therefore continue to exist. Not much research has as yet been carried out on how the new legislative system is to be implemented in practice and how these issues play out. In this contribution the consequences of the new legislative system in a particular area of EU law will be addressed: pensions law. More specifically we will focus on the second Directive on Institutions for Occupational Retirement Provision (IORP II).2 The role and competence of the EU in pension matters is highly politically sensitive3 and the revision of the initial IORP Directive has thus not only raised important matters of substance, but it also highlights various fundamental issues of the EU's legislative system. These include a) the competence of the EU to act in this area to begin with, b) the inclusion of powers for the Commission to adopt secondary legislation, but also c) the quasi-regulatory powers of the competent EU agency in the field: the European Insurance and Occupational Pensions Authority (EIOPA).

The structure of this contribution is as follows. First, a general analysis of the EU's legislative system is made, partly based on an analysis of the existing literature and the issues identified therein. Then, the revision of the IORP II Directive will be discussed in light of these issues. In concrete policy areas such as pensions law, such issues cannot be viewed in isolation (for example, only the IORP Directive), but must be seen in light of the underlying substantive controversies. In the case of the IORP II Directive, one of the main controversies is whether the EU (i.e. the EU legislature, the Commission as the main executive rule-making authority and EIOPA) should be able – for instance – to adopt capital requirements for pensions institutions. How this substantive controversy affects the general legislative issues identified in Section 2 will thus be the main focus of attention.

EXECUTIVE RULE-MAKING AFTER 'LISBON'

The Treaty System

The EU's legislative system is based on two main distinctions: the first between legislative acts and nonlegislative acts and the second between delegation (Article 290 TFEU) and implementation (Article 291 TFEU). Both delegation and implementation are qualified as 'non-legislative acts' in the terminology of the EU Treaty. According to Article 290 TFEU, a delegated act is an act of general application to supplement or amend certain non-essential elements of the legislative act. According to Article 291 TFEU, an implementing act is an act that ensures that legally binding Union acts are implemented subject to uniform conditions. Accordingly, both types of

Citation: van den Brink, T. & van Meerten, H., (2016). Executive Rule-Making and the Second Directive on Institutions for Occupational Retirement Provision. Utrecht Law Review. 12(1), pp.75–85. DOI: http://doi.org/10.18352/ulr.329.

secondary legislation are primarily defined in institutional and procedural terms, rather than in substantive terms.4 Definitions of and prerequisites for the various legal acts are determined by procedural conditions and institutional relationships.5 As delegated acts ('quasi-legislation') are clothed in stronger democratic guarantees, they may be viewed as instruments that carry more weight than implementing acts.6 Yet, the Treaties have not established a formal hierarchy between delegated and implementing acts.7 Strikingly, the definitions of delegated acts and implementing acts are not related.8 Delegated acts are defined on the basis of their scope of application (supplementing or amending nonessential elements of legislative acts), whilst the definition of implementing acts is based on their function and rationale (implementing acts allow legislative acts to be applied according to uniform conditions).9 These definitions partly overlap.10

The result of this has been that the substantive distinction between legislation, delegation and implementation had to be fleshed out further by the institutional practice. Apart from the EU's political institutions, also the role of the CJEU should be noted. Two decisions of the CJEU have shed more light on this issue. In the Schengen Borders Code case the CJEU ruled on the distinction between legislation and non-legislative acts11 and the decision in the Biocides case concerned the distinction between delegation and implementation.12

The Distinction between Legislative and Non-Legislative Acts

The distinction between legislative and non-legislative acts is not only for the EU legislature (Parliament, Council, Commission) to make. Indeed, with Article 290 TFEU the limitation of the EU legislature's freedom to delegate rule-making powers has been awarded Treaty status.13 The status of legislative acts has thus acquired a constitutional dimension, which is reflected in the fact that political scrutiny has become a key characteristic thereof.14 The substantive criterion is that 'essential elements' of an issue need to be regulated by the legislature itself whereas 'non-essential elements' may be delegated to the executive.

In the Schengen Borders Code case the CJEU made clear that it has a substantial role in defining the distinction between legislative acts and non-legislative acts. Long before the Treaty of Lisbon, the basis for that conclusion had already been developed in the case law of the CJEU in which 'essential' elements were distinguished from 'non-essential' elements.15 Although the terminology is quite open-textured, the findings as to which elements are essential are '(...) [to be] based on objective factors amenable to judicial review' (Paragraph 67).16 According to the CJEU, the decision of the Council supplementing the Schengen Borders Code (in the form of what we would now refer to as an implementing act) did indeed relate to essential elements. They should have been laid down in the basic act (i.e. a directive, secondary EU Law) and the decision of the Council therefore had to be annulled. The essential elements that had to be decided at the legislative level included the enforcement powers granted to border guards to take coercive measures. According to the CJEU, not only did the Council decision thus affect fundamental rights, but it also involved political choices: a balance had to be found between conflicting interests (protection of the migrant vs. the interest involved with checks at the EU's external borders).17 Political choices as a criterion for defining essential elements is, however, problematic: if only since political decision-making can never be fully excluded in the context of executive rule-making.18

In any case, the discretion of the legislature has been effectively restricted by the CJEU.19 This is obviously manifested first of all by the outcome of the case. Moreover, the CJEU did not review whether or not the Council, as the executive institution, had remained within the margins set by the EU legislature (the delegation provision from the Schengen Borders Code) but rather whether the EU legislature had respected the general, constitutional distinction between essential and non-essential elements. In other words, the CJEU focused on the limits on the legislature rather than on the limits on the delegate.

The dividing line between legislative and non-legislative acts is also relevant from an inter-institutional perspective. In a recent case the CJEU had to rule on the Commission's decision to withdraw a legislative proposal for a Regulation on macro-financial assistance to third countries.20 The Commission opposed the Council's and the European Parliament's amendment of the proposal to remove an implementing power from the proposal according to which the Commission would have the power to decide on the actual conferral of assistance. The European Parliament and the Council had lodged an appeal against the withdrawal of the proposal by the Commission. The Commission disagreed with the decision of the European Parliament and the Council in that the European Parliament and the Council were of the opinion that such decisions should be made via the ordinary legislative procedure (and thus took the position that such decisions were part of the essential elements of the Regulation). The CJEU, however, found that the Commission's withdrawal was justified. One of the main objectives of the proposal is to accelerate the decision-making on providing assistance and thus its effectiveness. In light of this, the implementing power was in fact an essential element of the proposal, according to the CJEU (Paragraph 91). Furthermore, the withdrawal was justified based on the Commission's position regarding the trialogues. In practice, these informal consultations between the three legislative institutions are of vital importance in order to reach consensus. The CJEU used the Commission's position during these trialogues as a justification for the subsequent withdrawal of the proposal. It did not answer the material question of whether this case involved essential or non-essential elements. The case should be seen as an answer to the question regarding the scope of application of the powers of legislative institutions to determine what elements of the regulation are essential.

The Distinction between Delegation and Implementation

The Treaty of Lisbon has introduced another distinction that relates to the distinction between delegation and implementation.21 This distinction, although it may appear as quite technical, has indeed become extremely politicised. A lack of consensus on the choice between delegation and implementation frequently leads to considerable delays in the legislative process. This has been the case in major legislative dossiers such as the Multiannual Financial Framework, the reform of the Common Agricultural Policy and the series of measures relating to the Single Market Act I (April 2011) and II (October 2012).22 The diverging and even opposing interests of EU institutions and the lack of clear substantive criteria and definitions in the Treaties are conducive thereto. Delegation is based for the most part on ex post control by the Council and the European Parliament.23 Depending on the legal basis, these institutions may have the power to object to a specific delegated act (as a result of which it cannot enter into force) or they may even have the power to revoke the delegation altogether. Moreover, a legislative act may provide that both of these powers are connected to a specific delegation. The power to revoke the delegation is a radical one as it essentially means that the Council and the European Parliament can unilaterally amend a legislative act. However, as far as the authors are aware, this power has not yet been actually exercised. Both the Council and the European Parliament have, however, raised several objections to specific delegated acts.24 Thus, delegated acts have certainly become included in processes of democratic oversight.25

Not surprisingly, the European Parliament strongly prefers Article 290 TFEU because of these ex post control mechanisms26 which it lacks under Article 291 TFEU.27 By contrast, the Member States prefer implementation over delegation because of the ex ante control mechanism which applies to implementing acts via committees of national experts (comitology). The Member States value this mechanism of ex ante control mechanism highly and have tried to apply it to the adoption of delegated acts as well. Although the Commission already promised in 2009 to 'systematically consult experts from the national authorities of all the Member States'28 – and this commitment has indeed been incorporated into various legislative acts29 – Member States view this as an insufficient guarantee. These diverging subjective institutional views on delegation and implementation now make the legislative choice for either Article 290 TFEU or 291 TFEU necessarily easy to understand. Moreover, control by the CJEU is limited as the Court grants the legislature a wide margin of discretion. In its decision in the Biocides case, the CJEU concluded that judicial control is limited to whether the choice of the legislature falls within the conditions laid down in Articles 290 and 291 TFEU.30 In a later case, the CJEU decided that whether the Commission has been granted a discretionary power or not (or, if so, the scope thereof) is not a relevant factor to determine whether Article 290 or 291 should apply.31

Despite the legislative discretion that determines the choice between Article 290 and 291 TFEU, Schütze has argued that delegation and implementation are fundamentally different in nature: in his view Article 290 TFEU concerns the delegation of legislative power (as it involves the power to amend primary legislation) whereas Article 291 TFEU concerns the delegation of executive powers (as it involves the implementation of primary legislation).32 The respective control mechanisms reflect this different status: control in the context of Article 290 TFEU focuses on democratic guarantees, whereas control by Member States is the key element in the context of Article 291 TFEU. The latter element can be explained by viewing implementing acts as a manifestation of executive federalism: Member States feel the need to be able to control the (supranational) Commission. Such an idea of a fundamental difference between delegation and implementation is difficult to reconcile with the EU's legislative practice. Delegation is limited to acts of general application but this does not imply that implementation may not include measures of general application as well.33 Moreover, whereas implementation is supposed to only give effect to existing provisions of primary legislation (and, thus, to refrain from adding new elements thereto), the reality is that it often inevitably involves value judgements and political choices.34 Thus, implementing acts and delegated acts are not easy to distinguish on the basis of their content.35

With the Interinstitutional Agreement on Better Law Making (IIA),36 the EU institutions have tried to remove some of the controversy by bringing the procedure to adopt delegated acts closer to that of the committee procedures under Article 291 TFEU in that:

- it is now an obligation for the Commission to consult Member State experts;
- the Commission is obliged to react to the consultation of Member State experts and will state how it will take the experts' views into consideration; and
- Member State experts have the right to give a new opinion in case of a change in the material content of a draft delegated act.

Consequently, Member States' opposition to delegation may be expected to diminish and, thus, the choice between delegation and implementation may be expected to be depoliticized to a certain extent. But the Commission had wished for more – and, for that matter, the European Parliament as well – and tried to introduce a more substantive delineation of delegation and implementation. To that end, it identified a set of objective criteria that should guide the choice between the two forms of secondary legislation. In its proposal for a new IIA37 the Commission identified a number of criteria that in fact directly flow from the Treaty system, such as the rule that measures designed to lay down additional substantive rules and criteria to be met can only be adopted by way of delegated acts as they supplement the basic act.38 Other criteria would indeed have clarified and further elaborated the existing legal framework, such as the rule that 'the annual and multiannual work programmes implementing financial instruments should be adopted by means of implementing acts'. However, all of the Commission's criteria have been removed from the final version of the text of the IIA, including those that in fact add little to the existing legal framework. Even a vague commitment to negotiate substantive criteria between the three institutions following the entry into force of the IIA has not made it to the final text.39

The legitimacy of EU secondary legislation is not only relevant from an interinstitutional perspective. The involvement of stakeholders and public consultation are increasingly seen as valuable elements of the decision-making on delegated acts in particular.40 The IIA, however, brings little new in this regard, and focused as it is on Member State expert participation. It only provides that decision-making on delegated acts 'may include' consultations with stakeholders.41 Experiences with obligations to that effect that already exist with regard to the powers of financial agencies of the EU have thus not found their way to the IIA. More in general, the IIA completely ignores the position of EU agencies in EU law making. The EU financial agencies that were set up in 2011 have been given quasi-regulatory powers and are authorized to propose draft delegated and implementing acts. The status of such draft acts is strengthened by legislative constraints on the discretion of the Commission. The Commission may not simply ignore such draft acts. Thus, the existence of such quasi-regulatory powers raises questions as to their exact status and scope, their legitimacy and the implications for the EU institutions. These questions have remained unaddressed by the IIA. This is all the more surprising since the basic Treaties have failed to recognize the status of EU agencies as well.42 Thus, no constitutional framework exists to regulate the position of agencies as recipients of (quasi-)delegated or (quasi-)implementing powers. The gap between the constitutional provisions and the actual institutional practice is only widening.43 We will analyse the effects of this gap on the position of the EU agency in the field of pensions: the European supervisory agency EIOPA (European Insurance and Occupational Pensions Authority).44

EXECUTIVE RULE-MAKING IN EU PENSIONS LAW

Resistance to Executive Rule-Making

Article 30 of the Commission's proposal to revise the IORP II Directive contains a legal basis for delegation for the Commission. Under this provision, the Commission may adopt a delegated act specifying, inter alia, the remuneration policy, the risk assessment for pensions and the pension benefit statement. Moloney45 concludes that delegation provisions are usually drawn up in very general terms and that it is therefore difficult to see how they relate to the requirements of Article 290 TFEU. Moloney's view is inter alia supported by the European Economic and Social Committee (EESC). In connection with the MiFid II proposal46 the EESC objected to the 'extreme and disproportionate use of delegated acts', as provided by Article 94 of the proposal.47 According to the EESC, delegated acts should relate to specific and well-defined affairs and should be exercised within a certain period of time. In the proposal for the MiFIR Regulation48 the EESC49 notes that there is a compatibility problem between Article 40 of the draft Regulation (the legal basis for delegation) and Article 290 TFEU.50 The number, content and provisions of the delegated acts are not consistent with the provisions of the Treaty and place too many fundamental aspects of the Regulation outside the scope of the normal legislative process, according to the EESC. The EESC therefore recommends examining how Article 40 of the proposal can be aligned with the requirements of Article 290 TFEU.

The EESC was also critical of the proposed legal bases for delegation in the IORP II proposal.51 The EESC urged the Commission to be particularly cautious when drawing up the delegated act mentioned in Article 54 of the proposal (regarding requirements for the pension benefit statement), 'given the potential costs of such a solution'. The Committee therefore suggested that when listing information requirements for scheme members, the Commission should take into account the nature of the schemes which they belong to.52 By doing so, the EESC essentially said that the Commission should be careful not to affect the essential elements of the rules. As to making information available to members and beneficiaries of pension funds, the EESC expressed concerns about the suitability of a statement of standardised information, and proposed that more experience should be gathered before the delegated act could be carried out.53

EIOPA and Executive Pension Regulation

As stated in Section 2, the EU financial agencies have powers to draw up draft rules in preparation of delegated acts and implementing acts.54 EIOPA55 has such powers too. They are somewhat controversial, mostly due to the fact that EIOPA deals with rather sensitive issues and seems to act, sometimes, on its own initiative. On its own initiative, EIOPA is currently working (in connection with the implementation of the current IORP Directive) on tightening the requirements for the solvency of pension institutions.56 These solvency requirements, set out in the 'Holistic Balance Sheet (HBS)', entail a mechanism that should facilitate a clearer comparison between European pension funds.57

In the course of its consultations EIOPA reiterated the Commission's statement that more technical information on the solvency of pension funds was required.58 EIOPA acted on this by starting these consultations on its own initiative, and emphasized that there was no connection with the Commission's proposal for IORP II. Pensions Europe, a representative body of national pension funds, has been critical of the EIOPA's plans for the HBS, and has even referred to the plan as being 'conceptually wrong.' It claims that the HBS is not an adequate regulatory instrument and moreover entails an 'unacceptable burden' for IORPs.59 Aside from the HBS, EIOPA issues several reports and guidelines, including ones on the costs of IORPs60 and individual value transfers between Member States.61 This last report62 identifies eight bottlenecks for cross-border individual value transfer for which EIOPA offers 'good practices'. These should be observed by the Member States. These EIOPA activities do not automatically lead to acts with legally binding effect. This could however be the end result, either through the mechanism of Article 290/291 TFEU, or otherwise (see the next section). This could give EIOPA a greater role than is perhaps assumed. This will be explained in what follows.

FURTHER CAPITAL REQUIREMENTS FOR IORPS?

As said, under the current measures of the European Commission and EIOPA, and based on the current draft text of the IORP II Directive, no new capital requirements seem to be imposed on IORPs.63 Nevertheless, as stated at the end of the preceding section, it cannot be ruled out that such requirements will eventually come into the picture. Three developments can be mentioned. First of all, Article 30 of the draft IORP II Directive empowers the European Commission to adopt implementing acts 'in cases not foreseen by this Directive'.64 In practice, the differences between the national capital requirements are a complicating factor when it comes to the cross-border provision of pension schemes. Precisely these differences could be a reason for applying Article 30 and imposing capital requirements. This is affirmed by the wording of the recitals of the IORP proposal that state that it is principally the sponsoring undertaking rather than the pension institution that either covers the longevity risk (for example) or guarantees certain benefits or certain investment performance. According to the this recital, however, in some cases it is the pension institution itself which provides such cover or guarantees and the sponsor's obligations are generally exhausted by paying the necessary contributions. In these circumstances, the recital continues, the products offered are similar to those of life-assurance companies and the institutions concerned should hold at least the same additional own funds as lifeassurance companies.65 Accordingly, although the scope of application of the legal basis for delegation is fairly broad, no essential elements of the regulation are in dispute in this sense. Partly in light of the recitals, the separation between legislation and executive rule-making would thus not be jeopardized.

In this light it is – in se – at least doubtful whether removing the delegation provision of Article 30 IORP II Directive would result in a situation in which no capital requirements can be imposed on IORPs.

Moreover, secondly, the Green Paper on the 'Capital Markets Union' is also relevant in this context.66 Pensions (albeit – so it seems, 3rd pillar, individual pensions) form a prominent position in the Green Paper.67 The European Commission views national pension measures as an important obstacle to the development of a capital market. In our view this also holds true for occupational pensions. An essential obstacle in this regard seems to be, for example, mandatory membership of a Dutch (!) pension fund for employees in the Netherlands (albeit 2nd pillar). It seems – regardless of whether it concerns 2nd or 3rd pillar – only a matter of time before the Commission deals with this discrimination in terms of nationality in light of the Capital Markets Union.68

Thirdly, account should also be taken of the possibility that another EU legislative instrument or mechanism is used to impose further capital requirements on IORPs. In that regard it should be noted, first of all, that it is possible to 'convert' the soft law instruments of EIOPA (such as the HBS) into executive rules,69 or that the CJEU adopts such soft law instruments, for example, by referring to them in the case law. This has happened before, e.g. in the fields of competition and state aid.70 The fact that this might also happen to, for example, the EIOPA reports seems all the more likely, as Article 16 of the EIOPA Regulation includes a 'comply or explain' mechanism. The first paragraph of this article provides that with a view to establishing consistent, efficient and effective supervisory practices within the ESFS, and to ensuring the common, uniform and consistent application of Union law, EIOPA issues guidelines and recommendations addressed to competent authorities or financial institutions. The same therefore applies to IORPs.71 Article 16(4) of the EIOPA Regulation then provides that the European Parliament, the Council and the Commission will be informed of the guidelines and recommendations that have been issued. EIOPA will state which competent authority has not complied with them, and outline how it intends to ensure that the competent authority concerned follows its recommendations and guidelines in the future (hence: comply or explain).

An example of how the comply or explain system can work out is found in the sphere of the Solvency II Regulation. Part of the adopted delegated act under the Solvency II Directive72 is a detailed description of the calculation of the solvency capital requirement and the minimum solvency requirement of insurers.73 The fact is that, pursuant to Article 4 of the current IORP Directive, certain pension insurers can operate in another EU Member State under a more favourable solvency regime than insurance companies from a Member State that does not apply Article 4 IORP.74 It cannot be ruled out in advance that EIOPA will use the power to adopt delegated acts under the Solvency II Regulation to deal with this uneven playing field between pension insurers. It should be noted, however, that in this regard it is relevant that this power of EIOPA must not concern the essential elements of the Solvency II Regulation.

EIOPA also has at its disposal the powers set out in Article 8 of Regulation 1094/2010 (the EIOPA Regulation).75 They are fairly broad, especially in relation to insurers and include a) advisory and coordinating powers, b) the development of drafting standards and c) independent supervisory powers. Article 1(2) of this Regulation moreover provides that EIOPA will act within the powers conferred by this Regulation and within the scope of secondary EU legislation (including the Solvency II Regulation and the IORP Directive), but also 'including all directives, regulations, and decisions based on those acts, and of any further legally binding Union act which confers tasks on the Authority'. The EIOPA Regulation moreover provides for a mechanism to resolve differences of opinion between national supervisory authorities.76 Where a national supervisory authority takes issue with the procedural or substantive terms of a measure taken (or not taken) by another national supervisory authority, EIOPA must assist the authorities at their request in reaching agreement within the timeframe determined by EIOPA.77 If the dispute continues, EIOPA must be able to settle the matter.78 These dispute resolution powers are broad and can therefore also extend to the interpretation of delegated acts. Via these powers too, the capital requirement can therefore fall within the scope of EIOPA's powers.

CONCLUSION AND CLOSING REMARKS

The distinction between legislative and non-legislative acts is not only relevant from a constitutional perspective, but defines concrete legislative dossiers as well. In EU pensions law a key issue is whether capital requirements for pensions institutions may be adopted by executive regulation. As we have contended, various legal bases and options exist that may allow for this. At least, they would not a priori prohibit such rules. Yet, given the political controversy it would be likely that setting such requirements would amount to regulating essential elements of the area. Indeed, the making of political decisions would be involved which is, according to CJEU, reserved for the legislature, albeit that the CJEU would look at the actual substantive political interests at stake, rather than at the existence of political controversy. The case of pensions law illustrates, moreover, that the demarcation between legislative and executive power is not only a matter of institutional powers, but affects the vertical power balance between the Member States and the European Union. This is a strong argument in favour of CJEU control over the issue at a level that is higher than the one we find in some domestic legal systems.

The distinction between delegated and implementing acts plays a role as well in the national opposition against delegated acts. Some governments have issued a critique on the proposed Article 30 of the draft IORP Directive, which provides for the power to adopt delegated acts.79 Arguably, the possibility that the Commission may invoke this provision to impose capital requirements on pension institutions is especially worrying for Member States in light of the lack of ex ante control via committee procedures (comitology) that does exist under implementing acts. Here, the new Interinstitutional Agreement on Better Law-Making may make a difference on the point of the consultation of Member State experts. In any case, the key element here is Member State control. The constitutional discourse on the nature of the difference between delegated and implementing acts seems to be playing no role whatsoever in the decision-making process on the Directive.

The political controversy over Article 30 of the Directive is relevant from another perspective as well. The legal basis for the adoption of delegated acts has become the focus of attention with the opposition to capital requirements. As we have argued, however, such capital requirements may, however, acquire an EU dimension in other ways than Article 30 alone. This seems to remain ignored. Thus, we may expect that the political salience of Article 290 TFEU will remain to be higher than Article 290 TFEU despite the horizontal rather than vertical divide between them. Finally, the role of EU agencies: this article has argued that EIOPA could have an important influence on the solvency requirements that may be imposed on pension institutions. This is not only due to the extensive quasi-regulatory powers that EIOPA possesses on the basis of numerous legislative acts, but is also due to its other powers (such as dispute resolution powers). In fact, this scenario is quite likely in view of EIOPA's actual activities in recent years. The lacuna in regulating EU agencies' position in rule-making in a more general way is thus manifested as an ever increasing problem.80 The role of the EIOPA is now being developed in an ad hoc way. The new Inter-Institutional Agreement on Better Law-Making fails to address the issue, however. In light of the controversy over executive rule-making powers, it would make sense if capital requirements for IORPs were directly and effectively regulated by the legislature itself. This would strengthen their legitimacy and be in line with the case law of the CJEU. As an essential element of the IORPs, capital requirements can also be regarded as an essential element of the regulation itself and as such they belong to the legislative domain.

NOTES:

1 The system is not entirely new: it is in part an explication of an existing situation.

2 Directive 2003/41/EC of the European Parliament and of the Council of 3 June 2003 on the activities and supervision of institutions for occupational retirement provision (Institutions for Occupational Retirement Provision, IORP), OJ L 235, 23.9.2003, pp. 10-21. See for more background information on the IORP Directive, inter alia, H. van Meerten & B. Starink, 'Cross-border problems and solutions for IORPs', (2011) EC Tax Review, no. 1; A. van den Brink et al., Regulating pensions; Why the EU matters, Netspar design paper no. 5 (2011) and H. van Meerten, 'The scope of the IORP Directive', in U. Neergaard et al. (eds.), Social Services of General Interest in the EU (2013).

3 Not only the Netherlands, but also the United Kingdom, Ireland and Belgium are sceptical of a IORP II Directive. IPE, 3 September 2014: 'The UK government has said it will challenge all proposals in the IORP II Directive that do not "add value" to the local pension system, a minister has warned.' To be found at: (last visited 22 January 2016).

4 A. van den Brink, 'Van rechtsinstrumenten naar rechtshandelingen: 'Lissabon' en de introductie van een Europees primaat van de wetgever', (2008) SEW. Tijdschrift voor Europees en economisch recht, no. 5, pp. 166-170.

5 Important in this regard are the extensive 'call-back' rights under the concept of delegation that allow the Council and the European Parliament, individually, to raise an objection against a delegated act, or even to withdraw the delegation itself (this section will elaborate on this in more detail).

6 It should be noted that an argument for that conclusion can also be found in the fact that the concept of the delegated act had to replace the most far-reaching kind of comitology, i.e. the Regulatory procedure with scrutiny (known under its French acronym PRAC).

7 J. Bast, 'New Categories of Acts after the Lisbon Reform: Dynamics of Parliamentarization in EU Law', (2012) 49 Common Market Law Review, no. 3, pp. 885-927 at p. 919.

8 T. Christiansen & M. Dobbels, 'Comitology and Delegated Acts after Lisbon: How the European Parliament lost the Implementation Game', (2012) 16 European Integration Online Papers (EIOP), article 13, p. 8, (last visited 22 January 2016).

9 Communication from the Commission to the European Parliament and the Council, Implementation of Article 290 of the Treaty on the Functioning of the European Union, COM(2009) 673 final, p. 3.

10 J. Bast, 'Is There a Hierarchy of Legislative, Delegated and Implementing Acts?', in C.F. Bergström & D. Ritleng, Rulemaking by the European Commission. The New System for Delegation of Powers (2016), pp. 157-172 at p. 167. 11 Case C-355/10, ECLI:EU:C:2012:516.

12 Case C-427/12, ECLI:EU:C:2014:170.

13 As it provides that delegation must be limited to non-essential elements and that the legal basis for delegation must explicitly define the objectives, content, scope and duration of the delegation of power.

14 Cf. J. Bast, 'New Categories of Acts after the Lisbon Reform: Dynamics of Parliamentarization in EU Law', (2012) 49 Common Market Law Review, no. 3, pp. 885-927, at pp. 893-894.

15 In particular, the decision in Cases 25/70, Köster, ECLI:EU:C:1970:115 and C-240/90, Germany v Commission, ECLI:EU:C:1992:408.

16 This wording shows traces of the wording developed by the CJEU in connection with the choice for the right legal basis (Case C-300/89, Titanium Dioxide, ECLI:EU:C:1991:244; Case C-376/98, Tobacco Advertising, ECLI:EU:C:2000:544). In practice, however, the judicial review of the choice of the Community legislature has remained restricted to a fairly marginal review, see: S. Weatherill, 'The Limits of Legislative Harmonization Ten Years after Tobacco Advertising: How the Court's Case Law has become a 'Drafting Guide'', (2011) German Law Journal, no. 3, pp. 827-864. As shown in what follows, the review of the CJEU is also more limited with

regard to the choice to delegate regulatory powers than the level at which it appears to aim with this wording.

17 The type of political choices that is reserved to the legislature also depends on the legal basis: K. Bradley, 'Delegation of Powers in the European Union. Political Problems, Legal Solutions?', in C.F. Bergström & D. Ritleng, Rulemaking by the European Commission. The New System for Delegation of Powers (2016), pp. 55-85, Section 4.2.2.

18 D. Ritleng, 'The Reserved Domain of the Legislature. The Notion of Essential Elements of an Area', in C.F. Bergström & D. Ritleng, Rulemaking by the European Commission. The New System for Delegation of Powers (2016), pp. 133-155 at p. 152. See also M. Chamon, 'How the concept of essential elements of a legislative act continues to elude the Court: Parliament v. Council', (2013) 50 Common Market Law Review, no. 3, pp. 849-860.

19 Ritleng, supra note 18 analysed more CJEU decisions and concluded that the CJEU applies a rather case-by-case approach.

20 Case C-409/13, ECLI:EU:C:2015:217.

21 According to the European Parliament, the introduction of the concept of the delegated act is the most important change that the Treaty of Lisbon has made to the European legislative system: see for more details the AG's Opinion in Case C-427/12, ECLI:EU:C:2014:170. See for a discussion of the 'old' system: H. van Meerten, 'Naar een nieuw Europees wetsbegrip?', (2001) Nederlands Tijdschrift voor Europees recht, no. 6, pp. 166-169.

22 See for the details of this: (last visited 22 January 2016).

23 Schütze has argued that the powers of the European Parliament with regard to Art. 290 TFEU amount to nothing less than a constitutional revolution, since the basic treaties never previously acknowledged any formal role for the European Parliament over executive legislation: R. Schütze, '"Delegated" Legislation in the (new) European Union: A Constitutional Analysis', (2011) 74 The Modern Law Review, pp. 661693 at p. 685.

24 A couple of examples: the Council has raised an objection against a delegated act of the Commission of 12 August 2014 regarding the format for submitting data on expenses for research and developments as referred to in Regulation (EU) 549/2013 on the European system of national and regional accounts in the European Union. In 2014, the European Parliament objected to a delegated regulation of the Commission regarding the definition of 'technically manufactured nanomaterials' that was based on Regulation (EU) 1169/2011 on the provision of food information to consumers.

25 The European Parliament has been looking to boost resources for the scrutiny of delegated acts, as well as to create greater uniformity between parliamentary committees in dealing with them. So far, the European Parliament's record has been poor in this regard: Th. Christiansen & M. Dobbels, 'Comitology and Delegated Acts after Lisbon: How the European Parliament lost the Implementation Game', (2012) 16 European Integration online Papers (EIOP), article 13, (last visited 22 January 2016).

26 As had been predicted by Craig: P.P. Craig, 'Delegated Acts, Implementing Acts and the New Comitology Regulation', (2011) 36 European Law Review, no. 5, pp. 671-687, at p. 675.

27 Art. 11 of the Comitology Regulation (Regulation 182/2011/EU) does provide for a mechanism to scrutinize implementing acts for the Council and the European Parliament: if either of these institutions indicates that a draft implementing act exceeds the implementing powers of the Commission provided for in the basic act, the Commission needs to review it. However, as Craig has noted, the limits of this mechanisms are notable, and do not extend to the Commission having to withdraw or amend an implementing act to which the Council or the European Parliament have objected: P.P. Craig, 'Delegated Acts, Implementing Acts and the New Comitology Regulation', (2011) 36 European Law Review, no. 5, pp. 671-687, at pp. 684-685.

28 Communication from the Commission to the European Parliament and the Council, Implementation of Article 290 of the Treaty on the Functioning of the European Union, COM(2009) 673 final.

29 For example, in the field of pensions in Directive 2013/14/EU (institutions for occupational retirement provision, undertakings for collective investment in transferable securities and managers of alternative investment funds). Recital 3 of the Directive provides: 'It is of particular importance that the Commission carry out appropriate consultations during its preparatory work, including at expert level, and that it publish the results of such consultations.'

30 Case C-427/12, ECLI:EU:C:2014:170. More in detail on the decision and a critique thereof: D. Ritleng, 'The dividing line between delegated and implementing acts: The Court of Justice sidesteps the difficulty in Commission v. Parliament and Council (Biocides)', (2015) 52 Common Market Law Review, no. 1, pp. 243-258.

31 Case C-88/14, ECLI:EU:C:2015:499.

32 R. Schütze, '"Delegated" Legislation in the (new) European Union: A Constitutional Analysis', (2011) 74 The Modern Law Review, pp. 661693 at p. 682.

33 Communication from the Commission to the European Parliament and the Council, Implementation of Article 290 of the Treaty on the Functioning of the European Union, COM(2009) 673 final, p. 4.

34 P.P. Craig, 'Delegated Acts, Implementing Acts and the New Comitology Regulation', (2011) 36 European Law Review, no. 5, pp. 671-687, at p. 686.

35 See also Bast: 'In terms of phenomenology, they [i.e. delegated acts, TvdB/HvM] closely resemble earlier implementing acts.' J. Bast, 'New Categories of Acts after the Lisbon Reform: Dynamics of Parliamentarization in EU Law', (2012) 49 Common Market Law Review, no. 3, pp. 885-927, at p. 916.

36 The three Institutions reached a political agreement on the text of the new Interinstitutional Agreement in December 2015. At the time of completing this contribution (January 2016) it still awaits formal approval. The provisional text is available at: (last visited 12 January 2016).

37 COM(2015) 216 final.

38 Annex I to the Commission's proposal COM(2015) 216 final, Common Understanding between the European Parliament, the Council and the Commission on Delegated Acts, consideration 8.

39 IIA, Common Understanding on Delegated Acts.

40 This could be viewed as a result of Art. 11 of the Treaty on European Union in which the principle of representative democracy is elaborated and supplemented by consultation and dialogue obligations (among other obligations). See for more details on this the proposal of the Research Network on EU Administrative Law (RENEUAL) to develop a general framework for the EU administrative procedure: the RENEUAL Model Rules 2014 (specifically: D. Curtin et al., 'ReNEUAL Model Rules on EU Administrative Procedure: Book II – Administrative Rulemaking'), available at: (last visited 22 January 2016).

41 Consideration 17 of the IIA.

42 H.C.H. Hofmann, 'Legislation, Delegation and Implementation Under the Treaty of Lisbon: Typology Meets Reality', (2009) 15 European Law Journal, no. 4, pp. 482-505, at p. 501.

43 Cf. Hoffmann, ibid., who signalled this development in relation to EU primary law, but six years later and with a new Inter Institutional Agreement that ignores the issue, the gap has only widened.

44 EIOPA has received little scholarly attention so far regarding its rule-making powers. This is different for ESMA (the European Markets and Securities Authority). See inter alia: M.P.M. van Rijsbergen (2014), 'On the Enforceability of EU Agencies' Soft Law at the National Level: The Case of the European Securities and Markets Authority', (2014) 10 Utrecht Law Review, no. 5, http://doi.org/10.18352/ulr.304, pp. 116-131.

45 N. Moloney, EU Securities and Financial Markets Regulation (2014), p. 904.

46 Opinion of the European Economic and Social Committee on the Proposal for a Directive of the European Parliament and of the Council on markets in financial instruments repealing Council Directive 2004/39/EC of the European Parliament and of the Council (recast), OJ C 191, 29.6.2012, pp. 80-83.

47 Ibid.

48 Markets in Financial Instruments Regulation, this Regulation 'comes' under MiFid.

49 Opinion of the European Economic and Social Committee on the Proposal for a Regulation of the European Parliament and of the Council on markets in financial instruments and amending Regulation (EMIR) on OTC derivates, central counterparties and trade repositories, OJ C 143, 22.5.2012, pp. 74-77.

50 Ibid., no. 1.7.

51 Ibid., no. 4.3.5.

52 Opinion of the European Economic and Social Committee on the Proposal for a Directive of the European Parliament and of the Council on the activities and supervision of institutions for occupational retirement provision, OJ C 451, 16.12.2014, pp. 109-115.

53 Ibid., no. 4.3.2.

54 See extensively: E.M. Busuioc, European Agencies: Law and Practices of Accountability (2013).

55 See note 3, supra.

56 This 'own initiative' is already controversial in some Member States. See: H. van Meerten & F. Valkenburg, 'Naar een Europese pensioenrichtlijn', (2015) Pensioenmagazine, no. 4.

57 Ibid.

58 Outcome of the consultations, EIOPA, 'Consultation Paper on Further Work on Solvency of IORPS', 13 October 2014, EIOPA-CP-14/040, No. 3.4.

59 Press release by PensionsEurope, 'PensionsEurope publishes Position Paper on EIOPA plans for further work on solvency of IORPs', 17 February 2015.

60 EIOPA, 'EIOPA Report on Costs and charges of IORPs', 7 January 2015, EIOPA-BoS-14/266.

61 Outcome of the consultations, EIOPA, 'Consultation Paper on a Report on Good Practices on individual transfers of supplementary occupational pension rights', 29 January 2015, EIOPA-CP-15/001.

62 Ibid.

63 P. Borsjé & H. van Meerten, 'Voorstel IORP II-richtlijn: aanzet tot hervorming van het Nederlands pensioenstelsel', (2014) Nederlands tijdschrift voor Europees Recht, no. 8, pp. 264-274.

64 See Para. 3.4 of the explanatory notes to the IORP II proposal (COM(2014) 167 final), 'Further explanation of the proposal, per chapter or per article', to Article 30 in Chapter 1 – Governance System.

65 Recital 30 in the Commission Proposal for the IORP Directive and included in the recitals, even after the Council's comprise, in no. 29 in the IORP II proposal (COM(2014) 167 final).

66 Green Paper, 'Building a Capital Markets Union', COM(2015) 63 final.

67 Ibid. 'This raises the question of whether the introduction of a standardised product, for example through a pan-European or "29th" regime, removing obstacles to cross-border access could potentially strengthen the single market in personal pension provision.'

68 That the Dutch mandatory membership is at odds with the EU law was discussed in: H. van Meerten, 'Vrij Verkeer Van Diensten: Solvency II Basic en de Verplichtstelling', (2012) Tijdschrift voor Financieel Recht, no 7/8, pp. 290-296.

69 Van den Brink and Senden have argued that a better system of checks & balances for the adoption and functioning of such soft law should be adopted: A. van den Brink & L. Senden, Checks and balances of soft rule-making in the EU, Study for the European Parliament, PE 462.433, March 2012, available at <http://www.europarl.europa.eu/RegData/etudes/etudes/join/2012/462433/IPOL-JURI_ET(2012)462433_EN.pdf?> (last visited 22 January 2016).

70 O. Stefan, 'Hybridity before the Court: a Hard Look at Soft Law in the EU Competition and State Aid Case Law', 2012 (37) European Law Review, no. 1, pp. 49-69.

71 We therefore agree with the view of the Dutch Council of State (Raad van State): IORPs are financial undertakings (Kamerstukken II 2011/12, 32182, 4). IORPs are also service providers within the meaning of Art. 56 TFEU. The fact is that according to the CJEU the IORP Directive aims at establishing

an internal market for occupational retirement provisions within the scope of which the institutions for occupational retirement provisions must be able to freely carry out services and investments, see: Case C-343/08, Commission v Czech Republic, ECLI:EU:C:2010:14, Para. 43.

72 Commission Delegated Regulation (EU) 2015/35 of 10 October 2014 supplementing Directive 2009/138/EC of the European Parliament and of the Council on the taking-up and pursuit of the business of Insurance and Reinsurance (Solvency II), OJ L 12, 17.1.2015.

73 Kamerstukken II 2014/15, 34100, 6.

74 How this works is elaborated in: H. van Meerten & B. Starink, 'Cross-border problems and solutions for IORPs', (2011) EC Tax Review, no. 1, pp. 30-40. Whether or not this leads to unfair competition was recently discussed (once more) in the Dutch Lower House (Tweede Kamer). The government concluded that this was not the case. Wrongly in our opinion.

75 Regulation (EU) 1094/2010 of the European Parliament and of the Council of 24 November 2010 establishing a European Supervisory Authority (European Insurance and Occupational Pensions Authority), amending Decision No 716/2009/EC and repealing Commission Decision 2009/79/EC.

76 Art. 21 Regulation (EU) No. 1094/2010 (the EIOPA Regulation).

77 That thereby takes account of any relevant time-limits from the relevant legislation and the urgency and complexity of the dispute: Directive 2014/51/EU of the European Parliament and of the Council of 16 April 2014 amending Directives 2003/71/EC and 2009/138/EC and Regulation (EC) No. 1060/2009, and (EU) Nos 1094/2010 and 1095/2010 in respect of the powers of the European Supervisory Authority (European Insurance and Occupational Pensions Authority) and the European Supervisory Authority (European Securities and Markets Authority ('Omnibus II').

78 Ibid.

79 P. Borsjé & H. van Meerten, 'A European Pensions Union: towards a strengthening of the European pension systems', in F. Pennings & G. Vonk (eds.), Research Handbook on Social Security Law (2015), pp. 385-412.

80 See, inter alia, Hofmann, supra note 42, who had identified this as one of the major challenges in EU administrative law and the RENEUAL proposals, supra note 40, in which the issue features prominently as well.

CHAPTER 14

OWNERSHIP OF COPYRIGHT IN WORKS CREATED IN EMPLOYMENT RELATIONSHIPS: COMPARATIVE STUDY OF THE LAWS OF COLOMBIA, GERMANY AND THE UNITED STATES OF AMERICA

Jose Roberto Herrera Diaz

Keywords: Copyrighted Works, Software, The Sovereignty and Territoriality Principles, Ownership of Economic Rights

INTRODUCTION

Great quantities of copyrighted works around the world are produced in the context of labor law Relationships. The ownership of these works has been regulated in different ways by the national laws of each country, and the only attempt of legal harmonization has been found in the European Community regarding computer programs created in the course of employment. The sovereignty and territoriality principles by with each country can enact its own laws in its territory to rule on the ownership question has been applied by countries. As an example, Germany and United States have regulated the subject in their respective national copyright laws. Nonetheless, there are similarities in the ways that these two countries regulate the ownership of economic rights. In other countries, such as Colombia, lawmakers have established a legal rule regarding the ownership of moral rights in copyrighted works, but have not ruled on the important issue of the economic rights in such works. This ambiguity has caused legal uncertainty, raising the question as to whether these types of rights belong to employees or employers.

This paper will make a comparative study of the laws of Colombia, Germany and the United States of America, taking into account the current issues that can arise in works created in employment relationships and the ensuing consequences. The structure of the comparison will be focused on the following two central points of analysis.

First, this thesis will concentrate on the differences in the laws and case law of the three countries with regard to the ownership of the copyright in employment relationships. In order to determine how each country addresses the ownership question, other aspects such as authorship and the differences between the author's right system and the Anglo American Copyright system (i.e., the treatment of moral rights) will be analyzed as well. Likewise, the diverging theories underlying the author's rights systems in these countries, with Colombia being a dualistic system and Germany being a monistic system, and the effect of the silence of the parties to a contract with respect to the point of ownership, are both issues that must be explored to render a thorough understanding of the subject. Secondly, not only the differences, but also the similarities between each system will be explored. In this regard, the paper will analyze whether, in works created in employment relationships, there is a tendency of the monistic and dualistic author's right systems to approach to the Anglo American Copyright System. In other words, any similarities between the laws and practices of Colombia and Germany and the American "work made for hire" doctrine will be addressed. Most important, if the philosophies by which the two main

Citation: Jose Roberto Herrera Diaz, Ownership of Copyright in Works Created in Employment Relationships: Comparative Study of the Laws of Colombia, Germany and the United States of America, Intangible Property magazine, No. 14, pp. 91-139, 2010.

copyright systems were created are currently applicable to works created in employment relationships. This issue will address whether the interest in protecting the human being's original expression and thus the interests of the employed authors prevails over the interest in protecting the utilitarian character of the works.

Furthermore, the study will focus on the topic of ownership as it relates to specific kinds of works, such as computer programs regulated in the European Community Directive 91/250. On this point for example, the same approach will be followed, analyzing whether the German implementation of this directive is creating a tendency for the author's right system to become similar to the American copyright system. Despite the fact that the focus of the paper is on copyright provisions, some aspects of labor law, such as scope of employment and employment relationships, will be analyzed in order to have a integral understanding of the topic. Since labor law provisions and copyright provisions are different fields of law, the difficulties that may arise in knowing which area of law to apply will be examined. Finally, issues concerning to works created by independent contractors in Colombia, Germany, and the United States will be analyzed, in particular the same copyright provisions regarding the ownership of the works that can apply to employees and independent contractors. In a similar context, the treatment of works created by public servants or private employees may reveal similarities and differences to the treatment of public employees in these three countries.

WHY WORKS CREATED IN EMPLOYMENT RELATIONSHIPS?

When the topic under study has been analyzed in the legal literature, the usual terms by which the authors refer to it are: works made for hire,1 works created by employees,2 or works created in employment relationships.3 This diversity of terms creates a difficulty to analyze the subject, as the significance of each expression may bring different results on the ownership point. For instance, the first option, work made for hire, is a popular term for common law countries in which the employer is considered the author and owner of the copyright. The problem using this term is that is of no use in continental tradition countries where in almost all the situations the authorship of the copyright vest in the employee, as well as the ownership of the moral rights. Regarding the second option, works created by employees, despite being common in the continental tradition countries, in which usually the authorship and ownership vest in the employee, one may find difficulty in establishing if the work is always created by an employee. In some cases, the original expression of the copyrighted work may come from the employer and the employee's freedom to produce the work can be limited by the employer's orders. For instance, an employer that is dictating a literary work to his secretary cannot be prevented from being the original author of the work, despite the fact the secretary fixed the expression of the copyrighted work. Thus, one must carefully observe the term creation, because in the context of an employment relationship, it can cause misleading interpretations such as, for example, that every function of an employee constitutes creation. For these reasons, it is more impartial to use the concept works created in employment relationships, since it addresses not only the employers' interests, but also the employees'.

WHAT IS AN EMPLOYMENT RELATIONSHIP?

Before entering into the analysis of the Copyright law, it is necessary to understand the concept of employment relationships. The International Labor Organization (ILO) has identified three common elements in labor law contracts around the world.4 Those elements are not always defined by the law or case law of each country. However, not only the ilo, but also the labor law doctrine in all the countries of the world, have established a consensus on the existence of three elements.5 The first element, called the personal element, means that only a natural person can be considered an employee.6 Second is the subordination element by which the employer is entitled to give orders to the employees; this element involves a hierarchical aspect. The third and final element is the salary that employers pay to their employees as a retribution for their work.7 Colombia is one of the countries by which said elements can be clearly found. Article 22 of the labor law code defines labor law contract as: "one in which a natural person promises to give his services to another legal or natural person, under continuous subordination (i.e., receiving orders from the employer), with remuneration in exchange for the services".8

When these three elements are present, there is a presumption of existence of a labor law contract. 9 In Colombia the main distinction of a labor law contract and other contracts is the so called subordination. In the course of services provided under civil law contracts, there are orders given to the person providing the services, but the autonomy that the provider of services has is broader than those in an employment contract.10

The term employment is not only linked to works created under a labor law contract. In most jurisdictions the term employment is a generic term by which not only labor contracts are included, but also contracts by which a person agrees to provide services to another are included.11 Despite the fact that the focus of this study is the employment relationships in the narrow sense, meaning, labor law contracts, one cannot ignore other kinds of agreements that are included within the generic concept of employment. For instance, works created by independent contractors in the United States or works created under contracts to provide services in Colombia, are mandatory examples that show the broad understanding of the term employment. Likewise, these other kinds of relationships can provide answers in some cases to ownership issues in the labor law contract.12 Thus, the following analysis will not only review labor law contracts, but also non labor law relationships in each country by which employment and works are created.

LABOR OR IP LAWS?

One important question for the analysis is whether the ownership of the copyright in works created in employment relationships should be regulated by labor or intellectual property laws. As the present topic combines both fields of law, intellectual property provisions can be found in labor law statutes and vice versa. One may ask if it is better if only one field of law rules on the topic or if it is better that both fields can rule some part of the topic. As we will see later, there are some issues that have been exclusively ruled by the labor or agency law. For instance, the definitions of an employee, a labor law relationship or the elements of a labor law relationship are usually found within employment statutes.

Regarding the central topic of study, some countries regulated the topic under a labor law statue. For example, Spain regulated the ownership of the copyright of the works created by employees in a labor law provision, the employees' statute.13 However, after some years, the Spanish lawmakers followed the global trend of regulating IP topics exclusively in IP laws. Thus, the Spanish Intellectual Property Law derogated previous labor law rules and provided an answer to the ownership of the copyright in employment relationships.14 As it will be shown in the next Chapters, Germany and the United States have regulated the ownership point on Intellectual Property laws (Copyright acts) following the mentioned global trend. In the case of Colombia, as there is not a specific answer to the economic ownership point, one cannot have certainty on whether the Author's Right law contains a provision that rules the topic.

GERMANY. LEGAL RULES AND ANALYSIS

Applicable Law

Germany has many different laws regarding the Copyrights. However, for the purpose of this study, the analysis will concentrate mostly in the Copyright and Related Rights Act of 1965. Although this Act has been modified by several amendments, the most pertinent for analysis is the Amendment of June 9, 1993, by which the E.C. Directive on the Legal Protection of Computer Programs was implemented. Regarding Labor Law provisions, Germany does not have a codified Labor Law Act. Instead, there are different legal sources such as the Federal Legislation, collective agreements, work agreements and case law.15 Likewise, the Civil Code is another important provision as it defines employment relationship16 in section 622 with the trilogy of elements previously analyzed.

Although the Civil Code sets forth the elements to define employment relationships, there is no definition of employee in Germany. However, German Courts have said that employee is a natural person that receives instructions on the way to do work17. Also, they have said that despite the fact that a person can be greatly autonomous in doing work, a clear indicia of classifying someone as an employee is the act of fulfilling a schedule ordered by the employer.18

The German Continental Law Tradition

The philosophy of the classical author's right system created under the continental legal models is based on the idea that the work is always of property of the author. Consequently, the author can only transfer or license his economic rights, and not his moral rights, to third parties.19 However, this is the Classical notion of the author's right system that is evident in France, representing some clear differences with Germany, where neither the economic and moral rights can be transferred.20 German Copyright Law is classified as continental law, as opposed to common law tradition. This enhances many differences among the Copyright system existing in Germany and non-continental countries such as the USA.

The first and the most important effect is that the continental tradition is based on the protection of rights of flesh and blood authors.21 This means that the main goal of the continental legal family is protecting the rights of natural persons that create copyrighted works. The continental Tradition does not directly protect the legal persons as they are not human minds that produce works. However, despite the differentiation of natural and legal persons, the continental System protects some economic rights of legal persons by the so-called "neighboring rights".22 The second effect of the continental legal system in relation to copyright law is strongly related to the first. As the focus of the protection is centered on flesh and blood authors, the law protects not only the economic basis of their lives, but also their intimate moral interests tied up in their works.23 For this reason, as Dietz says: "The German term Urheberecht, usually translated into English by copyright or copyright law, is better translated by the French term droit d'auteur, meaning "author's right" or author's right law". 24 Thus, the term author is a clue word in the continental system as it is focused merely on the protection of the personal and economic interests of the authors as natural persons.

The German Author's rights system and its effect on works created in Employment Relationships

The author's rights system structure was brought into practice in the German Law through Copyright and Neighboring Rights (Urheberrechtsgesetz, UrhG) in Article 11. This Article established that the ownership of the copyright belongs to the creator of the work, demonstrating how important it was for the German lawmaker to protect the traditional concept of author by giving him, in all cases, the ownership of the copyright. When Article 11 states that the "Copyright shall protect the author with respect to the intellectual and personal relationship with his work", 25 the personal aspect characterized in the author's right system is clearly shown. Even when there are matters by which the so-called works made for hire are present, the German law claims for the importance of recognizing the ownership to the natural person that creates the work.26 As will be seen later in the United States analysis, the work made for hire doctrine allows that a person other than the creator of the work can be considered as the author. Hence, in the United States, despite the fact that in some situations an employer may not participate in the creation of a copyrighted work, he can still be considered as the author and owner of a work created by an employee. An important difference between these two countries lies in the consequences of these differing systems. In Germany, if the parties do not agree otherwise, the economic rights will always be employee's property. By contrast, in the United States, if the parties do not agree otherwise, the copyright will belong to the employer. As one can see, on the same de facto situation, the results in these two countries may be the opposite.

For some commentators, like GOLDSTEIN, there is no significant difference in the results between common law jurisdictions and civil law jurisdictions. In the words of Goldstein:

> Civil law and most Common law jurisdictions take different roads to essentially the same result in assigning rights to works made in the course of an employment relationship. Common law countries provide that, absent an agreement to the contrary,

copyright in works created in the course of employment initially vests in the employer, not the employee.27 Goldstein further explains: "Civil law countries generally reverse the common law presumption and provide that copyright in works created in the course of employment vests in the employed author, so that a transfer by the employee is required for the employer to obtain copyright."28 Thus, in Goldstein's opinion, the difference lies in the way by which each system reaches the result, but not on the result as such, since usually the copyright ownership vest with the employer. We have to distinguish however, that in the author's rights system, what the employee transfers to the employer are not all rights upon the work. Only the economic rights are transferred and the employed author retains the moral or personal rights in the work.

Two German Particularities

Having addressed the generalities of the German Author's Right system, is the turn to focus on two characteristics in the German context of works created in employment relationships. The first important aspect to point out is that German law treats works created under employment relationships as works created on commission.29 Thus, a work created by an independent contractor in Germany will have the same copyright ownership as a work created by an employee. The copyright will still vest on the employee or independent contract, if there is no agreement otherwise. By contrast, as will be seen in chapters vi and vii, in the United States and Colombia, there are certain differences regarding the treatment of independent contractors and employees.

Second, the fact that Germany does not recognize initial ownership to employers does not mean that an employer cannot claim the rights of a copyrighted work created by an employee at his service. However, the way by which the employer can enjoy the economic rights is different in comparison to most of the countries with a continental law tradition. On this point, some commentators like Dietz said that this is due to the fact that Germany has the monistic theory of author's right, by which economic and moral rights are indivisible.30 In words of Dietz: German law governing copyright transfer is articulated in Subchapter 2 on "Copyright Licenses" within Chapter V of part I of the Copyright Act. The particular thrust of this law can only be understood against the background of the so-called monistic theory of German Copyright. According to this concept, copyright as a whole, that is, author's right, safeguard both the financial and the personal or intellectual interests of an author.31

On article 11 of the Copyright Act this monistic approach is applied when the article states: that the "Copyright shall protect the author with respect to his intellectual and personal relationship with his work, and also with respect to utilization of his work". In Germany, this rule leads to the conception of the Copyright as a whole, by including in one body the "personal relationships to the work" (moral rights) and the "utilization of his work" (economic rights). This feature of the German system is another important distinction from the traditional author's right systems, such as France or Belgium. In these two countries, the economic rights are freely alienable and employees can transfer their economic rights to the employer in the employment agreement or otherwise32. As was mentioned above, the inalienability of the economic rights does not mean that the employer does not has rights to a work created by an employee. By the so called "contractual right to use", German law makes it possible for the employer to exercise the economic rights in the work.33 The fact that the employer does not receive the ownership of these rights, because there is not a transfer of right, can raise some questions, such as whether the employer has standing to sue when there is a copyright infringement.34

The German Copyright Act only permits the transferability of the copyright by inheritance, but the law clearly states that no other means are possible. Article 29 of the Act provides: "Copyright may be transferred in execution of a testamentary disposition or to coheirs as part of the partition of an estate. Copyright shall not otherwise be transferable". Furthermore, the English translation of Article 3135 expresses that the author may grant the exploitation right to use to another. For Dietz, this is what the literal translation of the German provision must be, as the English term "license" cannot be used here. In the words of Dietz: "Although used in some English translations, the English term 'license' does not fully translate the German conception of such contractual transfer. The Copyright Act only speaks of the granting of 'simple or exclusive rights of use'".36

The exclusive right of use is twofold. On the one hand, Article 31 (2) refers to the non-exclusive exploitation right to use. On the other, Article 31 (3) refers to an exclusive right to use. The main difference of both provisions is that in the latter, the exclusive right gives the power to the party to exclude others from use, even to the author. Dietz compares these two provisions to the traditional notions of exclusive and simple licenses. However, he states that in comparison to the German contractual right to use, the contractual terms by which the parties negotiate their interests are in the framework of the copyright contract law37 located in subsection 2 of the Copyright act. The framework includes different rules oriented to protect authors in the contractual grants.

The first important rule of subsection 2 is the prohibition to grant uses that are not yet known at the time of a grant (Article 31 (4) German Copyright Act).38 Second, Article 31(5) establishes the principle of "purpose-restricted transfer." This principle states that the author is not to be held to have granted more extensive rights that would be required by the purpose pursued in the grant39. Finally, Article 3740 establishes that in cases of doubt concerning the extent of certain types of transfers, the authors retain specific rights. Usually, when the author grants the right to use, he reserves the rights to make it available to the public and to exploit derivative works. Likewise, when the author grants the right to reproduce, the author reserves the right to fix the work on sound or visual recording 41. For the purpose this analysis, one has to take into account that these rules also apply to the employer who is the party that would receive the right to use the work created by the employed author. Hence, it is important to stress that, in technical terms, there is no transfer of rights to the employer in Germany and the employer receives a right to use the work. The power of exercise that the employer has will be represented by an exclusive right to use or a simple right to use.

As will be seen later, to constitute a work made for hire for independent contractors in the United States, the law requires a written agreement. Likewise, in the following chapter, we will see that in Colombian law as well, the transfer of economic rights requires a written agreement. By contrast, the German Copyright Act does not provide general formalities for the grant of the exploitation rights.42 The only exception can be found in Article 4043 which requires a written agreement for the granting of exploitation rights in future works. Perhaps a possible explanation for the flexibility of the German system is that, as there is not a transfer of right, there is no need for the law to establish a strict formality to protect the interest of the author. Despite some limitation to the author, such as the impossibility to use the work in the case of an exclusive grant, he will still be considered as the author and owner of the work. Finally, regarding other formalities such as the registration of transfer,44 the German law does not impose any obligation to record transfers of copyrighted interests.45 By contrast, as we will see in Colombia and the United States, in some cases the process of registration may be necessary.

Article 43 of the German Copyright Act

Article 4346 of the German Copyright Act, together with Article 69b47, are the most important provisions for the German law analysis as they regulate expressly the topic of works created in employment relationships. As it was said before, the general rule in Germany is that the employee is the owner and author of the copyrighted work produced under the course of his employment. Likewise, if the employee wants to grant the right to use to the employer, he will have to do it by contract.

The copyright contract rules are established in subsection 2 (Exploitation rights) from Articles 31 through 42 of the Copyright Act. When Article 42 states that "the provisions of this subsection shall also apply if the author has created the work in execution of his duties under a contract of employment or service", it is referring to the rules of subsection 2 analyzed before. However, the provisions of subsection 2 may not be applicable to employment relationships as the second sentence of Article 43 states: "provided nothing to the contrary transpires from the terms or nature of the contract of employment or services". This second sentence has created some critics within the legal commentators. For example, Dietz states: "This somewhat vague and unsatisfactory final clause in Section 43 in practice merely serves as a means to make it easier to find and interpret implied clauses in favor of employers".48 Furthermore, Dietz remarks: "This provision may be read as containing a sort of indirect presumption to the effect that all rights necessary for the activities of the employer or the commissioning party have been granted".49 As we can see, it is not completely clear in Germany whether the employers have to expressly sign an agreement with the employees to receive the right to use the exploitation rights. The wording of the article may consequently produce situations wherein an implied grant is concluded.

However, as already mentioned, there is a clear consensus that the Copyright as a whole, moral rights and economic rights vest in the employed or commissioned author.50 Likewise, the rules of contracts of subsection 2 (e.g. prohibition to grant uses that are not known, principle of purpose restricted transfers, and favorability for the author in cases where it is unclear as to what type of grant) are applicable to the employed author and can help to minimize the effect of an implied clause that may grants rights to the employer, and hence, affects his interests.

The Scope of Employment Requirement

In addition to the grant of the economic rights that the employer has to receive from the employee, another important requirement in making a valid grant is that the work must be created in execution of the employee's duties. To determine the employee's duties or the scope of employment, labor law regulations, rules in union agreements and the labor law contract have to be analyzed.51 Likewise, courts have said that factors such as location and the time by which the employee creates the work (working hours) are not suitable criteria for evaluating the scope of employment.52 Thus, the functions that the employee has are the main factor to determine if a work was created under the scope of employment.53 The previous rule does not imply that the employee cannot grant the economic rights from works created outside the scope of employment. However, some commentators have noted that under this hypothesis, the employee will not be remunerated just with the salary, and extra remuneration will have to be given to the employee.54

The general tendency regarding the employee remuneration is that it is given within the current wage. No additional remuneration is provided. This is a topic under discussion, as some commentators state that paying the employee with only the wage will infringe the general principle by which the author must receive reasonable compensation for the exploitation of his work.55 This is an issue for debate, since another argument that can arise under an extra compensation theory will be that not all the works that employees produce are protected under copyrights. In fact, most of the works are not protected. Thus fixing a mandatory extra remuneration as a general rule can be a fair retribution to the employed author for accomplishing the intellectual property protection of his creation. Likewise, if a mandatory extra remuneration is created, employed authors will have an incentive to create. Also, the progress of arts, which is one of the main objectives of copyright law, could be easily furthered by stimulating creation for employees.

On January 18 of 2002 the last version of the Employees' Invention Act was enacted in Germany.56 The Act gives an extra remuneration to the employees that create patents. The employed inventors in Germany are not only remunerated by their salary, in virtue of the said act, Employed inventors received an extra sum that awards their creation, and at the same time creates an incentive for other employees to invent. Despite the fact, that the said act does not contain copyright provision, this is an example of an extra remuneration that may be reasonable to put into practice in the context of works created in employment relationships. As most of the times the employer exercise the economic rights, and the employee only receives its salary in return of his creations, an extra remuneration can be a fair solution to protect the interest of the employed authors.

The Rights Granted by the Employee

Typically in the employment contract, the employee grants the exploitation rights to the employer. If this is the case, preference has to be given to these agreements.57 Likewise, when the employee grants the use of economic rights to the employer, these rights are given exclusively to him.58 However, the tendency is that the parties do not agree on the ownership of the copyright in the contract, and the courts59 find implied clauses that grant economic rights to the employer. In fact, some commentators state that there is a general obligation in the employment contract for the employee to grant economic rights to the employer.60 For instance, Rojahn states that there are two arguments that may justify a general obligation for the employee to grant the economic rights to the employer. The first argument is that there must be an analogy with the Employees Inventions Act of 2004. In Section 18 and 19 of the Act, there is a general obligation for the employee to offer the license of rights to the employer.61 Thus, Rojahn states that the economic rights of the employee in the copyrighted work should be licensed to the employer, as in the patent right. Both are intellectual property rights, so there should be a general obligation to offer a license.

The second argument is based on the labor law principle by which there must be a general relationship of trust between employee and employer.62 Consequently, as Rojhan states, a demonstration of trust lies in the fact that the employee offered a license to the employer.

The topic of implied license has not only been analyzed by commentators but also addressed by courts. The Federal Court of Justice (decision reference: bgh grur 1974, 480/483) in fact went further and said that there was a presumption of a license when the employee has handed the work to the employer.63 Other criteria stated used to determine implied grants of economic rights, as stated by Kirchberger, include looking objectively to the labor law contract and checking if the works created are related to the normal functions of the employer company. By contrast, the subjective elements, such as the intention of the employee to grant the economic rights, are not taken into account.64 Apart from looking to the labor law contract, another tool used to determine implied clauses that grant economic rights to the employer in lack of express agreements can be found in Germany in Union Agreements (tarifvertraege).65 Some examples of Union Agreements in which economic rights are granted to the employer can be found in the following areas: press (newspaper, magazines), radio and television (public as well as private television companies), movie, theater and design.66

Fortunately for the employee, despite the implied grants of economic rights that a court may find or an employer may argue, some of the economic interests in the work can still be protected. As it was already mentioned there are different provisions in subsection 2 orientated to protect the interests of the author, such as the prohibition to grant uses that are not yet known at the time of a grant (Article 31(4) German Copyright Act);67 the principle of purpose restricted transfer68 and the principle of favorability to the author in case of doubts concerning the extent of certain types of transfers.69 Regarding the term by which the employee grants the use of the economic rights to the employer, Krasser states that the usual practice is that even after the end of the labor law contract, the employer keeps the economic rights.70 Likewise, Dreier calls attention that the employee cannot use the economic rights in the course of a new employment contract with a new employer, if in a previous contract the old employer was exercising the economic rights. The old employer will still have the power to exercise the economic rights of the work created by the employee.71 However, we have to take into account that, as the grant of rights is ruled by a contract, the employee can agree with the employer that after the contract comes to an end, the grant is concluded. This will depend on the negotiation of both parties.

The e.c. Directive 91/250 on the Legal Protection of Computer Programs and the Article 69 b) of The German Copyright Act

The E.C. Directive was issued in 1991 in response to the amount of differences existing in the legislation of the Member States regarding this kind of works. One of the differences in Member States' legislations was the authorship of this works. But the other one related to the topic under study, was works created in employment relationships.72 The main aim of the Directive however was to codify the special standard of protection to computer programs, as there were many differences in the level of originality required to protect this type of work.73 Germany was in fact one of the European countries characterized by its high originality requirements for considering a work protected under copyright. The German legislation required the author's personal intellectual creation that was interpreted by courts with a narrow standard oriented to a high originality level for protection.74

In fact, before the Directive the German Supreme Court said in 1998 in Computer Edge v Apple Computer, that only "above average" creative result in the field of programming, an estimated 20 to 30 percents of all programs, would be eligible for protection.75 Thus, the problem that German courts faced was in harmonizing the statutory standard of protection fixed in the Directive with the high originality standard. However, in implementing the Directive, the German government adopted the mandatory standards of the Directive in Article 69 of the German Copyright act.76 Article 69a(3) of the German Copyright Act set the new originality standard by saying that the computer program has to express the "author's own intellectual creation" as is also stated in Article 1(3)77 of the Directive.78

This topic is still under debate on the legal literature, because the interpretation of the terms "author's own intellectual creation" can vary between courts in different states.79 However, for the purpose of this study, it is important to take into account that if an employee in Germany creates a computer program in the execution of his duties, the terms that have to be used to analyze the level of originality required for protection is the one established in Article 69(a) of the German Copyright Act; that is, the work must reflect the author's (employee's) own intellectual creation. For the topic under analysis Article 280 of the Directive is the central focus of the analysis, as this Article contains the E.C. rule for Authorship and ownership in the employment relationships.

Article 69(b) of the German Copyright Act is the national implementation of article 2 of the EC directive. As already explained, there is an exception to the general rule of granting of economic rights, as the Article directly entitles the employer to economic rights. As in the case of works created by employees which are not computer programs, Article 69(b) requires that the works must be created in the execution of the employee's duties. In order to decide the scope of the obligations, the previous considerations under the subtitle, scope of employment, should be applied here, meaning that the labor law contract, the main area of business of the employer and union agreements, have to be taken into consideration.81 Just as in Article 42 of the German Copyright Act, Article 69(b) also applies to works created in the course of services contracts. However, one important difference with the directive should be made here, as the Directive do not regulate the topic of freelancers. However, Dreier states that the initial proposal of the directive was to include freelancers in article 2(3). In his words:

Contrary to the Commission's initial proposal, the directive does not specifically regulate the authorship of commissioned computer programs. The main reason seems to have been the intention not to impair too heavily the interests of freelance programmers, in order not to hinder programming activities in the EC. Consequently, in the absence of special regulation on the national level, authorship of commissioned works is vested in the person(s) who created the program and the exercise of the exclusive rights is left to contractual provisions.82 After reading the previous passage, another open question for analysis is: Why does the German lawmaker give the exercise of economic rights to the employer in service relationships if the Directive did not regulate this topic? Bearing in mind that the author's rights tradition of Germany by which the protection of the author may be considered bigger than in the Anglo-American Copyright System, the application of the same rules to the independent contractor may be considered contradictory.

Furthermore, Article 2 (3) of the Directive keeps silent on whether the fact that the employer exploits the economic rights means that he receives a license, a transfer of rights, or if it is an initial ownership of the exclusive right.83 As will be mentioned later in Chapter vi, in the United States, the employer has the initial ownership of the copyright if there is a work made for hire. Hence, in the United States the third result would be applied. In the German case, the most similar result under these three options is that the employee grants a license84 to use the work to the employer, but the employer would not have the ownership of the Copyright.

As previously stated, Article 69(b) establishes a clear rule that the economic rights in a computer program created by an employee can be freely exploited by an employer without the need for the employer to receive a contractual grant from the employee. The situation described in Article 69 is different from the situation of Article 43, in which the employee will have to agree with the employer the grant of the economic rights or the employer may have to find some implied argument85 that will grant him the exploitation rights. The situation is oppositely different in computer programs, since Article 69(b) allows employers and employees to agree otherwise, meaning that the general rule wherein the exercise of economic rights vest on the employer can be changed by the consensus of the two parties. Thus, the employee will still have a way to freely exploit the economic rights in virtue of the Directive. Moreover, the basic principle by which the author of a work is protected by copyright is also applicable in the case of computer programs.86

Regarding the general practice of remuneration for the employee by the creation of computer programs, the tendency is the same as Article 43 (non computer programs works created by employees). There is no extra remuneration for the employee in addition to the salary that the employer pays, and the employee cannot demand licensing fees.87 However, if the computer program is created outside of the employee's duties, and the employer is exercising his economic rights, the result is the same as in non computer program creations and an extra remuneration must have to be given to the employee.88 Despite the fact that the general practice in Germany is that the employee does not get an extra remuneration when he creates a computer program, one may conclude that under this hypothesis the practice should be different. The situation of computer programs sets forth a different hypothesis from the general rule of Article 43. In computer program created works, the employer has the power to exercise all the economic rights.89 Thus, in this case, it may be reasonable to consider an extra remuneration for the employee despite the fact that in practice it is not provided. As previously stated, the German Employee´s Inventions Act gives extra remuneration to employed inventors. In the case context of computer programs created by employees is even clearer to think about a similar mechanism, as the employer exercise directly the economic rights.

It is important to ask why the drafters of the Computer Programs Directive gave the employer the direct power to exercise economic rights. Some question to open the debate could be: Was it because the employee has less autonomy in creating the works in a computer as opposed to other kinds of works? Or is it because the normal practice before the directive was that by implied clauses or express agreements the rights were exercised by the employer, and thus, the drafter of the Directive saw this de facto situation and put it into the law? Furthermore, and most important, as it will be mentioned latter, the interests of the software industry companies which were usually based on an Anglo American Copyright System were taken into account in the negotiations of this directive.90 The solution that the Directive took can be considered however, a fair solution as it allowed the exercise of the economic rights to the employer, without giving him the ownership of the copyright. It can be considered a fair balance between the two main systems of Copyrights: the Anglo American Copyright System and the Author's right System.

The silence of the parties before the E.C. Computer Programs Directive

The Directive made a clear change to German copyright law in works created by employees depending whether the work is a computer program or not, as in the first case, without agreement of the parties the economic rights will rest with the employer. Before this Directive, silence of the parties in Germany did not give the economic rights to the employer. In other European Countries, the directive did not make any changes to the National law. That is the case of Spain, where before the Directive if employer and employee were silent about the ownership of a copyrighted work, the economic rights vested were transferred to the employer.91 Thus, Spain did not suffered a change with the computer programs works, as before the Directive employers were exercising the economic rights of all kind of works created by employees if there was not agreement to the contrary.

Moral Rights

As already mentioned, German law is based in the monistic theory of author's right by which both economic rights and moral rights are included in one body. Moreover, there are no assignments of these rights, and third parties can only acquire the exercise of economic rights by agreeing with the copyright owner on a contractual right to use. Regarding moral rights, the primary difference from economic rights is that they are completely inalienable and third parties cannot even exercise this type of right like they can with exploitation rights. Nonetheless, as will be addressed below, in certain types of works such as computer programs, some moral rights can be limited in their exercise.

The application of economic and moral rights is sometimes difficult to differentiate as the interests involved are related. As described by Dietz: "It is therefore not very easy to state precisely whether, as a general matter, many provisions of the Copyright Act partake more of a moral or more of an economic nature".92 The said difficulty to distinguish in some cases if an economic or personal right is recognized is applicable as well to employees who, as already mentioned, are authors and thus owners of the moral and economic rights. Regarding the point of moral rights in the E.C. Directive of Computer Programs, it is important to state that the directive remained silent on this point and left the power to Member States to regulate the topic.93 The German lawmakers do not mention in article 69 b) any provision regarding moral rights, hence, there is no difference at least by law, on the application of moral rights in computer programs.

The German Copyright Act primarily recognizes the two classical moral rights: the right of paternity or right of recognition of authorship (Article 13) and the right of integrity (Article 14). The Act also recognizes another important moral right, the right of publication or right to control disclosure (Article 12).94 Unlike the exploitation rights, as already explained, the moral rights are not alienable in any author rights system. Articles 43 and 69(b) of the Copyright Act, regarding works and computer programs works created in employment relationships, do not affect directly the moral rights in Germany. Nonetheless, as Kirchberger states, some moral rights can be limited in the exercise:

> ... the author has the right of recognition of authorship. This right can, in general, neither be transferred nor waived. It can, however, be limited to the extent of the special nature of the employment.95

Moreover, when Kirchberger refers to the effect of the computer programs Directive on moral rights, she states:

> ... the regulation deals solely with the economic rights and does not affect the moral rights of the creator as such. The execution of the personal rights can however be limited. The author's right to prohibit any distortion or any other mutilation of the work is often limited as computer programs are usually further developed and a prohibition to alter software programs would reduce the employer's possibility to do so.96

After reading the previous conclusion of Kirchberger, one may question if the differences between an author's right system and a pure copyright system are really clear. If one of the main difference of the copyright system from the author's right system is that the latter protects moral rights, it is important to evaluate how effective is this protection. On this regard, Prof. Lehman has commented on the difficulty to protect Moral Rights in computer program works. In his words: "Thus, given the rather industrial character of computer programs, in practice moral rights only play a subordinate role, and it has been argued that legally they should also have to stand back". 97 Another argument that has been raised to explain the reason why the integrity right is limited lies in the possibility of this right being waived.98 On this point, Dietz states: "the fact that the obligation to respect the integrity of a work subject to a license under Section 39 is made dependent on the condition that there is no agreement to the contrary shows that this moral right, to some degree at least, can be contractually waived".99

Thus, despite the effect of new technologies that affect the integrity moral right, the fact that this right can be waived creates the possibility for companies to alter the works of their employees without their authorization. Despite the weaknesses of the moral rights that can be presented in some works, in some situations there are authors that underline the importance of this right. For example, in the following phrase, Dietz calls attention to the importance of the moral right of public disclosure: "The separate statutory recognition of this right stresses the importance of this moral aspect of copyright law, which guarantees that no person other than the author himself is allowed to decide whether and in what way his work shall be disclosed, eventually to the public".100 Applying Dietz's statement to this study, the employed author is the only one that can decide the public disclosure of the work. However, this phrase can be clear under the hypothesis of an independent author in which the employer can exercise many of the exploitation rights and even, the employee has limitations on exercising his moral rights. Thus, another question for the debate is whether the right of public disclosure is limited in the exercise in the course of employment, and whether, for example, the employee cannot impede the employer to disclose a work in an unauthorized way.

Exercising the Right of Authorship, the author can determine whether his work is to bear his name, signature or other designation and what designation is to be used.101 In this situation, the same question raised earlier will be applied. In the case of an individual author, he will decide to put his name. However, in the course of employment, it is important to check if an employee has the power to decide this matter and request to the employer that his name should appear on the work. As already seen in the analyzed Computer Programs Directive, the computer industry was influencing the adoption of the Directive in order to give legal persons (employers) the exercise of economic rights. Thus, the right of authorship is in practice claimed to a far lesser extent than is possible because of the interest of the software house in question.102 One may conclude that the possibility for legal persons to exercise the economic rights in computer programs, gave a back door to the computer industry to limit the exercise of moral rights.

It is worth inquiring if in the computer software that we usually use, we can see the names of the employees who actually created those works. At least in the software created by Microsoft, an American Company, the names of the software developers are not mentioned. If one sees the product package or the dvd's or cds in which these programs are contained, there are no indications of the names of the employees who create those works. This is probably due to the fact that the copyright system in America does not recognize this moral right. Thus, the task will be to see if software created in an employment relationship under German law shows the name of the author or authors. A paradoxical situation is found in France, where limitations on moral rights are not only present in the usual practice as in Germany, but also the law provides a limitation. Article 46 of the French Author's right law provides that "unless otherwise stipulated, the author may not oppose adaptation of the software within the limits of the rights he has assigned nor exercise his right to correct or to retract".103 This rule can be considered as paradoxical because it contradicts France's reputation for staunchly protecting all of the author's moral interests. However, within Article 46 a 'personal rights protection' is not reflected, as parties waive their moral rights of integrity and revocation in the case of silence.

Furthermore, in spite of the previous critics of the application of moral rights in the studied topic, there are some cases in which there is a clear application of moral rights in Germany that can make a clear differentiation between the author's right system and the copyright system. For instance, German cases104 dealing with the integrity moral right in architectural and cinematographic works are famous examples of the application of this right. However, there are not known cases dealing with the application of moral rights in works created in employment relationships that can lead to the conclusion that there are big differences between author's right system and copyright systems. Thus, the legal theory can be different as the German law recognizes different moral rights. Nonetheless, the practice can bring very similar situations as the ones found in the Anglo-American Copyright System, where the employer is in most of the cases the one that exercises the economic rights.

After analyzing the current practice on moral rights, a question for future policy making is whether the legal system's philosophy regarding author's rights will recognize, not only the economic, but also the moral rights of employers. Examples of this can already be found globally. For instance, the Japanese Copyright Act in its Section 15 provides for the transferability to the employer of, not only the exploitation rights, but also the moral rights.105 This provision was made in order to centralize the rights of author on the employer and to facilitate exploitation.106 Finally, it is important to bear in mind that as Germany has the monistic theory of author's right, the duration of the moral right is the same as in the economic rights. Article 64 of the Copyright Act establishes that the duration of the rights is seventy years after the author's death. Thus, the heirs of the employee will only have 70 years of moral and economic rights. The heirs will not have a perpetual moral right as in the case of countries with dualistic theory of moral rights. As will be addressed below, Colombia adopted the French author's right system, in which moral and economic rights are divided, and thus, the heirs of an employee in Colombia will enjoy the perpetual moral right.

Works Created By Public Servants

The Works created by employees working for the German government are initially owned by employees, as is also the case with employees working in the private sector. On this point, German law keeps in line with the philosophy of the French author's right system, and does not recognize government or corporate works initially owned by legal entities.107 It is important to specify that the list of Government works in Article 5 of the German Copyright Act, which states those works not protected under copyright. Thus, what is protected are the works not listed in Article 5.108 Nonetheless, as it happens to the private employment relationships109, in the public employment relationships,110 the ownership of these works belongs to the employees and the government can only receive the exploitation rights to use the work.111

The German provision highlights a difference in comparison to United States and Colombia, where the State is the owner of the copyright in the United States and of the economic rights in Colombia, despite the Colombian author's right system.112 Consequently, another particularity of the German system lies in the fact that the copyright is given to the employed author and his interests prevail over the economic interests that the State may have on the work created by the public servant. An open question for debate will be why does article 69 (b) of the German Copyright gave the economic rights to the employer? If one may think that the interest of the state is more important that the interest of an employer that orders the production of computer programs?

United States. Legal Rules and Analysis

In a different sense from Germany and Colombia, which are continental law systems characterized by statutes as the only primary source of law, the United States is a common law system in which case law is the main source of law. In fact, in the United States, common law principles first established that the ownership of the copyright presumptively belongs to the person that commissioned a work.113 This rule was later brought under statute in the Copyright Act of 1909 that established that the employer is the author and initial holder of works made for hire.114 However, as Garlock says, the 1909 statute did not define terms such as employer or work made for hire.115 It was not until the 1976 Copyright Act that in the United States the term work made for hire appeared in a statute. This study will focus on the analysis of section 201 of the 1976 Act which is the current applicable law. An examination of the background surrounding the enactment of the law is essential as starting point.

Despite the fact that the topic under study is 'works created under employment relationships', in Germany and in Colombia, the term 'employment' is a generic term in which not only labor law contracts but other type of private law contracts can be included. In the United States one of the examples of a private law relationship by which great amount of works are produced, is the case of works created by independent contractors. These types of contractors are not subject to the normal direction and supervision that can be seen in a labor law contract. However, since the Bratlleboro case116 in 1966, the second circuit applied the work for hire doctrine to independent contractors.117 Years later, in 1974, in the Siegel case118 the second circuit developed a test to determine when an independent contractor was included into the 'work made for hire' doctrine. This was the so called 'instance and expense test' by which the employer was considered as the owner of the copyright if the employer was the motivating factor to produce the creation.119 Under this test, the employer did not need to direct and supervise the work he ordered. Simply having the right to control the process was enough to make him the copyright owner.120

Furthermore, in Murray v. Gelderman,121 the fifth circuit extended the work for hire doctrine under the 1909 act. In opinion of Garlock, after this case: "the common law interpretation of the work made for hire doctrine under the Copyright Act of 1909 developed into a virtually irrebuttable presumption that anyone who paid another to create a copyrightable work was the statutory author and thereby entitled to a copyright in the product".122 Thus, notwithstanding that the work made for hire was not defined in the 1909 statute, courts in the usa created this doctrine to give an answer to the ownership of the copyright question. Not only the direction and supervision factors were taken into account to determine a work made for hire, also the economic factor by which the one who paid the work can be considered the author were important elements for Courts to determine a work made for hire. The utilitarian aspect of copyright law, characterized by a copyright system, was clearly shown by giving the ownership of the copyright to the person that paid another one for the production of a work, even without having any labor law contract. This utilitarian aspect is also represented by the fact that the employer is considered the author of the work. The employee who may be sometimes the original creator of the work is not considered to be the author in the United States, as happens in continental systems such as Germany and Colombia.

However, in the United States, as Nimmer points out, there have been problems caused by naming an employer the author. In words of Nimmer, "According to some commentators, a constitutional question arises, given the notion of 'author' in the Copyright Clause, as to whether the employer is considered the 'author' of a work by operation of law or as the transferee of the Actual creator. See Scherr vs. Universal Match Corp".123

Despite criticism of naming an employer as the author of a work created by an employee, the fact that in the United States moral rights do not exist like those of a continental law system, can bring a justified explanation to this matter. The employee in the continental system will always be the author of the work, mainly because the employee is the owner of the moral rights in the work that are not transferable. There are only transfers or licenses of the economic rights in the work, but the employee will retain the moral rights, hence, the author title.

Section 201(b) , and 101of the Copyright Act of 1976 and The 1909 Copyright Act

As in the 1909 Act, section 201 (b) of the 1976 Act established that the employer is the author. 124 Likewise it recognized the exception to the general ownership rule, as it gave the possibility to the parties to agree otherwise, meaning that not only the employer or person from whom the work was prepared can be the owner of the copyright, but also others can be designated e.g. the employee. Section 101 of the 1976 Act created a big change in comparison to the 1909 Act as it was the first time that the 'work for hire' term was defined. 125 The definition included works created in employment relationships, a topic which was already covered by the 1909 Act. The most significant difference from the 1909 Act is that the definition of 'work made for hire' also included the works ordered or commissioned for use in nine categories of works.

Note that the nine categories of works do not apply to employees. If an Employee creates a different kind of work he can still be considered within the doctrine of work made for hire. The works of section 101 are only applicable to independent contractors, and are the only type of creations by which an independent contractor can be deemed to be considered within the doctrine of work made for hire. In fact, in the case May v. Morganelii-Heumann & Associates, the court stated that the list provided in the section 101 (2) was a closed and exhaustive list. 126

There is however the two following formalities that the 1976 Act included in the definition, in order to consider a copyrighted work as a work made for hire:

1- The parties have to agree that the work will be a work made for hire

2- The agreement of the parties must be in a written instrument and signed by them.127

It is important to take into account that in the first hypothesis of section 101 by which the work is created by an employee, there is no transfer of the copyrighted work as the employer is considered the author. However, for some commentators128 there is in fact a transfer, but in this case the transfer is operated by law as section 101 gives the ownership of the copyright to the employer. The discussion about whether there is a transfer or not is, however, impractical as the consequence will always be that if the employee and employer do not agree otherwise, the ownership of the copyright will vest on the employer. By contrast, in the majority of the countries with author's right systems the discussion of the transfer of rights is of extreme importance, as at first glance the employee is considered the author, and the employer can be the owner of the economic rights in virtue of a transfer of rights. As we already see, the German case is even more oriented to protect the author as the transfer of economic rights is not possible, and only by licensing an employed author can transfer his rights.

A recommended formality to be fulfilled is the record of the transfer document in the Copyright office129 to give third parties notice of the transfer.130 Despite the fact that registration is not a requirement for the existence of a work made for hire, this is a step by which owners of the right can easily prove the ownership of the work and claim rights over third parties (i.e. priorities).131 In countries like Colombia, as we will see in Chapter vii, the registration requirement has the same effect. Regarding the duration of the right in the United States for works made for hire, the duration of the copyright will be 95 years from the first publication or 120 years from creation, whichever of the two terms is shorter.132 By contrast, in other countries under analysis, as we already saw in Germany, the copyright term is considerably different. Likewise, as it will be mentioned in the following Chapter, the term that Colombia has differs from Germany and United States.

The Remaining Problem of the Independent Contractor after the Copyright act of 1976

The fact that the Copyright Act defined the term 'work made for hire' do not solve the problem of determining when a work created by an independent contractor was considered a work for hire. After the expedition of the 1976 Act, Garlock states that three different interpretations of the ownership of the works created by an independent contractor were made. 133 The first interpretation was the so-called "Conservative Approach", and it consisted in applying the previously mentioned instance and expense test, and the right to control test used by courts when the 1909 Act was in force.134 If the independent contractor made the work by the instance and expense of the buyer, and by his control, the work was considered as a work for hire.135 However, under this first approach the instance and expense and control tests were not enough. The works produced must fall also within the categories established in the section 101 (2) and there must be a written agreement in which the parties agreed that there was a work for hire.136 In opinion of O'Meara this first approach was intended to protect independent contractors from the expansive common law doctrine of 1909 by which the instance and expense test and the control test were enough to consider an employer as the copyright owner.137

The second interpretation138 was made in the Aldon Accessories vs. Spiegel case.139 The court ruled in this case that if an independent contractor is controlled and supervised by the party who ordered the work, then an employer/employee relationship exists, and section 101 of the 1976 Act has to be applied.140 This ruling was followed in two other cases: Evans Newton Inc v. Chicago Systems software141 and Brunswick Beacon v. Schoch-Hopchas Publishing Co.142 As in the Aldon v. Spiegel case, in these two cases the courts ruled that if supervision and direction were present, the relationship between the two parties will be deemed to be an employee/employer relationship and section 101 (1) will be applied. This interpretation is broader than the conservative interpretation and can be considered as very similar to the common law that existed during the 1909 Act. In this second interpretation courts did not take into account subsection (2) of section 101 and gave most importance to the traditional elements of an employer/employee relationship, that is, control and supervision. This issue will be explained in chapter vii when explaining the labor law principle of reality over forms. However, it is important to take into account that a similar situation comes into play here. Although an independent contractor is not an employee and in the formal legal language is not included within the labor law lexicon, the presence of control and supervision are realities that turn the formality (the independent contractor title) into an employee. In other words, the existence of control and supervision during the creation of a work will prevail over the fact that the person who created a work was called an 'independent contractor'. Thus, the independent contractor will be under the work made for hire doctrine because he will be considered an employee.

The third interpretation for the application of work made for hire in the independent contractor hypothesis143 was given by the Fifth Circuit in the so called Easter Seal Society case.144 The fifth circuit stated that section 101 (1) of the Act will be applied to the independent contractor only if he is an employee within the terms of agency law. Regarding section 101 (2) it will be applied only if the works fall into the ten categories of works and there was a written instrument signed by the parties stating that the work was considered to be for hire. The change of this third interpretation was that to determine who was an employee the fifth circuit remitted the question to the section 220 of the restatement of agency law of 1958 that defined the term servant and do not use the previous tests of instance and expense nor the control test. In words of Garlock: "In support of its own literal interpretation, the fifth circuit relies primarily on the Actual language of the statute." 145 Further, Garlock states: "The court also favors this literal interpretation because it unites the work made for hire doctrine with the comparatively settled law of agency". 146

Summarizing the third approach, the definition of employee was determinative to establish an answer for the problem with the independent contractor. If the elements of the definition of servant were present, the independent contractor will be deemed to be an employee for purpose of the work made for hire. It is interesting how the fifth circuit in this case used agency law and not the pure IP statute, the Copyright Act of 1976. Should the ownership of the copyright created by employees be regulated by an IP statute or a labor statute? This is a policy question that we will see later in the Colombian analysis.

The CCNV Case

The Community for Creative Non Violence (CCNV) v. Reid case147 has become the most important decision on the topic of 'work made for hire' in the United States.

After this case, the previous three different interpretations were no longer used and the CCNV decision became the applicable law.148 For Nimmer, with this case "a definitive method of construing the 1976 Act on point became cast in concrete".149 As this is an important case for our analysis, the following short mention of its facts will be made:

The CCNV ordered the production of a sculpture for James Earl Reid. The order stated that the sculpture must depict homelessness with precise words on the work. Furthermore, the order suggested variations during the process of elaboration and it also proposed humans as models from the sculpture. The legal problem began when the parties did not agree to whom the copyright would belong. Thus, the CCNV sued Reid claiming for a work made for hire on the production of the sculpture.150

In the CCNV judgment the Supreme Court did not use the exact elements of the definition of employee given in the Second Restatement of Agency law151 that were used in the Easter Seal case.152 By contrast, the Supreme Court did not tied up with the Restatement of Agency law to determine the definition of Employee, as the Supreme Court said that the elements provided in section 220 (2) of the Restatement were not determinative.153 In the words of the Supreme Court: In determining whether a hired party is an employee under the general common law of agency, we consider the hiring party's right to control the manner and means by which the product is accomplished. Among the other factors relevant to this inquiry are the skill required; the source of the instrumentalities and tools; the location of the work; the duration of the relationship between the parties; whether the hiring party has the right to assign additional projects to the hired party; the extent of the hired party's discretion over when and how long to work; the method of payment; the hired party's role in hiring and paying assistants; whether the work is part of the regular business of the hiring party; whether the hiring party is in business; the provision of employee benefits; and the tax treatment of the hired party. See Restatement ' 220(2) (setting forth a no exhaustive list of factors relevant to determining whether a hired party is an employee).31 No one of these factors is determinative. 154

The italicized part shows how the Supreme Court did not use the exact definition of the restatement of agency law. The ratio decidendi of the present case ruled on Reid's benefit as the work was not considered for hire. Thus, it concluded that Reid was an independent contractor and not an employee.155 The United States Copyright office in the Circular # 9, by using the CCNV decision has classified the following three factors to determine when a work is made for hire:

1) Control by the employer over the work (e.g., the employer may determine how the work is done, has the work done at the employer's location, and provides equipment or other means to create work)
2) Control by employer over the employee (e.g., the employer controls the employee's schedule in creating work, has the right to have the employee perform other assignments, determines the method of payment, and/or has the right to hire the employee's assistants)
3) Status and conduct of employer (e.g., the employer is in business to produce such works, provides the employee with benefits, and/or withholds tax from the employee's payment).156

Nonetheless, the Copyright Office in the said circular states that in the CCNV decision the Court do not settle on which factors were determinative in order to prove an employment relationship.157 Coming back to the CCNV case, the Supreme Court also studied the second approach made in the case Aldon Accessories v. Spiegel case already mentioned. The Supreme Court said that the control and supervision arguments that were made in that case, were not sufficient to determine if there was a work made for hire. In words of the Supreme Court: The Actual control test, articulated by the Second Circuit in Aldon Accessories, fares only marginally better when measured against the language and structure of section 101. Under this test, independent contractors who are so controlled and supervised in the creation of a particular work are deemed "employees" under section 101(1).158 Thus, for the Supreme Court it was not enough that the employer had a formal control over the employee. There must be a direction and supervision like the one that was used later in the case of Quintanilla v. Texas Television case, meaning that the employer must supervise the manner and means in which the creator performs his job.159

Finally, despite the fact that the Supreme Court reached the conclusion that Reid's sculpture was not a work made for hire, this did not mean that the only owner of the work was Reid. The court, however, suggested that that this could be a case of joint authorship as the CCNV also contributed in the creation of the work.160

It is important to point out that when American courts conclude that there are not works made for hire, the joint authorship solution is not always the outcome. There are cases in which the authorship can be deemed only on the independent contractor or the employee.161 In some countries, like Mexico, there is a especial situation as the result is not joint authorship, the general rule is that the employee is the author, but the economic rights are shared equally between the employer and the employee.162 Thus, another question for debate will be whether it is fairer to rule the ownership question by creating a 50/50 rule and give both employer and employee economic benefit from the work.

After the CCNV decision, the case law on the work made for hire has not gone through major changes as in previous times. In fact, there are cases that back up the CCNV decision like Carter v. Helmsley Spear. In this case it was said that despite the parties having signed a labor law contract, it is important that the elements of the works made for hire determined in the CCNV decision are present.163 We can see here, how the already mentioned principle of the 'reality over the forms' comes into play again. Earlier, we talked about the situation in which an independent contractor can be considered an employee. In the previously cited case we find the opposite situation. The formality would be that the parties agreed there was a labor law contract, and the reality would be that there was not an employee/employer relationship for the purpose of the work made for hire, since its elements were not present.

Critics after the CCNV Case

The legal uncertainty of what is considered a work made for hire was minimized with the CCNV case. However, there are still questions and critics of the work made for hire doctrine. In fact, the Copyright office in the already mentioned Circular 9, stated that as there is "no precise standard for determining whether or not a work is made for hire under the first part of the definition, consultation with an attorney for legal advice may be advisable". 164 This shows that the definition of the work made for hire term is not definitely clear.

Some commentators, like Assaf, say that the elements of determining a work made for hire fixed in the CCNV decision, have caused legal uncertainty. The main reason for this conclusion is that the test used by the Supreme Court is based on Tort Law principles which are not compatible with the philosophy of Copyright Law.165 Furthermore, Assaf does not only criticize the current test fixed on the CCNV decision. He also proposes the following ideas to transform the work made for hire doctrine using arguments focused on copyright principles rather than agency law: My proposal is that the 'work made for hire' doctrine should be applied from the vantage point of Copyright Law. The test should focus on incentives to create on the one hand and public access to created works on the other. These are the goals of Copyright Law as stated in the Constitution. Thus, the new test should re-interpret the term 'employee' in a manner that complies with the needs of Copyright Law. Most importantly, 'employee' should be interpreted to give the first entitlement to the party most apt to achieve the goals of the Constitution: Instead of using agency test factors such as employee benefits and tax treatment, the courts should consider factors such as the parties' relative incentive to create new works, public accessibility, transaction costs, and the parties relative ability and motivation to disseminate works to the public. The partnership of individual creativity with the employer's resources yields a significant engine for creative production in society. Revising the 'work made for hire' test would re-align this important issue with the rest of intellectual property law.166

As we can see, despite the existence of the CCNV decision, there are however some critics in the United States regarding the 'work made for hire' doctrine. We would be right in stating that the general topic under study, in some cases when the law applies, the outcome is not entirely certain in the United States. The reason is mainly because finding a consensus between the definitions and principles of Copyright Law and Labor Law has not been an easy task. This conflict between the two fields of law is not only present in the United States. As we will see in the next Chapter, the Colombian situation can be seen as even more ambiguous, as there is a legal gap on the ownership point that has created a series of positions, some coming from the labor law side and others coming from the author's rights side.

Common Examples of works that fall under the Work for Hire Doctrine

– The Copyright office in the cited Circular 9, states that nowadays, the common examples of works of hire are the following:

A software program created within the scope of his or her duties by a staff programmer for Creative Computer Corporation.

A newspaper article written by a staff journalist for publication in the newspaper that employs him.

A musical arrangement written for xyz Music Company by a salaried arranger on its staff.167

The first example proposed by the Copyright Office is of extreme importance and relevant around the world. As we already see in the German Chapter, the European legislator gave the ownership of the economic rights to the employer in this particular kind of works. Despite the fact that the directive only gives economic rights to the employer, this is the most similar provision to the work made for hire system in relation to countries which have a continental law system (e.g. Germany). The question will be whether the author's rights system is becoming more similar to the copyright system or if the situation is vice versa, with the copyright system creating more traditional author's right provisions. In our analysis we will continue to see more similarities between the two systems to finally determine which the prevailing one is.

The Importance of the Scope of Employment Element to Determine a Work Made For Hire

In the William vs. Weisser case the court ruled that if a professor writes his lecture during business hours and without any kind of supervision, that work is not considered to be for hire, despite the fact the professor is an employee of the University working in business hours.168 The requirement that the created work be bound within the scope of the labor law contract, is put into practice in this case. On this point Nimmer says that: "Given the requirement that works for hire fall within the scope of employment, it follows that if an employer and employee agree that even works prepared outside such scope will be considered works for hire, those provisions of the contract are invalid."169 Thus, if an employer wants to allege the rights on a work created by an employee, it is a mandatory requirement that the work falls within the scope of the contract. The protection of the employee's rights that Nimmer suggests would prevail over the freedom of the parties. At a first glance, the copyright system in comparison to the author's rights system can be considered as less protective to the employed author. Thus, this kind of protection is paradoxical and we could ask ourselves whether there are similar commentators in line with Nimmer, applying this argument to the author's right system.

Salary as an Element in Determining the Employment Relationship

In the CCNV decision, one of the elements in determining the employment relationship was the "method of payment to the hired party".170 Thus, as in the continental labor law traditional doctrine, not only the existence of control and supervision, but also the fixation of a salary is considered an indication of the existence of the labor law contract. However, in Brown v. Cosby171, it was stated that despite the presence of a fixed salary, if an employer does not pay the salary to an employee, there is a breach of contract that will not give the ownership of the copyright to the employer.172 This case was ruled before the CCNV decision. Thus, it would be interesting to ask ourselves if, under current law, the same consequence would apply or the employee will simply have to enforce the right to get paid and loose the right on the created work. As we can see, this is another ruling in order to protect the employed author, which at first glance would be more likely found in an author's right system. In the law of continental systems, however, there are no labor or IP law provisions like this. The stated common law rule can be considered not only as a fair price to an employee that do not get paid, but also as a method of penalizing the employer for not fulfilling his labor law obligations, despite the fact that there are in each country other ways to punish the employer for not paying the employee.173

Colombia. Legal rules and analysis

We begin the Colombian legal analysis by stating that the two topics of study under examination, employment and copyright, are protected under the Colombian Constitution of 1991. The constitution of Colombia guarantees a right of employment and protection of one's ip. The term 'employment' is defined in article 25 of the Constitution. Under this provision employment is a constitutional right, and it is an obligation for the state to protect all forms of employment. The first question that we have to raise after reading the previous provision is: what does the Constitution meant by 'all forms of employment'? 174 The answer for this is the same as in Germany and in the United States; employment is a generic term, encompassing labor law contracts and private law contracts.175

In addition, article 61176 of the Constitution creates an obligation for the Colombian state to protect Intellectual Property rights. This provision does not distinguish between the three traditional IP rights of copyrights, patents and trademarks, but the legal doctrine includes these concepts under the generic concept of Intellectual Property rights. With referal to the Copyright tradition that has been used in Colombia, the same analysis that was made in Germany applies here, as Colombia is a continental law system. Thus, the proper way to name the right which an employee may have for the works created is author's' right and not copyright. However, as it was previously said, in the German analysis, for practical reasons the term copyright may be used here as well. Although the aim of this analysis is not to consider what constitutes an employment contract in the analyzed countries, some generalities of the Colombian law can be pointed out: As mentioned, the traditional three main elements of the labor law contract that have been analyzed in United States and Germany are present also in Colombian law in the article 22 of Labor Law Code.177

Likewise, as stated above, the term employment is a generic term in civil law relationships, in which is included the situation where persons provide services to others. In Colombia the most common civil legal law relationship in which copyrighted works are created is the so called contract to provide services or contract of services, a literal translation from the Spanish term: Contrato de prestación de servicios. The elements of this type of contracts are not defined in a specific provision, but it is of frequent application as it is a legal way by which the one that orders a work is not legally obliged to pay different sums usually related to the Colombian Social Security Regime. However, it is important to take into account that the person who wants to receive the services does not treat the provider as an employee, otherwise he will run the risk of being under a labor law contract even without even signing one as the substantive reality prevails over the practice.178 The contract to provide services is not specifically defined in a legal provision; however, there are rules that explain its origin and its philosophy. The first rules that mentioned the topic were Articles 2053 and 2063 of the civil code.179 The first refers to the lending of services to create a tangible work and the latter refers to intangible forms.

The Colombian Commercial Code also includes provisions related to contracts for services. The most important is article 968.180 However, the only legal norm that has an approximate definition of the contract to provide services can be found in article 32 paragraph 3 of the Law of States' Contracts. For our purpose, the important element of this definition is the express exclusion of labor law contracts when it states: "in any case, these contracts do not create labor law relationships".181 The cited provision clearly shows the legislator's intention to differentiate this contract from labor law contracts. The previous rules are the basic legal provisions by which a person in Colombia can create work for an employer or for someone that has not the title of employer, but receives the services under a non labor law relationship.

The Gap in Colombian Law Regarding the Ownership of Economic Rights in Works Created In Employment Relationships

None of the Colombian legal rules above provide a clear answer regarding the ownership of the copyright of works created by employees. The only reference that can be found in the Labor law code in relation to IP is related to the employee obligation to maintain confidentiality.182 Neither the civil code nor the commercial code established a legal rule that provides a clear answer about the ownership of the copyright in Works created by employees. The Colombian Author's Right Law number 23 of 1982 has in its article 20183 a specific rule concerning the ownership of the copyright in contracts to provide services, however, the law does not mention any express rule about the situation under an employment contract. A literal translation of article 20 will be:

When one or more authors during a contract to provide services make a work under the directions of a natural or legal person, the author or authors will only receive the fees that they agreed by contract. Just by this fact, the author or authors transfer their rights on the work, without prejudice of article 30 letters a) and b).184

Two consequences will derive from this provision:

1- That just by signing the contract, the provider of the services will transfer the economic rights.
2- As Colombia is an Author's Right system, the dualistic theory of rights by which the law differentiates between Moral and Economic rights will be applied here. Thus, the author in this case will retain the moral rights of integrity (a) and paternity (b).185

In spite of the previous provision, according to some commentators, like Fernando Zapata López, article 183 of the law under study, fixes a formal requirement to make the transfer of the economic rights effective in the course of the contract to provide services.186 Article 183 states that every act, in which there is a partial or total transfer of the author right, must be made by public instrument or by a private document certified by a Notary.187 In addition, to have effect on third parties, the documents have to be registered in the National Office of Author's Right.188 On this regard there is a big difference with United States and Germany. As previously mentioned on these two countries, the registration of a transfer or a grant at the respective Copyright Office is not a mandatory requirement for the validity of the transfer.

In Zapata´s opinion, article 20 does not establish a legal presumption of transferal of the economic rights.189 The argument that he relies on to reach this conclusion is that legal presumptions are formed by facts, and in the present case this legal presumption is created by a contract (the contract of services) but not by a fact, so technically it is improper to talk about a legal presumption under this analysis.190 Moreover, he states that what article 20 is establishing is the effect of signing a contract to provide services, but this does not mean that the parties do not have to fulfill the formalities established under article 183.191

Thus, the questions to ask after reading these two legal provisions are:

Why does the law mention in article 20 that simply by signing the contract to provide services, the economic rights will be transferred, if later, in article 183 it establishes an extra requirement for the economic rights transfer? Does articles 20 and 183 have to be used in order to solve the economic rights problem, or other legal arguments can be used? There has been different interpretations to resolve this question. However, for the purpose of the study, only the following 4 main approaches are going to be mentioned:

The Application of the Latin Maxim the Special Law Prevails Over the Generic Law 'Lex Specialis Generalem Deroga'

The author Carlos Hernán Godoy states that article 183 does not apply to contracts to provide services.192 He uses the legal principle by which the special law prevails over the generic law lex specialis generalem deroga in order to solve the ambiguity.193 The special provision is Article 20 by which the lawmaker was only regulating the contract to provide services. Thus, in Godoy's opinion there will be no need to require a public instrument or other formalities for a transfer of economic rights in the course of a contract to provide services.194 Notwithstanding the need for the requirements of article 183 in a contract to provide services, Godoy emphasizes the importance that the three following conditions of article 20 are fulfilled in order to transfer the economic rights:

1- The contract has to include a clear work plan. The reason for this is to avoid situations in which undefined rights shall be transferred. This is of importance because if the author agreed to broad work, then he may run the risk of lost economic ownership on works that were not meant to be transferred.

2- The elaboration of the work should be under the risk of the person that orders it.

3- The price that the parties agree must be clearly specified in the contract.195

If as Godoy says, the lawmaker is referring to contracts different from the agreement to provide services in article 183, the question for our purpose will be, what if one of these types of contracts was a labor law contract?

Regarding this question Godoy states that article 20 is not applicable to the labor law agreement,196 because of the following two arguments: – In spite of the fact that the text of article 20 is ambiguous because it refers to contract of services, the word fees (honorarios in Spanish) marks a clear distinction between the contract of services and the labor law contract, as in the latter the money that the employer pays to the employee is by essence called a wage, but never fees. If the law maker distinguished the word fees, it should be inferred that it was referring to service contracts.197

There is not a specific rule for the labor law agreement on the Author's right law. This fact means that we have to apply the general provision of article 183. The wording of Article 183 states that "every act" ("Todo acto" in Spanish) of transfer must fulfill the requirements established herein. When the law refers to 'every act' it must be interpreted as every act different from the contract of services where there is a specific rule.198 Thus, in Godoy's opinion article 183 applies to the labor law agreement, and if the employer wants to receive the economic rights, the agreement will have to fulfill the two requirements already mentioned, that is: it has to be made by public instrument or in a private document certified by a notary, and will have to be registered in the Author's Right National Office to have effects on third parties. To summarize Godoy's approach: There is no specific provision in the civil, commercial and author's right law that will tell us to whom the economic rights should belong in an employment relationship. As there is no special provision, article 183 is the general rule that we will have to apply for the labor agreement.

Transferability of the Economic Rights in Virtue of Article 20 of the Author's Right Law

The Colombian Consejo de Estado199 in the year 2003 provided an opinion200 to the question of the application of articles 20 and 183 in the employment relationships. The opinion can be considered as opposite to Godoy's interpretation mentioned above. This is because the Consejo de Estado avers that article 20 is enough to say that the employee transfers the economic rights to the employer. By the sole fact of having a labor agreement the employer can receive the economic rights on the work, and there is no need to fulfill the requirements of article 183.201 The following are some of the main reasons that the Consejo de Estado uses to justify the opinion:

– Despite the fact that there is no internal law that refers to the situation in the labor law contract, there must be an harmonious interpretation with the following articles of the author's right law: Article 4 of the author's right law permits in some situations that a legal or natural person has the economic rights when he, she or it orders the production of the work at his own risk. Article 92 establishes that if in the course of an employment contract, a collective work is created, and if it is impossible to determine the ownership, the property of the economic rights will belong to the person that ordered the work. Thus, the said harmonic interpretation will apply if the lawmaker regulates the situation in these rules; they have to be applied to the employment contract too without seeing if the created work is collective or not. The result is that the economic rights of the employee are transferred to the employer with the sole act of signing the labor contract202.

– The Colombian Constitutional Court in the judgment C-278 of 1996 said that article 20 of the author's right law was enough to transfer the economic rights to the natural or legal person who ordered the work. This judgment was confirmed in a later case (C- 155 of 1998). These judgments must be also extended to the labor law contract.203

– The Andean decision # 351 of 1993 in its article 10 provides the same legal presumption of transfer of economic rights, not only when there is a work that is ordered in the course of a civil relationship, but also in a labor law agreement.204

Regarding the application of the previously mentioned article 183 of the author's right law, the Consejo de Estado states that this norm could be a mistake by the lawmaker, because the truth of the matter is that the transfer of economic rights in civil law and labor law agreements by which an employer or non employer orders a work, do not require the formalities established in article 183.205

The Favorability Principle of the Labor Law and Author's Right Law

This approach does not use articles 20 or 183. On the contrary, under these interpretations the favorability principles established in the Author's right law and the labor law code are the legal arguments that give the employee the ownership of the economic rights.

Regarding the favorability in the labor law code, Riveros states that the gaps of the legislation may not be interpreted in a manner which is contrary to the interests of the employee who produced the work in an autonomous way or produced the work in accordance with a given plan.206 The favorability principle protected under labor law bestows on the employee a claim over the economic rights of a work when there is no agreement in which the employee has transferred such rights to the employer.207

Likewise, article 257 of the Author's Right Law establishes that any doubt regarding the application of the law will be interpreted in favor of the author. As this is clearly a case where there is not a specific rule that gives an answer, and as the employee in Colombia is the author, he will be the one that benefits from this principle.208 By contrast, as it was explained in the previous Chapter, the author in the United States is the employer. Thus, there will be an important difference in this point as the application of the said principle in the United States will be in favor of the employer.209

Labor Law Approach in favor of the Employer

As the previous interpretation this approach does not use article 20 or 183, it states that the philosophy under the labor law norms implies that every work created by an employee should be property of the employer.

One of the proponents of this philosophy is the Argentinean professor Delia lipzyc who recognizes that despite the difficulty of finding an answer to the question of ownership of works created in employment contracts, the principles of labor law should prevail over the principles of author's law.210 According to the general principles of labor law, every fruit produced by an employee must belong to an employer, although the moral rights will be always remain the property of the employee.211 The Colombian Professor ARCADIO PLAZAS, shares Lipzyc's approach, and adds that one must differentiate between authorship and what he calls title of rights212. The authorship of a work can only vest with the employee, as he is the one who creates the work. The second element, title of rights, belongs to the employer, so the employer will be the direct owner of the economic rights unless the employer agrees differently with the employee.213 Moreover, Plazas states that employer and employee both satisfied their immediate economic interests because, on the one hand, the employee received a wage for his work and, on the other hand, the employer received the fruits of the works for which he was paying.214 Another justification that Plazas uses to support the idea of the ownership of the economic right residing with the employer, is the fact that the employees create copyrighted works, not only according to instructions given by the employer, but also with material tools provided by the employer. Thus, the effort of the employer should be recognized by giving him the ownership of the economic rights.215

The previous four theories concerning the ownership of the copyright in works created in employment relationships created can be summarized as follows:

1- Article 20 of the author's right law is not enough to transfer the economic rights to the employer. For an employer in order to be the owner of the economic rights, he has to fulfill the requirements provided in article 183 of the author's right law. By contrast, in the contract to provide services there is no need to fulfill the requirements fixed on article 183. However, some commentators like Zapata216 argue that even in the contract to provide services the formal requirements of article 183 have to be fulfilled in order to transfer the right to the person that ordered the work.

2- In virtue of article 20 of the author's right law, it is clear that an employee is an author that retains the moral rights, however the economic rights are automatically transferred to the Employer. The same conclusion applies to the contract to provide services.

3- The principles of favorability of the labor law code and the author's right law give the employee the economic rights on its creation. The employer will only have the ownership of the economic rights if the employee decides to transfers them to him.

4- The labor law should prevail over the author's right in this case, and the economic rights should belong to the employer for the sole fact of signing a labor contract with an employee.

Works Created By Public Servants

Notwithstanding that the Author's right law did not provide a legal answer for the ownership of the economic rights in works created in private employment relationships, Article 91 regulates the subject in works created by public servants. In this situation, we are under the hypothesis that an employee from the state creates a protected work. The legal consequence is that the State is the owner of the economic rights. This provision can probably contains one of the few exceptions of the moral rights in the law, as it says that "the moral rights will belong to the authors (the employees) as long as their exercise is compatible to the legal duties and rights of the public offices involved". 217 The philosophy under the norm is protecting the public interest of the state, however, there are no known cases related to this matter in which a public company has claim something from an employee because of an incompatible exercise of the moral right.

The situation in Colombia regarding works created by public servants is more similar to the Anglo America Copyright System as the State is the owner at least of the economic rights. By contrast, and despite the fact that Germany is an author's right system like Colombia. The ownership in works created by public servants in Germany is different, as the economic and moral rights vest with the public servants.218

CONCLUSIONS

Main Differences in the Law of the Analyzed Countries

As Germany and Colombia are countries based on the author's right system, the employee will always be considered the author of a work created under the scope of employment. Likewise, the employed author will always be a natural person. By contrast, in the United States, the employer is considered the author of a work created under the scope of employment, and he can be a legal entity or a natural person.219 With respect to the issue of ownership, since Germany and Colombia are both based on the author's right system, the employee will always be the owner of the inalienable moral rights in these countries. Since there is no express recognition of moral rights in the United States, the employees cannot enjoy such types of rights.

Since Germany is a monistic author's right system, the moral rights and the economic rights are represented in one sole right that belongs to the employee.220 Consequently, an employee in Germany can only grant the right to use the economic rights, since he will always be considered the owner of economic rights , and no transfer will be possible. By contrast, Colombia is classified under the dualistic theory of moral rights by which moral and economic rights are not merged into a unitary right, and thus, the employee can transfer or license the economic rights to the employer.221 The silence of the employer and employee regarding the ownership of the copyrighted works may also bring different results in each country. In the United States, the general rule is that if the parties did not agree to anything otherwise, the employer will be the author and owner of the work. In Germany, if the parties were silent, the employee will exercise the economic rights. However, an important exception to the general rule in Germany can be found in computer programs created by employees.222 In this case, the silence of the parties will give the exercise of the economic rights to the employer. In Colombia, the law does not tell where an employee and employer are silent on the topic of economic rights, resulting in different interpretations by commentators. Some commentators prefer to give the ownership of the economic rights to the employer while others aim to vest the employee with these rights.

Finally, regarding the duration of the copyright, Colombia has the longer protection, since the economic rights last 80 years after the death of the employee or 80 years after the death of the employer if the economic rights were transferred to him and the employer is a Natural person.223 With respect to the moral rights, since Colombia follows the dualistic author's right system, the duration of these rights is perpetual. The monistic theory of author's rights in Germany has a different result, whereby the moral and economic rights last 70 years after the employee's death.224 The United States provides the minimum protection, as the right lasts 95 years from the publication of the work or 120 years from the creation of the work, without taking into account the death of the employer.225 This can be considered as one clear difference revealing how important is for an author's right system to observe the interests of the authors by giving them longer terms than in a copyright system.

The Tendency of the Author's Right Law Systems like Germany and Colombia to Become Similar to the Anglo American Copyright Systems

The fact that the German law recognizes the employer's ability to exercise economic rights in computer programs, leads to a clear approximation to the American work made for hire doctrine. The employer in Germany is not the author, but the power to exercise the economic rights in these works is enough to reveal a similarity to the Anglo American system, as the economic interests of the employer prevail over those of the employee, who in most cases is the natural person creating the copyrighted work. Likewise, for other types of works, the usual practices in Germany can lead to the same conclusion. In most of the cases, not only have employees granted the use of the economic rights to the employer, but by "implied clauses" or presumptions, the employer finds a means of exercising the economic rights.226

Despite the fact that the E.C. computer programs directive leaves the regulation of moral rights to the national law of each member state, the reality in Germany is that the use of the moral rights in software created by employees is being diminished,227 revealing another similarity to the Anglo American Copyright system where these types of rights are not recognized.

The E.C. computer programs directive also left another issue to the member states, that of computer programs created by independent contractors. On this regard, Germany gave the exercise of the economic rights to the person that orders the work,228 highlighting another similarity to the Anglo American Copyright system in which the copyright vests in the person that ordered the work, if the conditions of a work made for hire are present. In the case of Colombia, it is difficult to take a position regarding an approximation to the Anglo American copyright system regarding works created by employees serving private companies. This is due to the fact that the law does not provide a clear answer, and legal commentators have expressed different interpretations about the ownership of the economic rights in employment contracts. By contrast, in works created by public servants, the law in Colombia is clear and shows an approximation to the Anglo American Copyright system, since the economic rights vest in the Nation. Likewise, the moral rights in such public employment contracts are limited, as their exercise is permitted if they do not conflict with the normal exploitation of the work. 229

Thus, it can be considered paradoxical that two author's right systems like Colombia and Germany do not have uniform rules on the topic, and by contrast, both countries have strong similarities to the Anglo American copyright system. If the Colombian lawmakers decide to amend the law and fill the legal lacunae, the philosophy of the author's right system should not be forgotten. The economic and moral interests of the employed authors have to be conserved. Otherwise, it would be inconsistent to call the system an author's right system which was created to protect the original creation of the human being. Likewise, lawmakers should consider solutions to protect the interests of the authors in industries where employees cannot freely exercise moral and economic rights (i.e. computer programs). Some solutions may lie in creating mechanisms that give extra remuneration to the employees for their work, as is the practice in Germany with inventions created by employees.230 Another fair and probable solution that can balance the interests of employees and the employers in these kinds of works may consist of dividing the ownership of the economic rights by half, as is the practice in countries like Mexico.231 One must not forget that it is not every day that an employee is creating works that are protected under copyright. The creation should be rewarded, and in most of the cases the salary is not a great enough incentive. Mechanisms to simultarneously reward authors and stimulate creation are necessary.

Other Types of Similarities between the Countries under Study: Scope of Employment, Employment Relationships and the Use of IP Statutes

In the three countries analyzed, one may conclude that the expression "scope of employment" has a similar meaning. The important indicator in considering whether a work was created under the scope of employment lies in whether the employee created the work in execution of his duties. Other factors, such as the creation of the work in the place of work or during working hours, are subsidiary facts that are not clear indicia to prove that a work is created in an employment relationship. Likewise, the understanding of a labor law relationship is similar in Colombia, Germany, and the United States. The element of dependency, characterized by the fact that the employer gives orders to the employee in how to do their work or fulfill a schedule, is present in all three countries.

Similarly, the principle of reality over the forms232 is applied in the three countries, as it does not matter if one party uses a different formality from a labor contract to order another party to produce work. If elements such as supervision, control, or dependency are present, the reality shows that there is in fact a labor relationship.

Naturally, in all the countries, it is mandatory to observe labor law provisions such as labor law contracts, labor law codes, and union agreements. This fact has created critics in the United States who believe it is a mistake of courts to take into account agency law in the "work made for hire" doctrine.233 Nonetheless, one may affirm that the tendency at least in Germany and in the United States has been to regulate the issue of ownership mostly by using Copyright justifications and the National Copyright acts. Since Colombia has not provided a clear answer to the ownership question, if the lawmakers decide to fill in the legal gap, it would be recommendable to follow the legal trend and amend the Copyright provision, that is, the author's right law.

NOTES:

1. Goldstein, Paul: International Intellectual property law. Cases and Materilas - New York : Foundation. 2D. 2008, at 214.
2. Christine Kirchberger, Ulrika Nyh, Silvina Penaloza, Hanna Sepanen and Kerli Tults. Ownership of the Copyright and the Patent Right in Works Created by Employees. Finland, Sweden, Austria, UK, Estonia, and Argentina. Sanna Wolk (ed.) 2002, at 1.
3. Yu Du and Matthew Murphy. mmlc Group. Intellectual Property in the Employer and Employee Relationship in China. at: http://www.hg.org/article.asp?id=5341.
4. oit. Contratos de Trabajo, at http://www.ilo.org/public/spanish/dialogue/themes/ ce.htm#ci.
5. Efren Cordova, Naturaleza y Elementos del Contrato de Trabajo. México. unam, Série B, Estudios Doctrinales Núm 188. 1997. Chapter 16, at 302.
6. Likewise, the employee has to be free on his decision to work, there cannot be any form of forced labor. On this point see id, at 306.
7. Cordova, supra note 5 at 306.
8. Original text of Article 22 reads: "Art. 22. – Definición. 1. Contrato de trabajo es aquél por el cual una persona natural se obliga a prestar un servicio personal a otra persona natural o jurídica, bajo la continuada dependencia o subordinación de la segunda y mediante remuneración (Código sustantivo del trabajo)". Text translated by the author.
9. The theory by which the presence of the three said elements form a labor law contract was born in Germany in the first quarter of the previous century, soon after the first labor laws were enacted. For further information See El derecho del Trabajo en España. Ideologías Jurídicas y Contrato de Trabajo. Madrid, Instituto de Estudios Sociales, 1981. at 127, 128, 129 & 130.
10. For further information see supra note 5, at 309.
11. Id, at 312.
12. For instance, as it will be mentioned in Chapter VII, in Colombia, to solve the legal gap on the ownership point, there are some theories who by way of analogy translate the ownership rules of the contract to provide services to the labor law contract.
13. A. Martin Valverde, F. Rodríguez- Sañudo y J. García Murcia. Derecho del Trabajo. Madrid. Ed. Tecnos, 14 Edición, 2005, at 642.
14. Id, at 642.
15. National Labor Law Profile: Federal Republic of Germany. Contributed by Liliane Jung. Last update, April 2001. at http://www.ilo.org/public/english/dialogue/ifpdial/info/ national/ger.htm
16. Id.
17. Schricker. Urheberrecht Kommentar (2006) 3. Auflage, at 887 section 13.
18. Id. at 887 section 13.
19. Goldstein. supra note 1, at 214.
20. Id. at 214.
21. Adolf Dietz, German Chapter of the book Compilated by Nimmer, Melville. International Copyright Law and Practice. b. volume 2 1997/2000, at 19.
22. Juan Pablo Riveros Lara. Derecho de Autor en Colombia.. Ed Hojas e Ideas, at 38.
23. Dietz, supra note 21, at 19.
24. Id, at 19.
25. German Copyright Act of 1965 Article 11: "Copyright shall protect the author with respect to his intellectual and personal relationship with his work, and also with respect to utilization of his work". Translation provided by wipo. Text Available at: http://www.iuscomp.org/gla/statutes/UrhG.htm.
26. Dietz, supra note 21 at 20.
27. Goldstein, supra note 1, at 214.
28. Id. at 214.
29. Dietz, supra note 21 at 47,48
30. Id, at 51. Not only the German law predicts the indivisibility of these two rights, but the term of both rights are the same, 70 years after the death of the author. By contrast, in others authors right tradition Countries like Colombia and France, the moral rights are perpetual, and the term of the economic rights last with time.
31. Id, at 51.
32. Goldstein, supra note 1, at 214.
33. Dietz, supra note 21, at 51.
34. The courts usually have decided if the licensee has the right to sue third parties for infringement. One of the examples by which the court gave the right to sue to a licensee is in one decision of the bgh of June 17 of 1992, (vgl. hierzu bgh grur 1992, 697, 698 F- Alf.). Despite the plaintiff in this case was not an employer. General rules of contracts will apply also if the plaintiff were an employer.
35. German Copyright Act. See also supra note 25.
36. Dietz, supra note 21, at 52.
37. Id, at 52.

38. Id, at 53.
39. Id, at 54.
40. See supra note 35.
41. Dietz, supra note 21, at 54.
42. Id, at 53.
43. See supra note 35.
44. We have to bear in mind that despite referring to registration of transfers in the citation. The proper term to be use in Germany would be registration of the grants of the contractual right to use the exploitation rights.
45. Dietz, supra note 21 at 55.
46. Article 43 German Copyright Act. See supra note 35.
47. Article 69b German Copyright Act. See supra note 35.
48. Dietz, supra note 21, at 50.
49. Id, at 54.
50. Id, at 50.
51. Kirchberger, supra note 2, at 14.
52. Schricker, supra note 17, at 890 Section 23.
53. Dreier, Schulze. Urheberrechtsgesetz 2 auflage (2006), at 54 lines 24 to 25.
54. Schricker, supra note 17, at 905 section 65
55. Id, at 902 section 64.
56. German Employees' Inventions Act of January 18 2002.
57. Kirchberger, supra note 2, at 14.
58. Dreier, Schulze, supra note 53, at 56 Lines 22 to 30.
59. The German Supreme Court have said that the there is a presumption to an implicit transfer of economic rights. Case Reference: rgz 153,1/8. For further information see Schricker, supra note 17.
60. Schricker, supra note 17, at 894 sect. 38.
61. Id, at 921 section 101.
62. Id, at 921 section 101.
63. Id, at 894 sect 41
64. Kirchberger, supra note 2, at 14.
65. Rojahn, Urheber In Arbeits – Oder Dienstverhaeltnissen In Urheberrecht Kommentar, at 683
66. Olenhusen v., a. G., der Urheber- und Leistungsrechtsschutz der Arbeitehmeraehnlichen Personen, grur 2002, book 1at 15.
67. Dietz, supra note 21, at 50.
68. Id, at 50.
69. Id, at 50.
70. Krasser, Urheberrecht in Arbeits-, Dienst- und Aufragsverhaeltnissen (1999), at 97.
71. Dreier, Schulze, supra note 53, at 53 lines 20 to 25.
72. Dreier. The international Development of Copyright protection for Computer programs. 1993, at 225.
73. Dietz, supra note 21, at 33.
74. Dreier, supra note 72 at 221.
75. Id, at 227.
76. Scholz, Implementation of the European Community Software Directive in Germany. (1993) 34 Copyright World, at 36 .
77. Article 1 E.C. Directive for the legal protection of Computer Programs, at http:// eurlex.europa.eu/smartapi/cgi/sga_doc?smartapi!celexapi!prod!CELEXnumdoc&numdoc=31991L0250&model=guichett&lg=en.
78. Dietz, supra note 21 at 33.
79. For further information regarding originality requirements and the E.C. Directive see Scholz, supra note 76, at 36.
80. Article 2 E.C. Directive for the Legal Protection of Computer Programs. Supra note 77.
81. Kirchberger, supra note 2, at 15.
82. Dreier. The Council Directive of 14 May 1991 on the Legal Protection of Computer Programs. [1991] 9 eipr, at 3.
83. Id, at 2.
84. However, as already mentioned the German Copyright Act does not refer to the term license, and the nearer English translation is a grant of the contractual right to use.
85. The implied arguments that the employer may alleged are in other words the determination of the scope of employment that was previously analyzed. On this regard, it was said that the labor law contract, the unions agreements and the main area of business of the employer are factors to take into consideration.
86. Kirchberger, supra note 2, at 15.
87. Dreier, Schulze, supra note 53 Line 15 to 17 at 53.
88. Lowenheim. Schricker Urheberrecht Kommentar 3. Auflage at 1353 section 15.
89. Id. at 1351 sect. 11.
90. Dreier, supra note 72, at 221.
91. Alberto Valdés Alonso. Propiedad Intelectual y Relación de Trabajo: La Transmisión De Los Derechos de Propiedad Intelectual a través del Contrato de Trabajo: Artistas, Programadores Informáticos Y Producción Audiovisual De, Civitas, 2001, 1ª ED. at 32.
92. Dietz, Supra note 21, at 87.
93. Dreier, supra note 82 at 2.
94. There are other moral rights on the copyright act such as the right of revocation for non exercise (article 41) and Right of revocation for changed conviction (article 42) however, in the chapter of moral rights, the mentioned 3 previous rights are the three rights classified as moral for the act.
95. Supra note 2, at 15.
96. Id. at 15.
97. Lehman. The legal protection of Computer Programs in Germany: A Summary of the present situation. (1988) 19 iic 473, at 478.
98. Dreier, Schulze, supra note 53, at 54 Lines 8 to 10.
99. Dietz, supra note 21, at 90.
100. Id, at 88.
101. Id, at 88
102. Dreier, supra note 72 at 221.

103. French Copyright Law of 29/03/1972.
104. For further Information see supra note 21, At 89, 90, 94, 95 & 96.
105. Edited By Peter Ganea, Christopher Heath and Hiroshi Saito, Japanese Copyright Law. Writings in honour of Gerhard Schricker.. Kluwer Law International (2005) at 36.
106. id, at 36.
107. Dietz, supra note 21 at 48.
108. For instance in the case of the bgh of October 9 of 1976 an informational pamphlet published by a government organization was protected by copyright, as it was not under the list covered in article 5.
109. German translation: Arbeitsverhaeltnis.
110. German translation: Dienstverhaeltnis.
111. Dietz, supra note 21, at 35.
112. On chapters vi & vii the American and Colombian provisions will be analyzed.
113. See. Dillman v. White, 102 Fed. 892 (c.c.d. Mass 1900).
114. Steve E Garlock. The work made for hire doctrine under the copyright Act of 1976: What about the independent contractor? 1988. Washington University Law Quarterly vol 66.423. at 423.
115. Id, at 423.
116. Bratlleboro Publishing Co. v. Winmill Publishing Corp, 369 F.2d 565 (2d Cir) (1966).
117. Garlock, supra note 114, at 424.
118. Siegel v. National Periodical Publications, Inc., 508 F.2d 909 (2d Cir. 1974).
119. Garlock, supra note 114, at 424
120. Id, at 424.
121. Murray v. Gelderman 566 F. 2d 1307 (5th Cir. 1978).
122. Garlock, supra note 114, at 424.
123. Nimmer, Melville, International Copyright Law and Practice. B. Volume 2 1997/2000. United States Chapter, at 48.
124. "Works Made for Hire. In the case of a work made for hire, the employer or other person for whom the work was prepared is considered the author for purposes of this title, and, unless the parties have expressly agreed otherwise in a written instrument signed by them, owns all of the rights comprised in the copyright".
125. "A 'work made for hire' is —
126. a work prepared by an employee within the scope of his or her employment; or
127. a work specially ordered or commissioned for use as a contribution to a collective work, as a part of a motion picture or other audiovisual work, as a translation, as a supplementary work, as a compilation, as an instructional text, as a test, as answer material for a test, or as an atlas, if the parties expressly agree in a written instrument signed by them that the work shall be considered a work made for hire. For the purpose of the foregoing sentence, a "supplementary work" is a work prepared for publication as a secondary adjunct to a work by another author for the purpose of introducing, concluding, illustrating, explaining, revising, commenting upon, or assisting in the use of the other work, such as forewords, afterwords, pictorial illustrations, maps, charts, tables, editorial notes, musical arrangements, answer material for tests, bibliographies, appendixes, and indexes, and an "instructional text" is a literary, pictorial, or graphic work prepared for publication and with the purpose of use in systematic instructional Activities".
128. May vs Morganelii-Heumann & Associates. 618 F2D 1363 C.A.Cal., (9th Cir. 1980) see at 1368. In this case the appellant (May) was considered by Court as an independent contractor per-se. The drawings that he created were not works included in the list of section 101 (2) see at 1369.
129. Nimmer, supra note 123, at 54.
130. Id, at 54.
131. On this regard section 205 (c) of the 1976 Copyright Act requires that the document adequately identifies the work which it relates and that a registration has been made for a work.
132. us Copyright Office. Circular 1. Notice of Copyright, at http://www.copyright. gov/circs/circ1.html#noc.
133. Id.
134. Circular 15 (a) of the United States Copyright office provides a summary of the provisions related with the duration of the copyright under the Copyright Act of 1976, see at: http://www.copyright.gov/circs/circ15a.html.
135. Garlock, supra note 114, at 425.
136. Id, at 425.
137. Id, at 425.
138. Id, at 426.
139. William O'Meara "Works made for Hire" under the Copyright Act of 1976.. Aus: Creighton Law Review. Vol. 15, 1981 - 1982, 2, at 533.
140. Garlock, supra note 114, at 426.
141. Aldon Accessories Ltd. v. Spiegel, Inc. 738 F. 2d 548 (2d Cir. 1984).
142. Garlock, supra note 114, at 426.
143. Evans Newton Inc. v. Chicago Systems Software, 793 F.2d 889 (7th Cir. 1986).
144. Brunswick Beacon v. Schock-Hopchas Publishing Co. 810 F. 2d 410 (4th Cir. 1987).
145. Garlock, supra note 114, at 429.
146. Easter Seal Society for Crippled Children and Adults of Louisiana, Inc v. Playboy Enterprises. 815 F. 2d 323 (5th Cir. 1987).
147. Garlock, supra note 114 at 431& 432.
148. Id, at 431& 432.
149. Community for Creative Non-Violence vs.Reid. 490 U.S. 730. 109 S.Ct. 2166, U.S.Dist.Col., (1989) (Hereinafter ccnv case).
150. Nimmer, supra note 123, at 49.
151. Id, at 49.
152. ccnv case, supra note 148. See facts of case at 733.

153. It is important to take into account that since 2006 the current Agency Law is the third Restatement that replaced the Second Restatement of 1958. The ccnv case only analyzed the Second Restatement from 1958. See Third Restatement at http://74.125.39.104/search?q=cache:Cphn2VXToxQJ:www.wmitchell.edu/academics/curriculum/courses/assignments/Restatement%2520Third%2520of%2520Agency.pdf+restatement+third+of+agency+law&hl=en&ct=clnk&cd=2&client=firefox-a

154. As already see in Germany and as will be explained in the Colombian Chapter, the definition of employee that the law used is only establish by a labor law regulation. The fact that in the United States the Court creates a specific definition for employee for purpose of the work made for hire is a big difference between the countries under analysis.

155. CCNV case, supra note 148, at 751

156. Id, at 751.

157. CCNV case, Supra note 148, at 742.

158. US Copyright Office Circular 9. See at: http://www.copyright.gov/circs/circ9.html.

159. Id. The circular also underline that as the CCNV decision states; supervision alone is not enough to establish a work made for hire, and that if all or mostly all the elements are proved there is a work made for hire.

160. CCNV case, supra note 148, at 742.

161. Quintanilla v. Texas Television 139 F.3d 494C.A.5 (Tex.), (5th Cir. 1998), at 497. In this case the appellant (Quintanilla) claimed that he was the exclusive owner of the copyright in a videotape because he supervised the work that Texas TV made for the creation of this work. See complete background of the case at 495 & 496.

162. CCNV Supra note 147, at 2168 & 732.

163. For instance, in the case William v. Weisser, the ownership of the work was only for the employed professor. See infra note 169.

164. Mexican Federal Author's right Law Art 84.

165. Carter v. Helmsley Spear 71 F. 3d, C.A.2 (n.y.), 1995. (2nd Cir. 1995). See at 85 & 86.

166. Circular 9, See supra note 156.

167. Assaf Jacob. 2008. tort made for hire - reconsidering the ccnv case. Preliminary Draft, Later version pending. See at 1. Available at: http://works.bepress. com/assaf_jacob/1.

168. Id. at. 1 & 2.

169. Circular 9, supra note 156.

170. William v. Weisser, 273 Cal. App. 3d 726 Cal. Rptr. 542, (Cal. Ct. App. 1969) at 739, 742.

171. Nimmer, supra note 123, at 50.

172. ccnv case, supra note 148, at 151.

173. Brown v. Cosby 433 F. Supp. 1331 d.c.Pa. 1977. (Distr. Ct. 1977) see at 1343 & 1344.

174. Nimmer, supra note 123 at 51.

175. In comparative labor law, the employer usually has to pay high interests for not paying salaries. For instance, In Colombia if an employer does not pay the employees its monthly salary, the law 789 of 2002 establishes that the employer will have to pay the employee two times of the salary and for two years, and after that time a financial interest will be charged. Thus, another policy question for debate is if labor law illegal behaviors can be punished by affecting other type of rights, like in the present cases, IP rights.

176. Art. 25 of the Colombian Constitution reads: "Art. 25 - El trabajo es un derecho y una obligación social y goza, en todas sus modalidades (All forms of employment), de la especial protección del Estado. Toda persona tiene derecho a un trabajo en condiciones dignas y justas".

177. e.g. In the United States what is known as 'work for commission' may be included within the work made for hire 101 provision. See supra note 125.

178. "Art. 61.- El Estado protegerá la propiedad intelectual por el tiempo y mediante las formalidades que establezca la ley".

179. Colombian Labor Law Code, See supra note 8.

180. The real conditions of a legal relationship prevail over the forms that the parties select. Thus, it is a recognized principle of labor law that even if parties sign other types of agreements, if the three elements mentioned above are present, the contract is deemed to be a labor law contract. See supra note 5, at 302.

181. Colombian Civil Code of 1873

182. Colombian Commercial Code of 1971

183. Law of State's Contracts # 80 of 1993. Art "3. Contrato de prestación de servicios... En ningún caso estos contratos generan relación laboral ni prestaciones sociales y se celebrarán por el término estrictamente indispensable".

184. Colombia Labor Law Code in its Articles 58 provides an obligation for the employee of not disclosing confidential information to third parties. In Article 62 (8) it is stated that revealing trade secrets and confidential information can lead to termination of the labor law contract. It is important to clarify that trade secrets and know-how are different concepts, but the Colombian provision refers to both. Thus, the employee will have to show loyalty to his employer by not revealing to third parties this kind of information.

185. Article 20 Author's Right Law number 23 of 1982.

186. It is important to note that article 20 starts with the word 'authors', this is without doubt an example of an author's right provision where there is no need to distinguish the transfer of the moral rights as it is implied that the moral rights are inalienable and the author or authors will retain them.

187. Despite the fact that the Author's right Law recognizes other types of Moral Rights, these are the only moral rights that the law recognizes to the author that creates a work under a contract to provide services.

188. Zapata López Fernando. El derecho de Autor y la Marca. Universidad Externado de Colombia. Revista de Propiedad Intelectual. Centro de Porpiedad Intelectual Primer Semestre 2001. Revista 2, at 21

189. Article 183 Colombian Author's Right Law number 23

of 1982.

190. Id.

191. Zapata, supra note 187, at 9

192. Id, at 9. This opinion has been criticized in the opinion of the Colombian Consejo de Estado stating that a contract is a fact, so a presumption can exist. See infra note 201 at 14

193. Zapata, supra note 187 at 9.

194. Carlos Hernán Godoy. El Contrato Laboral y de Prestacion de Servicios ¿Herramienta Idónea Para La Transferencia de Derechos?. Conferencia para el Semniario Internacional organizado por la pontificia Universidad Javeriana, at 7.

195. Id, at 7. The law 57 of 1887, is the Colombian law to solve conflicts between laws. Article 5 (1) states that when there are incompatible provision within the law codes, the legal provisions that refer to an specific matter will prevail over the ones that have a general character.

196. Id, at 7.

197. Id, at 9.

198. Id, at 13.

199. Id, at 15.

200. Id, at 14.

201. The literal translation in English of Consejo de Estado will be State adviser. This organ is the head of the administrative Jurisdiction in Colombia. One of its functions is to give opinions on legal questions that the government makes. The initiative to consult this issue came from the Minister of Justice. It is important to clarify that despite the fact that usually the citizens, courts and other institutions follow these opinions, they are not binding and only constitute recommendations. See Juan Carlos Galindo Vácha, Lecciones de Derecho Procesal Administrativo, Publicado por Pontificia Universidad Javeriana, 2006. See at 190.

202. Consejera Ponente Susana Montes, consultancy number 1538 of October 23 of 2003.

203. Id, at 7.

204. Id, at 10.

205. Id, at 15.

206. Id, at 18.

207. Id, at 13.

208. Riveros, supra 22, at 124.

209. Id. at 124.

210. dnda, Consultancy # 12879 2001. at 56.

211. For the application of this Principle in the United States, see supra 1, at 222.

212. Lipzyc, Delia, Derechos de Autor y Derechos Conexos. Ediciones unesco at 93.

213. Id. at 93.

214. Plazas, Arcadio, Estudio sobre derecho de autor, reforma legal Colombiana, Bogotá, Temis, 1984, at 220.

215. Id. at 220.

216. Id, at 220.

217. Id, at 220.

218. Zapata, supra note 187.

219. Article 91 Colombian Author's Right Law # 23 of 1982.

220. See works created by public servants in Germany in Chapter V (H).

221. See supra note 124.

222. See supra note 31.

223. See art 20 Colombian Author's Right Law.

224. See article 69 (b) German Copyright Act.

225. See articles 29 & 30 Colombian Author's Right Law. Regarding Legal Persons article 27 establishes a term of 30 years after the first publication of the work.

226. See article 64 German Copyright Act.

227. See supra note 132.

228. See Dietz, supra note 48.

229. See Kirchberger, supra note 95.

230. See Dietz, supra note 29.

231. See supra note 218.

232. See supra note 56.

233. See supra note 163.

234. See supra 179.

235. See supra note 166.

CHAPTER 15

MONITORING AND SURVEILLANCE IN THE WORKPLACE: INVESTIGATING THE INTERNATIONAL LEGAL POSITION

Verine Etsebeth

Keywords: Information security, legal issues, monitoring and surveillance, privacy

INTRODUCTION

There are various legal issues that are embedded in workplace monitoring and surveillance. Mainly, there are two main schools of thought that exist on this subject-matter. On the one hand there are those that argue that employers are the owners of the computing equipment, resources and systems and they therefore have a right to monitor how their property is being used, and then there are those that argue that employees' rights to privacy should weigh more than that of any employer. When examining the relevant statutes, case law and regulations it becomes apparent that in most jurisdictions a notice requirement exist, but this notice of surveillance and/or monitoring is rarely sufficient. This paper will examine Internet and e-mail related surveillance and monitoring in the workplace from a comparative legal perspective. Ultimately, the aim of this paper is to inform readers of the current legal position existing in some of the most important jurisdictions world-wide, thereby enabling readers to make up their own minds on which approach their country should follow, and enabling readers to understand the legal consequences embedded in each approach.

JUSTIFICATION FOR MONITORING AND SURVEILLANCE IN THE WORKPLACE

"Surveillance technology is neither inherently bad nor good, but ...there is both good and bad surveillance."

When considering the legal implications of monitoring and surveillance in the workplace, the question may be asked why companies deploy computer surveillance and monitoring in the first place. Several reasons may be put forward to justify why more than 80% of all major American firms monitor employee e-mails and Internet usage. The first reason centers around employee productivity. As a result of the Internet and e-mails employee productivity has decreased. This is a major concern for employers, as Internet use surveys continue to indicate that the majority of employees spend anywhere from 10 minutes to an hour every day surfing sites unrelated to doing their jobs – using their work computers to read virtual newspapers, or go online shopping, or even viewing naked woman. Secondly, network performance must be considered. Employees that download video or audio files from the Internet are taking up a great amount of bandwidth. It therefore makes sense that employers spend money on Internet monitoring tools rather than on increasing the bandwidth. Thirdly, the very real risk exists that a company may be held legally liable for the online activities performed by its employees. For example the brokerage firm of Morgan Stanley was exposed to $70 million lawsuit because of racist jokes that appeared on the company's e-mail system. Also, Dow Chemicals discovered through computer surveillance technologies that 50 employees

Citation: Verine Etsebeth, Monitoring and Surveillance in the Workplace: Investigating the International Legal Position, http://ojs.jdfsl.org/index.php/jdfsl/article/view/197.

were using the company's computers to store and send sexual or violent images, resulting in the termination of all of these employees. Fourthly, all companies are faced with the ever present 'insider threat'. It is therefore understandable that companies will go to great lengths to protect the confidentiality of its corporate information and trade secrets even if it is from its own employees.

MONITORING AND SURVEILLANCE – THE CANADIAN PERSPECTIVE

Introduction

It is generally accepted that in terms of Canadian law employees enjoy very little to no privacy protection in the workplace when it comes to computer and email surveillance. MacIsaac observes: "...many employers consider electronic mail sent and received using company computer equipment and stored on company computer networks to be the property of the employer. From the employer's perspective this is a business resource paid for by the employer and is to be used only for business purposes. Therefore, e-mail messages and telephone conversations made on behalf of the employee in the course of business should be made available for review for legitimate business and security reasons. For these reasons, an employee acting on behalf of their employer should have no reasonable expectation of privacy". This view was supported in an arbitration case in which a college lab technician's employment was terminated after sending unwarranted allegation against other employees to the campus-wide email message board. The case finding reiterated the principle of 'office e-mail: no reasonable expectation of privacy'.

Today however, a definite move towards finding a balance between monitoring and privacy may be observed in Canadian law. As stated in the previous chapter, the most important source of privacy protection in Canada is found in the Personal Information Protection and Electronic Documents Act (PIPEDA) 2000. PIPEDA recognizes the importance of finding a balance between an employer's need to collect certain personal data, and an employee's need for privacy protection. The Act states: "...the purpose of this part [Protection of Personal Information in the Private Sector] is to establish, in an era in which technology increasingly facilitates the circulation and exchange of information, rules to govern the collection, use and disclosure of personal information in a manner that recognizes the rights to privacy of individuals with respect to their personal information and the need of organizations to collect, use or disclose personal information for purposes that a reasonable person would consider appropriate in the circumstances".

Regulatory Framework – PIPEDA

When evaluating employee surveillance within the ambit of PIPEDA the following observations should be made:

- Firstly, the provision in PIPEDA of 'appropriate purpose' limits the use, collection and disclosure of personal information to situations which a reasonable person would deem to be appropriate under the circumstances. Within the ambit of the workplace this would imply that mere consent by an employee to surveillance is no longer sufficient as the provision clearly states that a reasonable person must consider the circumstances to be appropriate. Therefore it may be argued that where surveillance takes place under the façade of creating and maintaining a harassment free and safe working environment, it is likely that the courts will declare such surveillance to be unlawful because of the absence of a known issue in response to which surveillance takes place;
- Secondly, PIPEDA requires of companies must appoint a privacy officer who will be responsible for ensuring that the company complies with its privacy obligations. The act suggests that the collection of personal workplace data no longer falls within the exclusive jurisdiction of the company's technology personnel, but the privacy officer must also be involved;
- Thirdly, the act contains specific provision relating to the notification of employees of workplace surveillance. It is expected of companies to: (a) identify the purpose for which the data is being collected; (b) obtain consent prior to collection; and (c) to limit collection of personal data to that which is necessary for the purposes as set out by the company. The aim of these provisions are to: (a) limit the type of information a company may collect; and (b) demand of companies to inform their employees of the surveillance policies of the company. The act does however contain an exception to the general rule that notice must be given to employees before surveillance may take place. Section 7(1)(b) of the act states: "...an organization may collect personal information without the knowledge or consent of the individual only if ...it is reasonable to expect that the collection with the knowledge or consent of the individual would compromise the availability or the accuracy of the information and the collection is reasonable for purposes related to investigating a breach of an agreement or a contravention of laws of Canada or a province".
- Fourthly, the Act requires that "personal information shall be retained only as long as is necessary for the fulfillment of the [identified] purpose". Therefore, this provision regulates an employers' use of information after collection thereof. Employers are furthermore prohibited from keeping personal information for an unlimited time period.

Employee Monitoring and Surveillance – The Present Position in Canada

The Canadian court's commitment to privacy protection has come to the fore in recent years. In 1999 the B.C. Supreme Court ruled in the Weir case that email does enjoy a reasonable expectation of privacy. Also in that same year the case of Pacific Northwest Herb Corp v Thompson 1999 BCJ No 2772 came before the court. Thompson was an employee of Pacific Northwest who used the company's computer in his home for business and personal purposes. After termination of his employment he continued using the company computer for personal purposes. Amongst the documents on the computer was a file containing documents relating to the wrongful dismissal action he was planning to institute against Pacific

Northwest. Before returning the computer to the company he hired a computer consultant to erase all the data on the hard drive. His attempts were however unsuccessful, and after returning the computer to Pacific Northwest the company was able to restore the data. Thompson sought an interdict to prevent Pacific Northwest to exploit the data, claiming that his right to privacy and solicitor-client privilege has been infringed. The judge in this case concluded that Thompson had a reasonable expectation of privacy regarding documents that were created for personal use.

In R v Duarte 1990 1 SCR 945 the judge concluded that although the right to privacy was not absolute, it must be "judged against what is reasonable in the circumstances and, amongst other things, is dependant upon competing interests such as the relationship between the parties". The court went even further and stated that in order to determine what would amount to 'reasonable in the circumstances', three considerations must be kept in mind: (i) whether it was reasonable to request surveillance; (ii) whether the surveillance was conducted in a reasonable manner; and (iii) whether any other alternatives to surveillance were available to the employer.

This case has been approved in many other cases. In St Mary's Hospital and HEU 64 LAC (4th) 382 an electrician discovered a video camera in the ceiling of a manager's office. The local union was outraged at this surreptitious surveillance, and filed a grievance. The arbitrator found in this case that surveillance can be characterized in three ways: (a) benign surveillance which would entail surveillance done for the benefit of the employee; (b) security surveillance which has as its main aim to ensure the protection of employees as well as the employer; and (c) surreptitious surveillance which represents the most intrusive force of surveillance. The arbitrator was of the opinion that this form of surveillance requires strict justification. Furthermore, in Re Toronto Transit Commission and ATU Loc 113 (Belsito) 95 LAC (4th) 402 and in New Flyer Industries Ltd and CAW Canada Loc 3003 (Mogg) 85 LAC (4th) 304 the court acknowledged that "surveillance by an employer may, in certain circumstances, infringe upon an employee's right to privacy to an unreasonable extent".

The Privacy Commissioner has made his views on workplace surveillance, the privacy of e-mails and the reasonable expectation of privacy clear. The Commissioner states: "I don't accept that the protection necessarily translates into wholesale surveillance of e-mails or computer use. We accept that there are stringent limits on an employer's rights to read employees' mail, eavesdrop on their telephone calls or rifle through their desk drawers. I think we have to look closely at e-mail communications to see what principles should apply there as well".

The Commissioner went on to comment on the practice of some companies to state in their email policies that the employees should have no reasonable expectation of privacy when using the e-mail systems: "[t]he law of privacy has developed around the notion of the 'reasonable expectation'; one of the ways that the courts determine whether privacy has been violated has been to determine first whether a person could have reasonable expected privacy in a particular place and time. But I don't agree that it follows that an employee's or anyone's privacy can be simply eradicated by telling them not to expect any. While management has the right and the responsibility to manage, it has to operate within limits, including respect for fundamental rights. It is not for management alone to determine whether an expectation of privacy is reasonable". Therefore, a clear shift in the pendulum in Canadian law may be observed. In the past emphasis was placed on whether or not the employee had a reasonable expectation of privacy, today emphasis is placed on the question whether or not the surveillance is reasonable. It is now accepted that workplace surveillance, whether it be by video camera, server-side computer monitoring, or client-side computer monitoring, cannot be justified by simply giving notice to an employee. An investigation will have to be launched into the reasonableness of the surveillance.

Geist identifies six factors which may be taken into consideration when wanting to determine whether or not the computer or email surveillance is reasonable in terms of Canadian law:

- The target of the surveillance – Consideration must be given to whether computer surveillance will be conducted across the company as a whole or if it will be targeted against specific employees;
- (Purpose of the surveillance – Companies that install new surveillance technologies must be able to show how these technologies support their objectives;
- Alternatives to surveillance – It is suggested that other surveillance technologies that are much less intrusive on an employee's right to privacy in the workplace must first be investigated;
- The surveillance technology – The choice of surveillance technology must be reasonable taking into account the purpose of the surveillance;
- Adequacy of notice – in terms of the Criminal Code as well as PIPEDA consent must be obtained from the employee. This would entail not merely informing employees of the fact of surveillance but also giving them an accurate description of the company's surveillance practices; and
- The implementation of the surveillance activities – the company will have to ensure that unauthorized persons are not able to gain access to the surveillance information.

Conclusion

From the above it may be concluded that in Canadian law neither the right to privacy nor the right to surveillance is absolute. Canadian law attempts to find a balance between the interest of the employer and the rights of the employee by focusing on the reasonableness of the surveillance.

MONITORING AND SURVEILLANCE IN THE WORKPLACE – THE AMERICAN POSITION

Introduction

At present the position in America is that no employee has any constitutional, federal or common law legal remedies for redress where an employer abuses email and Internet monitoring and surveillance.

Constitutional Protection against Employee Monitoring and Surveillance

Federal Constitution

The US Constitution does not afford anyone the right to privacy expressly. The constitution only recognizes privacy as a penumbral theory. This explains why the right to privacy has not been extended to protect an employee's electronic communications. Cherminisky observes: "[m]ost Americans would be surprised to learn that there is no right to privacy granted in the United States Constitution. The Fourth Amendment protects privacy in limiting police searches and arrests, but privacy in terms of autonomy and the right to be left alone by the government is not mentioned in the text of the Constitution".

Consequently, the present position in the United States is that employees, in a private workplace, are not afforded any protection against electronic surveillance because of the doctrine of state surveillance. In contrast to this public sector employees have a certain degree of constitutional protection against abusive monitoring in the workplace. Included in this would be the right to reasonable searches and seizures. American courts have even gone so far as to state that public sector employees have a reasonable expectation of privacy regarding their emails and Internet communications.

State Constitution

Privacy protection in respect of state constitutions vary to a great extend. It is however important to bear in mind that to date no court has extended state constitutional protection of privacy to email monitoring and surveillance in the workplace. Most states do not require employers to give employees any form of notification when monitoring their emails and Internet communications.

Federal Legislation – The ECPA

Title I of the ECPA – The Federal Wiretap Statute

In terms Title I (The federal Wiretap Act) of the ECPA interception of electronic communications such as telephone calls and emails are prohibited. The Act prohibits the following activities:

- intercepting or endeavoring to intercept electronic communications;
- disclosing or endeavoring to disclose intercepted electronic communications; and \
- using the content of intercepted information.

It therefore follows that if an employer intercepts email or monitors Internet communications of his/her employee, his actions will fall within the ambit of the ECPA. The following important observations must be, made in this regard. First, it is required that the interception and/or monitoring should be made intentional. Secondly, the content of the communication is only protected as long as it is under transmission. Consequently, Title I will not be applicable where an employer searches an employee's stored emails. Two exceptions are contained in Title I. First, the ECPA allows service provides to intercept and disclose electronic communication if either the sender or the receiver consented thereto, or the 'ordinary course of business' exception can be applied. The latter exception however, proves to be highly problematic.

In order for an employer to make use of the 'ordinary course of business exception' it is expected of the employer to proof the following:

- the device used to intercept the electronic communication is "a telephone or telegraphic instrument, equipment or facility, or a...component thereof," provided or installed by the employer himself/herself; and
- that the specific device is employed by the employer in his/her ordinary course of business.

It must furthermore be borne in mind that an employer is only authorized to intercept the communication for long enough to determine the nature of the conversation. Once the employer has determined that the communication is personal in nature he/she must immediately terminate interception.

Title II of the ECPA – The Stored Communications Act of 2005

Title II of the ECPA (The Stored Communications Act of 2005) provides guidance when wanting to obtain access or disclosure of electronic communication, such as messages left on a voice machine, once in storage. A violation of Title II will result in civil liability for any person who (a) intentionally accesses, without authorization, a facility through which an electronic communication service is provided; or (b) intentionally exceeds an authorization access and thereby obtains, alters, or prevents authorized access to a wire or electronic communication while it is in electronic storage. As soon as an electronic message has been stored the SCA will regulate the situation. This is irrespective of the length of storage.

When considering the operation of Title II it becomes evident that emails are generally considered to be stored communications in terms of American law. Consequently, employers are authorized to access electronic communications under this title. However, this means that Title I of the ECPA is in actual fact rendered useless. From the above discussion it may be concluded that in virtually all cases decided by American courts in the last decade it has been decided that employees do not have a reasonable expectation of privacy. In some instance American courts have gone so far as to validate employee monitoring even where advance warning was not given to the employee. The following American case law supports this statement:

Employee Monitoring and Surveillance without Notice

In Restuccia v Burk Technology 1996 Mass Super LEXIS 367 (Super Ct (Mass) Aug 13 1996) the employer neglected to have an email policy stating the possibility that emails can be monitored, stored on back-up or that emails may not be used for personal messages. When viewing back-up files the employer discovered email messages containing nick-names for the president of the company and references to an extra-marital affair with another employee. The president of the company terminated the two employee's employment based on the fact that they were using the email system too much. The ex-employees argued that they had a reasonable expectation of privacy because of the fact that they had personal passwords to access their message system. the court found that the president's action of reading the email messages on the back-up system constituted an infringement of the privacy of the ex employees. In this case the ex-employees were successful in their claim, but in every other workplace interception case the defendant's were awarded summary judgment in a claim that workplace surveillance invaded a plaintiff's right of privacy.

Furthermore, in Smyth v Pillsbury Co 914 F Supp 97 (ED Pa 1996) an employee was fired after having made negative comments about a sales manager in an email. The email contained treats to "kill the backstabbing bastards". The company had, on various occasions, assured its employees that all emails are confidential and privileged. The company based the termination of employment on "transmitting what it deemed to be inappropriate and unprofessional comments over the company's e-mail system". The employee however argued wrongful termination. The federal court decided that the termination of the employee was justified, as the employee had no expectation of privacy in the employer's email system. The court went even further to state that even if the employee had a reasonable expectation of privacy it would not amount to invasion of privacy if an employer intercepted messages on a system it owned.

Moreover, in McLaren v Microsoft Corp Microsoft 1999 Tex. App. LEXIS 4103, 1999 WL 339015 (Tex. Ct. App. 1999) accessed personal folders on a network in order to investigate claims of sexual harassment. The employee claimed that Microsoft had violated his reasonable expectation of privacy. The emails that Microsoft eventually uncovered did provide evidence that the employee was engaging in a "systematic pattern of sexual harassment". The court held that it was not going to recognise a cause of action for invasion of privacy, even though the employee had a special password and the files were marked 'personal'. The court stated in this case that the decisive factor was that the computer was the property of the employer and formed part of the computer environment. The court furthermore stated that because of the fact that the folder was transmitted over the network, it was inevitable that it would be accessed by a third party at some stage. Consequently, the plaintiff had no expectation of privacy with regards to the files marked 'private'.

Employee Monitoring and Surveillance with Notice

By implementing an email and Internet policy companies safeguard themselves against any privacy-based claims by employees. In Bourke v Nissan Motor Corp Nissan California Court of Appeals, Second Appellate District, Case No. B068705 (July 1996) made every employee sign a waiver form in which they had to acknowledge that they understood that Nissan's email system was to be used for business purposes exclusively. In this case the court decided that this waiver was fatal to any claim an employee can bring based on invasion of privacy.

Furthermore, in Garrity v John Hancock Mutual Life Insurance Company 2002 US Dist. LEXIS 8343 (D Mass. May 7, 2000) two long term employees forwarded sexually explicit jokes to third parties. One of their co-workers complaint after receiving such an email. The company had an email policy providing that "messages that are defamatory, abusive, obscene, profane, sexually orientated, threatening or racially offensive" are prohibited. The two woman's employment was consequently terminated. The court dismissed the privacy based action brought by the two women stating that employees do not have any reasonable expectation of privacy pertaining to work related emails. The court furthermore made a very harsh statement by stating that the fact that the company had an email policy was irrelevant. The court concluded that the employer's right and duty to limit harassment in the workplace outweighs any rights the plaintiffs' though they had in respect of privacy.

Moreover, in Thygeson v US Bancorp 2004 US Dist. LEXIS 18863 (D. Ore. Sept 15, 2004) the bank's employment handbook stated that employees were prohibited to "use US Bancorp computer resources for personal business". The handbook furthermore stated "do not access inappropriate internet sites and do not send emails which may be perceived as offensive, intimidating, or hostile or that are in violation of Company policy". One of Bancorp's employees were spending more than four hours a day visiting non work related Internet sites on his work computer. The company furthermore discovered that he was viewing "inappropriate emails containing pictures of nudity and sexually offensive jokes". The employee was subsequently fired. The employee brought an action against the bank arguing that they invaded his privacy as well as the federal Employee Retirement Income Security Act (ERISA) by firing him without awarding him severance pay. The court found that the employee had no expectation of privacy when his employer accessed the files on its network that the plaintiff saved using a personal password, then this employee had no expectation of privacy in his email 'merely labeled personal' without even creating a password.

Conclusion

The conclusion must be reached that when it comes the subject matter of workplace monitoring and surveillance, all indication are that it is proemployer. Employees have no real remedies for the abuse of email and Internet monitoring and surveillance. Furthermore almost all courts in America have held that employees do not have a right to privacy in the workplace. Courts continue to justify their position by stating that since business computers are the property of its employers, employers have an unfettered right to monitor its usage. American employees will furthermore be unable to find any relief in the US constitution, common law of torts or the ECPA.

MONITORING AND SURVEILLANCE IN THE WORKPLACE – THE UNITED KINGDOM'S PERSPECTIVE

Introduction

The United Kingdom is a member of the European Union.

Consequently, the United Kingdom has to comply with EU directives on the subject matter of employee monitoring and surveillance. In terms of the European Community Treaty it is expected of the UK to propagate enabling legislation which will give effect to the fundamental rights as set forth in the Council of Europe Convention for the Protection of Human Rights and Fundamental Freedoms of 1950 (ECHR) and legislation of the EU.

Regulatory Framework

Because of the operation of the doctrine of vicarious liability, the UK government has accepted that employers do have the right to monitor their employees. However, in contrast to the approach followed in America, the right of an employer to monitor is balanced with the employee's right to privacy.

The legal framework for Internet monitoring in the United Kingdom comprises of five main statutes and almost no case law on the subject matter.

The Data Protection Act of 1998

All British employers must comply with the United Kingdom's implementation of the European Union Directive on Data Protection in the form of the Data Protection Act of 1998. In terms of the DPA data controllers are compelled not only to inform the employee of the monitoring system, but also to protect the data processed in accordance with the Data Protection Principles (DPA).

In terms of the DPA electronic monitoring has to comply with the following requirements:

- the monitoring must be lawful and fair;
- the monitoring program must be necessary; and
- the monitoring program must be proportionate to achieving the legitimate business objective while simultaneously protecting the right to privacy of the individual employee.

In terms of the DPA only one exception exists regarding the notification requirement: if electronic monitoring is done with the aim of preventing a specific crime the employer will not have to adhere to the notice requirement.

The Human Rights Act of 1998

The DPA furthermore takes cognizance of the Human Rights Act of 1998. In terms of this Act the privacy of any private communication, telephone conversation and email communication is expressly protected. It is important to observe that the Human Rights Act draws a distinction between public and private sector employers. If the employer falls within the ambit of the public sector, the employee will have a direct cause of action in terms of the Human Rights Act. Employees in the United Kingdom enjoy further protection in terms of article 8 of the ECHR. In terms of article 8 of the Act "everyone has the right to respect for his private and family life, his home, and his correspondence". This convention affords private employees with a legal remedy to challenge abusive monitoring practices. The European Court of Human Rights has extended the definition of 'private life and correspondence' to include business relations, emails and other electronic communications.

Furthermore, the United Kingdom's chief regulatory agency (OFTEL) issued in 1999 Guidance on recording on private conversations. The aim of these guidelines was to provide employers with guidelines when wanting to implement electronic monitoring without violating their employees' right to privacy.

The Regulation of Investigative Powers Act of 2000

In terms of this Act it is a criminal offence to intercept data without authorization. It is however important to keep in mind that RIP is not applicable to private telecommunications systems such as intranets and Virtual Private Networks. Moreover, no provision in RIP addresses electronic monitoring in the workplace expressly. In general employers are permitted to intercept emails and to monitor Internet access as long as both the sender and receiver agree thereto. Employers may furthermore only intercept emails and Internet communications if the monitoring is conducted in order to carry out the employer's business activities.

The Lawful Business Practice Regulations (LBPR)

This Act governs the rights and responsibilities of businesses relating to monitoring electronic communications. This Act provides certain exceptions to the RIP Act. The most important of which is that monitoring without compliance with the notice requirement can take place. In terms of this exception companies may monitor and keep record of Internet communications in order to comply and adhere to regulatory or self-regulatory practices and procedures. There is however a limitation placed on monitoring activities by providing that such activities may only take place if a company employee uses the computer system within the scope of his/her duties. Furthermore, in terms of the LBPR interception without consent is authorized if the interception has one or more of the following purposes:

- to establish the existence of facts, to ascertain compliance with the regulatory or self-regulatory practiccs or proccdures (quality control and training);
- to prevent or detect crimes;
- to investigate or detect unauthorized use of telecommunication systems;
- to secure; and
- to determine whether or not the communications are business communications.

It should furthermore be kept in mind that interception will only be authorised if the controller of the telecommunication system (employer) made reasonable efforts to inform potential users that interception may take place. Also the scope of application of this Act is limited to business communication therefore the interception of personal communications will not be legal in terms of this act.

Conclusion

In terms of the RIP Act, LBPR and the DPA it would appear that an employer will only be authorized to lawful intercept communications if it is done 'in the course of transmission'.

The legislature therefore encourages UK companies to have a clearly Internet and email usage policy in place. If an employee wants to base his/her claim on infringement of privacy, the Code of Practice will be the most effective regulation for him/her to rely on.

CONLUSION

It is evident from the preceding discussion that Canada, the United States and the United Kingdom have very different views on the protection that should be afforded to employees when dealing with monitoring and surveillance in the workplace. In America a pro-employer regime is applied in terms of which employees have lost all their privacy based actions. Consequently, employees in America have no reasonable expectation of privacy. It would appear as if American employers have an absolute immunity against the constitution, common law and federal statutory remedies for abusive surveillance practices. In terms of American law it is evident that everything including electronic communications on a work computer belongs to the employer. Furthermore, business and private communications are deemed to be the property of the employer. Therefore, employers are permitted to monitor any electronic communication even if the employer has no e-mail and/or Internet usage policy in place which could serve to notify employees of the fact that their electronic communications are being monitored.

In stark contrast to the American position, in the UK the monitoring and surveillance of employees are strictly proscribed. In the EU and consequently in the UK, electronic monitoring must be reasonably based, proportional, transparent and non-discriminatory. The European Court of Justice feels that it is very important for companies to have written e-mail and Internet usage policies stating what the company's position is regarding employee surveillance and monitoring. This is in contrast with the position in America where courts have allowed the surveillance of emails even in situations where the company guaranteed its employees privilege and confidentiality. The Canadian position relating to employee monitoring and surveillance fits in comfortably somewhere between the UK and the USA. Although this country have enacted legislation regulating employee monitoring and surveillance, with a built-in notification requirements. The biggest deficiencies encountered in these statutes are that they only contain a notification requirement and not a consent requirement.

The question may be asked which approach is correct? Although from a legal perspective most academics would insist that the United Kingdom's approach is correct, the writer is of the opinion that the current political and social climate must play a very important role in deciding which approach a country should take to this subject matter. Moreover, when considering the fact that a company can incur legal liability for the illegal and inappropriate acts performed by its employees when making use of the corporate computer resources and systems, the writer feels that an employer should have the right to monitor e-mail and Internet usage without too many restraints being placed on him/her. Therefore, the writer is in favor of the American position pertaining to this subject matter. Perhaps countries such as the United Kingdom and Canada should rather ask themselves if they are not empowering employees too much, because at the end of the day, it is still the employer's computer resources and systems that are being used, so why should an employer not be afforded the right to protect its own assets through monitoring and surveillance, especially when considering the fact that an employer can be faced with numerous lawsuit based on the inappropriate use of its computer assets and resources?

REFERENCES

1. Blackman and Franklin (Aug 1993) "Blocking big brother: proposed law limits employer's right to snoop" NYLJ 5
2. Ciocchetti (2001) "Monitoring employee e-mail efficiency workplace vs employee privacy" Duke Law & Technology 0026 6
3. Greenberg "Comment, e-mail and voice mail: employee privacy and the federal Wiretap statute" American University Law Review 22 219, 247-48
4. Harnden "Office e-mail: no reasonable expectation of privacy" FOCUS: Employment Law No 3 7
5. Newton "Proposed NSW workplace surveillance bill extends employees' protection from surveillance in the workplace" (2004) Workplace and Employee Relations Law Update
6. Sneddon and Troiana "New tort of invasion of privacy and the Internet" (2003) Internet Law Bulletin 6(6) 1
7. Wilborn, S.E. (1998) "Revising the public/private distinction: employee monitoring in the workplace" Ga L Rev 32 825
8. Chemirinsky, E. (2003) "Privacy and the Alaska Constitution: failing to fulfill the promise" Alaska Law Review 20 29

CHAPTER 16

INTERNATIONAL LEGAL REALITIES OF MIGRANT LABOUR RIGHTS

Giovanni Di Lieto

Keywords: International labour law, migrant labour rights, migration governance, labour mobility, decent work, ILO

THE INTERNATIONAL LAW OF LABOUR MIGRATION: ILO'S MINIMUM STANDARDS

International regulation and direction play a crucial role in shaping contemporary patterns in the international movement of workers and constitute the essential foundation for legislation, policy and practices at the national level. Besides the vast array of international standards already in place to provide parameters for the regulation of cross-border migration, numerous complementary instruments present more specific frameworks in the areas of labour and human rights, which are relevant to this study. The present regulatory system displays the struggle to protect migrant workers' rights, addressing the related issues from national through to bilateral, regional and multilateral levels. The comprehensive ILO system of standards, combined with a tripartite supervisory mechanism comprising of scrutiny by independent legal experts, is the pivotal crossroad of the multilayered apparatus of international regulation concerning migrant workers.

Overall, all ILO fundamental principles and standards apply to migrant workers, although Conventions No. 97 and No. 143 and their accompanying recommendations are specifically relevant to people moving in search of employment. The ILO developed these two comprehensive standards in 1949 and 1975, marking two dissimilar approaches to labour migration due to the different political contexts in the wake of the Second World War and of the 1973 oil crisis respectively. The provisions of the Migration for Employment Convention (Revised), 1949 (No. 97), and the supplementing Recommendation (Revised), 1949 (No. 86), were induced by the concern of managing (and facilitating) the movement of surplus labour from a struggling post-war Europe to other regions of the globe, therefore focusing on the standards applicable to the recruitment of migrants for employment and their conditions of work.

Less than 30 years later, unemployment and an increase in irregular migration had become major concerns of governments, who were interested instead in restraining migrant flows and enforcing the curb on unauthorised migration and employment. Indeed, the Migrant Workers (Supplementary Provisions) Convention, 1975 (No. 143), and the Migrant Workers Recommendation, 1975 (No. 151), were the first multilateral instruments aimed at regulating the irregular migration phenomenon and calling for sanctions against traffickers. However, Conventions No. 97 and No. 143 both deal with the migratory process as a whole, from emigration through transit and immigration, applying to people on the move from one country to another in search of being employed otherwise than on their own account.

With few exceptions, the instruments of the two conventions do not differentiate between permanent or

Citation: Giovanni Di Lieto, International Legal Realities of Migrant Labour Rights, ISSN: 1843-5610.

temporary migrants.1 Besides, the included provisions are not based on reciprocity and cover refugees and displaced persons to the extent that they work outside their home country. In particular, Convention No. 143 not only reaffirms that Member States have a general obligation to respect the basic human rights of all migrant workers and that they should be entitled to equal treatment, it also prescribes more specifically the protection of equality of opportunity, which entails access to employment, trade union and cultural rights, and individual and collective freedoms. The general provisions of Part II of Convention No. 143 do not cover trainees and employees who enter the host country on a short-term basis to carry out specific duties or assignments, in addition to the categories already excluded from its scope of application by Convention No. 97, such as seamen, frontier workers, artists and members of the liberal professions.2

With regard to the application of the above-mentioned instruments, an ILO general survey found that governments tended to consider these obstacles to ratification, especially arts 6 and 8 of Convention No. 97, affirming equality of treatment for foreign and national workers, as well as the maintenance of residence rights for permanent migrant workers in the event of incapacity for work. In addition, arts 8, 10 and 14(a) of Convention No. 143 are concerned with the protection of lawfully admitted migrant workers in the event of loss of employment, equality of opportunity and treatment, and the right of migrant workers to geographical and occupational mobility.3 Arising from the very fact of membership of the organisation and regardless of the ratification of specific conventions, all ILO Member States have the obligation to respect, realise and promote core labour rights and principles. The 1998 Declaration on Fundamental Principles and Rights at Work and its follow-up identifies four categories of such principles and rights: freedom of association and the effective recognition of the right to collective bargaining; the elimination of all forms of forced or compulsory labour; the effective abolition of child labour; and the elimination of discrimination in respect of employment and occupation.

These fundamental principles and rights at work are universal and applicable to all people in all countries. It therefore applies to all migrant workers, regardless of their legal status. Additionally, the 1998 Declaration specifically refers to migrant workers as a group with special needs.4 As a result of the successful ILO campaign for the universal ratification of its core conventions in the past 20 years, a critical mass of labour rights and standards covering migrant workers along with all other workers is currently binding on the vast majority of ILO Member States. With regard to freedom of association and collective bargaining, the CEACR and the Committee on Freedom of Association (CFA) have repeatedly affirmed the fundamental rights of migrant workers (even if irregular)5 to form and join trade unions and to be protected against any act of discrimination on the grounds of trade union activities. The denial of trade union rights by countries that have ratified the Freedom of Association and Protection of the Right to Organize Convention, 1948 (No. 87), and the Right to Organize and Collective Bargaining Convention, 1949 (No. 98), have also been addressed by the CEACR and CFA, claiming that representation and voice at work are crucial to guarantee labour rights and the improvement of labour conditions for migrant workers. Therefore, restrictive provisions on nationality deprive migrant workers of the right to elect their representatives and take up trade union office, in most cases even after a reasonable period of residence in the host country, particularly in sectors where they are the majority of the workforce.6

On several occasions, the ILO supervisory boards have expressed concern about the absence or inadequacy of legislation and measures taken against forced labour of migrants and for the elimination of child migrant labour. Practices that are against the Forced Labour (1930, No. 29 and 1957, No. 105) and Child Labour (1973, No. 138 and 1999, No. 182) Conventions usually include, for instance, the use by employers of excessive power over migrant workers in an irregular situation, the retention or non-payment of wages, contract substitution and retention of passports, long working hours and physical violence.7 The ILO supervisory bodies have also frequently affirmed that migrant workers, irrespective of their legal status, are protected by the instruments developed to battle discrimination based on race, sex, religion, political opinion, national extraction and social origin in employment, occupation and wage remuneration, as set out in the Discrimination (Employment and Occupation) Convention, 1958 (No. 111), and the Equal Remuneration Convention, 1951 (No. 100).8 Besides the above fundamental principles and rights at work and the standards dedicated to migrant labour, all other ILO standards are in principle applicable to migrant workers regardless of their specific reference.9 In addition, comments by the supervisory bodies of the ILO substantiate the practical application of instruments especially relevant for migrant workers. For example, the Private Employment Agencies Convention, 1997 (No. 181), asserts that the recruitment and placement of migrant workers through private employment agencies should be free of charge to prevent abuses, although certain exceptions are allowed in respect of specific types of services and categories of workers.

The Protection of Wages Convention, 1949 (No. 95), also applies in this context where it prohibits deductions from wages for payment to fee-charging agencies for the purpose of obtaining or retaining employment.10 The CEACR has raised issues in relation to deductions made from the salaries of plantation workers that are mostly migrants,11 and to non-payment of wages to workers forced to return to their country because of war.12 The Employment Promotion and Protection against Unemployment Convention, 1988 (No. 168), strongly affirms the promotion of full, productive and freely chosen employment through the equal and non-discriminative treatment of lawfully resident migrant workers, and the more recent Safety and Health in Agriculture Convention, 2001 (No. 184), also explicitly covers temporary and seasonal migrant workers. Nonetheless, other aspects particularly relevant to the payment of wages to migrant workers such as periodicity, modes of payment, deferred payments in foreign currency and appeals still do not seem to be dealt with in depth, since, for instance, no specific standards can be found with specific regard even to domestic workers.

THE INTERNATIONAL HUMAN RIGHTS LAW OF MIGRANT WORKERS: THE UN'S ICRMW

Since its establishment in 1919, the ILO recognised in the preamble of its constitution the need to protect the interest of "workers employed when in countries other than their own", drawing international attention to the practical significance of the rights of migrant workers. The two major ILO treaties concerning migrant labour mentioned above (1949, No. 97 and 1975, No. 143) have been described as innovative, rich in detail and ground-breaking, but have been largely ignored by the international community thus far.13 The Conventions register a poor record of adoption, generally occurring in origin rather than destination countries, where the protections are most needed.14 It is argued that this lack of attention is due to the generality of the Conventions, the enduring preference for a State's own nationals in economic matters, and principally the concern that treaty obligations may hinder the regulation and enforcement of irregular immigration.15 The ILO itself has acknowledged that the Conventions do not effectively face the challenges raised by contemporary migration issues, such as regional integration, commercialisation and privatisation of recruitment and the increase of female labour migration.16

In the past two decades, the importance of the ILO Conventions has been overshadowed by the conclusion and growing adoption of the International Convention on the Protection of the Rights of All Migrant Workers and Members of their Families (ICRMW), which follows the latest trend of adopting specific human rights treaties to protect groups of vulnerable people on the grounds of gender, age or other particular circumstances, such as women, children, persons with disabilities and indigenous peoples.

The ICRMW is a comprehensive convention opting for a new approach to migrant labour, focused on the human rights of migrant workers rather than minimum standards at work, as per the ILO's usual methodology. Indeed, although some countries wanted the drafting of the new convention to take place at the ILO, a larger number of (origin) countries advocated for the treatment of migrant workers as subjects of a broader set of rights and to expand protection to their families. Therefore, the ICRMW was drafted under the auspices of the United Nations General Assembly, with many provisions echoing the civil and political rights of the related International Covenant of Civil and Political Rights (ICCPR) and the International Covenant of Economic, Social, and Cultural Rights (ICESCR).

Beginning in 1980, the drafting process was lengthy and reflective of tensions raised by diverging interests and perspectives of the diverse countries involved. The first draft was issued in 1984 and further discussion went on for another six years. Meanwhile, rapid and unforeseen changes in global migration dynamics influenced government policies and subsequently modified their attitudes towards transnational labour mobility. Both earlier progressive and traditional countries of emigration that started to receive migrants began to be concerned with the increased flows of undocumented migrant workers and became more restrictive and conservative, thus influencing the text.

The ICRMW was eventually adopted by the United Nations on 18 December 1990. Contrary to other major human rights treaties, in which universalism and multilateralism were pledged, virtually only the G77 non-aligned movement from the late 1970s was the driving force behind the studies and initiatives that led the General Assembly to initiate the Convention.17 In general terms, the ICRMW extends existing rights and creates new ones in providing for the prevention and elimination of the exploitation of all migrant workers and members of their families throughout the whole migration process, including preparation to migrate, adjustments in the receiving country, and access to social and medical services.18

The ICRMW is composed of nine parts: scope and definitions; nondiscrimination with respect to rights; human rights of all migrants (also including the rights of migrants in an irregular or 'undocumented' situation); other rights of migrants who are documented or in a regular situation; provisions applicable to particular categories of migrants; the promotion of sound, equitable, humane and lawful conditions in connection with international migration; application of the Convention; general provisions; and final provisions.

This index shows the comprehensiveness (which might well be seen also as undue complexity) of the ICRMW as an international treaty on labour migrants' human rights, produced by an unprecedentedly thorough combination of factors. Existing legally binding agreements, as well as United Nations human rights studies, resolutions, recommendations and debates on the migrant worker issue, all combined to inspire the formulation of the treaty.19 The ICRMW offers for the first time an international definition and taxonomy of migrant workers and members of their families.20 In viewing migrants as more than labourers or mere economic entities and assets, it admirably fills a conceptual gap in the protection of situations of vulnerability. Minimum universal human rights standards are affirmed for all migrant workers, including those who are undocumented, and further rights are expanded to documented labour migrants and members of their families, especially in the area of employment and equality of treatment in a number of legal, social, political and economic matters.21

The ICRMW identifies a core of non-negotiable rights directly derived from the International Bill of Human Rights.22 Most articles on civil and political rights included in Part III of the ICRMW on human rights of all migrants virtually correspond to articles in the International Covenant on Civil and Political Rights. Equivalent articles on the right to physical and moral integrity and the right to procedural guarantees can also be found in the Convention against Torture (Part I, arts 1–16).

In the ICRMW, included in the fundamental set of rights applicable to both documented and undocumented migrant workers and members of their families, are a number of provisions such as the right to life (art 9); protection from torture or cruel, inhuman or degrading treatment or punishment (art 10); freedom of thought, conscience and religion (art 12); the right to liberty and personal security and protection against arbitrary detention (art 16); freedom from slavery, servitude or forced or compulsory labour (art 11); and the right to procedural guarantees (art 18). Article 18 is also significant as it explicitly entitles all migrant workers (including those who are illegal) to another basic human right that applies to all people: the right to equality before the courts and to a fair trial by an independent and impartial tribunal established by law (arts 6 and 7 of the UDHR, and art 14 of the ICCPR).

Only a few rights had not specifically been formulated in previous human rights instruments, as they inherently relate to migrant workers. For example, it is unlawful for anyone, other than a public official duly authorised by law, to confiscate, destroy or attempt to destroy identity documents, documents authorising entry or stay, residence or establishment in the national territory, or work permits (art 21). The ICRMW also provides a shield for other civil and political rights specific to the condition of migrant workers, such as the right for migrants to have recourse to the protection and assistance of the consular or diplomatic authorities of their State of origin whenever the rights recognised under the ICRMW are impaired (art 23), and the right to protection against collective expulsion (arts 22 and 56).

In addition, the ICRMW designs its core socio-economic provisions on the basis of the International Covenant on Economic, Social and Cultural Rights, with certain measures added to meet the specific issues of migrant workers. For instance, upon termination of their stay in the State of employment, migrant workers and members of their families shall have the right to transfer their earnings and savings and their personal effects and belongings (art 32). Moreover, in the event of death, State Parties shall facilitate, whenever necessary, the repatriation to the State of origin of the bodies of deceased migrant workers and members of their families (art 71).

Another set of specific rights addresses important issues of migrant workers in regular situations, such as the right to be fully informed by their States of origin and employment about conditions applicable to their admission and concerning their stay and the remunerated activities in which they may engage (art 37).23 In addition, they can form trade unions (art 40); they can participate in the public affairs of their State of origin and vote or be elected at elections of that State (art 41); they may enjoy some political rights in the State of employment (art 42); and they may have the same opportunities and treatment as nationals in relation to various economic and social services (art 43).

Under art 44, State Parties are obliged to facilitate family reunification and to take appropriate measures to ensure the protection of the unity of the families of migrant workers. Regular migrants have to be able to choose their remunerated activity (art 49), while enjoying the same protection as nationals against dismissals and being entitled to similar unemployment benefits (art 54). Lastly, labour migrants are entitled to a clear level of guarantees and protections against expulsion (art 56). The ICRMW required 20 ratifications to come into force (art 87), which occurred in 2003. The ICRMW was negotiated by the United Nations General Assembly precisely with the goal of attracting more support than it would have as a convention drafted by the ILO, and it actually did.24 Nearly as many States have adopted the ILO's Conventions No. 97 over 60 years as have ratified the ICRMW in only 20 years.25 Nevertheless, in examining the list of the States currently party to the convention, it is striking to note the absence of any Western democracies, although (or perhaps because) these are the politically prominent countries receiving foreign migrant labour. As was the case with the ILO conventions, it is evident that the success of the ICRMW relies ultimately on the support of highly developed destination countries.

Among the various reasons for this poor adoption rate are the incompatibility with existing national legislation; technical and financial challenges of implementation; coordination problems between government departments because of shared responsibility for migrant workers;26 lack of awareness of the convention; failure of the convention to differentiate sufficiently between regular and irregular migrant workers; and a general lack of political will.27 Other authoritative research goes even further in addressing, for instance, selfperpetuated ignorance about ICRMW provisions and peer pressure for nonratification.28

BEYOND CONVENTIONS AND INSTITUTIONS: A NEW INTERNATIONAL REGIME ON LABOUR MIGRATION

The limits of the ILO Conventions and the ICRMW discussed above have nonetheless prompted additional measures to ensure protection for migrant workers through the development of a soft law framework.29 In 2005, the ILO introduced a Multilateral Framework on Labour Migration to provide guidance to migration policy makers through a collection of principles, guidelines and best practices. Respecting the latest trend in the area, the framework develops a rights-based approach to labour migration, but does so within a non-binding framework that does not interfere with the sovereign right of all countries to dictate their own migration policies. For instance, Principle 9 states that national laws and regulations should be inspired by the underlying principles of ILO Conventions No. 97 and No. 143, as well as the ICRMW, to be fully implemented if ratified by the State concerned. This softer language certainly fits better with both intrinsic dissimilarities between States and the need for gradual implementation. The long-term goal of the framework is to positively influence State practice towards the better protection of migrant workers, without the strictures of binding legal instruments. The development of such world best practices and standards is supposed to spread out widely and to be advanced through inter-agency programmes. Similarly, other United Nations mechanisms aimed at protecting human rights often make detailed recommendations on the situation of migrants, based on numerous non-discrimination clauses in respective human rights treaties. For example, the independent expert bodies set up to supervise the implementation of core human rights treaties, also known as treaty monitoring bodies (TMBs), have specifically addressed the application of relevant treaty provisions to undocumented migrants in European countries, while urging a more general and basic protection for legally residing migrants in the Middle East.30

The International Organization for Migration (IOM) was established in 1951 on the basis that there was a need to manage the resettlement of millions of Europeans displaced by the Second World War. In its original role as a logistical agency, it helped to transport and resettle nearly one million Europeans during the 1950s, largely to the Americas and Oceania. The IOM assumed its present name and revised its constitution in 1989, expanding its scope to become one of the leading international agencies working with governments and civil society to advance the understanding of migration issues and conducting operations on a global scale to encourage social and economic development through migration, as well as to uphold the human dignity and wellbeing of migrants.

The IOM is not an entity within the United Nations system, but is an intergovernmental organisation (IGO) whose members are bound by a constitution, under which membership is confined to States with a demonstrated interest in the principle of free movement of persons, together with States that were previously members of the Intergovernmental Committee for European Migration. There are currently 157 Member States, and numerous other entities have observer status (including ten States).31

Article 1 of IOM's constitution identifies its core functions as: making arrangements for the organised transfer of migrants, refugees and displaced persons; providing migration services to States upon request (including services for voluntary return migration or repatriation); and providing a forum for the exchange of views and coordination of efforts on international migration issues. To facilitate the coordination of international activities, the IOM cooperates closely with international organisations concerned with migration, refugees and human resources. Critically, the IOM provides an approach to forced and voluntary migration based on assistance rather than rights, with no formal protection mandate, as is the case of the UNHCR in dealing with forced migration and asylum. Notably, because the dividing line between forced and voluntary migrations has been becoming finer than ever since the end of the Cold War, the IOM is assuming an increasingly protective role in relation to refugees, virtually overlapping with the role of UNHCR.32

Thus far in this study, the ILO and IOM have been identified as the foremost labour migration organisations. Nevertheless, an array of other international institutions is concerned with the free movement of migrant workers. This proliferation of specialised institutions can lead to conflicting considerations. From one side, tensions occurred between the ILO and the United Nations General Assembly in the negotiation of the ICRMW, during which promoting countries bypassed the traditional role of the ILO.33 This is a good example of what can result from overlapping bodies in terms of duplication of effort, wasted resources and gaps in responsibilities.34 Conversely, it can be argued that from proliferation of the international institutions, such organisations gain expertise, develop effective networks, fill the gaps in the system and focus on their specialised tasks without the bureaucracy and inefficiency typical of larger organisations with their extended chains of command.35

The only common feature of such different perspectives is perhaps the call for a new international regime for labour mobility and migration. Globalisation is the factor most taken into account, as it is presenting the need for supranational regulation and international response to issues that cannot only be solved within national borders. Recent literature generally advocates well-balanced and comprehensive multilateral frameworks in labour mobility, combined with global minded migration policies, although it seems difficult to find any detailed and elaborated proposal.36

More realistically, in 2005, the Global Commission on International Migration (GCIM) expressly considered the question of appropriate global institutions to provide a framework for the formulation of a coherent, comprehensive and global response to international migration.

In the same year, the GCIM reported to the United Nations SecretaryGeneral the conclusion that, in the long term, a fundamental overhaul of the current institutional architecture relating to international migration will be required, both to bring together the disparate migration-related functions of existing United Nations' and other agencies within a single organisation, and to respond to the new and complex realities of international migration.37 The GCIM professed a preference for institutional consolidation by envisioning the amalgamation of the IOM with UNHCR and the individuation of a spearhead agency from among existing institutions. However, no specific recommendation was made on this matter aside from bringing the IOM into the United Nations system, to be put at the cutting edge of the voluntary migration regime, but not out of the context of a thorough on-going reform of the United Nations.

Beyond these long-term consolidating options, the GCIM took forward the combination of operational efforts rather than institutional structures and advocated the establishment of a short-term, inter-agency facility to strengthen cooperation between all international institutions dealing with migration.38 The Secretary-General first put this suggestion into action in 2006 with the transformation of a limited-membership Geneva Migration Group into a larger GMG. This would involve 14 relevant agencies and a number of recent inter-state and inter-agency initiatives, such as the United Nations High Level Dialogue, which started in 2006.39

This is a new approach in some cross-agency areas of the United Nations that aims to achieve better coordination of efforts. Initiating new programmes without establishing new organisations can provide more flexible structures in building new processes for coordination. Hence, the call for a versatile Joint United Nations Programme on International Migration seems well founded on the spur of the useful development of the coordination efforts of the GMG, jumping over the hurdles of starting up a new international organisation and providing crucial settings for consolidating existing principles and promoting new concepts of international labour migration law40 .

BILATERAL AND REGIONAL AGREEMENTS REGULATING CROSS-BORDER LABOUR MIGRATION

The multilateral context of international standards and mutual support at bilateral, regional and multilateral levels are paramount in the operation of agreements regulating transnational labour migration and addressing the protection of migrant workers. In connection with its application, Convention No. 97 asks States to enter into bilateral agreements to regulate issues concerning migration. Additionally, the accompanying Recommendation No. 86 sets out a model agreement covering major features of the whole migratory process and offers contents for model contracts of employment.

Bilateral agreements adhering to such standards aim to provide protection for migrant workers, especially with regard to specific areas, like social security and protection of more vulnerable groups, as previously discussed. Until the economic turmoil of the oil crisis in the 1970s, bilateral agreements were current practice in managing migration flows and resolving related issues between two countries. In the following two decades, much looser framework agreements, memoranda of understanding, and declarations of mutual cooperation on the contracting and protection of foreign workers largely superseded bilateral agreements.41

It is difficult to discern whether the concomitant upsurge

of the more integrated approach of international law in migration affairs is the cause or effect of the decline of bilateral agreements. Nevertheless, in the 1990s, there has been a global, although geographically irregular, growth in the number of bilateral agreements. For instance, in the last decade of the 20th century, OECD countries registered a fivefold increase42 and Latin American countries doubled the number of bilateral agreements, while Asian countries did not present the same expanding figures.43 Noticeably, Central-Eastern European States and the Former Soviet Republics marked a significant use of bilateral agreements not only with neighbouring or other regional countries, but also with States on other continents.44 This latest generation of bilateral agreements usually seeks to address broader economic and social issues, although the objectives may focus on a more specific range, such as preventing irregular migration or regulating seasonal work in agriculture, at the same time raising hopes and prompting criticism in the arena of global migration governance.45

Similarly, subregional and regional bodies have established an array of measures at various levels with regard to the management of transnational migratory flows, addressing in their agendas pivotal issues such as the conditions of admission, stay and treatment of foreign workers. In place in all continents (although to different extents, such as in Asia), regional standards usually comprise both the protection of migrant workers and the governance of migration, showing converging interests and approaches towards progressive harmonisation, especially in terms of processes of regional and subregional economic integration. Indeed, in the last decade, regional inter-state economic integration and frameworks increasingly developed or implemented agreements regarding labour mobility at both administrative and formal legal levels.

In the Asia-Pacific area, the purpose of the Labour and Social Protection Network is to foster strong and flexible labour markets and strengthen social protection to address sustainable human resource development across Asia-Pacific Economic Cooperation (APEC) member economies. Labour mobility between New Zealand and Australia creates an excellent opportunity for the development of labour flows in accordance with migration issues and conventional economic theory. Over recent years, there have been large movements of people in both directions, as they have sought to achieve their objectives through employment in the other country. This provides an excellent opportunity for a study of the likely effects of the free movement of labour upon migrant workers' rights, although both countries are comparable in wealth and employment standards.

The Association of Southeast Asian Nations Labour Ministers' (ASEAN-LM) Work Programme provides the framework to prepare the region's labour force to face the challenges of globalisation and trade liberalisation. One of the six broad priorities set in the Work Programme is in the area of labour mobility. The 2007 ASEAN Declaration on the Protection and Promotion of the Rights of Migrant Workers mandates that member countries promote fair and appropriate employment protection, payment of wages, and adequate access to decent working and living conditions for migrant workers. The 2009 ASEAN-Australia-New Zealand Free Trade Agreement also represents an opportunity to improve dialogue and conduct cooperative activities, including the promotion of labour rights and obligations and decent work conditions.

In Europe, there is a complex set of workers' circulation standards and migration policies, particularly within the framework of the EU. After the entry into force of the 1992 Maastricht Treaty on the EU, as amended by the treaties of Amsterdam, Nice and Lisbon, the evolution from a common economic space moved the European labour migration apparatus from the intergovernmental level to the community level. The freedom of movement for workers is one of the four pillars of the EU, as art 45 of the Consolidated Treaty on the Functioning of the EU (ex-art 39, European Community—EC Treaty) entitles about 500 million people to move and stay freely in 27 different countries for the purpose of employment. Hence, the EU can be deemed as quite an advanced prototype of labour citizenship established within intergovernmental organisations, conferring status, participation, solidarity and identity on all those who have the right to be engaged in a remunerated activity in a Member State of which he or she is not a national.

Outside the EU framework, the European Committee on Migration (CDMG) is theCouncil of Europe body working with governments to develop common policies on the challenges of migration and the human rights of migrants. The CDMG's task is to develop European cooperation on migration and social integration of populations of migrant origin, aiming through its work to influence government policy and practice in the Member States of the Council of Europe. Its target group is therefore essentially government policy makers and public officials responsible for delivering services to migrants at both the national and local level.

In Africa, continental organisations embraced the concept of free movement, fundamental to Africa's integration objective, as can be seen in several instruments, including art 43 of the 1991 Treaty Establishing the African Economic Community and the African Union's Priority Programme on Free Movement of Persons as detailed in the 2004–2007 Plan of Action to Speed Up Integration of the Continent, promoting the free movement of people. At the subregional African level, there is a clear influence of the EU model for the free circulation of labour. For instance, the Southern Africa Development Community (SADC) drafted a Protocol in 2001 on free movement of labour, which, although the Member States did not subsequently adopt it, forms the negotiation basis for new initiatives addressing labour migration in the area.

In 2003, the Central African Economic and Monetary Community (CEMAC) unsuccessfully sought new measures to put into effect its agreement on the free circulation of labour, all but implemented since its adoption in the 1980s. Further, the treaty establishing the East African Community in 2003 affirms free circulation and residence of labour for nationals of member countries. Within the American continents, the Permanent Council of the Organization of American States (OAS) established in 2007 a Committee on Migration Issues as a strategic platform for the discussion and analysis of the patterns of human migration in the Americas and the impact of these movements on Member States. The Secretariat of this Special Committee on Migration is in the stage of gathering information and producing a matrix of existing legal frameworks and, as appropriate, migration regulations, policies and programmes for OAS countries, with a view to creating a compendium of best practices with respect to migration.

The TN (Trade NAFTA- North American Free Trade Agreement) status is a special non-immigration status unique to citizens of the US, Canada and Mexico, created by virtue of the 1994 NAFTA. It allows American, Canadian and Mexican citizens the opportunity to work in each other's countries in certain professional occupations. In South America, the Mercado Comun Del Sur (MERCOSUR) countries approved an agreement on residence for their nationals in 2002 in order to implement the integration process, and similarly, the Andean Community adopted in 2003 a revised Andean Instrument for Labour Migration. More comprehensively, the Labor Consultative Council of the newly formed Union of South American Nations pursues the attainment of fuller participation in the construction of an integration process leading to the creation of a common market. The member countries have decided to join efforts to ensure that their inhabitants are able to move freely through the subregion for purposes of work, adopting measures aimed at the promotion of intra-community mobility.

In general terms, only few of all the subregional and regional agreements draw on relevant international standards, because not all Member States of these regional bodies have ratified ILO Conventions No. 97 and No. 143. Not incorporating international standards clearly presents the risk of putting in place legal measures that undermine existing norms and reiterate the transnational inconsistencies that these norms were designed to avoid.46 For instance, recent literature noted that many countries in the Global South (especially in Asia) prefer to operate bilaterally on the basis of Memoranda of Understanding, which is not conducive to the promotion and upholding of migrant workers' rights at all.47

SOCIAL SECURITY RIGHTS FOR MIGRANT WORKERS: ILO INSTRUMENTS

As social security rights are usually related to periods of employment and residence, the situation of migrant workers, especially if they do not enjoy permanent or legal status is particularly difficult to manage at the national level and in compliance with the international regulation on labour and social rights. In general, the ILO instruments encourage the development of model contracts to manage effectively the issues that arise from the circumstances of migrating for employment. For instance, art 22 of the Model Agreement on Temporary and Permanent Migration for Employment, including Migration of Refugees and Displaced Persons, annexed to the Migration for Employment Recommendations (Revised), 1949 (No. 86), affirms that bilateral agreements should provide measures concerning the equal treatment of migrants and nationals and appropriate arrangements for acquired rights in the area of social security.

Migrant workers' social security rights are particularly vulnerable, as their benefits and entitlements are at stake not only in origin countries, due to their absence, but also in the host country, where restrictive conditions for the inclusion of alien residents in the national social security system may apply. For migrant workers' social rights, protection is crucial for equal access to and coverage by national entitlements, to maintain and export acquired rights when leaving the country, and to be able to accumulate the benefits obtained in different countries.48

As for labour rights, all current ILO social security standards apply in terms of their scope of coverage irrespective of nationality and residence status, in most cases including similar clauses on equality of treatment for nationals and foreign workers in the host country. Moreover, the ILO supervisory bodies have made specific reference to migrant workers in the context of their regular supervision in the social security area.49 Conversely, although the Equality of Treatment (Accident Compensation) Convention, 1925 (No. 19), and the similar Equality of Treatment (Social Security) Convention, 1962 (No. 118), establish the right to equality of treatment for foreign workers in respect of compensation for industrial accidents and social security, signatory countries grant equality of treatment with their own nationals only to nationals of any other Member State on the provision of reciprocity.50

Under the Maintenance of Social Security Rights Convention, 1982 (No. 157), and Recommendation, 1983 (No. 167), State Parties have to ensure the maintenance of acquired rights for the nationals of other members in any branch of social security in which the concerned countries have legislation in force. Convention No. 157 and its relevant Recommendation No. 167 establish an international framework for the maintenance of not only acquired rights, but also rights in the course of acquisition for workers who cross borders, entailing the effective provision of their benefits abroad even when they return home. Essentially, Convention No. 157 advocates the conclusion of bilateral or multilateral social security agreements, while Recommendation No. 167 offers a model provision for the definition of such agreements.

Other special non-discrimination clauses are dealt with in Part XI of the Social Security (Minimum Standards) Convention, 1952 (No. 102), which affirms that national and non-national residents should have the same rights to social security, although with some acceptable exclusion of foreign people when benefits are funded entirely by public resources (art 68). In conclusion, migrant workers' opportunities for maintaining and exporting social security benefits differ markedly according to the country and branch of social security being considered, although regular and permanent migrants usually enjoy equality of treatment with nationals. As delineated in the previous sections, restrictions mostly occur in the unemployment benefits area.

CONCLUSION

This paper provided a picture of the development and content of domestic and international legal instruments and programmes relating to migrant labour, to the extent that the freedom to choose where to work and to do so in decent conditions can enter the legal reality on several normative levels. The analysis focused on the current tendency of domestic legal systems to broadly incorporate such a conception, and to support it at an international level. Finally, the investigation revolved around the extent to which the established legal frameworks at both levels (national and international) recognise or incorporate the notion of decent work equally for domestic and migrant workers.

Nonetheless, for the past few decades, the preservation of working rights and social provisions is increasingly becoming economically unsustainable across the globe. Where the migrant labour cost is not able to compete with the sum of outsourced labour and logistics expenses, exporting production is more advantageous than importing labour. Hence, industry production has been largely reallocated to countries that have abruptly improved their socio-economic development, skipping the intermediate steps of the modernisation process that beforehand took the outsourcing countries more than a hundred years to achieve.

As a further development, the answers of this study could take into account the often under-estimated social capital created by transnational migrant labour in our society. Considering this may help us understand why both old and new immigration countries are not advancing a thoroughly integrated and farsighted approach to global labour migration affairs. In such perspective, the pivotal matter is whether, at this present stage, these migrant-receiving countries are merely taking advantage of what historically is just a moment, where the migrants' social capital (i.e. the value of migrants' social relations and cooperation) transferred through generations of labour migration has not yet been dissipated, while at the same time trying to prolong this moment as much as possible by cutting or not bearing the social costs of workers on the move. Such a short-sighted approach may well present in the near future the awkward situation in which the social costs of labour migration will no longer be sustainable, while its entire social capital will be lost irreversibly.

Over the long term, the failure in the global management of labour migration may also result in developed societies not being socio-economically sustainable, whilst not being able to grow without cross-border migrant workers. In other words, immigration may become socio-economically unsustainable, although still necessary for maintaining the current levels of human development in receiving countries.

In connection to the issues discussed in this paper, open-ended configurations of transnational production and variable processes of economic globalisation are increasingly putting a strain on the already weak capability of domestic labour law to ensure justice at work for migrants. This situation may be seen as a call for migrant labour rights to comprehensively enter the international legal reality.

NOTES:

1 Article 8 of Convention No. 97 states: "1. A migrant for employment who has been admitted on a permanent basis and the members of his family who have been authorised to accompany or join him shall not be returned to their territory of origin or the territory from which they emigrated because the migrant is unable to follow his occupation by reason of illness contracted or injury sustained subsequent to entry, unless the person concerned so desires or an international agreement to which the Member is a party so provides.2. When migrants for employment are admitted on a permanent basis upon arrival in the country of immigration the competent authority of that country may determine that the provisions of paragraph 1 of this Article shall take effect only after a reasonable period which shall in no case exceed five years from the date of admission of such migrants", available at <http://www.ilo.org/ilolex/cgi-lex/convde.pl?C097>; and Article 11.2(e) of Convention No. 143 does not apply its provisions to "employees of organisations or undertakings operating within the territory of a country who have been admitted temporarily to that country at the request of their employer to undertake specific duties or assignments, for a limited and defined period of time, and who are required to leave that country on the completion of their duties or assignments", available at <http://www.ilo.org/ilolex/cgi-lex/convde.pl?C143>.

2 The ILO defines „liberal profession, or „professional service as "those services supplied by professional workers, often self-employed, such as doctors, lawyers, accountants, architects, etc." International Labour Organization, ILO INFORM, Bureau of Library and Information, ILO Thesaurus 2005, available at < http://www.ilo.org/public/libdoc/ILOThesaurus/english/tr4621.htm>.

3 International Labour Organization (ILO), General Survey on migrant workers, Report III (Part 1B), International Labour Conference, 87th Session (Geneva, 1999) at para 101.

4 International Labour Organization, ILO Declaration on Fundamental Principles and Rights at Work - 86th Session (Geneva, June 1998): "Whereas the ILO should give special attention to the problems of persons with special social needs, particularly the unemployed and migrant workers, and mobilize and encourage international, regional and national efforts aimed at resolving their problems, and promote effective policies aimed at job creation;" available at <http://www.ilo.org/declaration/thedeclaration/textdeclaration/lang-- en/index.htm>.

5 With respect to migrant workers in an irregular situation, the Committee on Freedom of Association considered that Article 2 of Convention No. 87 "recognize[d] the right of workers, without distinction whatsoever, to establish and join organizations of their own choosing without previous authorization. The only permissible exception to Convention No. 87 [was] that set out in Article 9 concerning the armed forces and the police". International Labour Organization (ILO), 327th Report of the Committee on Freedom of Association, Governing Body, 283rd Session (Geneva, March 2002) at GB.283/8, para 561.

6 International Labour Organization (ILO), Freedom of association and collective bargaining: General Survey, Report III (Part 4B), International Labour Conference, 81st Session (Geneva, 1994) at para 118.

7 Inter alia see International Labour Organization (ILO), Report of the Committee on the Application of Standards, International Labour Conference, 88th-91st Sessions (Geneva, 2000-03).

8 Inter alia see: Committee of Experts on the Application of Conventions and Recommendations, CEACR Report, International Labour Conference, 89th Session (Geneva, 2001), individual observations concerning Conventions Nos. 97 and 111, pp. 369-374 and 493-495.

9 Remarkably, in 2003 the Inter-American Court of Human Rights issued a far-reaching advisory opinion which clearly reinforces the application of international labour standards to non-national workers, particularly those of irregular status. The Court found that nondiscrimination and the right to equality are „juscogens and applicable to all residents regardless of immigration status. See further in Inter-American Court of Human Rights (IACrtHR) Advisory Opinion on Juridical Condition and Rights of the Undocumented Migrants, OC-18/03, (San Jose, Costa Rica, 17 September 2003) available at

<http://www.unhcr.org/refworld/docid/425cd8cb4.html>

10 International Labour Organization (ILO), Protection of wages: Standards and safeguards relating to the payment of labour remuneration, General Survey of the reports concerning the Protection of Wages Convention, 1949 (No. 95), and the Protection of Wages Recommendation, 1949 (No. 85), Report III (Part 1B), International Labour Conference, 91st Session (Geneva, 2003) at para 267.

11 Committee of Experts on the Application of Conventions and Recommendations, CEACR Report, International Labour Conference, 87th Session (Geneva, 1999) at p. 313; and CEACR Report, International Labour Conference, 89th Session (Geneva, 2001) at p. 357.

12 Such as in the case of a number of Egyptian workers in Kuwait during the Gulf War: CEACR Report, International Labour Conference, 89th Session (Geneva, 2001) at p. 358.

13Cholewinski, R., Migrant Workers in International Human Rights Law: Their Protection in Countries of Employment, Clarendon Press (Oxford, 1997) at 135.

14 As of January 2015, Convention No.97 has been ratified by 49 countries and Convention No. 143 by 23 countries. For an updated list of adopting countries, see: ILO at http://www.ilo.org/dyn/normlex/en/f?p=1000:11300:0::NO:11300:P11300_INSTRUMENT_I D:312242 and <http://www.ilo.org/dyn/normlex/en/f?p=1000:11300:0::NO:11300:P11300_INSTRUMENT _ID:312288>.

15 Fitzpatrick, J., The human rights of migrants in T. Aleinikoff and V. Chetail (eds), Migration and International Legal Norms, TMC Asser Press (The Hague, 2003) at 169-184.

16 Leary, V., Labor migration in T. Aleinikoff and V. Chetail (eds), Migration and International Legal Norms, TMC Asser Press (The Hague, 2003) at 227-239.

17 On the ICRMW draftingprocesssee: Battistela, G., La naissance dune Convention: les difficiles relations entre migrations et droits de lhomme, in Hommes & Migrations, Cité nationale de lhistoire de limmigration (Paris, 2008) at 1271:20-30.

18 Nafziger, J., and B. Bartel, The Migrant Workers Convention: its place in human rights law in International Migration Review 25, Wiley-Blackwell (Hoboken, NJ, 1991) at 771–799.

19 Office of the United Nations High Commissioner for Human Rights (UNHCHR), FactSheet No 24(Rev.1), The International Convention on Migrant Workers and its Committee (Geneva, 2005).

20 Article 2(1) ICRMW defines a „migrant worker as „a person who is to be engaged, is engaged or has been engaged in a remunerated activity in a state of which he or she is not a national, available at OHCHR, <http://www2.ohchr.org/english/law/cmw.htm>.

21 For further reference see: December 18, International NGO Platform on the Migrant Workers Convention, A Guide for Non-Governmental Organisations on the Implementation of the UN Migrant Workers Convention, Updated (Brussels, 2007) available at <http://www.december18.net/sites/default/files/Guide_for_NGOs_en.pdf>.

22 The so-called (informally) International Bill of Human Rights consists of the Universal Declaration of Human Rights (adopted in 1948), the International Covenant on Civil andPolitical Rights (1966) and the International Covenant on Economic, Social and Cultural Rights (1966). On their link with the ICRMW see further: Grange, M., Strengthening Protection of Migrant Workers and their Families with International Human Rights Treaties – A do-it-yourself Kit, International Catholic Migration Commission (Geneva, 2006) at Table IV: 44-49.

23 Arguably, it is not explained how migrants native states would know and manage all this information about other countries.

24 Lönnroth, J. The International Convention on the Rights of All Migrant Workers and Members of Their Families in the context of international migration policies: an analysis of ten years of negotiation, International Migration Review 25: 710–736, Wiley-Blackwell (Hoboken, NJ, 1991), at 728.

25 As of March 2013, the ICRMW accounts for 35 signatories and 46 parties. For an updated list of adopting countries see UN Treaty Collection, at <http://treaties.un.org/Pages/ViewDetails.aspx?src=TREATY&mtdsg_no=IV-13&chapter=4&lang=en>.

26Cholewinski, R. The rights of migrant workers, in R. Cholewinski, R. Perruchoud and E. MacDonald (eds), International Migration Law: Developing Paradigms and Key Challenges, TMC Asser Press (The Hague, 2007), at pp.255-274.

27 Pécoud A. and P. de Guchteneire, Migration, human rights and the United Nations: an investigation of the obstacles to the UN Convention on Migrant Workers,, Rights, in Global Migration Perspectives No. 3. GCIM (Geneva, 2004) at 4 and 13, available at http://portal.unesco.org/shs/en/files/6611/10962899451GCIM.pdf/GCIM.pdf.

28 UNESCO, UN Convention on Migrants Rights, Information Kit, International Migration Programme, UNESCO Publications (Paris, 2005) at 12-14, availableat <http://unesdoc.unesco.org/images/0014/001435/143557e.pdf>.

29 Betts, A., Towards a soft law framework for the protection of vulnerable migrants. New Issues in Refugee Research, UNHCR Research Paper No. 162, (Geneva, 2008) at 12-18.

30 Guimont, A., M. Silvestri and Proli, P., The UN Treaty Monitoring Bodies and Migrant Workers: a Samizdat, UNESCO-December 18 vzw (Brussels, 2008) at 2.2:10.

31 As of January 2015, for updated figures see: International Organization for Migration (IOM), at <http://www.iom.int/cms/en/sites/iom/home/about-iom-1/members-andobservers.html>

32 Perrouchoud, R., Persons falling under the mandate of the International Organization for Migration (IOM) and to whom the organization may provide migration services, International Journal of Refugee Law (Oxford, 1992) at 4:205–215.

33 Böhning, R., The ILO and the new UN Convention on Migrant Workers: the past and future, International Migration Review, Issue 25, Wiley-Blackwell (Hoboken, NJ, 1991) at 698–709.

34 Blokker, N., Proliferation of international organizations: an explanatory introduction, in Blokker, N. and H. Schermers (eds), Proliferation of International Organizations: Legal Issues, Kluwer Law International (The Hague, 2001) at 1-49.

35 Schermers, H., Final remarks, in Blokker, N. and H. Schermers (eds), Proliferation of International Organizations: Legal Issues, Kluwer Law International (The Hague, 2001) at 551. For a more recent and thorough appraisal on global governance of migrations see in particular: Grugel, J.B. and Piper, N., Critical Perspectives on Global Governance: Rights and Regulation in Governing Regimes, Routledge (London, 2007) at 3:41-64.

36 For example see: Ghosh, B. (ed.) Managing Migration: Time for a New International Regime? Oxford University Press (Oxford, 2000) at 227.

37 Global Commission on International Migration (GCIM), Migration in an Interconnected World: New Directions for Action (Geneva, 2005) at 75.

38 See Global Commission on International Migration (GCIM), above n 37, at 76-78.

39Neilsen, A., Cooperation mechanisms, in R. Cholewinski, R. Perruchoud and E. MacDonald (eds). International Migration Law: Developing Paradigms and Key Challenges, TMC Asser Press (The Hague, 2007) at 405-426.

40 Opeskin, B., The Influence of International Law on the International Movement of Persons, Human Development Research Paper 2009/18, UNDP (Geneva, 2009) at 6:127.

41 Abella, M., Sending workers abroad, International Labour Organization(Geneva, 1997) at 6.1:63-67.

42 Bobela, D. and Garson., J., Migration for Employment, Bilateral Agreements at a Crossroad, Organisation for Economic Co-operation and Development (OECD), (Geneva, 2004) at 11-29.

43 See International Organization for Migration (IOM), World Migration Report 2003, Managing Migration - Challenges and Responses for People on the Move (Geneva, 2003) at 11:195-212.

44 See IOM, above n 43, at 13:239-256.

45 See for example: Commonwealth Caribbean and Mexican Agricultural Seasonal Workers Programme in Canada: Martin, P., Managing labour migration: Temporary worker programmes for the 21st century, International Institute for Labour Studies (Geneva, 2003) at 26-35.

46 ILO, Towards a fair deal for migrant workers in the global economy, Report VI, International Labour Conference, 92nd Session (Geneva, 2004) at 264.

47 See for instance Wickramasekara P., Labour migration in South Asia: A review of issues, policies and practices, ILO, International Migration Paper No. 108 (Geneva, 2011) at 3.4.1:23-24.

48 Humblet, M., and R. Silva, Standards for the XXI century – Social security, International Labour Organization (Geneva, 2002) at 41-45.

49 Inter alia, with respect to application of the Employment Injury Benefits Convention, 1964 [Schedule I amended in 1980] (No. 121) and of the Medical Care and Sickness Benefits Convention, 1969 (No. 130).

50 For example, Convention No.19 provides for the export of covered benefits of foreign workers only when the ratifying State undertakes the grant of such export of benefits for its own nationals. In addition, Convention No.118 advocates the maintenance of acquired rights when stating that a member country has to ensure the provision of social security benefits abroad for its own nationals and for the nationals of any other State that hasaccepted the obligation of the Convention, regardless of the place of residence of the beneficiary. Relevant literature on "portable rights" includes Grugel, J. and Piper N., Global governance, economic migration and the difficulties of social activism, in: International Sociology, SAGE (London, 2011) at 26(4): 435-454.

CHAPTER 17

THE NORMATIVE CONCEPT OF LABOUR CITIZENSHIP AS A DETERMINANT OF THE GLOBAL VALUE OF ECONOMIC MIGRATION

Giovanni Di Lieto

Keywords: Labour theory of value, Economic migration, Industrial citizenship, Global governance of migration, Transnational labour citizenship, Cross-border labour mobility

NORMATIVE DEVELOPMENTS IN THE LABOUR THEORY OF VALUE

The concept of labour as a normative source and as a determinant of social and economic value does not appear in ancient literature. It was only in the Middle Ages that labour assumed a distinct analytical role as one of the sources of an ethical, but also practical, theory of value. In Ancient Greek philosophy, Aristotle only conceptualised labour as deriving from the notions of poiêsis (production, making) and praxis (doing, action).1 Life was praxis and slaves, or those who worked for others, were involved in poiêsis. Only praxis wasentitled to full participation, membership and identity within the political, economic and cultural spheres of the polity (in other words, to citizenship).

On both the subjective and objective levels, the theory of value in labour can also be traced back to Aristotle.2 The Greek philosopher was the first to speculate over the logical linkage of labour (or product, ergon) with trade (or equivalent exchange, catallaxis). Aristotle went further in arguing that a common measure was the precondition for commercial association, as the exchange of needs (chreia) would bring the contracting parties together. However, he could not find a common measure for things that were dissimilar, for instance a shoe and a house for a builder and a shoemaker respectively.3

This is because the very concept of labour as an abstract category did not exist in Greece, nor later in Rome.4 The ancient economy was inclined to reason in terms of use and value, as it was the object of the work that mattered, not the labour of the producer. Under the Roman mentality, activity (officium) by full citizens (cives) was not considered labour, but rather a productive manifestation of leisure (otium). This approach always prevented the ancient Romans, as for the Greeks before, from conceptualising labour as a distinct measure of value, let alone recognising that there was a distinction between free and slave labour, since the latter did not have to be valued in the same way unless it was hired out to others. Certainly, in the later Roman Empire there were aspects of labour law present in relation to the contractual hire of menial and slave labour, and the legal concept of specificatio conferred rights of property under certain conditions to those who transformed raw materials into a new product (nova species) by their own labour.5 However, neither a hypothesis of labour as one of the possible explanations of value, nor any analytical treatment of labour as a distinct conceptual category, emerged until the 13th century under Scholastic philosophy.

At that time, philosophers such as Albert Magnus and Thomas Aquinas wrote extensive commentaries on Aristotle, adding a second basis for value, namely the factors of labour and expenses.6 Labor et expensae were offered as a possible

Citation: Giovanni Di Lieto, The Normative Concept of Labour Citizenship as a Determinant of the Global Value of Economic Migration, ISSN: 1843-5610.

measure of what should constitute the just price (justum praetium) in commercial transactions.7 The Scholastics ultimately believed that the just price of a thing should reflect the common estimation of the community, such that those who produced it and those who bought it preserved their status (dignitas) in the divinely ordained social hierarchy.8 This implied a purely ethical theory of price determination within a static economy, not suited for the later development of a dynamic economy based on trade, in which merchants were required to save their immortal souls and their profits altogether, justifying even usury as remuneration for labour (stipendium laboris).9

Subsequently, mercantilist and natural law theorists argued that a utility and scarcity theory of value existed alongside a cost and labour theory. However, a proper labour theory of value eventually developed only under the influence of Locke's theory of property, and it became a prominent part of what is known as the classical political economy. Based on the concept of labor et expensae persisting in natural law philosophy, the labour theory of value became more articulate, as the price of things was meant to "usually have a Regard to the Pains and Expenses the Merchants and Traders have been at".10 Nevertheless, in the classical political economy, non-market factors (such as the dignity and fame of the artisans, and the needs of the contracting parties) were still largely contaminating the labour theory of value in terms of scarcity (indigentia) and utility or difficulty of acquisition.11 Furthermore, the role of labour was seen as a dimension of production, rather than used to explain value.12

John Locke, often seen as the originator of the labour theory of value,13 when arguing for a right to property, affirmed that labour "puts the difference of value on every thing", and that "of the Products of the Earth useful to the Life of Man 9/10 are the effects of labour".14 In the post-mercantilist period, theories of a natural price of labour emerged, thus advancing the notion of a self-organised economy mediating through the market between different classes of people.15 Hence, the principles of exchange needed an explanation in terms of demand and supply, measured only by 'arguments of sense' (i.e. 'number, weight or measure').16 Other authors went further in affirming that "Industry and Labour are the only real Riches, ... Money therefore being nothing more than a Certificate of Labour".17

As a medium of exchange for other labour and any commodities, labour was also seen as "more proper to be made a measure of value" than money, "thus the riches of a country are to be valued by the quantity of labor its inhabitants are able to purchase, and not by the quantity of silver and gold they possess".18 Following the early theories of exchange within the general concept of value as a ratio composed of scarcity and utility, labour ('fatica') could be seen as the main determinant of scarcity, and thus the "sole object that gives value to things".19 In the classical political economy, propounding the idea of labour as the single determinant of value required major analytical efforts to demonstrate how a labour theory of value might work in a capitalist economy.

Adam Smith was the first to link goods exchange to labour value by asserting that wealth depends upon what one can command from the labour of others. In other words, in a capitalist economy there is division of labour and each worker must rely on the labour of others by acquiring goods through exchange. The analytical hurdle was that, despite the assertion that labour is the measure of the value of everything, the exchange value of commodities was still measured by traders in terms of money. Another issue was the difficulty to equate and measure types of labour differing in skill and hardship. The answer was found in the market prices and quantities that imputed value to underlying labour, which was comparable between time periods and relatively permanent. However, Smith argued that labour only determines the exchange value of things in an 'early and rude' state of society where, for instance, "beaver and deerskins are exchanged in a ratio inversely proportional to the labour time required to hunt and skin them".20 Once, however, we are in a society with capitalists and landlords, profits and rents along with wages must be paid, so that the price of commodities ends up being the sum of the value of the three components. Labour is reduced to reflect the concept that "the real price of every thing, what every thing really costs to the man who wants to acquire it, is the toil and trouble of acquiring it".21This argument shows its inconsistency, as the value of labour is only imputed, not determining but determined, and as such it cannot be a measure of value.

A few decades later, David Ricardo reformulated the concept developed by Adam Smith into the foundational part of a consistent theory of value and distribution. To address Smith's analytical contradictions, Ricardo looked for instance at the agricultural sector, whose commodities were measured in physical units, aggregating both the produce and the cost of production, including wage and rent costs. It was therefore demonstrated that the labour theory of value would apply to "such commodities only as can be increased in quantity by the exertion of human industry, and on the production of which competition operates without restraint".22 This meant that the labour theory of value was not to be limited to the 'early and rude state of society', but was applicable also to a competitive capitalist economy. Furthermore, it implied the assumption that determination of the level of wages takes place outside the sphere of exchange and production, separating analytically the question of distribution from that of value determination.

Based on these assumptions, Karl Marx moved forward to a philosophical conception of labour as the affirmation and actualisation of the human essence.23 Labour was seen as "a process in which both man and Nature participate, and in which man of his own accord starts, regulates, and controls the material re-actions between himself and Nature".24 While "Labour is not the source of all wealth. Nature is, ... the first source of all means and subjects of labour, as an owner, treats her [nature] as belonging to him [the man], his labour becomes the source of use values, and also of wealth".25 Here it is clear there is a distinction between concrete labour (i.e. the technical-material labour process), and abstract labour, to be equalised through the process of exchange. Later commentators argued that, in a commodity economy, exchange value is determined by the distribution of labour, which in turn "is indirectly regulated through the market and the exchange of things".26 This argument fits well with the famous Marxist distinction between abstract labour and labour power, which is the potentiality of labour to be realized in the labour process and purchased (i.e. exploited) by the capitalist. In other words, for the first time in modern history labour (power) was recognised as a commodity. This became the major point of either attack on or appraisal of the political implications of Marx's system. However, labour had finally achieved the status of a major analytical concept in the explanation of value.27

The concept that labour was the sole determinant of value could not be tolerated for long, as it implied the ideologically dangerous postulate that labour has a rightful claim to the full product. A new politically harmless paradigm was found in the economic concept of marginal utility, which involved the labour theory of value only indirectly, as it was empirically based on the direct experience of market exchange and consumption of goods.28 To the traditional and 'more philosophical' taxonomy of 'agents of production' including 'labour' and 'nature', an empirical classification was added that subsequently became conventional: 'labour, capital and land'.29 However, in the light of the marginal utility theories, the very notion of agents of production implies that labour alone is not the sole producer of value. In other words, it is not labour that determines scarcity,30 but instead labour creates value whenever there is scarcity.31 This shifting assumption marks the beginning of the downward turn of the theory of labour value, increasingly seen as determined solely through the exchange of things in the market, as such expanding the Marxian theory of distribution of labour value but without the distinctive feature of labour power.32 This completed the loss of the centrality of the concept of labour in the current political economy, a process that started with the commodification of labour and the regulation of its price through the market on a par with all the other factors of production. Following the theories of marginal productivity, which maximised individuals under different situations and levelled the factors of production with commodities, even the very concept of labour was fading away, being substituted by the subjective absence of leisure. This subjective component in the determination of value led the focus of the analytical treatment of labour towards its impact on utility-producing final goods for exchange between trading bodies.33 Such a view obliterated the agents of production (labour, capital and land) concept in favour of a "space of economic goods"34 where workers' services and tools were on the same level. In other words, labour was just one more economic good and was considered only in relation to its ability to produce goods that themselves produce value in use (i.e. the utility of consuming a good),35 a concept further renamed 'derived demand' in the theory of wages.36

However, before the advent of marginal productivity theories, wages were determined outside the market system, according to the concept of a 'natural wage' above a moral minimum reflecting the historical "habits and customs of the people", 37 or, as more recent literature pointed out, as a result of social and power relations.38 Conversely, the concept of marginal productivity ruled out the postMarxist theories of labour exploitation by assuming that all factors of production were paid their marginal value of use. Accordingly, labour as a factor of production was also to be remunerated according to its actual contribution to the socioeconomic system based on production and exchange of commodities.39 The argument that workers must be paid their diminishing marginal product40 was assumed not on the "interdependence between the quantity and the cost of production of a commodity produced under competitive conditions", but rather on the "change in the basis of the theory of value, from cost of production to utility".41 This is a theory of marginal productivity of labour that appears to have inspired most of the industry-driven bilateral and regional agreements regulating crossborder labour migration, as it looked at managing migratory flows in terms of diminishing marginal utility and reward of capital. The notion of utility in labour theory conveyed a further analytical alteration through its opposite, labour as disutility, or as the absence of leisure. At the theoretical level, this approach not only related the equation of labour to all other agents of production and its rewards to those of any commodity, but also led to labour being considered as a "special case of the general theory of value" to the extent that the analytical interpretation of labour dissolved into the subjective and immeasurable notion of absence of leisure.42

In the post-war decades, the theoretical basis of neoclassical revisionism (until the 1960s) and later experimental economics focused on the effects of social structures and behaviour on economic structures, thus recognising the worker as a sentient being and not just as an agent of production or utility.43 However, little analytical development was devoted to the operation of competitive labour markets, as the debate focused on the "strength and effectiveness of competition in actual labor markets".44 Therefore, it appears that this approach did not really examine labour as part of a social process, but rather hypothesized a worker outside of the social process, with instrumental rationality and preferences created outside the work environment. It is true that labour market anomalies, such as wage setting under competitive conditions, and the deviation between wages and the value of marginal product, were explained in light of the openness and indeterminacy of the employment relationship, to be cleared through the lenses of 'efficiency wages or earnings' with the function of 'motivating and retaining' labour.45 Thus, the notion of efficiency wages links to a concept of labour implying an employment relationship based on a wage-effort contract maximizing the worker's utility function (positive in wages and negative in effort).46 However, industrial relations literature points out that the determination and monitoring of effort is hard and costly to quantify,47 that workers react strategically to control by management, and that the motivation of workers is ultimately linked to issues of trust and fairness, which do not fit well with an instrumentally rational (i.e. opportunistic) worker.48 Thus, in such a labour environment where there is no social scope for workers' preferences and behaviour, the contractual employment relationship is seen merely as an optimal incentive to make the worker commit to a level of effort otherwise unrealisable.49 This approach contrasts with later research in experimental economics rejecting the notion of instrumental rationality in labour in light of an 'economics of reciprocity', implying that a simple contractual arrangement is insufficient to regulate employment.50 This theory has a significant impact on the industrial relations and labour standards spheres of legal systems fostering the collective bargaining of trade unions and the statutory protection of individual employment rights, which are driven by the social interest in protecting the employment relationship from the inherently asymmetric contractual power between employer and employee.51

The Emerging Concepts of Citizenship at Work

T.H. Marshall first introduced the concept of industrial citizenship in the aftermath of the Second World War in his famous account of the relationship between citizenship and social class.52 According to Marshall's perspective, citizenship in general refers to the membership of a national community of individuals equally enjoying civil, political and social rights. More specifically, industrial citizenship relates to employees having the equal right to engage in a variety of actions in pursuit of improved conditions of employment.53 Only a relatively small body of literature developed the concept of industrial citizenship, however, largely because it was seen as secondary to civil and social citizenship, and it could not be equated to ideas of industrial democracy.54

The above-mentioned lack of interest in developing the concept of industrial citizenship can be found in Marshall's account in the first instance. This explains much of the subsequent scholarly attitude in separating the dimensions of civil, political and social citizenship. Thus, in terms of the established framework of rights, industrial citizenship is maintained as a secondary feature at the cultural level, and an anomaly at the normative level.55 Despite the recent resurgence of legal interest in the issue of citizenship in a globalising world,56 to date, the discussion of workers' rights raised by the idea of citizenship appears to be confined to a merely aspirational rather than analytical conceptualisation.57 This normative indeterminacy can permeate citizenship with a broad (and vague) range of positive values, such as a sense of identity, inclusion, self-governance, equal membership and entitlement to rights.58 However, such indeterminacy does not help address the opposing issues of exclusion entailed in the notion of citizenship.59 Well before the effect of globalisation became visible, a vast body of literature was already able to demonstrate how, in the first place, citizenship is the outcome of political struggles,60 and consequently, its nature is often affected by racial, ethnic and gender patterns.61

Therefore, much of the work on citizenship focused on the criticism and modification of its various dimensions of inequality and exclusion.62 When structural social changes relating to globalisation and welfare state decline occurred,63 the scholarly debate about citizenship again conceptualised the related social inequalities and conflicts largely in terms of culture. This approach neglected the more specific context of industrial citizenship and its nexus with cross-border workers' mobility.64

In summary, the literature on citizenship is mainly divided between those who maintain the validity of T.H. Marshall's scheme, believing that social citizenship is all-embracing and the most desirable form of citizenship, and those who remark that such a concept of citizenship is not gender or racially neutral.

The Transnational Evolution of Normative Theories of Labour Migration

A substantial area of literature is also emerging on the global aspects of citizenship at work and migration. Moving ahead of the traditional concept of industrial citizenship, the key theoretical development underlying this study is the recent conceptualisation of "transnational labour citizenship" by J. Gordon.65 This innovative notion seeks to incorporate the role and views of civil society organisations, including those working on behalf of migrant workers' rights. By contrast to the state-centric definitions of economic/industrial citizenship outlined above, Gordon describes labour citizenship as "the status of membership in a workers' organization, and to the act of participation in the decision making processes of that organization, with the goal of improving wages, working conditions, and the dignity of work." Gordon also adds "a fourth component, identity, as participants come to identify with their organization and with their fellow 'labour citizens'".66

According to Gordon's account of transnational labour citizenship, at the present stage only union members are, in practical terms, full industrial citizens. Thus, Gordon's theory of supranational industrial citizenship conceptualises new purpose-formed unions to accommodate a constant flow of new migrants through a model that would tie immigration status to membership in organisations of transnational workers, rather than to a particular employer or a national union. These memberships would entitle migrants to transnational services, benefits and rights. The creation of multinational and multilevel labour networks would conglomerate the interests of national and cross-border workers equally.67 According to Gordon, a successful management of global labour mobility can best be achieved through the implementation of comprehensive and cooperative policies that uphold justice at work for migrants. Ensuring global labour mobility, and its full economic and human potential, is paramount in order to protect the human rights of migrants. The liberalisation of labour migration would entitle migrants to services, benefits and rights that cross borders just as the workers do, promoting transparent recruitment and employment policies essential to upholding the rights of migrant workers.68

In the area of migration and human rights, existing studies take critical perspectives on global governance of labour mobility, especially with regard to policies and regimes of temporary and guest work in relation to socio-economic development. For instance, researchers such as K. Hujo and N. Piper focus on the important issue of 'South-South migration', despite the fact that migration debates occur mostly in the context of flows from developing to developed countries.69 Other studies focus on issues from a migrant rights perspective, such as guest and temporary work programmes leading to the commodification of workers and the privatisation of migrant worker schemes. According to this perspective, such national migrant worker programmes increase the number of 'forever temporary' migrants, maintaining barriers and discrimination between guests and residents and substantially privatising immigration.70

Moreover, other studies criticise the concept of free trade agreements including provisions on labour mobility, such as deals that allow for a limited number of workers' categories into host countries on a temporary basis, prompting critics to argue that such deals merely institutionalise commodification, exploitation and international trade in workers.71

CONCLUSION

The academic development and practical viability of the research question calls for comprehensive and multi-layered responses that are based on a better understanding of the socio-economic and institutional forces at play in shaping working conditions across different industrial sectors and geographical regions. This study was intended to single out the elements necessary for a sound analytical framework for managing labour migration globally, identifying in particular multilateral and inter-state cooperation, labour market regulation and harmonisation, and effective mobilisation of all concerned social actors.

The variety of analytical treatments of the concept of labour, citizenship and migration spanned from ancient Greek philosophy through to the Scholastics and mercantilists, to the forerunners of the classical political economy, and finally to present labour economics, law and political science. Such an interdisciplinary approach challenges the traditional hypothesis of labour as a basic analytical category in which the worker is increasingly invisible, and where the price of labour is regulated through the market in a manner similar to other factors of production. The vast body of existing literature combining citizenship and migration issues suggests that a key factor driving the management of borderless labour movement schemes will be the composition of migration flows, meaning the evaluation of the timing, duration and frequency of the aggregate of individual migration projects. Also, the migrant workers' intentions regarding their plans call for a more precise interpretation at the policy making level. In fact, the circularisation of global migration patterns assigns the migrants a major role as vehicles of technological advancement and knowledge transfer, thus recognising migrant workers as investors of human capital rather than commodified agents of production.

The successful management of global labour mobility can best be achieved through the implementation of comprehensive and cooperative policies that ensure protection of the rights of migrant workers. Well-informed choices by migrants, governments, home and host communities, civil societies and the private sector can help realise the positive potential of migration in social, economic and political terms. Academic research has a crucial role in giving society directions for better management of global labour mobility through action-oriented approaches to manage labour mobility for the benefit of all. Therefore, the main challenge of further studies in this field is to understand whether, how and to what extent a soft-bordered concept of industrial citizenship can be formulated as the foundation for a new deal of labour mobility governance, with a view to harmoniously embrace economic migration in the global social contract.

In addition, there are points to be drawn from contrasting current transnational labour arrangements with guest and temporary work programmes across the world, both of which inevitably maintain barriers between guests and residents. Ultimately, there is scope to go beyond current theories of industrial citizenship to develop the conceptual premise for the establishment of postnational labour networks, conglomerating both national and cross-border workers for a complete, fair, advanced and dynamic approach to migration issues.

NOTES:

1 See Aristotle, EN1140a2 ff., Pol.1254a5 ff., found in Cartledge, P., The political economy of Greek slavery in P. Cartledge, E. E. Cohen and L. Foxhall (eds), Money, Labour and Land: Approaches to the Economies of Ancient Greece, Routledge (London, 2002) at 156–166.

2 Gilibert, G., Necessary price in Kurz, H. and N. Salvadori (eds), The Elgar Companion to Classical Economics, Edward Elgar (Cheltenham, 1998) at 166–177; see also Meikle, S., Aristotle's Economic Thought, Clarendon Press (Oxford, 1995) at 190.

3 See further on Aristotle's Book V of the Nicomachean Ethics, as commented byTheocarakis, N. J., Nicomachean ethics in political economy: The trajectory of the problem of value, in History of Economic Ideas, 14 (1), Fabrizio Serra Editore (Pisa, 2006) at 9–53

4 See for example Sadlek, G. M., Idleness Working: The Discourse of Love's Labor from Ovid Through Chaucer and Gower, Catholic University of America Press (Washington, DC., 2004) at 71; and Applebaum, H., The Concept of Work: Ancient, Medieval, and Modern, State University of New York Press (Albany, N.Y., 1992) at 93.

5 Gaius, Gaii Institutiones or Institutes of Roman Law by Gaius, with a Translation and Commentary by Poste, E., Fourth edition, Clarendon Press, (Oxford, 1904) at 167.

6 Baldwin, J. W., The medieval theories of the just price: Romanists, Canonists, and Theologians in the twelfth and thirteenth centuries, in Transactions of the American Philosophical Society (Philadelphia, 1959) at 49 (4), 74.

7 See for example Baeck, L., The Mediterranean Tradition in Economic Thought, Routledge (London, 1994) at 157; and Kaye, J., Economy and Nature in the Fourteenth Century: Money, Market Exchange, and the Emergence of Scientific Thought, Cambridge University Press (Cambridge, 1998) at 68.

8 See for example Wilson, G. W., The economics of the just price, in History of Political Economy, Duke University Press (Durham, 1975) at 7(1) 56–74; and Worland, S.T, Justum pretium: One more round in an 'endless series', in History of Political Economy, Duke University Press (Durham, 1977) at 9(4) 504–521.

9 Le Goff, J., Your Money or Your Life: Economy and Religion in the Middle Ages, Zone Books (New York, 1988) at 73.

10 Grotius, H., The Rights of War and Peace (1625), edited and with an introduction by Tuck, R., from the edition by Barbeyrac, J., Liberty Fund (Indianapolis, 2005) at ii.xii §14.

11 Carmichael, G., Supplements and Observations upon Samuel Pufendorf 's On the Duty of Man and Citizen (1724) in Moore,J. and M.Silverthorne (eds), Natural Rights on the Threshold of the Scottish Enlightenment: The Writings of Gershom Carmichael, Liberty Fund (Indianapolis, 2002) at 106.

12 See further in Meek, R. L., Studies in the Labour Theory of Value, Lawrence and Wishart, Second edition (London, 1973) at 94-107.

13 Marx, K. Theorien über den Mehrwert (Theory of revolution) vol. 26.1 in Marx-Engels, Volume IV of Das Kapital (The Capital), 1863 available at Marxist website, .

14 Locke, J., Two Treatises of Government, (1689) edited by Laslett, P., Cambridge University Press, (Cambridge, 1988) at §40-45.

15 See Meek, R. L., above n 12.

16 Petty, W., Political Arithmetick (1690)edited by Hull, C., Cambridge University Press (Cambridge, 1899) at (1) 244.

17 Tucker, J., The Elements of Commerce and Theory of Taxes (1755)in Schuyler R. L., (ed.), Josiah Tucker: A Selection from

His Economic and Political Writings, Columbia University Press (New York, 1931) at 147.

18 Franklin, B., A modest inquiry into the nature and necessity of a paper currency (1729) in Sparks, J., (ed.), The Works of Benjamin Franklin, Hilliard, Gray, and Company (Boston, 1836) at (II) 264.

19 See Galiani, F., Della moneta. Libri cinque, published anonymously by G. Raimondi editore (Naples, 1751), in Caracciolo, A. and Merola, A. Della moneta e scritti inediti, Feltrinelli (Milan, 1973) at 36.

20 Smith, A., An Inquiry into the Nature and Causes of the Wealth of Nations, (1976) in Campbell, R. H., Todd, W.B. and A.S. Skinner (eds), Glasgow Edition of the Works and Correspondence of Adam Smith (Clarendon, Oxford, 1979) at (2) I.v.2.: 47–48

21 See Smith, above n 20.

22 Ricardo, D., On the Principles of Political Economy and Taxation in Sraffa, P. and M. H. Dobb (eds), The Works and Correspondence of David Ricardo, Cambridge University Press (Cambridge, 1951) at (1) 12.

23 See further in Wood, A. W., Karl Marx, Second edition, Routledge (New York, 2004) at 16- 30.

24 Marx, K., Capital: A Critique of Political Economy. Volume I: The Process of Capitalist Production, (1867),translated by Moore, S., and E. Aveling, Charles H. Kerr and Co. (Chicago, 1909) at 197–198.

25 See Marx, K., above n 13 at 15.

26 Rubin, I. I., Essays on Marx's Theory of Value, Black-Red (Detroit, 1972 - translated from the third Russian edition, 1928), available at Marxist website <http://www.marxists.org/archive/rubin/value/index.htm> at 18.2.

27Sweezy, P. M., (ed.) Karl Marx and the Close of His System by Eugen Von Böhm-Bawerk and Böhm-Bawerk's Criticism of Marx by Rudolf Hilferding, Augustus M. Kelley (New York, 1949) at 1–118.

28 Marshall, A., Principles of Economics, Eighth edition, Macmillan (London, 1920) at (I) IV.

29 Edgeworth, F.Y., Agents of production (1894) in Palgrave's Dictionary of Political Economy, Macmillan (London, 1926) at (1) 21–22.

30 See Galiani, F., above n 19.

31 Walras, A., De la nature de la richesse et de l'origine de la valeur, Furne (Paris, 1832) at 167.

32 See Rubin, I.I., above n 26.

33See further in Jevons, W. S., The Theory of Political Economy, Third edition, Macmillan (London, 1888) at 27.

34 Menger, C., Principles of Economics, (1871) translated by Dingwall, J., and B.F. Hoselitz, Ludwig von Mises Institute, (Auburn, Alabama, 2004) available at at 57.

35 See Marshall, A., above n 28.

36 See further in Hicks, J. R.The Theory of Wages, Second edition, Macmillan (London, 1963) at 241.

37 See Ricardo, D., above n 22 at (1) 97.

38 See further in Bharadwaj, K., Wages in classical economics in Eatwell, J. et al, Cambridge University Press (Cambridge, 1987) at (4) 843–846; and Stirati, A., The Theory of Wages in Classical Economics: A Study of Adam Smith, David Ricardo and their Contemporaries (Elgar Publishing, Aldershot, UK, 1994) at 80.

39 Böhm-Bawerk, E.V., Kapital und Kapitalzins, Fourth Edition (G. Fischer, Jena, 1884 - Oxford University, 1921) at 327.

40 Lester, R. A., Shortcomings of marginal analysis for wage employment problems, American Economic Review (Pittsburgh, 1946) at 36 (1) 63–82.

41 Sraffa, P., On the relations between cost and quantity produced (1925) in Pasinetti L.L. (ed.), Italian Economic Papers, Vol. 3, Oxford University Press (Oxford, 1997) at (3) 325.

42 See Hicks, J. R., above n 36 at 1.

43 See further in Kerr, C., The social economics revisionists: The "real world" study of labor markets and institutions' in Industrial Relations, Kerr, C., and P. D. Staudohar (eds), Georgia State University - Wiley (Atlanta, 1994) at 66–108; and Dunlop J. et al, Kaufman, B. E. (ed.), How Labor Markets Work: Reflections on Theory and Practice, Lexington Books (Lexington, 1988) at 85.

44 Reynolds, L.G., The problem of relative wage rates in Reynolds, L.G., Taft C.H. and R.M. MacDonald, The Evolution of Wage Structure, Yale University Press (New Haven, 1956) at 2.

45 Marshall, A. and Marshall, P.M., The Economics of Industry, Macmillan (London, 1879) at 17.

46 Lazear, E.P., Personnel economics: Past lessons and future directions, Journal of Labor Economics, University of Chicago Press (Chicago, 1999) at 17(2), 199–236.

47 See further in Baldamus, W., Efficiency and Effort, Tavistock, (London, 1961) at 114-122.

48 See for example Fox, A., Beyond Contract: Work, Power and Trust Relations, Faber (London, 1974) at 386-408; and Hyman, R. and Brough, I., Social Values and Industrial Relations: A Study of Fairness and Inequality, Blackwell (Oxford, 1975) at 262-277.

49 Parsons, D.O., The employment relationship: Job attachment, work effort, and the nature of contracts, in O.C. Ashenfelter and R.Layard (eds), Handbook of Labor Economics, NorthHolland (Amsterdam, 1986) at 789–848.

50 See further in Fehr, E. and Gächter, S., Fairness and retaliation: The economics of reciprocity, Journal of Economic Perspectives (Pittsburgh, 2000) at 14 (3), 159–181.

51 Brown, W. A., Industrial relations and the economy in Floud, R. and P. A. Johnson (eds), The Cambridge Economic History of Modern Britain, Volume 3: Structural Change and Growth, 1939–2000, Cambridge University Press (Cambridge, 2004) at 400.

52 See Marshall, T.H., Citizenship and Social Class, Cambridge University Press (Cambridge, 1950) at I (1-85).

53 See Marshall, T.H., above n 52, at 114.

54 Amongst the few commentators on industrial citizenship see: Barbalet, J.M., Citizenship Rights, Struggle and Class Inequality, University Minnesota Press (Minneapolis, 1988) at 22- 7; Gersuny, C., Industrial Rights: A Neglected Facet of

Citizenship Theory, in Economic and Industrial Democracy, SAGE Publication (Uppsala University, Sweden, 1994) at Vol. 15, No. 2: 211-26; Muller-Jentsch, W., Productive Forces and Industrial Citizenship: An Evolutionary Perspective on Labour Relations, in Economic and Industrial Democracy, SAGE Publication (Uppsala University, Sweden, 1996) at Vol. 12, No. 4: 439-467; Streeck, W., Industrial citizenship under regime competition: the case of European works councils, in Journal of European Public Policy, Routledge (London, 1997) at Vol. 4,4: 643-64; Woodiwiss, A., Behind Governmentality: Sociological Theory, Pacific Capitalism and Industrial Citizenship, in Citizenship Studies, Routledge (London, 1997) at Vol. 1,1: 87-114.

55 See Marshall, T.H., above n 52, at 14.

56 For example see: Bosniak, L., Critical Reflections on 'Citizenship' as a Progressive Aspiration, in Labour Law in an Era of Globalization: Transformative Practices and Possibilities, J. Conaghan, M. Fischl, and K. Klare, eds., Oxford University Press (Oxford, 2002) at 339–349.

57 For example see: McCallum, R., Collective labour law, citizenship and the future, Melbourne University Law Review (Melbourne, 1998) at 22:(1) 42-61.

58 On the inclusive meaning of citizenship for migrants, see for instance: Barbalet, J.M., above n 54, at 99.

59 Lister, R., Inclusion/Exclusion: The Janus Face of Citizenship, in Towards a Gendered Political Economy, J. Cook, J. Roberts, and G. Waylen, eds., MacMillan (Houndsmills, Baskingstoke, UK, 2000) at 98-120.

60 Turner, B., Contemporary Problems in the Theory of Citizenship, in Citizenship and Social Theory, B. Turner, ed., SAGE Publications (London, 1993) at 1-18.

61 For example see: Baines, D., and N.Sharma, Migrant Workers as Non-Citizens: The Case Against Citizenship as a Social Policy Concept in Studies in Political Economy, Carleton University (Ottawa, 2002) at 69.75-108; and Orloff, A.S., Gender and the Social Rights of Citizenship: The Comparative Analysis of Gender Relations, American Sociological Review, SAGE Publication (Thousand Oaks, CA, USA, 1993) at 58(3), 303–328.

62 See for example: Isin E.F., and P.K.Wood, Citizenship and Identity, SAGE Publications (London, 1999) at 1-24; Nash, K., Contemporary Political Sociology: Globalization, Politics, and Power, Blackwell (Oxford, 2000) at 4:131-192; Sypnowich, C., The Culture of Citizenship, in Politics and Society, N.Stevenson ed., SAGE Publications (London, 2001) at Vol 28, 4 (2000), 531-555.

63 See further the discussion of "The rise and fall of the welfare state for migrants" in chapter 3.9.

64 See Roche, M., Rethinking Citizenship: Welfare, Ideology and Change in Modern Society, Polity Press (Cambridge, MA 1992) at 26; Delanty, G., Citizenship in a global age: Society, culture, politics, Open University Press (London, 2000) at 79-92; Glenn, E., Citizenship and Inequality: Historical and Global Perspectives, in Social Problems, University of California Press, (Berkeley, 2000) at Vol. 47, No. 1: 1-20; Urry, J., Sociology Beyond Societies: mobilities for the twenty-first century, Routledge, (London, 2000) at 7:161-187.

65 Gordon, J., Transnational Labour Citizenship, Southern California Law Review, (Los Angeles, 2007) at Volume 80 pp.503-587.

66 See Gordon, J., above n 65, at 510-511.

67 See Gordon, J., above n 65, at 578.

68 See Gordon, J., above n 65, at 561-578.

69 Hujo, K. and Piper, N. (eds), South-South Migration – Implications for Social Policy and Development, Palgrave Macmillan (London, 2010) at 8-15.

70 Grugel, J. and Piper, N., Critical Perspectives on Global Governance: Rights and Regulation in Governing Regimes, Routledge (London, 2007) at 3:41-64; furthermore, this strand of literature may be linked to seminal work framing the discourse on the international governance of migration in terms of reclaiming State's sovereignty, rather than ceding it, see for instance: Newman, K., The governance of international migration: mechanisms,processes and institutions, Migration Policy Institute, Global Commission on International Migration (Geneva, 2005) at 17.

71 See in particular Chi, X., Challenging Managed Temporary Labor Migration as a Model for Rights and Development for Labor-Sending Countries, New York University Journal of International Law and Politics (New York, 2008) at 40(2): 497-540.

CHAPTER 18

HOW WOMEN WORK: THE SYMBOLIC AND MATERIAL REPRODUCTION OF MIGRANT LABOR CAMPS IN UNITED STATES AGRIBUSINESS

Robert CARLEY, Hilario MOLINA II

Keywords: Labor, immigration, capitalism, agriculture, women, exploitation, gender theory, significant symbols

INTRODUCTION

A good part of the cultural and social norms of the United States were founded, in no large part, through the cultivation and the expansion of agriculture. For example, the Civil War was a conflict over the issue of cheap labor between the plantation states in the southern part of the United States and emerging industries in the north (Silberman, 2003). Generations of African Americans enslaved in the southern United States experienced exploitation and cruel working and living conditions well after the end of the Civil War. Given the racial ideology in America during this time, their maltreatment simply didn't register at the level of either general worker's concerns or a larger public moral sentiment. However, during the Great Depression and mass migration of "Okies" and "Arkies" to California's agricultural sector resulted in general public outrage. The mistreatment of White workers by foreman and farmers along with the sub-standard living and working conditions of these White Americans was popularly portrayed in John Steinbeck's novel Grapes of Wrath published in 1940. When the United States was young, Mexican labor was also responsible for a good deal of agricultural production in what now comprises the southwestern United States; now, the migration of Whites and African Americans into the farmwork sector has been replaced by Mexican and Mexican American labor (Gonzalez, 2000). These migrant farm workers find themselves in working and living conditions similar to their predecessors. Farmers have a vested interest in the maintenance of a mass-migrant system of labor because it permits them to exploit farm workers while maintaining high profits and without the additional need to regularly invest in new technology. Given the history of labor exploitation within this industry, why has there not been mass sustained labor unrest? The most likely explanation is that the agricultural industry encourages patrimonial authority to flourish within the migrant farm worker communities—labor camps.

DIFFERENCES FROM MIGRATION AND LABOR LITERATURE

Previous studies on migrant labor focus on economic relations even where gender is a salient variable (Donato et al., 2006; Hondagneu-Sotelo, 1994, 2001, 2003a, 2003b; Mahler and Pessar, 2001b; Pessar and Mahler, 2003) or they focus on the migrant experiences of specific ethnic-national groups (Castellanos and Boehm 2008; Boehm 2008; Karjanen 2008; Castellanos 2008; Seif 2008). Our analysis looks at migrant labor, in the context of a single labor camp (where ethnicnationalities are multiple but linguistic communities are shared) from a cultural, communal, symbolic perspective. We also consider the role of economics as the primary context that comprises the social formation of the camp. Our theoretical focus is oriented around:

Citation: Robert CARLEY, Hilario MOLINA II, How Women Work: The Symbolic and Material Reproduction of Migrant Labor Camps in United States Agribusiness, ISSN: 1843-5610.

1. Gender formation: In our work women are seen as agents of the social structure and not as ancillary to it. We view the role of women as central to maintaining the authority structure in the camp.
2. Theory of power/authority: Our analysis expands the definition of power beyond the social and economic structure to encompass culture and cultural meaning through symbolic interaction. In doing so, we explain how power works within the context of the camp and to the advantage of the farmer/owner who employs the camp as an aggregate labor force.
3. Level of analysis/empirical focus: We focus our analysis at the level of the camp and not "labor force" and are able, then, to understand labor at a cultural and communal level not, exclusively, as a capital-labor relation. Our theoretical focus is on ethnic identity, custom/tradition, language and symbols and interaction.

The un-evenness of capital labor relations provide a descriptive context and are discussed in detail in the theoretical overview section Our theoretical perspective (discussed in the section subsequent to the "theoretical overview" and entitled "theoretical orientation") is, in many ways, unique to this literature. It relies, primarily, on symbolic-interactionism, but also includes other feminist-based theoretical approaches that discuss symbols and power. The total theoretical framework links culture, tradition and symbols to gender and power, specifically gender and the analysis of micro-power (Mead 1932/1962; Douglas 1966; Dalla Costa 1973; Irigaray 1977; Weber 1978; Hartman 1981; Kristeva 1982; Butler 1990; Rubin 1997). In the following two sections we discuss or theoretical framework in detail.

THEORETICAL OVERVIEW

In Economy and Society (1978) Max Weber describes the traditional authority of patrimonial system as having the capacity to preserve legitimate degrees of authority within a given community. Through traditional authority migrant farm workers are kept in a subordinate position; they "freely" subsume themselves under the total authority of the farmer and the institution. As a result, the farmer's pursuit for profit in the United States enables him to have a "handsoff" approach with regard to the management of migrant farm worker communities. Contained within the patrimonial system, families exercise authority though a patriarchal structure, in this case ironically, within a larger society that advocates gender equality.

The socio-economic structure of small farms depends upon the capitallabor relation and, hence, the exploitation of labor and extraction of surplus value can be understood as a legitimate and automatic form of systemic authority. This authority structure is not visible but, rather, a given aspect of the social structure that limits choice within its own terms (Przworski 1985). Labor exploitation has a pervasive structural presence that is legal and economic; it resides within the very foundation of modern civil society. The extraction of surplus value from labor is a right to those who employ labor power and that surplus is converted into profit. Profit represents the difference between costs, including labor, and earnings. According to Karl Marx, capitalist institutions profit from the economy at a greater degree by investing in variable over fixed or constant capital at the beginning of a production cycle. This changes with investment, capital concentration and centralization however, in the context of this study, investment is largely represented in investment in labor power alone. As a result, when variable capital is higher than fixed capital, more value is produced and, by extension, a greater potentiality for profit (Marx, 1970: 209). Over time, this process becomes more complex. The question remains, why would capitalists seek to introduce new technologies into the production process if it would, ultimately, result in—on the one hand—greater input expenditures and—on the other hand—a lower rate of profit on capital invested?

Marx discusses this issue further in Chapters 8 and 25 of Capital. In short, producers revolutionize their means of production, within a given branch of production, in the interest of competing for ever-greater shares of a particular market. Producers often gain the lion-share of profit by introducing a new product onto the market. However, over time, when the use of this new innovation in production becomes available to other producers, the average rate of profit declines. Furthermore, and most importantly, the introduction of this new product and the concomitant productive technologies forces innovation on the part of other producers with the compounded threat of overall success to an individual producers business. And, finally, Marx points out that while the average rate of profit on capital invested at the beginning of production cycles within a given branch of production may decline, the volume of profit in the economy will increase since it is the case that more output can be produced and sold in a given period, using new technology. However, in the context of this study, the camps were either subsidiary producers for larger agribusiness or small-scale "petitebourgeoisie" farming enterprises that relied upon a large-scale, cheap, and compliant labor force. In other words, agribusiness allows for certain sectors of production to innovate while others may be profitable, in a "primitive" sense, by exploiting cheap labor through certain tasks: e.g. picking and packing. Hence, in this case, labor power represents the primary means of investment, on the one hand, but also it is the primary function of people in the camps and, hence, it is also the primary social factor in this study.

Since the majority of the migrant farm workers are first generation immigrants, a patrimonial authority structure does not seem as unfamiliar as the language or customs of the host society. Therefore, a patrimonial system permits migrant farm worker men to govern the affairs of the family in the camp. Through patrimonial authority the traditional norms govern the affairs of the community. Men assume a position of authority while women are subsumed beneath male authority (patrimonialism). Thus, the fact that men have power over the affairs of the family reinforces the status quo within the labor camps and facilitates the structure of profit and production. Patrimonial authority functions like a frame, delimiting the norms and values that are then reproduced within the second generation of migrant farm workers through significant symbols. It allows the camp to maintain an endogenous set of social relations and, as a result, it facilitates the capital-labor relation since the latter requires little or no "alien" social control in the form of labor rationalization. In short people work because the society of the camp works for them. Although other theories about economic power and social structure regarding agricultural labor, generally, have been advanced in other similar studies (Shaffner 1995; Bardhan, 1991a; Bardhan,

1991b; Bardhan, 1983) the dimensions, focus, and deployment of our theory differs significantly.

THEORETICAL ORIENTATION

At the macro-sociological level, the mode of production (capitalist, agriculture) confers upon our theoretical framework determinate social relations which explain the presence of the camp, this material configuration of socially necessary labor, the role of the capitalist, etc. At the meso-sociological level, the structure of patrimonial authority explains the normative moral totality of the social structure—it is an 'idea type' and, as such, a frozen abstraction. At the microsociological level—which is the focus of this paper—we explain the reproduction of the social structure through Mead's discussion of symbolic structures and significant symbols (1932/1966) as well as the role that symbolic violence plays in maintaining patrimonial authority (Douglas 1966; Dalla Costa 1973; Irigaray 1977; Hartman 1981; Kristeva 1982; Butler 1990; Rubin 1997).

Significant symbols are instrumental in the development and the "moral" or normative maintenance of the individual and their connection to the general community. Indeed, significant symbols enable the individual to learn how to communicate with other members of the group while simultaneously conveying the customs of the group (Mead 1932/1966). The locus and the primary distributive mechanism of significant symbols remain women, specifically mothers or matrons (women can serve in this latter social role whether or not they have any biological children or, if their children are now adult and mostly autonomous). This burden, relegated to gender roles, is described in second wave feminist literature, specifically through the work of Lacanian oriented theorists (Irigaray 1977; Kristeva 1982; Butler 1990; Rubin 1997). Lacanian oriented feminist theory locates patrimonial authority structures within the "symbolic" which is configured or presided over by the phallus: a master-code of authority structures in the names, and their associated kin-meanings (Rubin 1997). Whereas patrimonial authority represents an "ideal type" the phallus, like the patrimonial authority structure, is a static and abstract conceptual category that confers law—a symbolic structure or frame, border, or boundary—upon the process of identity construction or, in the language of Lacanian theory, "subjectivity." The primacy of this law is to differentiate men from women in such a way that the man is dominant due to his access to the phallus and hence to the law itself; this renders these boundaries "natural" (Douglas 1966; Kristeva 1982; Rubin 1997: 47). In this sense, the earlier statement that through patrimonial authority men's social role is to frame the structure of values and norms—delimiting the nature of the reproduction of the system itself—is entirely commensurable with the Lacanian feminist theoretical orientation. As such, women are "responsible" for producing and maintaining symbolic content limited, in situ, by the patrimonial authority structure or phallic law (i.e. phallogocentrism).

The relationship between our theory and data leads to the following analysis: We examine how significant symbols have produced a system of endogenous (socially symbolic) consciousness within the patrimonial system of the migrant labor camps; a system which doubly exploits women, first in their responsibilities to rear children through symbolic content and second through the labor they provide in the sphere of the camp and family. Their double exploitation contributes to the preservation of the societal status quo whereby the needs of women are subordinated to those of their families. What follows is an investigation into the roles of women in the camp through our deployment of Mead's symbolic theory of social situations.

ARGUMENT

Farmers do not worry about labor resistance because the patrimonial system endogenous to the camp ensures a beneficial capital-labor relation. The data demonstrates that one farmer may preside over several camps but the boundaries between the camps are more than geographic. Within a single camp shared linguistic, religious, or cultural symbols (or all three, simultaneously) form a normative strata (i.e. a single camp may contain Mexicans, or Mexicans and Guatamalans, or Hatians but not Mexicans and Hatians). But, more significantly, the endogenous patrimonial authority structure also ensures the removal of individuals who may threaten it. In other words, the endogenous authority structure not only forms a compliant relationship between capital and labor but it has its own internal mechanisms to reproduce a compliant relationship within the camp itself through either language, religion, culture, tradition, or some combination of these factors. In the camps workers organize authority structures in a patrimonial fashion, i.e. around a "head of household." A traditional familial structure is reproduced, willy-nilly, in the camps. Anyone who does not abide by the endogenous authority structure is pushed out by means of negative sanctions. Furthermore, as sanctioned workers are being pushed out of the camp new, first generation, immigrants are entering the labor camps. In other words the endogenous authority structure within the camp, which is expressed through forms of symbolic exchange, renews the labor side of the capital-labor relation: new immigrant farm workers replace those who are exiting. Also, this enables the camp to preserve the traditional authority structure the farmer/owner is sated with a new labor force. Sanctions which ensure the exclusive nature of patrimonial authority within the camps are, at the same time, examples of strong social cohesion, communal authority and identity. This general theory of the social and economic structure of migrant labor is supported by more quantitative analyses of Mexican labor in the U.S. agricultural sector (US Dept. of Labor, 2005; Martin, 2002).

Structure of the Paper

The following section provides detailed ethnographic accounts of the symbolic and cultural mechanisms that reproduce the circuitry of subjection and exploitation. One of the most basic and salient examples of gender identity and visibility comes from Tom Conover's book Coyotes (1987). As Conover is initially greeted by members of the community he studies he states that he, "...glanced toward the women, expected them, too, to be introduced, but it was not to be...when the men had the floor, women were silent" (173). In addition, this paper will also describe the ways in which women work, how they provide economic wealth for families by either working alongside of their spouse, by cooking for the single men in the camp, or by selling home-made food, such as elotes (corn on the cob). Through negotiations and the creation of small, yet effective, businesses within the camp women have been able to address men on a more equal basis, despite the persistence of a negative social stigma regarding women, gender, and autonomy.

In the following sections (the literature review, methodology, field research, discussion and conclusion) we discuss others' ethnographic contribution to the literature on gender formation, exploitation, and capitalism—especially central contributions from Chicana feminism. Our methodological claims our based in the information collected by observing the daily interaction of migrant farm works in three labor camps in North Carolina. The fieldwork section provides a descriptive and narrative analysis of central events in the context of the labor camps: episodes that demonstrate how gender identity issues from out of symbolic, non-material, cultural forms. This paper ends with a discussion of the findings and a conclusion section that makes suggestions for future theoretical contributions.

LITERATURE REVIEW

The structure of the migrant farm worker culture is such that it places the values and the needs of the family above the needs of the woman (Segura 1978; Cromie 1987). For migrant farm workers, North American culture is alien to their family structure, because of the particularities through which it advocates specific values/norms of achievement and independence. North American norms do enter the camps through second-generation, younger, laborers who have entered the U.S. public schooling system. Regardless, these values situate the husband-father as the exclusive authoritative breadwinner and view women as a submissive wifemother who cares for the home and rears the children (Zavella 1987). Gloria Anzaldúa discusses the consequences of deviating from these norms:

...I heard mothers and mothers-in-law tell their sons to beat their wives for not obeying them, for being hociconas (big mouths), for being callerjeras (going to visit and gossip with neighbors), for expecting their husbands to help with the rearing of children and the house work... (38).

Women in a migrant farm worker community are expected to comply with beliefs that support the patrimonial structure. They assume the role of a "good woman" Violators, as Anzaldúa points out, are sanctioned through symbolic (if not through the suggestion or administration of real) violence. As a result, the migrant farm worker woman is trapped in a torrent of values; a combination emerging from out of both the host culture and native culture. A mediation of sorts is witnessed in the development of a middle ground where the woman is allowed to work but does not have the authority to question her husband's decisions (Thompson 1985). For example, if the husband's wage is insufficient to meet the families' expenses, then the woman is encouraged to contribute to the family income by working too. Yet, the woman still remains primarily responsible for the care of the family and the home (Thompson 1985; Cobas 1987).

While it remains beyond question that the women can perform the same complicated work as their male counterparts, the social recognition, prestige, or "social capital" gained by men for completing this work is absent from women's' contributions to the migrant farm worker culture. This is demonstrated by Villaseñor (1991) who recorded an interaction between two young migrant farm workers. The young woman was helping her mother with the dishing after a day in the work field:

...the young girl, Lydia, who was a senior in high school and not much of a good student, said, 'Please, tell me one thing before you go.' Roberto stopped. She brushed back her hair with the back of her hand. Her hand was still covered in white wet suds...He had not really noticed this girl all evening. She was still in boots and pants and long-sleeve shirt. She looked more like a boy than a girl... (194).

Thus, the division of labor, especially at the site of the household, exposes a bias toward migrant farm worker women. The value of done by is of diminutive value compared to the work performed by men (Segura 1978). Anthony Giddens (1971) also notes that socialistic and moralistic distinctions are instrumental to establishing and maintaining the value of one's labor (i.e. labor differentiation in specific contexts). Moral individualism is contextual; it describes an individual's understanding of right and wrong within, in this case, the migrant farm worker community. One's moral understanding is limited by what the patrimonial culture defines acceptable or unacceptable. Therefore, in situation of production, the division of labor in the workplace mirrors the relegation domestic tasks, where women perform tasks similar in complexity to those at home. In case of Lydia and Roberto, Lydia performed her domestic chores dressed as a boy. Since she contradicted Roberto's understanding of gender and attire (i.e. gender and representation) Roberto overlooked her.

The feminization of labor cuts both ways. Men apply this moral individualism to the division of labor when assigning themselves tasks in an industrial or post-industrial context. For example, Carmen Ramos Escandón notes, "...of the distribution of labor between men and women...men claimed exclusive use of new device, relegating women...to other activities..." (74). Therefore, in the migrant farm worker community, a man will, if given the opportunity to learn, operate the heavy equipment, such as a tractor, and a woman will perform the least skilled job, hand picking the crop.

Although women are limited in their capacity to question the decision making process of their husbands they are, however, encouraged to provide means to assist in meeting family expenses. This contradiction is mitigated by relationships which they develop within the enclave of the migrant farm worker community. Since the capacity to provide significant surplus assistance is embedded in a gendered network of social relations within the women's enclave, the men need not acknowledge it as a legitimate contribution. Moreover, women who work must find the means to mitigate negative social stigmas to which they inadvertently expose themselves as they contribute to the family (Reitz and Sklar 1997). This somewhat tenuous relationship has its effects on young, first generation, girls in the camp who are establishing their identities as workers and semi-autonomous members of the family. According to George Herbert Mead ([1932]1962) the development of the self starts to take shape as the individual begins to develop a socialized identity. He states the following:

What goes to make up the organized self is the organization of the attitudes which are common to the group. A person is a personality because he belongs to a community, because he takes over the institutions of that community into his own conduct (162).

The development of the self occurs through role playing with others. Girls, then, learn roles through significant symbols by, for instance, partaking in social rituals described, by Mead, as "stages." Mead refers to these stages as play and games. In the play stage, based in imitation or mimesis, the girl plays at "being" a mother, often through the repetition of activities, while in the game stage she learns not only the role of her mother but also more complex levels of social interaction between her mother, father, and everyone in the orbit of the community. In these instances, the development of "the" self is, in actuality, the development of "a" cultural self; imbedded within the development are the cultural values that define, implicitly, what a self is within the boundaries of a specific cultural form.

This ability to understand the relations between the self and the community is referred to, by Mead, as the generalized other. Given the patrimonial frame, the girl learns, implicitly, to accept a subordinated role. Internalizing these norms is a kind of passive and mimetic learning. By imitating the activities of their gender peers, they learn to accept the commands of their male siblings and father (Vold Bernard & Snipes 1998; Mead 1962). The young girl learns skills that would be applied, in later years, to the role of wife and mother. She also learns that the men do not assist in the daily duties of the house. The men must maintain a traditional machismo, in the presence of his peers, and that gender role does not include housework or childcare tasks (Hawks & Taylor 1975; Zavella 1987).

A negative effect produced through patrimonial authority is that it fails to confer social capital on women. Social capital requires the recognition of an individual's financial contribution to both the household and the community. There are social rewards that are visible within the migrant farm worker community, such as the title of "Don" (Mr.) and Doña (Mrs.). However, the title Don, which confers prestige upon the husband (and which can be gained through the recognition of services provided by his wife to the community), the word Doña merely signifies that a woman, in the migrant farm worker community, is married to a Don (Light, Sabagh, Bozorgmehr, & Der-Martirosian, 1994). When a woman is addressed as Doña, that honor is based on the recognition of her husband's social capital, not hers.

METHODOLOGY

The evidence comes from observing approximately 25 females (children, young adults, and married women) in three major migrant farm labor camps in North Carolina. In the summer of 2004, for a duration of six weeks (spending two weeks in each camp), one of the researchers lived, slept, ate, and worked in a migrant farm worker community. The majority of the women in this study consist of first and second generation immigrants. Regarding the issue of language, mothers only spoke Spanish while non-mothers (women over the age of fifteen) spoke both Spanish and English.

Thus, we feel confident that those women who only spoke Spanish were first generation immigrants and the "non-mothers," who spoke both languages, were second generation immigrants (Portes 1995). Regardless of age, women spoke Spanish with members of their family and with camp community members. Yet, there were times they spoke English to people of their own age. The prevalence of English speaking could be credited to states' educational laws requiring all children to attend school if they are of the rightful age during the regular school year. As a result, for these children, their lives consist of two different worlds. In the morning, they worked in a school environment; in the evening, they worked alongside their families until sunset.

With regard to the interviews, most of the field notes presented in this study consist of conversations that occurred in the presence of the researcher conducting the ethnography or they were comments addressed to the researcher without him initiating the conversation. This situation was conducive to the time frame of the harvest and the patience of the contact (gatekeeper) in North Carolina as well as the bureaucracy of the Internal Review Board (IRB). As such, an official patterned questionnaire was not developed (Molina, 2004). As a result, the author conducting the ethnography was unable to ask questions because it would have been required of him to develop, in advance, an approved IRB questionnaire. The dilemma introduced through this approach could be referred to as a "come as you are" style of social encounters. However, since there was no prior knowledge as to what would be an appropriate question to ask (i.e. questionnaire-based interaction), the study would have been limited to patterned questions. Also, anything else not mentioned, questions which would have been found important while conducting the field study, could not have been used in the study because it would have violated the agreement with the IRB.

While this might seem to be an obstacle, the nuance of the life-style within each of these communities was grasped through participant observation and conversation as well as reliance upon Mead's theory of significant symbols as the means of communication: e.g. body language, gestures, and speech. Furthermore, we believe that the forced adoption of a first person account may have spared us from a well-recognized tendency among ethnographers to provide accounts based on particularities which might raise doubts about the validity of these accounts (Geertz 1983; Shokeid 1997).

Field Research

As mentioned above, significant symbols provide a social control mechanism through which migrant farm worker women are configured within a nexus of exploitation. In addition, symbols manifest learned behavioral patterns through interaction with elder women peers, such as mothers, grandmothers, or extend relatives (aunts). Significant symbols are renewed when a girl learns to clean, cook, and learns other skills which will form the basis of domestic responsibilities. For example one morning, in Camp B's kitchen a conversation, between older women, and younger girls, took place. This discussion provides an example of how women reinforce domestic responsibilities. We describe the event below:

Lying in a room surrounded by thin plywood, I hear the sounds of pans and female voices coming from the kitchen (which is located at the end of the single men's sleeping area). I try to return to my sleep, but I wonder about the conversation taking place in the kitchen. Everyday is the same thing. For them, the day starts before the break of dawn while the rest of the camp is still asleep. At times, one hears children's voices—girls, most of the time, from the kitchen. Sometimes, the adult's voice says, "no, do not play with the pan that way; if you want to play with the pan, then use it the right way. "Esa es mija (that is my daughter)," the mother says when the daughter does something well. The child's laugher echoes through the rooms.

In this case, the girl learns that a pan has a specific use and purpose. When the child plays with the pan correctly, she is praised by her mother. Hence, play has both putative and confirmatory aspects, the effect of which is to strengthen the mother and daughter bond. For the child, the activity becomes associated with a positive experience and, later in life, she may associate knowing how to cook with an affirmative learning relationship. Through the play stage, the child begins to develop a concept of self that will later provide positive association between playing with pans and becoming the wife of a domestic farm worker.

Women not only cook for their family they often cook for the single men in the camp as well. Women can receive a regular fee for providing breakfast, lunch, and/or dinner to the single men in the camp. This fare is similar to what she might provide to her own family which, most of the time, consists of eggs, beans, flowertortillas, rice and, when available, meat. The services of wives are offered up at the discretion of her husband. For example, this service was offered to me while I moved from one cucumber field to another:

I was approached by one of the married men in the camp and, in a proud and ostentatious manner, he told me that his wife could cook breakfast, lunch, and dinner, five days a week, for a fee of $40. We were in the back of the crew leader's pickup when he made me the offer. I was confused at the offer since, most of the time that I'm on the bus, I noticed that his wife never speaks with anyone or makes eye contact with any of the other males in the camp. Now he, seated next to me, is smiling and eagerly awaiting my reply to a prospective agreement in which, I assumed, his wife had no say. Seeing that I was going to decline his offer he augmented his sales pitch, "My wife is a good cook; if you do not believe me, ask some of the men in the camp, she cooks for them too," he said in an excited tone of voice.

This represents a typical business transaction between married men and single men whereby the object mediating the interaction is the women's skill; the woman is present through an invocation of her skill but physically and symbolically absent. In the presence of women, the interaction between married and single men is altered when boarding and disembarking from the work bus but this social principle remains salient: there is no direct interaction between the migrant farm worker women and the single males. For example, every morning while boarding the bus, buenos dias (good mornings), are exchanged among those getting on and those already seated. The majority of the time, greetings are made exclusively to family men by women; either husbands or eldest sons.

Women do not interact with the single men in the camp. Husbands reserve the privilege of negotiation with other men because any interaction between single men and women is considered shameful and disrespectful to the family. In some instances preceding a business transaction the husband will seek out the approval of the wife. He may, for instance, ask her if she could handle an extra client before advertising his wife's services as a cook. For the husband, there is nothing worse then making an agreement with another man having, only later, to renege. Subsequent to the offer made to me I was told of such an incident which had occurred in the camp before my arrival. The other men in the camp referred to this married man as mandilon (a slang word for a submissive husband) because the wife told him that it was not okay for her to cook for another man despite him having made the agreement in advance.

The symbolic exchange that takes place as men are greeted by the women on the bus bears further discussion. Contained within this interaction is a gendered policing function. Its purpose is to insure that boundaries are not being violated. The demonstration of symbolic exchange produces a tacit enforcement and communal harmony. The communal, daily, and almost ritualistic interactions around the bus represent a microcosm where Mead's concept of the generalized other functions in such a way—as a kind of ritualistic repetition—to maintain harmony in the migrant farm worker community. The men, every morning, are obliged to place themselves in the shoes of one another. This "me," which, according to Mead, consist of the unit of all the men present, is advanced towards the women present. On the bus, men protect and insure that another man will neither violate nor overstep a boundary. This would include a man doing the same thing to the women of his household (mother and/or sisters) and, as such, represents a "frame maintenance" principle which is not habitual but requires the care to recognize and not transgress boundaries established within the given context.

This literal daily departure of the men from the domestic sphere confers a set of behavioral patterns upon the boy which are further magnified through the play stage. This crucial daily event highlights a social fact: that mom and dad do not share the same daily routines and responsibilities. These behavioral patterns become solidified in the game stage. Here, the young boy views manhood as the responsibility to work, protect his family, and serve as the authoritative figure in the household. Through a negation (the absence of certain responsibilities from men's lives) it is understood that cooking, cleaning, and washing are all the responsibilities of wives and sisters. Again, in a negative form, boys learn from their parents that daily duties of the household must not involve assisting women. The positive content of this negation results in maintaining traditional machismo in front of peers. Walking to toward the restroom after hard days work in the field we disclose an event which further illustrates this point: this incident took place in the wash area next to the male restroom:

The sun is setting after a hard day's work in the field, as the women move clothes up and down a washboard in a rubbing motion; they splash water all over the walls and the floor. The lack of sunlight creates puddles, which in turn become nesting grounds for mosquitoes and other insects. These damp conditions draw out mosquitoes. In the distance, one can hear the sound of hands slapping flesh as women try to kill the insects which interfere with their daily obligations. Refusing to quit, they endure the annoying insects. However, the crying children make them stop: a sign that the mosquitoes have become too much to endure; the women call it quits. However, now the wash for the next day has increased to include the unfinished wash from the previous day.

As some women excuse themselves, the other children stay close to the more persistent mothers. Now the mosquitoes swarm around them—placing them in an uncomfortable situation. The children pull on their mother for comfort and support as the mosquitoes gnaw at the smaller group. The scene intensifies as the children tug, more and more, at their mother's clothes and the mother tries gracefully to comfort the child and wash clothes at the same time. Some mothers ignore the crying children and attempt, hastily, to finish the wash because the women know that the longer it takes them to finish, the longer their children have to suffer. The men know what is happing but they do nothing. In one case a frustrated woman yells to nearest child, "Go tell your father to come and get your little brother".

The child returns within minutes and behind her appears the father. He walks slowly as if he had all the time in the world. He looks at his wife and says, "Are you almost finished? I'm hungry and so are the children." He picks up the child and walks away. The woman returns to the wash. The other women do not speak.

Often women spend a hot summer's day doing some form of agricultural work with the rest of the men however, their evenings also consist of washing and cooking for their families while the men socialize and rest. M. Melville, the author of Mexicans at Work in the United (1988), notes that women have a "double day" of work in the field and in the house hold while their labor, seen only as a second income, (extra money) is not considered to be of equal importance. This valuation of women's work is also evident in the example given above. This fragment from the ethnographic record raises other important issues. The child observes, through interactions between the mother and the father, that his father does not help with the housekeeping, that he can freely express his desires (e.g. to be fed, through a demand for gratification) and, finally, that other women present do not interject—they continue to wash in silence. A male child may seek the protection of his mother but he also notices that his presence is not reflected in the washroom. Exchanges of this sort are instrumental in enframing the future development of the self. What follows is an observation of a similar situation:

It is Sunday and I am seated outside of the wooden dormitory nursing my wounds from the previous day. A few yards away, four little girls are playing and laughing among themselves. They are not running around the campsite like the boys their age but, rather, are seated on the wild green grass, near their sleeping area, and they remain within view of their mothers who, like each previous evening, cook in the kitchen.

From within the kitchen, a small boy walks toward the girls playing on the grass. The other boys are running in circles near the girls. Each step this boy takes is firm; sure. He pays no attention to the other boys who, by this time, have motioned their hands in every way to get his attention. Several times, the boys call-out to him "vente a jugar" (come play). This boy is not easily distracted by the screaming of the other kids as they try to get his attention. I would guess that he is either seven or eight. His focus remains on the group of girls playing in the grass.

He stands over one of the girls who is seated, legs crossed, on the grass. As he stands there, the other three girls stop smiling and conversing with each other. Standing over the girl he tells her, "Mom wants you to help her in the kitchen." The other girls do not protest her departure. As she and follows her brother toward the kitchen, she pushes him in a playful manner. He immediately he turns to face her. His face is unmoved by the playful gesture, and he looks up to meet the eyes of his hermana (sister). He stands there motionless until she breaks eye contact. The fun ends abruptly and the smile slowly vanishes from the girl's face. He stands even more erect and proceeds to walk, while his sister drops her eyes to the ground. At a silent pace, they walk toward the kitchen, him leading and her quietly following.

This story addresses several things but most specifically it illustrates the authority that was bestowed upon the male child by either the mother or the father. To the extent that this authority trumped the other social activities of his sister he takes the role of a responsible adult. Thus, he ignores invitations to play because in that particular moment he is not a child but rather a male adult who has been given the responsibility to get his sister. In reaction to his presence, his sister fails to intervene in his authority and is acquiescent to his wishes. Her brother's reaction to her pushing him—a playful attempt to subvert his authority— simultaneously exposes and re-inscribes the patriarchal frame. She, then, identifies with and understands the message her brother is conveying with his facial expression or gesture. The sister encounters authority "in raw form" the younger male sibling is supported by an authoritative frame. Her brother's invocation of authority denies any possibility of revolt; a revolt against her parents—and the patrimonial authority. In this case, the boy is cognizant of receiving these privileges and acts in such a way that he may be permitted more "male" responsibilities.

These symbols reinforce or renew social boundaries for the actors in the community which requires the social control of women. Individuals who attempt to brake or who accidentally violate these boundaries are bombarded with negative sanctions. The sanctions come from members of the community who share the patrimonial system with the violator. The violation of cultural norms, i.e. transgressions, results in ridicule by members of the migrant farmer worker community. Such a case of sanctioning occurred while during cucumber picking:

A Mexican family, with three children, picks cucumbers near me. I cannot help but admire the mechanical proficiency: they have divided their work like an assembly line: the mother and young children place the cucumbers in the red plastic basket, while the eldest child and father carry the full baskets to the truck. However, they are one of few families whose eldest child is female. The men tap their head wear as she approaches (trucker or baseball caps, or cowboy straw-hats). They act "chivalrous" around her by removing their hats and by allowing her, and the other women, to dump their cucumbers before them. The men permit the women to cut in front of the line where the cucumbers are being dumped and they place their buckets on the ground to assist the woman in dumping out their baskets.

However, today one man fails to allow the woman behind him to dump her bucket first. He also does not assist her with the dumping of the bucket. In fact, in one instance, he walks at a faster pace passing and cutting in the line before the young woman who was picking with her family. The other men, who see this, they ridicule him for his lack of learning appropriate manners from his father and mother. One of the men comments, “Because we work like animals, it does not mean we should act like one.” Consequently, this individual became the butt of jokes and comments (specifically addressed to his manhood) for the duration of day.

The presence of young women working in a largely male sphere results, in this case, in a soft, gestural form of a policing of the patriarchal frame manifest through teasing and ridicule. The substantive form of this sanction, disclosed above, addresses the transmission of manners through the family. It highlights the diminished potential of change (within the workplace through imagining forms of equality) within a patriarchal social structure. In the case above, the worker overlooked the young girl and, de facto, treated her as an equal partner in the work process, as just another cucumber picker, but as the other men policed the symbolic boundaries of the patriarchal structure her gender required, from him, a different, formal, interaction.

The reaction of the women working in the field was also significant. They also partook, indirectly, in the sanctioning of the male individual through a complicit secondary means of supporting the sanction, e.g. smiles and laughter. The women’s tacit agreement with the men, was based a perception that the act (of cutting and not assisting in the dumping of the cucumbers) did, in fact, show a lack of respect and manners (he may have behaved out of ignorance or an expectation of equality based on an assumption of age or experience—it is impossible to know for sure). The common identity of workers plays handmaiden to gender.

There is more to the story. The young girl was not aware of any impropriety. She responded to the event, after the fact, with confusion. This, in and of itself, is salient to a discussion of “the self.” First the girl was called back by her father to where her family was standing in the field. Second she began to look around to see if she had done something wrong. Finally, confident that she has done nothing wrong, (e.g. shamed herself) she participated in the ridicule leveled at the man who had cut in front of her. The logic of this effect of authority (though in regard to the state, it is analogous to other systems of social organization) has been described by Louis Althusser, (using Lacan’s work) specifically in his discussion of “interpolation.” In this case, the injunction by the father resulted, immediately, in the subjection of the young woman to the patrimonial system mitigated only through her gradual recognition that she, in this instance, was not guilty of a transgression (Althusser 1971). However, as Althusser indicates, the sanctions do not emerge from the act; rather they emerge from out of the structure and are already embedded in the form and potentiality of the exchange.

Gender inequality is also rendered visible in the form through which financial contribution that women make to the household is represented and recognized. Put simply, women are not rewarded for identical work. For example, as described earlier, women receive a fee for supplying the single men in the camp with regular meals. Women may transform this type of work into small businesses that cater to the migrant farm worker community, regularly selling elotes (cooked corn with lemon, cream, butter, and red chili pepper powder in a cup) and other food. Despite these accomplishments—the keeping and maintaining of a business, which could be considered admirable and even confer upon the women some degree of social capital—women’s’ financial contributions to the family is viewed as nothing special.

A wife’s contribution to the financial stability of the family is accomplished through qualities (traditional traits) already vested in her, such as her ability to cook. The apex of social capital is reserved for married women in the camp; it is represented by the title, Doña. Doña was first used by the Spaniards and it maintained its venerable connotation, through the colonization process for the indigenous acculturated community. It symbolizes a certain amount of respect that should be warranted toward the individual. The credentials of the title are related directly to the contribution and skills of married women beyond the sphere of the family to the community. Given our discussion of women’s “double day,” it is obvious that the title is warranted. However, men, in this instance, are rewarded with the title Don which, while it also implies respect; the degree of respect is always greater, despite the fact that the title is conferred upon him based entirely on his wife’s merit. The title, across the Latino community, is warranted only for individuals who are of older and/or married. However, the title Don carries more weight than Doña, this means, de facto, that a man’s indirect contribution to the migrant farm worker community was marring someone who can cook. There are other couples in the camp where the wives do not cook for the men and these couples are referred to by their first name or by their proper name. These titles are not conferred upon or after marriage but are always already present as a feature of patrimonial authority. They are linked fundamentally and formally to the structure; coupled to one another and to the marital function.

There are, however, women who openly challenge the male dominated migrant farm worker culture. They are prostitutes. The nature of these women’s interaction with men in the camp is significantly different from all other gender based forms of social interaction. These women mitigate all social interaction through business transactions—sex for money. Below, is a detailed account of how these women interact with men in the labor camp. A visit to visit an informal “brothel” yielded the following event. Below we describe how the men gathered around in the living room, in a house farthest from the rest of the camp. It was a house intended for a large family, but the crew leader had converted it into a single man’s house. The kitchen had been made into a storage room and the rest of the house contained many beds which allowed for little personal space.

On the weekend, the house is clean and so are the men. Everyone is covered in cheap cologne. They laugh, tease and push each other around like children at a playground. None of men in the room say anything about who will go first. It became obvious, when one of the older men tells a thin, dark-skinned young man, “Go tell him that they are here!” As the door opens, the men’s eyes widen and they excitedly rub their hands together.

Two figures stand in the doorway; their large size blocks the view of the women making their way toward the living room. The wood creaks with each step they take. The women enter the room and exchange greetings with the men. They ask the men about their work since working men can spend more money on sex. They stand in the living room discussing prices. The men pick the women they want after prices were agreed upon. The room falls silent.

They all stand there waiting for the crew leader's right hand man (the alpha male) to arrive. After a few minutes, the much anticipated man makes his way to the front door of the house and stands there looking at the women. In the living room, the woman who seems to be the pack leader separates herself out from the others and makes her way toward the dark-skinned man.

They greet each other and go into one of the rooms together. After they leave the common room, two of the men, known to be the fastest pickers, grab the remaining women and take them to another room. I, still seated in the common room, can hear heated conversations that were coming from inside the other rooms. "I have told you before, no condom: no sex." The same conversation was taking place in the other room between the alpha male and alpha female. The voices of the men complaining could also be heard, "I do not need a stinking condom because I'm a man and condoms are for stupid teenagers and not for a man like me."

The nature of the relationship between the women and the men here gives rise to a distinct symbolic economy. In this case, by leveling a sexual prohibition, the women predominantly control the context of interaction; to the extent that the men finally give in to the demand that they wear condoms. The women's grievance, "why it's always the same chingadera (fucking) thing about the condoms," is part of a larger discussion regarding Mexican/Mexican American condoms use is also found in Norma Williams' (1988) study of Mexican/Mexican American families. However, the case above demonstrates how a single symbolic register that persists outside of "illegitimate sexual acts" (in the family, as in William's discussion) is context based; these men engage and interact under a different set of terms with these women than with the women in the labor camp. Although, in their personal life, the women in the above case were/are somebody's daughter, mother, sister, and/or wife, they produce a different symbolic framework within the male migrant farm worker community. The relationships embedded within this particular context give rise to a distinctively different symbolic economy. As a result, these women can gain a seemingly equal ground in the context of the exchange describe above, although their behavior could be view as deviant and the "equal ground" gained comes with a series of risks which represent non-normative communal transgressions and could be met with (or which threaten) dangerous repercussions that remain contained in a male context. The informal nature of sex work opens up greater levels of violence and risk for these women (Sanchez 1997).

DISCUSSION

The purpose of the paper was to covey how the gender formation in the migrant farm worker camps provides 1. a compliant labor force; 2. does so "naturally" through existing forms of patrimonial authority. The capital-labor relation depends upon leaving the symbolic (e.g. cultural, traditional, linguistic, religious etc.) structure of the host cultures intact and providing that context through the labor camp. The fieldwork demonstrates that in farm worker communities capitalism and patrimonial authority make strange though acceptable bedfellows. Significant symbols are the means of a social control mechanism that are limited by the patrimonial frame; they have the capacity to transcend generations. Cultural transmission, in migrant farm worker communities, requires little or no alteration to the patrimonial family structure.

This cultural transmission happens "naturally" as parents interact with their children, the group's values and norms are exchanged and passed on to the next generation. For example, at the wash area, the children observed through parental interactions that the father is excluded from assisting with domestic duties. The father's lack assistance with domestic duties signals a compliance with the norms of masculinity and is not viewed as insensitivity. Boys learn that one gender has exclusive access to social power (Irigaray 1977; Kristeva 1982; Rubin 1997). They internalize the roles of all the members of the family in "the game stage" through the development of an adult self.

In each of the passages above that detail gendered interaction (micro power) it is evident that men had more social, economic, and symbolic power than women. At an early age both boys and girls learn about their present and future roles; they experience their relation to the larger group which is, in turn, associated with the patrimonial structure that codes authority as gendered power. Taking the example of the girl who tried to "horseplay" with her younger brother, as the interaction unfolded, she accepted his authority as legitimate. Did she have a choice? Her younger brother bears abstract conceptual category that confers law/power—a symbolic structure or frame, border, or boundary—upon the process of identity construction. Therefore, the little brother recognizes that there are certain privileges in being a "man," and these privileges increase as he partakes in more male responsibilities which, in turn, gives him more authority over his older sister.

In addition, power and control is pre-coded but is reified and imbedded within the socialization process any challenges posed against expected gender roles are met by collective negative sanctions. Henceforth, through sanctions, the group reinforces the status quo which in turn benefits the male dominant culture as well as the economic (labor-capital relations) context. Consider the two examples from the fieldwork section of the paper: the man who overlooked the young woman in the fields, and the younger boy staring-down his older sister. Violations are quickly, if almost automatically, corrected. Minimizing in-group instability, both men and women depend on these symbols to negotiate transgressions as well as group membership—to the extent that any violation of norms is punishable by negative sanctions. In consequence, an individual is limited to act within the symbolic system and any attempt to alter those boundaries results in ridicule by other men and women, as in the case with the man in the field.

CONCLUSION

In summary, the goal of this study has been to demonstrate how patrimonial authority structures (Weber 1978), which are endogenous to the camps work, to maintain traditional power structure. Gender is the fulcrum upon which traditional authority structures rest (Mead 1932/1962; Douglas 1966; Dalla Costa 1973; Irigaray 1977; Weber 1978; Hartman 1981;

Kristeva 1982; Butler 1990; Rubin 1997). The policing of gender norms, intrinsic to the community in the camps, has the "value added" effect of community coherence so that it can function, well, as a community that ultimately labors for one another as well as another: the employer. We claim that those who exploit labor are actually exploiting an entire cultural structure as opposed to individual workers. The reason that the camp-form is so successful is because: 1. it allows members of the camp to maintain the illusion of cultural autonomy by maintaining its own authority through traditions and the symbolic structure; 2. it does not require any strict form of labor rationalization on the part of the employer.

REFERENCES

1. Althusser, Louis. "Ideology andIdeological State Apparatuses(Notes towards an Investigation)." Lenin and Philosophy and Other Essays, trans. by Ben Brewster, 127-242. New York: Monthly Review Press, 1971.
2. Anzaldúa, Gloria. Borderlands/La Fontera: The New Meitiza. San Francisco: Aunt Lute Books, 1999. Bhattacharjee, Anannya. "The Public/Private Mirage: Mapping Homes and Undomesticating Violence Work in the South Asian Immigrant Community." Feminist Genealogies, Colonial Legacies, Democratic Futures, edited by Alexander and Mohanty, 308-327. New York: Routledge, 1997.
3. Bardhan, P, "A Note on Interlinked Rural Economic Arrangements." In: The Economic Theory of Agrarian Institutions, edited by P. Bardhan, 237-242. Clarendon: Oxford, 1991a .
4. Bardhan, P, "On the Concept of Power in Economics." Economics and Politics 3 (1991b): 265-277.
5. Bardhan, P, "Labor-tying in a Poor Agrarian Economy: A Theoretical and Empirical Analysis." Quarterly Journal of Economics98 (1983): 501-504.
6. Boehm, Deborah A. "'Now I Am a Man and a Woman!': Gendered Moves and Migrations in a Transnational Mexican Community." Latin American Perspectives January 2008 35: 16-30
7. Butler, Judith, Gender Trouble: Feminism and thc Subversion of Identity. New York: Routledge, 1990.
8. Castellanos, M. Bianet. "Constructing the Family: Mexican Migrant Households, Marriage, and the State." Latin American Perspectives January 2008 35: 64-77
9. Castellanos, M. Bianet and Deborah A. Boehm. 2008. "Engendering Mexican Migration : Articulating Gender, Regions, Circuits." Latin American Perspectives 35: 5, pgs. 5-15.
10. Cobas, J, "On the Study of Ethnic Enterprise: Unresolved Issue." Sociological Perspective, 30 (1987): 467-472
11. Conover, T, Coyotes. New York: Random House, 1987.
12. Cromie, Stanley, "Motivations of Aspiring Male and Female Entrepreneurs." Journal of Occupational Behavior, 8 (1987): 251-261.
13. Dalla Costa, Maria Rosa, "Women and the Subversion of the Community." The Power of Women and the Subversion of the Community. Bristol: Falling Wall Press, 1973.
14. Donato, Katharine M., Donna Gabaccia, Jennifer Holdaway, Martin Manalansan IV, and Patricia R. Pessar. "A glass half full? Gender in migration studies." International Migration Review 11 (2006): 3–26.
15. Douglas, Mary. 1966. Purity and danger. New York: Ark Publication. Ehrenreich, Barbara and Arlie Russell Hochschild (eds.)
16. Durand, J. and Massey, D., "Mexican Migration to the United States: Critical Review." Latin American Review, 27 (1992): 3-42.
17. Giddens, Anthony, Capitalism and Modern Social Theory: An Analysis of the Writings of Marx, Durkheim and Max Weber. Cambridge: Cambridge University Press, 1971.
18. Gonzalez, J, Harvest of Empire. Penguin: New York, 2001.
19. Goss, J. and Lindquist, B., "Conceptualizing International Labor Migration: A Structuration Perspective." International Migration Review, 29 (1995): 317-351.
20. Guerrero, Marie Anna Jaimes, "Civil Rights Versus Sovereingty: Native American Women in Life and Land Struggles." Feminist Genealogies, Colonial Legacies, Democratic Futures, edited by Alexander and Mohanty, 101-121. New York: Routledge, 1997.
21. Hart, E, Barefoot Heart: Story of Migrant Children. Tempe, Texas:Juerez-Lincoln Center, National Migrant Information Clearing House, 1999.
22. Hartman, Heidi, "The Unhappy Marriage of Marxism and Feminism." Women and Revolution. Boston: South End Press, 1981.
23. Hawkes, G. and Taylor, M., "Power Structure in Mexican American Farm Labor Families." Journal of Marriage and the Family, 37 (1975): 807-811
24. Heaps, W, The Wandering Worker: The Story of Migrant Farm Workers and Their Problems. New York: Crown Publishers, 1968
25. Hondagneu-Sotelo, Pierrette. Gendered Transitions: Mexican Experiences of Immigration. Berkeley: University of California Press, 1994.
26. Hondagneu-Sotelo, Pierrette. Doméstica: Immigrant Workers Caring and Cleaning in the Shadows of Affluence. Berkeley: University of California Press, 2001.
27. Hondagneu-Sotelo, Pierrette. "Gender and immigration: a retrospective and introduction," pp. 3–19 in Pierrette Hondagneu-Sotelo (ed.), Gender and U.S. Immigration: Contemporary Trends. Berkeley: University ofCalifornia Press, 2003a..
28. Hondagneu-Sotelo, Pierrette. (ed.) Gender and U.S. Immigration: Contemporary Trends. Berkeley: University of California Press, 2003b..
29. Irigaray, Luce, "The Sex Which is Not One." Ce Sexe que n'en est pas un. Paris: Editions Minuit, 1977.
30. Karjanen. David. "Gender, Race, and Nationality in the Making ofMexican Migrant Labor in the United States." Latin American Perspectives January 35 (2008): 51-63
31. Kossoudji, S, "Immigrant Workers Assimilations: Is It a

Market Phenomenon." The Journal of Human Resources, 24 (1989): 494-52.

32. Kristeva, Julia. 1982. Powers of horror: An essay on abjection. New York: Columbia University Press.
33. Light, I., Sabagh, G., Mehdi, B., and Der-Martirosian C., "Beyond the Ethnic Enclave Economy." Social Problems, 41 (1994): 65-80
34. Littlefield, C. and Stout, C., "A Survey of Colorado's Migrant Farmworkers: Asses to Health Care." International Migration Review, 21 (1987): 688-708.
35. Martin, Philip, Mexican Workers and U.S. Agriculture: The Revolving Door. International Migration Review, 36 (2002): 1124-1142.
36. Marx, Karl, Capital, Volume 1. London: Lawrence and Wishart, 1970.
37. Mead, G., Mind, Self, and Society. Chicago: University of Chicago Press, [1932]1962.
38. Melville, M, editor. Mexicans at Work in the United States. Houston, TX: Mexican American Studies Program: University of Houston, 1988.
39. Mohanty, Chandra Talpade. "Women Workers and Capitalist Scripts: Ideologies of Domination, Common Interests, and the Politics of Solidarity." Feminist Genealogies, Colonial Legacies, Democratic Futures, edited by Alexander and Mohanty, 3-29. New York: Routledge, 1997.
40. Molina, H., The Working and Living Conditions of Farm Workers. Master's thesis, University of Texas-Pan American, 2004.
41. Nicholson, Linda, "Feminism and Marx: Integrating Kinship with the Economic." Praxis International (January 1985): 367-380.
42. Portes, A., The Economic Sociology of Immigration. New York: Russell Sage Foundation, 1995.
43. Przeworski, Adam. 1985. Capitalism and Social Democracy. Cambridge: Cambridge University Press.
44. Raijman, R., "Determinates of Entrepreneurial Intentions: Mexican Immigrants in Chicago." Journal of Social-Economics, 30 (2001): 393-411
45. Reitz, J. and Sklar, S., "Culture, Race, and the Economic Assimilation of Immigrants." Sociological Forum, 15 (1997): 233-277
46. Rubin, Gayle, "The Traffic in Women: Notes on the Political Economy of Sex." The Second Wave: A Reader in Feminist Theory. Ed. Nicholson. New York: Routledge, 1997.
47. Sanchez, L.E., "Boundaries of Legitimacy: Sex, Violence, Citizenship, and Community in a Local Sexual Economy." Law & Social Inquiry, 22, (Summer, 1997): 543-580.
48. Segura, D., "Chicanas and Mexican Immigrants Women in the Labor Market: A Study of Occupational Mobility and Stratification" Doctoral dissertation, University of California, Berkeley, 1978.
49. Seif, Hinda. "Wearing Union T-Shirts: Undocumented Women Farm Workers and Gendered Circuits of Political Power." Latin American Perspectives January 2008 35: 78-98,
50. Silberman, Matthew, Violence and Society: A Reader. Upper Saddle River, NJ: Prentice Hall/Pearson Education, 2003.
51. Stanford, A., "He Speaksto Whom? Inscription and Reinscription of Women in Visible Man and the Salt Eater." Malus,18 (1993): 17-31
52. Villaseñor, Victor. 1984. Macho!. Houston: Arte Público Press
53. Vold, G., Bernard, T., and Snipes, J., Theoretical Criminology 4th Edition. New York: Oxford University Press, 1998.
54. Weber, Max. Economy and Society: An Outline of Interpretive Sociology. Berkeley,. CA: University of California Press, 1978..
55. William, Norma, "Role Making among Married Mexican American Women: Issue of Class and Ethnicity." The Journal of Applied Behavioral Science, 24(1988): 203-217.
56. U.S. Department of Labor, "Profile of U.S. Farm Workers." Congressional Digest, June 94 (2005): 169-170.
57. Zavella, P., Women's Work and Chicano Families: Cannery Workers of the Santa Clara Valley. Cornell University Press: Ithaca, 1987.

CHAPTER 19

NON-DISCRIMINATION ON THE GROUND OF NATIONALITY IN SOCIAL SECURITY

Frans Pennings

Keywords: Discrimination, nationality, social security, ECHR, coordination of social security

INTRODUCTION

The negotiations on the accession of the European Union to the European Convention on Human Rights (henceforth: ECHR or Convention) raise several complicated questions of a formal nature, e.g. on the relation between Member State(s) and the Union in a particular procedure before the European Court of Human Rights (ECtHR) and on the coordination of the interpretation of EU law by the EU Court of Justice and the Court of Human Rights.1 These issues will not be addressed here, since some of them will be discussed in other contributions to this issue and some have been discussed elsewhere.2 Instead, I will study the effect of the accession on a material area of EU law. Currently an instrument of EU law can already be the subject of cases before the Court of Human Rights in so far as a Member State has implemented this instrument. However, after the accession of the EU to the ECHR, EU law itself can be the subject of procedures before the Court of Human Rights.3 This means that EU rules and practice must satisfy the provisions of the Convention. For our purpose it is therefore relevant to investigate the areas where EU law allows discrimination on the ground of nationality while the ECHR does not. In exactly this area it can be expected that the accession of the EU to the Convention may have certain effects. This approach thus requires a comparison of EU law and the Convention, including the case law, concerning discrimination on the ground of nationality. In this contribution, I will discuss which effects follow from the EU's accession to the Convention for a particular fundamental right, i.e. non-discrimination on the ground of nationality in the area of social advantages. The comparison is therefore not a complete one of all cases of discrimination on the ground of nationality, but focuses on those areas where differences can be expected. Thus the central question of this contribution is whether cases of discrimination on the ground of nationality which are allowed under EU law are problematic for the Convention.

Discrimination on the ground of nationality is of special interest, since the EU makes use of the nationality condition in order to define the scope and the contents of several of its instruments, in particular also in relation to social advantages. The application of this condition may be different from that under the Convention and therefore it is worthwhile studying this issue. Both EU primary and secondary instruments and the ECHR have non-discrimination clauses, but these may have different scopes and interpretations. Moreover, there is a difference with other fundamental rights which 'double up' in the Treaty and the Convention, such as the prohibition of discrimination on the ground of gender. Therefore the prohibition of discrimination on the ground of nationality deserves special attention. Of course, this prohibition is also relevant in areas other than social advantages,4 but the topic is of special interest since exactly this area is of a highly politically sensitive nature, because states wish to remain exclusively competent with regard to the organisation of their welfare system.

It is furthermore useful to keep in mind that the non-discrimination provisions within the EU context differ in several aspects from that in the ECHR context. Within the

Citation: Frans Pennings, Non-Discrimination on the Ground of Nationality in Social Security, DOI: http://doi.org/10.18352/ulr.217.

EU, non-discrimination on the basis of nationality is closely related to the free movement of EU citizens. For these citizens the non-discrimination rule is a fundamental right vis-à-vis another Member State. Secondly, EU law itself distinguishes between EU citizens and non-EU citizens (third-country nationals), although currently some (specific) non-discrimination provisions address third-country nationals as well. In the ECHR context the non-discrimination clause is not related to a particular purpose and does not distinguish between categories of citizens. Within the ECHR context the prohibition of discrimination on the ground of nationality is – as a fundamental right – a more general concept, and for distinctions between different nationalities to be allowed a justification is needed. Since the EU instruments can be brought before the ECtHR after accession, it is interesting to see whether the two different approaches can be reconciled. In the following sections I will first discuss the case law of the Court of Human Rights (Section 2); then I will address the EU provisions and case law (Section 3); in Section 4, I will analyse the differences and Section 5 will provide some conclusions.

THE CASE LAW OF THE ECTHR

Introduction: the Applicability of Article 14 to Social Advantages

Article 14 ECHR provides that the enjoyment of rights and freedoms set forth in this Convention shall be secured without discrimination on any ground such as sex, race, colour, language, religion, political or other opinion, national or social origin, association with a national minority, property, birth or other status. Thus nationality is a forbidden ground for making a distinction.

Article 14 is not a free standing provision, but it complements the other substantive provisions of the Convention and the Protocols. Thus it has effect solely in relation to 'the enjoyment of the rights and freedoms' safeguarded by these provisions. Consequently, this provision cannot be applied in any case of alleged discrimination.5 The Court has consistently held this approach in its case law, e.g. in the Gaygusuz judgment.6 However, the discrimination provision can be applied in social security cases since in the Gaygusuz judgment the Court also ruled that a benefit can be within the ambit of Article 1 of the First Protocol, i.e. the protection of property, and thus within the scope of the Convention.7 Article 1 reads:

'Every natural or legal person is entitled to the peaceful enjoyment of his possessions. No one shall be deprived of his possessions except in the public interest and subject to the conditions provided for by law and by the general principles of international law. The preceding provisions shall not, however, in any way impair the right of a state to enforce such laws as it deems necessary to control the use of property in accordance with the general interest or to secure the payment of taxes or other contributions or penalties.'

The Gaygusuz case concerned the refusal of so-called emergency assistance, a kind of Austrian social assistance, to Mr Gaygusuz, on the ground that he did not have Austrian nationality; instead, he had Turkish nationality. In this judgment the Court required, for the protection of property to be acceptable, that a link can be established between the financing method and the benefit concerned, more specifically that contributions had been paid. In this case the link between the contributions paid and the emergency assistance was an indirect one, but it was considered to be sufficient by the Court. The link was created by the fact that the emergency assistance was payable only after the right to (contributory) unemployment benefit had expired. Therefore, in the Court's view, the emergency benefit was linked to the payment of contributions to the unemployment insurance fund and, as a result, this benefit was within the ambit of the Protocol and, consequently, Article 14 was applicable to this case.

In later cases the Court abandoned the requirement of a link between a benefit and contributions as an accession requirement for Article 14. A landmark decision was the Stec judgment,8 which concerned an issue of discrimination on the ground of gender, but is also relevant to our topic, since its major relevance lay in the Court's new view on the scope of the protection of property. In this judgment, the Grand Chamber accepted that the Gaygusuz judgment had caused confusion relating to the criteria which are applicable for income protection and that it was necessary to 'examine afresh' the question whether a claim to a non-contributory welfare benefit should attract the protection of Article 1 of the First Protocol. For this purpose the Court acknowledged that there exists a wide range of social security benefits designed to confer entitlements which arise as of right. Given the variety of funding methods, and the interlocking nature of benefits under most welfare systems, the Court considered that it appears increasingly artificial to hold that only benefits financed by contributions to a specific fund fall within the scope of Article 1 of the First Protocol. In the modern, democratic state, many individuals are, for all or part of their lives, completely dependent for survival on social security and welfare benefits. Many domestic legal systems recognise that such individuals require a degree of certainty and security, and provide for benefits to be paid – subject to the fulfilment of the conditions of eligibility – as of right. Where an individual has an assertable right under domestic law to a welfare benefit, the importance of that interest should also be reflected by holding Article 1 of the First Protocol to be applicable (emphasis added).

So this is the new criterion: is there an assertable right to a welfare benefit? If the answer is in the affirmative, Article 14 (the non-discrimination rule) can be applied. However, Article 1 of the First Protocol is not only an admissibility provision, but also has a material content, i.e. the protection of property. I will address this latter dimension in Section 2.3, since some of the issues relating to (indirect) discrimination on the ground of nationality can also be covered by the property protection rules. Below I will discuss the interpretation of Article 14 and the interpretation of the right to property.

Article 14 ECHR

Direct Discrimination on the Ground of Nationality

In the already mentioned Stec judgment, the Court considered that Article 14 does not prohibit a Member State from treating groups differently in order to correct 'factual inequalities' between them; indeed, in certain circumstances a failure to attempt to correct inequality through different treatment may in itself give rise to a breach of the article. Then the Court continued, and used the argument already introduced in the Gaygusuz judgment and later judgments, that a difference in treatment is discriminatory, for the purposes of Article 14, if it has no objective and reasonable justification, that is if it does not pursue a legitimate aim or if there is not a reasonable relationship of proportionality between the means employed and the aim sought to be realised.

It added that Contracting States enjoy a certain margin of appreciation in assessing whether and to what extent differences in otherwise similar situations justify different treatment. The scope of this margin will vary according to the circumstances, the subject-matter and the background.9 A wide margin is usually allowed to the state under the Convention when it comes to general measures of economic or social strategy. Because of their direct knowledge of their society and its needs, the national authorities are in principle better placed than the international Court to appreciate what is in the public interest on social or economic grounds, and the Court will generally respect the legislature's policy choice unless it is 'manifestly without reasonable foundation'. However, and now the Court comes to an important criterion: very weighty reasons would have to be put forward before the Court could regard a difference in treatment based exclusively on the ground of nationality as compatible with the Convention (emphasis added).

In the Gaygusuz case the Austrian Government had submitted that the statutory provision in question was not discriminatory. It argued that the difference in treatment was based on the idea that the state has special responsibility for its own nationals and must take care of them and provide for their essential needs. Moreover, the Unemployment Insurance Act laid down certain exceptions to the nationality condition. Lastly, at the material time, Austria was not bound by any contractual obligation to grant emergency assistance to Turkish nationals. The Court did not find this argument to be persuasive, now that Mr Gaygusuz was legally resident in Austria and worked there at certain times, paying contributions to the unemployment insurance fund in the same capacity and on the same basis as Austrian nationals. The authorities' refusal to grant him emergency assistance was based exclusively on the fact that he did not have Austrian nationality. Apart from this he was in a like situation to Austrian nationals as regards his entitlement to the emergency benefit. The difference in treatment between Austrians and non-Austrians as regards an entitlement to emergency assistance was thus not based on any 'objective and reasonable justification'. Another judgment which is relevant to the non-discrimination rule is that of Koua Poirrez v France.10 It concerned a person with Ivory Coast nationality who had been physically disabled since the age of seven and had been adopted by a French national. He was assessed as being 80% disabled. In May 1990 he applied for an allowance for disabled adults. His application was refused on the ground that he was neither a French national nor a national of a country which had entered into a reciprocity agreement with France.

It is interesting that the case was first brought before the Court of Justice. In a judgment of 16 December 1992 this Court issued a ruling that the refusal to award the benefit to the applicant was not incompatible with the relevant articles of the EEC Treaty. It pointed out that the applicant's adoptive father could not claim to be a 'migrant worker', which was the category to which the European provisions in question applied, since the applicant's adoptive father, being French, had always lived and worked in France.11 In doing so, the Court did not examine the question whether the refusal to award the applicant the allowance was, in general, compatible with Community law or not. In 1998, according to a new Act the nationality condition was lifted for awards of non-contributory allowances. After several procedures Poirrez was awarded benefit as from June 1998. Now his claim for the preceding period led to a procedure before the Court of Human Rights and a judgment. Before the Court, the Government had submitted that the distinction made, prior to the 1998 Act, between nationals and foreigners when awarding the allowance for disabled adults pursued a legitimate aim, which was a balance between the state's welfare income and expenditure. The requirement of proportionality had also been satisfied since foreign nationals had not been deprived of all resources since they were entitled to, among other things, the minimum welfare benefit.

The Court repeated its formula that very weighty reasons would have to be put forward before the Court could regard a difference in treatment based exclusively on the ground of nationality as compatible with the Convention. In this case the domestic authorities' refusal to award him the allowance in question was based exclusively on the fact that he did not have the requisite nationality. The Court found the arguments advanced by the respondent Government unpersuasive. The difference in treatment regarding entitlement to social benefits between French nationals or nationals of a country having signed a reciprocity agreement and other foreign nationals was not based on any 'objective and reasonable justification'. Finally, also in the Luczak v Poland judgment the Court accepted that the direct discrimination which existed in this case was inconsistent with Article 14.12 The applicant, who was a French national of Polish origin, had moved to Poland in about 1984. After years of employment, he started a farm, but was excluded from the social security scheme for farmers since he did not have Polish nationality.

The Government pointed out that the distinction at issue pursued the legitimate aim of protecting a vulnerable group by allowing its members to have access to and benefit from the scheme subject to the payment of a modest contribution and the condition of having Polish nationality prior to 2004 and had played a vital role in directing state support to those in particular need. The farmers' scheme was 95% financed from the budget and constituted a heavy burden on taxpayers and the economy alike.

The Court attached importance to the fact that the applicant was permanently resident in Poland, had previously been affiliated to the general social security scheme and had contributed as a taxpayer to the funding of the farmers' scheme. It reiterated that very weighty reasons would have to be put forward by the respondent Government in order to justify a difference in treatment based, as in the present case, exclusively on the ground of nationality. The creation of a particular social security scheme for farmers that is heavily subsidised from the public purse could be regarded as pursuing an economic or social strategy falling within the state's margin of appreciation, but legislation regulating access to such a scheme must be compatible with Article 14 of the Convention. Where it is shown that there are reasonable and objective grounds for excluding an individual from the scheme, the principle of proportionality will then come into play. In particular, even where weighty reasons have been advanced for excluding an individual from the scheme, such exclusion must not leave him in a situation in which he is denied any social insurance cover, whether under a general or a specific scheme, thus posing a threat to his livelihood. Indeed, to leave an employed or self-employed person bereft of any social security cover would be incompatible with current trends in social security legislation in Europe. The Court also noted that the Government argued that the difference in treatment at issue was justified by the social and economic policies pursued prior to 2004, when Poland was obliged to change the relevant law following its accession to the European Union. The Government had not however explained, the Court remarked, why its public policy goals in respect of the farmers' scheme suddenly lost their relevance after 2004. The Court concluded by saying that the Government had not provided any convincing explanation of how the general interest was served by refusing the applicant's admission to the farmers' scheme during the period in question.

It has been argued that the Mousaquim case13 could be an argument that the Court of Human Rights will not consider preferential treatment for EU nationals to be contrary to the Convention, since there is an objective and reasonable justification for this as Belgium belongs, together with those states, to a special legal order. This case concerned a Moroccan man who had been deported from Belgium, who then stayed for a couple of years in Sweden, and who wished to have the deportation order revoked. Thus the right to enter and stay in the country was at stake, which is very different from the area of social security, since it is generally accepted that the right to equal treatment does not concern the right to enter a particular country.14 As far as social security is concerned, the issue of equal treatment only arises after a person has the right to stay legally in a country. Or, in other words, the very weighty reasons that can justify unequal treatment still allow differences in access to the country. Therefore, from this judgment we cannot derive that a difference between third country nationals and EU nationals is generally allowed, although it is certainly not impossible that the EU context may be, in particular circumstances, a justification for making distinctions, provided they constitute very weighty reasons.

Conclusion. The Court decided that very weighty reasons would have to be put forward before the Court could regard a difference in treatment based exclusively on the ground of nationality (i.e. direct discrimination) as being compatible with the Convention. Even if EU law does not require Member States to treat third country nationals equally with nationals, this may be required on the basis of the Convention (Gaygusuz, Poirrez). Even if EU law can explain why persons are excluded, or have to be included, that is not decisive (Luczak). Despite the room for states to have margins of appreciation to have a particular policy or scheme, for limiting access to the scheme on the ground of nationality the criterion of very weighty reasons applies.

Indirect Discrimination

In its case law, the Court of Human Rights has not (yet) developed a concept of indirect discrimination, a concept which is so well known from the Court of Justice's case law and which is now also laid down in EU instruments. For instance, in terms of the Directive on the implementation of the principle of equal opportunities and equal treatment of men and women in matters of employment and occupation,15 indirect discrimination shall be taken to occur where an apparently neutral provision, criterion or practice disadvantages a substantially higher proportion of the members of the other sex, unless that provision, criterion or practice is objectively justified by a legitimate aim and the means of achieving that aim are appropriate and necessary (Article 2(1)(b)). An obvious example for indirect discrimination on the ground of nationality is a residence condition, e.g. for receiving a benefit, since this will normally affect foreigners more than nationals, since it will be more often the case that foreigners do not live in the state where they work. So this is the approach within EU law

The LB v Austria judgment of the Court of Human Rights shows that this Court is not so sensitive to rules with discriminatory effects which are not directly discriminatory. The case was that of an Austrian national of Hungarian origin who complained that the Austrian authorities had refused to allow him to pay contributions for the time that he had been in school and studied in Hungary. The Court did not accept that the difference in treatment was based on national origin. It considered that the legislation in question did not distinguish on the basis of nationality and found that making participation in an insurance scheme dependent on employment in a specific country was not unreasonable or arbitrary.16 If a distinction is made that does not constitute direct discrimination on the ground of nationality or one of the other mentioned grounds, this can also be assessed on a ground other than nationality, since Article 14 does not only mention specific forbidden grounds, but also prohibits discrimination due to 'other status'.17

A recent case where this clause was applied to a situation where residence conditions were disputed is the Carson case.18 The case concerned 13 pensioners who had often spent long periods of their working life in the UK (during which they had paid social security contributions), before emigrating to another country (outside the EU), e.g. South Africa and Canada. After having become entitled to their pension, the pension was no longer upgraded if they left the UK, and therefore it became considerably lower than if it had benefited from upgrading. The Act required the upgrading to maintain its value 'in relation to the general level of prices obtaining in Great Britain'. For non-residents there was no such upgrading, unless they lived in a country with a bilateral reciprocal social security agreement with the UK.

The Court considered that it had established in its case law that only differences in treatment based on an identifiable characteristic, or 'status', are capable of amounting to discrimination within the meaning of Article 14,19 and there must be a difference in the treatment of persons in analogous, or relevantly similar, situations.20 Such a difference in treatment is discriminatory if it has no objective and reasonable justification; in other words, if it does not pursue a legitimate aim or if there is not a reasonable relationship of proportionality between the means employed and the aim sought to be realised. The Contracting State enjoys a margin of appreciation in assessing whether and to what extent differences in otherwise similar situations justify different treatment. A wide margin is usually allowed to the state under the Convention when it comes to general measures of economic or social strategy. The Court was not concerned, it continued, with an assessment of the effects, if any, on the many thousands in the same position as the applicants, but its role is to determine the question of principle, namely whether the legislation as such unlawfully discriminates between persons who are in an analogous situation.

The Court then had to decide whether a distinction on the ground of residence could fall under the ground 'or any other status'. The words 'other status' have a wide meaning so as to include, in certain circumstances, a distinction which is made on the basis of the place of residence. The second question was whether the applicants were in a relevantly similar position to pensioners receiving up-rating. As the Court has established in its case law, in order for an issue to arise under Article 14, the first condition is that there must be a difference in the treatment of persons in relevantly similar situations. The applicants' principal argument in support of their claim to be in a relevantly similar situation to pensioners who receive up-rating was that they had also worked in the United Kingdom and had paid compulsory contributions to the National Insurance Fund. The Court considered, however, that unlike private pension schemes, where contributions are paid into a specific fund and where those contributions are directly linked to the expected benefit returns, National Insurance contributions have no exclusive link to retirement pensions. It is impossible to isolate the payment of National Insurance contributions as a sufficient ground for equating the position of pensioners who receive up-rating and those, like the applicants, who do not. The payment of National Insurance contributions alone was insufficient to place the applicants in a relevantly similar position to all other pensioners, regardless of their country of residence. Given that the pension system is primarily designed to serve the needs of those who are resident in the United Kingdom, it was difficult to draw any genuine comparison with the position of pensioners living elsewhere, because of the range of economic and social variables which apply from country to country. Neither did the Court consider that the applicants were in a relevantly similar position to pensioners living in countries with which the United Kingdom has concluded a bilateral agreement providing for up-rating. Such treaties are entered into on the basis of judgments by both parties as to their respective interests and may depend on various factors. Where an agreement is in place, the flow of funds may differ depending on the level of each country's benefits and the number of people going in each direction. It follows that there had been no discrimination and, therefore, no violation of Article 14 taken in conjunction with Article 1 of Protocol No.1.

Conclusion. The Court of Human Rights does not apply a concept of indirect discrimination in its case law. Instead, it considers whether the disputed ground itself is a form of direct discrimination. In respect of discrimination on such grounds, which are not sex or nationality, the Court gives ample room for a margin of appreciation for the state and therefore such cases are not successful for the applicant.

The Right to Property

In Section 2.1 the right to property was mentioned as a possible way to address issues of (in) direct discrimination. The Court of Human Rights approaches this article as follows. Article 1 of Protocol No. 1 does not include a right to acquire property. It places no restriction on the Contracting State's freedom to decide whether or not to have in place any form of social security scheme, or to choose the type or amount of benefits to be provided under any such scheme. If, however, a state has legislation in force which provides for the payment, as of right, of a welfare benefit, that legislation must be regarded as generating a proprietary interest falling within the ambit of Article 1 of Protocol No. 1 for persons satisfying its requirements.21

So far, invoking the right to property protection has led to little success in the area of social security. An example where there was a positive result for the applicant was the Ásmundsson judgment. This concerned a person in Iceland who had become fully disabled in 1978 as a seafarer and became entitled to disability benefit. A 200-kilo boulder had fallen on his leg. After his accident the applicant joined a transport company, Samskip Ltd., as an office assistant, and became employed there as head of the claims department. In 1992, new legislation changed the way the applicant's disability was assessed for the purposes of his pension, so that it was to be based not on his inability to perform the same work, but work in general. Under the new rules, the applicant's disability was reassessed and his loss of capacity for work in general was found to be 25%; this was below the minimum level of 35% which was the accession requirement and therefore his benefit entitlement was terminated. Of the 336 reassessments the disability pension of 104 persons was changed and 104 pensioners lost their pension altogether. Thus the measure affected the applicant in a particularly harsh manner, the Court considered, in that it totally deprived him of the disability pension he had been receiving on a regular basis for nearly 20 years and which, at the time, constituted one third of his gross monthly income.

Against that background, the Court found that the applicant was made to bear an excessive and disproportionate burden which could not be justified by legitimate community interests relied upon by the authorities (emphasis added). It would have been otherwise had the applicant been obliged to endure a reasonable and commensurate reduction rather than the total deprivation of his entitlements. One can have some doubts as to this approach, since it is very well possible that the fact that the benefits of a small group are affected is, from a policy point of view, a justified outcome. After all, Ásmundsen could still earn a considerable income alongside his benefit. In addition, one may wonder why it is decisive, from the perspective of property protection, whether only a very small group loses all entitlement. It seems that the Court's approach can be explained as a typical human rights' perspective – 'is the outcome problematic in an individual case?' – rather than developing consistent criteria for when the infringement of benefit rights is allowed and when it is not.

This impression also appears from the Moskal judgment,22 which concerned a Polish woman who had received a Polish early retirement benefit since her son suffered from, inter alia, asthma, and therefore needed a lot of care. About 10 months later the benefit administration decided to terminate the benefit, since it now doubted whether the medical situation of the child indeed required permanent care. The Court considered that the total loss of benefit was too abrupt, and that the new benefit to which she would be entitled would be much lower. For this reason the Court decided that a fair balance between the requirements of the general interest and those of the protection of the fundamental rights of the individual were lacking and that Article 1 of the Protocol had therefore been infringed. This means that stopping the payment of an unrequired benefit is seen as an infringement of the right to property. However, we can hardly expect that this is the case in any instance of such undue payment; any general rules are lacking on this, however. Thus the Court is more focused on the individual situation than on making a more general rule on when and under which circumstances the withdrawal of a benefit is allowed.

In other cases, the Court has not held a general recourse to property protection to be successful. An example was the Valkov judgment,23 concerning the capping of pensions in Bulgaria (a pension was not paid for the amount exceeding a ceiling). As a result these persons were in some cases not paid two- thirds of their pension; the remaining pension was quite low (€ 81 a month in the case of Valkov). The Ásmundsen criteria might have led to the conclusion that their property rights had been infringed: the loss of pension rights was a major loss and the rule affected a small number of pensioners only. However, their claim was dismissed: they had not lost their full pension and they belonged to the 'top earners' among pensioners.

So the outcome in their individual situation – these were not really poor people – was considered more relevant than a consistent application of certain criteria. After all, different from Mr Ádmundsson, the pensioners had no other income, compared to other pensioners they had relatively high incomes, but this was indeed relative, since the pensions were so extremely low! Easier to understand is the argument also mentioned by the Court that the measure was a transitional measure, in view of Bulgaria's transition to a market economy.

Conclusion. The protection of property is not directly linked to discrimination on the ground of nationality, although if a benefit is withdrawn or reduced it may be indirectly concerned with nationality, e.g. because of residence. In this case the Court only provides protection if the measure cannot objectively be justified and the applicant is made to bear an excessive and disproportionate burden which could not be justified by the legitimate community interests relied on by the authorities.

THE PLACE AND APPLICABILITY OF THE NON-DISCRIMINATION RULES IN EU LAW

Introduction

In the Treaty on the Functioning of the EU (TFEU) and its predecessors, the prohibition of nondiscrimination on the basis of nationality is a fundamental principle laid down in Article 18 TFEU and Article 45 TFEU.

Direct Discrimination against EU Nationals

Workers

Article 45 TFEU ensures the free movement of workers and non-discrimination in the area of working conditions. Restrictions are only allowed if these can be justified on the basis of public order, public safety or public health. Article 45 also prohibits indirect discrimination. In the area of statutory social security, Regulation 883/2004 prohibits non-discrimination on the ground of nationality. Social assistance does not fall within the scope of the regulation and the regulation is restricted to traditional forms of social security, including unemployment benefit, an old-age pension, sickness benefit, survivors' benefits, and family allowances. Advantages such as study grants and housing benefits are thus not covered.

With respect to social advantages not within the scope of Regulation 883/2004, another regulation may be relevant, i.e. Regulation 492/2011, which prohibits all discrimination on the ground of nationality for workers (with EU nationality). The objective justifications in case of discrimination are limited: public order and public health, and these have been consistently given a narrow interpreted by the Court of Justice. For non-workers Article 18 TFEU is relevant as it reads that within the scope of application of the Treaties, and without prejudice to any special provisions contained therein, any discrimination on grounds of nationality shall be prohibited. In connection with the provision on European citizenship, Article 21 TFEU, Article 18 can be invoked by all EU citizens.

EU Citizens

Invoking Article 18 TFEU is possible on the basis of the provisions on European citizenship, Articles 20 and 21 TFEU. Before discussing this, it is important to point out the priority order. If Article 45 TFEU is applicable, Article 21 is not applicable. This is important as the application of Articles 18 and 45 may have different outcomes.

Article 18 TFEU provides that within the scope of application of this Treaty, and without prejudice to any special provisions contained therein, any discrimination on grounds of nationality shall be prohibited. In the Martínez Sala judgment,24 a landmark decision, the combination of these provisions led to an interesting outcome: a person who was no longer employed could invoke a non-discrimination rule, i.e. the predecessor of Article 18 (thus far, only employees and self-employed could do so), when she was refused child-raising benefit. The Court argued that Article 21 TFEU attaches to the status of a citizen of the Union the rights and duties laid down by the Treaty, including the right, laid down in Article 18 TFEU, not to suffer discrimination on grounds of nationality within the material scope of the Treaty. Also in the Grzelczyk judgment Articles 18 and 21 TFEU (the present numbering) were relevant.25 The Court of Justice considered that discrimination solely on the ground of nationality is in principle prohibited by Article 18 TFEU.

Article 21 TFEU indeed has important effects. Whereas a Member State was previously required to assume full social responsibility and provide welfare for those who had already entered its employment market and who thus made some contribution to its economy, such financial solidarity is now in principle to be extended to all Union citizens lawfully resident on its territory. Yet it should be noted that certain limits remain. As regards assistance covering the maintenance costs of students, the Court accepted in the Bidar judgment26 that Member States are permitted to ensure that the granting of social assistance does not become an unreasonable burden upon them and that the granting of such assistance may be limited to students who have demonstrated 'a certain degree of integration'. This was further elaborated in the Förster judgment.27 Jacqueline Förster, a German national, was confronted with the Dutch rule that study finance may be granted to students who are a national of a Member State if, prior to the application, they have been lawfully resident in the Netherlands for an uninterrupted period of at least five years. The Court investigated whether such a requirement can be justified by the objective of the host state's policy of ensuring that students who are nationals of other Member States have, to a certain degree, integrated into its society. The Court decided that this condition is appropriate for the purpose of guaranteeing that the applicant is integrated into the society of the host state.

Thus, Article 18 in conjunction with Article 21 does not remove all discrimination on the basis of nationality; instead, Member States may require a certain degree of integration by a claimant into its society before this Article can be invoked. Five years is considered to be a period which is proportional. In the Charter of Fundamental Rights of the European Union the non-discrimination principle is also mentioned (Article 21). This provision is elaborated in the provisions mentioned in this section.

Conclusion. Direct discrimination on the ground of nationality is not allowed under EU law for economically active persons apart from very limited exceptions. Also for EU citizens, protection against discrimination on the ground of nationality will apply. These rules apply to EU nationals only.

Indirect Discrimination against Workers

An example of the application of the prohibition of indirect discrimination can be seen in the Pinna case,28 where the Court decided that the coordination regulation for social security29 was not allowed to provide that persons employed in France received family benefits at the level of the state of residence. As a result, persons employed in France received for their children residing, for example, in Greece, child benefit in accordance with the Greek rules, which meant a lower benefit. The Court considered that the principle of equal treatment prohibits not only overt discrimination based on nationality, but all covert forms of discrimination which, by applying other distinguishing criteria, in fact achieve the same result.

Under EU law in case of a distinction which raises a suspicion of indirect discrimination an objective justification is possible. Consequently, indirect discrimination is not generally forbidden.

Indirect discrimination occurs, in the area of nationality, in particular as a result of residence conditions. Residence conditions generally affect larger numbers of persons with a nationality other than that of the state which imposes this condition. Also the regulation itself has examples of residence conditions and these may be reconsidered. Generally under EU law residence conditions are forbidden, and objective justifications relating to costs, administrative problems, comparisons between national workers and foreign workers and population policy are not accepted.

A major case in which the Court did not decide that a discriminatory rule under the regulation was inconsistent with the Treaty concerned unemployment benefit for wholly unemployed frontier workers. Wholly unemployed frontier workers are subject to the legislation on unemployment benefits in their country of residence, even if they seek work in the country of their last employment in addition to seeking work in the state of residence. For frontier workers wishing to be available to the employment services in the state of employment, this rule is unsatisfactory, as it implies that they are deprived of the rights they acquired by virtue of the legislation of the state of employment. In the Mouthaan judgment30 the Court held that the rule was not inconsistent with the Treaty. The Court accepted (actually: it itself invented) an objective justification: since frontier workers have better opportunities on the labour market in their country of residence it was allowed to determine that their unemployment benefits are also according to the legislation of this country.

Conclusion. In case of indirect discrimination, objective justifications are allowed, though only if there is an objective justification. However, such cases may imply a loss of benefit rights, and thus an infringement of the protection of property.

Discrimination against Third-Country Nationals

The provisions concerning non-discrimination in Articles 18 and 45 TFEU can be invoked by EU nationals only. For Article 45, this is the result of the fact that Article 45 is part of the section on the free movement of persons, which is one of the fundamental freedoms essential to the EU, and therefore for EU citizens. Also the scope of Article 18 TFEU is limited to EU citizens. As we have seen in the description of the ECtHR's case law, there are several cases where a person in an EU Member State was excluded from a particular benefit, whereas at the material time of the case recourse to EU law was not successful (e.g. in the case of Gaygusuz).

Let us first consider the current EU law. Also at present the nationality condition is essential for being covered by the coordination regulation for social security for migrant workers (Regulation 883/2004). This regulation contains an important non-discrimination rule in the area of statutory social security (social assistance benefit is excluded from the material scope). Thus this rule prohibits different treatment for EU nationals (and EEA and Swiss nationals). As a result a third-country national cannot invoke this rule to combat discrimination on the ground of nationality. This nationality condition has been severely criticised for excluding third-country nationals. A major point of discussion was whether Article 42 EC (now Article 48 TFEU) could be a suitable legal basis for an extension of the coordination regulation to third-country nationals. This issue was solved by the Court of Justice in the Khalil judgment.31 From this judgment it follows that Article 48 TFEU cannot be a legal basis for extending the personal scope to third-country nationals, since the Court decided that the scope of this article is limited to EU nationals. Only they enjoy the freedom of movement guaranteed by the Treaty.

The Court made an exception for stateless persons and political refugees, which were the appellants in this case. They could rely on the regulation, since they were mentioned in the regulation and because of the UN conventions on stateless persons and refugees this (limited) extension was allowed. The appellants applied for child benefit in Germany, which was refused to foreigners who did not have a residence entitlement or residence permit. Those involved were, among others, Kurdish and Palestinian refugees from Lebanon, who had already lived for ten years in Germany when they were confronted with this law.

However, although they were within the personal scope of the regulation, their claim was still not successful. This was because the Court referred to its case law, the Petit judgment in particular,32 in which it concluded that Article 51 EC Treaty (now Article 48 TFEU) and Regulation 1408/71 do not apply to situations which are confined within a single Member State. This is in particular the case where the situation of a worker has factors linking it solely with a non-member country and one single Member State. Consequently, the refugees and the stateless persons in this case could not rely on the rights conferred by the regulation now that they were in a situation which was confined in all respects within one Member State. This means that stateless persons and refugees can benefit from this decision only when their situation involves two Member States. The European Commission thereby made a new proposal, this time based on Article 63(4) EC (now Article 79 TFEU). This article concerns the conditions for the admission and residence of third-country nationals to the Community. This legal basis for making a regulation was accepted by the Council and in 2003 Regulation 859/2003 was adopted.33 This regulation meant that third-county nationals can, under certain conditions specified below, invoke the non-discrimination rule. When Regulation 883/2004 was adopted a new regulation on third-county nationals was necessary; after long and intensive discussions this was adopted, i.e. Regulation 1231/2010.34

Both regulations provide that the coordination regulation shall apply to nationals of third countries who are not already covered by those regulations solely on the ground of their nationality, as well as to members of their families and to their survivors, provided that they are legally resident in the territory of a Member State and are in a situation which is not confined in all respects within a single Member State (emphasis added). The italicised condition is of decisive importance since it means that the regulation can only be applicable if a situation concerns facts in at least two Member States (e.g. a worker from France who goes to work in the Netherlands). If, however, a person has come from a non-EU state and has remained in one and the same EU Member State, then the regulation is not applicable.35 Therefore the non-discrimination rule is for third-country nationals still of limited value. In other words, they can still be discriminated against without the possibility of invoking an EU non-discrimination rule.

Conclusion. For third-country nationals, invoking EU law is limited. For the coordination regulation an opening has been made, since invoking the regulation is possible if the facts of the case are not limited to one Member State. For other instruments the exclusion is still absolute.

COMPARISON OF THE EU AND ECHR APPROACHES

The Prohibition of Direct Discrimination

In the case of direct discrimination against persons with EU nationality the approach of EU law and the Convention do not differ significantly. The ECtHR requires that there must be 'very weighty' reasons to justify discrimination, whereas under EU law there is a specified number of exceptions to the prohibition of discrimination. We may assume that these terms will largely overlap, although the EU grounds are more specific.

Still, in terms of scope the approach to discrimination differs considerably. This has to do, for a large part, with the framework within which the discrimination terms occur. For the EU the nondiscrimination rule is basically linked to free movement, i.e. initially of EU workers and self-employed. As of 2010 this has been extended in the area of statutory social security to the free movement of persons, active or inactive, but still to EU citizens only.

Article 18 TFEU is also of use, in that it removes nationality conditions for benefits not within the scope of Regulation 883/2004, for instance for social assistance. This is relevant for those who are not workers. In these cases there is, in the Court's case law, more room for an objective justification than in the case of the regulations. In the Förster judgment,36 the Court decided that the condition that the applicant must have a certain degree of integration into the society of the host state is acceptable as an objective justification for a residence condition. This condition must be well reasoned, adequate and proportional.

There is, as yet, no comparable ECtHR case law. Since the condition which was applicable in Förster was applied to foreigners only, it is a form of direct discrimination, and thus would require very weighty reasons had it been a case before the ECtHR. How this Court would decide the case is still not clear. The criteria and arguments of the Court of Justice are well founded and satisfy the proportionality criterion. Still, the criterion of the degree of integration applies to foreigners only (and not to persons with the nationality of the host state); thus the distinction that is made between economically active persons and others is different from the ECtHR's case law so far. Whether these constitute 'very weighty' reasons remains to be seen.

Another distinction is between EU nationals and non-EU nationals. We have seen that gradually the scope of the non-discrimination rule has been extended to non-EU nationals, but only if the facts of the case are not restricted to one Member State (in statutory social security), or depending on whether there is an agreement. The condition that the facts must not be restricted to one Member State also applies for EU nationals, but for the latter it is much easier to satisfy this condition. It can therefore be disputed whether the criterion for third-country nationals is a very weighty reason. I will discuss this in the next section. In other areas (Article 18 TFEU) the exclusion of third-country nationals is an absolute one.

Can the ECHR Lead to Different Outcomes?

Can cases of direct discrimination which do not fall under EU law or which are still allowed by EU law be addressed by the Convention? If we look again at the Gaygusuz case, it has to be noted that EU law has changed to the extent that a regulation on third-country nationals (Regulation 1231/2010) has been adopted, which did not exist at the time of the Gaygusuz decision. This regulation extends the non-discrimination provision of the coordination regulation to third-country nationals such as Mr Gaygusuz. A particular problem, however, is that this emergency assistance is probably a form of social assistance and is thus excluded from the scope of the coordination regulation. However, and this is of more general importance, the mentioned regulation only applies if not all the facts of the case are limited to one Member State. Even if this emergency benefit is within the scope of the regulation, Mr Gaygusuz could not contest his exclusion from the benefit by means of the new regulation either.

Also the EU citizens provision (Article 18 TFEU) is limited to EU nationals. Mr Gaygusuz could not invoke this rule successfully either. Therefore, invoking the Convention is still necessary in such a case if benefit is refused on the ground of nationality.37 Therefore, the very limitation of the equal treatment rules to EU nationals constitutes a form of discrimination which may be tested against the Convention. As we saw, in respect of statutory social security this discrimination has been lifted to a considerable extent, the main difference is that the situation must not be limited to one Member State. Are there weighty reasons for this difference? The rule that the regulation is only applicable if the facts of the case are not limited to one Member State was established in the Petit judgment.38 In this case an employee was confronted with conditions on the use of language to be used in legal procedures in Belgium. The Belgian law on languages to be used in legal proceedings prescribed the Dutch language in a case like this. The use of another language would make the case of the person concerned inadmissible. When Mr Petit challenged this it was considered that he had Belgian nationality and had never been employed in a state other than Belgium. The Court of Justice decided that the rules of the Treaty ensuring the free movement of workers and the coordination regulation were not applicable to activities all elements of which are restricted to the territory of a single Member State only. This criterion was also at stake in the Government of the French Community and Walloon Government v Flemish Government Judgment. 39

In the Khalil case40 (see Section 3.4) the Court reiterated this condition and Regulation 1231/2010 has reproduced it. This means that only if a situation concerns facts in at least two Member States (e.g. a worker from France who goes to work in the UK) is the regulation applicable. If, however, a person has come from a non-EU state and has remained in one and the same EU Member State, then the regulation is not applicable. This limitation can also be found in the Khalil judgment, and earlier in the Petit judgment. Still, this limitation could be criticised, as, different from these two cases, the regulation on third-country nationals is not based on Article 48 TFEU, but on Article 63(4) EC. This separate legal basis is not related to the right to free movement, which is indeed related to the economic freedoms established within the EU. Therefore the question arises why at least the facts of two Member States have to be involved. For third-country nationals the effect of this requirement differs from that for EU nationals, such as Mr Petit in the Petit judgment,41 as the former persons are from a third country and are therefore much more likely to be discriminated against on grounds of nationality. The third-country nationals cannot, as a result of the condition that two Member States must be involved, invoke the regulation in, for instance, a case of discrimination on grounds of nationality which occurs within a Member State if s/he does not work, reside or stay in another Member State.

One can therefore doubt whether the difference within this EU instrument constitutes a weighty reason for making a distinction.42 Regulation 1231/2010 would probably not be of help in the Poirrez case either. In respect of the father it was argued that he was not a migrant worker. Under the new formula one would say that the facts of the case did not involve two Member States. Thus neither the father nor the son could invoke the regulation. The Polish case of Luczak v Poland would, of course, lead to a different outcome now that Poland is a member of the EU. The Court seemed to tease the Polish Government by saying that it had not explained why its public policy goals in respect of the farmers' scheme suddenly lost their relevance after 2004, since the answer is obvious: Poland was no longer allowed to make this distinction towards other EU nationals after it acceded to the EU. However, this remark is still relevant to us, since it shows that EU membership itself is no longer a self-evident ground, at least for the ECtHR, for making or not making differences.

Regulation 1231/2010 is relevant only to benefits within the scope of this regulation. Discrimination occurring in areas not covered by this regulation can be combated by means of Regulation 492/2011 or Article 18 TFEU (in combination with EU citizenship). The personal scope of both instruments is limited to EU nationals. Also here one can doubt whether this is consistent with the Convention. Are there very weighty reasons to exclude third-country nationals (who are legally staying in a Member State) from invoking EU law rules? As we saw in respect of the coordination regulation, there was a great deal of doubt as to whether this regulation could be based on Article 48. Only after the Court of Justice decided that in view of the place of the legal basis for the regulation in the Treaty (i.e. in the chapter on free movement, a freedom created for EU nationals) did it decide that third-country nationals could not be involved.

This argument need not constitute, in itself, a very weighty reason, and it is certainly not sufficient to justify any form of discrimination. Therefore we may expect that when third-country nationals wish to invoke EU rules and are refused on basis of nationality, the Convention may provide an instrument to fight this discrimination successfully.

Residence Conditions

There are some residence conditions that are accepted in the coordination regulation, for instance in the case of wholly unemployed frontier workers. As we have seen, the justification for this residence condition lies in the fact that frontier workers have a better position on the labour market in the country where they reside. The Court of Human Rights does not apply a concept of indirect discrimination. Therefore it is unlikely that it will consider the coordination rule to be contrary to the prohibition of discrimination on the ground of nationality. In cases of residence conditions the Court of Human Rights compares the situation of persons claiming that they are treated differently from other persons, e.g. the position of persons whose pensions are upgraded and that of those whose pensions are not upgraded. This comparison is quite complicated and has thus far not led to positive results for the persons concerned in residence cases. It is not likely that the Court of Human Rights would come to the conclusion, in the (rare) cases where the Court of Justice has accepted residence conditions, that these would infringe Article 14 ECHR, because of the reticence of the Court of Human Rights to award the claims of appellants and also because the Court of Justice mentions elaborated grounds of justification. If such a case would reach the Court of Human Rights, however, it has to assess the objective justification given by the Court of Justice, and this might influence the way it constructs its argument.

The use of these objective justifications made by the Court of Justice seems to be more satisfactory in case of indirect discrimination (in any case when residence conditions are concerned), than the use of a comparison of situations which is performed by the ECtHR. First of all, as a general problem it is often difficult to compare situations since it is difficult to know which elements have to be taken into account. The Carson situation clearly shows these problems. Secondly, is it not because it is indirect discrimination rather than direct discrimination that situations are difficult to compare? In other words, should we not use a different instrument? This is not unimportant, since the British rules had a large negative effect on the pensions in Carson. A well-elaborated justification that there is no infringement of the discrimination rules is desirable. Whether the accession of the EU to the ECHR will lead to changes in views by the ECtHR on the way discrimination cases have to be dealt with is uncertain at this moment in time. Given the differences in approaches such changes could be possible and it would even be desirable if such effects would occur.

Protection of Property

Protection of property in social security is not an issue regulated by EU law as such. The protection of property is mentioned in the Charter of Fundamental Rights of the EU (Article 17), but so far it has not been interpreted as pertaining to social security. In some cases before the Court of Justice, however, the principle of the protection of property was invoked vis-à-vis social security, and therefore it is interesting to compare the Court's approach with that of the Court of Human Rights. The Testa case43 involved the rule that an unemployed person can seek work abroad (while remaining in receipt of unemployment benefit) for three months. However, if he returns too late he loses all remaining benefit rights. Thus the EU rules deprive him of benefit rights acquired on the basis of national legislation. The effects of a late return can thus be quite harsh, depending on the duration of the benefit entitlement involved. The Court discussed – in answer to the national court's questions – whether the disputed article (Article 69(2) of the then coordination regulation) infringed the fundamental rights guaranteed in this manner by Community law, i.e. Article 14 of the German Basic Law with regard to the protection of the right to property. Although the property protection rule was at stake, no reference was made to the ECHR.

The Court considered that the question of a possible infringement of fundamental rights by a measure of the Community institutions can only be judged in the light of Community law itself, since fundamental rights form an integral part of the general principles of the law, the observance of which it ensures. One of the fundamental rights which is accordingly protected under Community law in accordance with the constitutional concepts common to the Member States and in the light of international treaties for the protection of human rights is the right to property. In order to determine whether Article 69(2) might infringe the fundamental rights guaranteed in this manner by Community law consideration should first be given to the fact that the system set up by this article is an optional right, which applies only to the extent to which such an application is requested by a worker, who thereby foregoes his right of recourse to the general system. The consequences are made known to the worker.

The penalty under Article 69(2) must likewise be judged in the light of the advantage of a worker by Article 69(1), which has no equivalent in national law. Moreover, in exceptional cases the three-month period may be extended, this ensures that the application of Article 69(2) does not give rise to disproportional results.44 Therefore the Court accepted an objective justification for the radical loss of benefit rights. The test of the Court of Human Rights would, in this case, be difficult to apply. If we apply its criterion, it can be said that there seems to be an excessive burden on a particular group (of late returners), who lose all remaining rights and who may no longer have an alternative income. Still, indeed, they have an advantage of which the loss of rights if they do not satisfy the rules is the counterpart. Therefore, if such a case would be brought before the Court of Human Rights, the question is whether its own criterion can be usefully applied. Therefore it is interesting to see which criterion the Court will apply.

Conclusion. The approach in the case of direct discrimination against EU nationals does not seem very different. In the case of third-country nationals there is an important difference. There is also a difference in the case of situations which would constitute indirect discrimination for the Court of Justice or an infringement of property.

CONCLUSION

In this contribution it was investigated which effects follow from the EU accession to the Convention for discrimination on the ground of nationality in the area of social advantages. In other words, are cases of discrimination on the ground of nationality, which are problematic under the Convention, allowed under EU law? As was explained in Section 1, after accession to the Convention, EU law has to be interpreted so that it is consistent with the Convention, and therefore the comparison is useful to identify the differences. From the present study it appears that the accession of the EU to the Convention on Human Rights will probably not have effects in all areas discussed here. This was to be expected, first since human rights have already played a role for a considerable time in Community law, and second because otherwise the EU would not have decided to accede to the Convention.

The main differences seem to lie, in the area of the prohibition of discrimination on the ground of nationality, in the treatment of third-country nationals. They are still treated differently from EU nationals in several respects in EU law. A difference in treatment on the ground of EU nationality cannot be found in the case law of the ECtHR. The Moustaquim judgment does not support such a difference, as was explained in Section 2.2.1 supra. This may lead to decisions in which the ECtHR decides that EU law, e.g. the exclusion of nonEU nationals from the coordination regulation, from Regulation 492/11 or from the application of Article 18 TFEU, has to be well reasoned. These grounds have to be 'very weighty', and it is possible that this criterion cannot be satisfied, since economic reasons – used within the EU context – are difficult to reconcile with the human rights approach of the ECtHR. Also in the cases before the Court of Human Rights discussed in Section 2.2 economic arguments were put forward by the state and it appeared that these were not accepted. Is it not likely that it will make a difference when an international organization uses an economic argument.

Also cases on residence conditions and the loss of benefit rights which were allowed by EU law can be brought before the Court of Human Rights. From the study it also appears that the courts use different types of reasoning. Since the Court of Justice's case law on indirect discrimination is quite strict, and that of the Court of Human Rights on situations that could amount to indirect discrimination is not so strict, we cannot expect many cases here.

In case of an infringement of property rights, the Court of Justice sometimes accepts such infringements. It is not clear whether the criteria of the Court of Human Rights would lead to the same outcome as that of the Court of Justice, since the Court of Human Rights uses different criteria. In any case, it seems that the Court has to change its reasoning if it wishes to accept the outcome of the case law of the Court of Justice. Thus the case law of the international courts may influence each other after the accession of the EU to the Convention. In this respect it is interesting that the Court of Human Rights has been criticized due to its ad hoc approach to cases on discrimination. Mel Cousins45 has called the case law 'advocacy of palm tree justice' in cases concerning social security as a property right. By palm tree justice he means a pragmatic approach to justice that is entirely discretionary and transcends legal rights or precedent, enabling the court to make such an order as it thinks fair and just in the circumstances of the case.

Indeed, also in the preceding sections the lack of consistent rules has been pointed to. Closer contacts between the courts and the need to take the EU dimension and case law into account may force the ECtHR to develop a clearer framework for the application of its criteria. The outcome is not easy to predict, but it may lead to interesting improvements for the EU, which has to mention new justifications for some forms of discrimination, and the Court of Human Rights, which has to take the reasoning of the Court of Justice into account and is thus challenged to systematize its reasoning.

NOTES:

1 See for a recent draft text of the accession agreement, CDDH-UE(2011)10 on the website of the Council of Europe, (last visited 7 December 2012).

2 See, for instance, T. Lock, 'Walking on a tightrope: the draft ECHR accession agreement and the autonomy of the EU legal order', 2011 CMLR, pp. 1026 et seq.; see also J.P. Jacqué, 'The accession of the European Union to the European Convention on Human Rights and Fundamental Freedoms', 2011 CMLR, pp. 995 et seq.

3 For a more precise description of the liability of Member States under the current law, see also Leonard Besselink, 'The EU and the European Convention of Human Rights after Lisbon: From 'Bosphorus' Sovereign Immunity to Full Scrutiny?', SSRN, or .

4 The term social advantages is chosen since our topic is not limited to social insurance or social security, but includes all benefits on the basis of whatever instrument or financing method.

5 Protocol 12 has introduced a more general equality clause. However, few countries have so far ratified it, and it is not a Protocol which is part of the EU accession agreement.

6 No. 39/1995/545/632, Reports 1996-iv, p. 1129. On this judgment, see also S. van den Bogaerd (ed.), Social Security, Non-discrimination and Property, 1997; H. Verschueren, 'EC Social Security Coordination Excluding Third-Country Nationals: Still in Line with Fundamental Rights after the Gaygusuz Judgement', 1997 cmlr, p. 991; F. Pennings, 'The Potential Consequences of the Gaygusuz Judgment', 1999 ejss, p. 181.

7 The First Protocol is part of the accession agreement.

8 Nos. 65731/01 and 65900/01, ECHR 2006.

9 See for example Petrovic v Austria, judgment of 27 March 1998, Reports 1998-II, § 38, where the authorities' refusal to grant parental leave allowance to a father, on the ground that the allowance was only available to mothers, was not found to have exceeded the margin of appreciation allowed to them.

10 No. 40892/98, judgment of 30 September 2003, ECHR 2005.

11 Court of Justice 16 December 1992, Case C-206/91, [1992] ECR 6685.

12 No. 77782/01, judgment of 27 November 2007.

13 No. 12313/86, judgment of 18 February 1991.

14 Relevant is also that Protocol 4 to the Convention itself makes a difference as far as nationality is concerned, since persons having the nationality of a country cannot be expelled from that country.

15 Directive 2006/54/EC of the European Parliament and of the Council of 5 July 2006, OJ L 204, 26.7.2006, p. 23.

16 LB v Austria, no. 39802/98, judgment of 18 April 2002.

17 M. Cousins, The European Convention on Human Rights and Social Security Law, 2008, p. 67.

18 Carson v United Kingdom, no. 42184/05, (2009) 48 E.H.R.R. 41. See also, M. Cousins, 'The European Convention on Human Rights, NonDiscrimination and Social Security: Great Scope, Little Depth?', 2009 Journal of Social Security Law 16, pp. 118 et seq.

19 Kjeldsen, Busk Madsen and Pedersen, judgment of 7 December 1976, Series A no. 23.

20 D.H. and Others v.the Czech Republic [GC], no. 57325/00, § 175, ECHR 2007; Burden v.the United Kingdom[GC], no. 13378/05, § 60, ECHR 2008

21 Kopecky v Slovakia [GC], no. 44912/98, § 35, ECHR 2004-IX.

22 Judgment of 15 September 2009, no. 10373/05.

23 Judgment of 25 October 2011, nos. 2033/04, 19125/04, 19475/04, 19490/04, 19495/04, 19497/04, 24729/04, 171/05 and 2041/05, EHRC 2012, no. 22, p. 255.

24 Case 85/96, [1998] ECR I-2691.

25 Case 184/99, [2001] ECR I-6193.

26 Case C-209/03 [2005] ECR I-2119.

27 Case C-158/07, Jacqueline Föster, [2008] ECR I-8507.

28 Case 41/84, [1986] ecr 1.

29 Article 73(2) of Regulation 1408/71.

30 Case 39/76, [1976] ECR 1901.

31 Case 95/99, [2001] ecr I-7413

32 ECJ 22 September 1992, Case 153/91, [1992] ECR I-4973.

33 OJ L 124, 20.5.2003, p. 1. See the preparatory work in Com (2002) 59.

34 OJ L 344, 29.12.2010, p. 1.

35 An interesting question is what the position of Denmark, the UK and Ireland is in this respect. It is clear, of course, that a third-country national cannot invoke the regulation if s/he first works in Belgium and then moves to Denmark, in order to have periods of insurance aggregated. However, what about the reverse situation? If s/he moves to Belgium, can s/he have his or her Danish periods added to the Belgian ones?

36 Case C-158/07, Jacqueline Föster, [2008] ECR I-8507.

37 Decision 3/80 of the Association Council will provide the same result since this decision has the same material scope as the coordination regulation. The decision will be beneficial for other types of benefits, but for Turkish nationals only. So for other third-country nationals linked to one Member State only, the Convention provides a result which is different from EU law.

38 Case 153/91, [1992] ecr I-4973.

39 Case C-212/06, [2008] ECR I-1683. See on this judgment also H. Verschueren, 'De regionalisering van de sociale zekerheid in België in het licht van het arrest van het Europese Hof van Justitie inzake de Vlaamse zorgverzekering', 2008 Belgisch Tijdschrift Sociale Zekerheid, no. 2, pp. 177-232; I. van der Steen, 'Zuivere interne situaties: geen omwenteling, wel inperking', 2008 NTER, no. 11, pp. 301 et seq.

40 Case 95/99, [2001] ecr I-7413.

41 Case 153/91, [1992] ECR I-4973.

42 Some Member States can exempt themselves from the Regulation: Denmark, the UK and Ireland. We will not go into this issue too deeply here, but it is doubted whether these states can now refuse to apply the equal treatment principle if the Union is bound by the Convention. As a result the non-discrimination law will also affect their reservations to the Regulation.

43 The Testa, Maggio and Viale judgment, Cases 41/79, 121/79 and 796/79, [1980] ecr 1979.

44 Regulation 883/2004 has a novelty: the person who returns too late loses all entitlement to benefit, unless the provisions of that legislation are mover favourable. Indeed, Member States may have their own rules on the period after which benefits are lost after a late return. These are applicable if they are favourable for the person concerned.

45 M. Cousins, 'Overview of recent cases before the European Court of Human Rights and the European Court of Justice (January-March 2012)', 2012 EJSS, p. 124.

INDEX